History Alive!®
The Ancient World

TCi™

Chief Executive Officer: Bert Bower

Chief Operating Officer: Amy Larson

Director of Curriculum: Liz Russell

Managing Editor: Laura Alavosus

Editorial Project Manager: Nancy Rogier

Project Editor: Pat Sills

Copyeditor: Susan Arnold

Editorial Associates: Anna Embree, Sarah Sudano

Production Manager: Lynn Sanchez

Art Director: John F. Kelly

Senior Graphic Designer: Christy Uyeno

Graphic Designers: Sarah Wildfang, Don Taka, Victoria Philp

Photo Edit Manager: Margee Robinson

Photo Editor: Diane Austin

Production Project Manager: Eric Houts

Art Editor: Mary Swab

Audio Director: Katy Haun

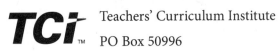

Teachers' Curriculum Institute

PO Box 50996

Palo Alto, CA 94303

Customer Service: 800-497-6138

www.teachtci.com

ISBN 978-1-58371-904-6

2 3 4 5 6 7 8 9 10 -MLI- 14 13 12 11

Program Director

Bert Bower

Program Author

Wendy Frey

Creative Development Manager

Kelly Shafsky

Contributing Writers

John Bergez

Mark Falstein

Diane Hart

Marisa A. Howard

Amy Joseph

Curriculum Developers

Joyce Bartky

April Bennett

Nicole Boylan

Terry Coburn

Julie Cremin

Erin Fry

Amy George

Anne Maloney

Steve Seely

Nathan Wellborne

Reading Specialist

Kate Kinsella, Ed.D.
Reading and TESOL Specialist
San Francisco State University

Teacher Consultants

Melissa Aubuchon
Indian Trail Middle School
Plainfield, Illinois

Anthony Braxton
Cruickshank Middle School
Merced, California

Amy George
Weston Middle School
Weston, Massachusetts

Randi Gibson
Stanford Middle School
Long Beach, California

Lisa Macurak
New Windsor Middle School
New Windsor, Maryland

Sherry Owens
Lubbock Independent School District
Lubbock, Texas

Acknowledgments

Scholars

Dr. Anthony Bulloch
University of California, Berkeley

Dr. Mark W. Chavalas
*University of Wisconsin,
La Crosse*

Dr. Eun Mi Cho
*California State University
Sacramento*

Dr. Steve Farmer
Palo Alto, California

Dr. Bruce Grelle
California State University Chico

Dr. David N. Keightley
University of California, Berkeley

Dr. Brij Khare
*California State University
San Bernardino*

Dr. Gary Miles
*University of California,
Santa Cruz*

Dr. Daniel Veidlinger
California State University Chico

Dr. Jed Wyrick
California State University Chico

Dr. Joel Zimbelman
California State University Chico

Assessment Consultants

Denny Chandler
*Curriculum and Assessment
Specialist
Cold Spring, Kentucky*

Julie Weiss
*Curriculum and Assessment
Specialist
Elliot, Maine*

Assessment Consultants

Melanie Pinkert
*Music Faculty
Montgomery College, Maryland*

Cartographer

Mapping Specialists
Madison, Wisconsin

Internet Consultant

Amy George
Weston, Massachusetts

Diverse Needs Consultants

Erin Fry
Glendora, California

Colleen Guccione
Naperville, Illinois

Cathy Hix
*Swanson Middle School
Arlington, Virginia*

**Unit 6
Ancient Rome**

How to Use This Program:
History Alive! The Ancient World

Teaching with the TCI Approach means shifting to a student-centered, activity-based classroom. To meet this exciting challenge, this introduction to the Lesson Guide for *History Alive! The Ancient World* will give you the basics you need to start teaching this program with confidence right away.

The TCI Approach

Why is the TCI Approach so effective at igniting students' passion for learning? The TCI Approach consists of a series of instructional practices that allow students of all abilities to experience key social studies concepts. It has eight features.

Theory- and Research-Based Active Instruction

Lessons and activities are based on five well-established theories.

Understanding by Design   Grant Wiggins and Jay McTighe maintain that teaching for deep understanding must begin with planning the big ideas students should learn. That's why you will see an Essential Question at the start of every chapter in *History Alive! The Ancient World*.

Nonlinguistic Representation   Research by Robert Marzano and colleagues demonstrates that teaching with nonlinguistic activities helps improve comprehension and retention. Use of graphic organizers and movement are both key to TCI lessons.

Multiple Intelligences   Howard Gardner believes that all students are intelligent —just not in the same ways. TCI activities address Gardner's seven intelligences: verbal-linguistic, logical-mathematical, visual-spatial, body-kinesthetic, musical-rhythmic, interpersonal, and intrapersonal.

Cooperative Interaction   Elizabeth Cohen's research shows that cooperative groupwork leads to learning gains and higher student achievement. Working in small groups is a cornerstone of TCI activities.

Spiral Curriculum   Jerome Bruner championed the idea of the spiral curriculum, in which students learn progressively—understanding more difficult concepts through a process of step-by-step discovery. TCI questioning strategies spiral from simple recall to higher-order thinking skills such as analysis and evaluation.

Standards-Based Content

Dynamic lessons that integrate hands-on learning and content reading build mastery of state and national social studies standards.

Preview Assignments

Short, engaging assignments at the start of the lessons help you preview key concepts and tap students' prior knowledge and personal experience.

Multiple Intelligences Teaching Strategies

TCI activities incorporate six multiple intelligences teaching strategies:

- Visual Discovery
- Social Studies Skill Builder
- Experiential Exercise
- Writing for Understanding
- Response Group
- Problem Solving Groupwork

These six strategies are explained in detail on the following pages.

Considerate Text

Carefully structured reading materials enable students at all levels to understand what they read. Uncluttered pages present content in digestible "chunks." Engaging images reinforce content, while consistent vocabulary development improves student comprehension.

Graphically Organized Reading Notes

Easy-to-understand graphic organizers help students record key ideas and make meaning out of what they read. By using graphic organizers that display the underlying logic of and interconnections among concepts, students improve their comprehension and retention of content.

Processing Assignments

End-of-lesson assignments, involving multiple intelligences and higher-order thinking skills, challenge students to apply what they have learned in a variety of creative ways.

Assessments to Inform Instruction

Carefully designed chapter tests move students through a progression of thinking skills, from comprehension to skills application to critical thinking. Test results in these three areas show you where students are succeeding and where they need more instruction.

Multiple Intelligences Teaching Strategies

The TCI Approach uses the six teaching strategies described here to bring learning alive. All six appear in the *History Alive! The Ancient World* Lesson Guide with detailed, step-by-step instructions. Support materials for the chapter activities appear in the Lesson Masters, visuals, and placards; on Sounds of History; and online at TeachTCI (see page xxvi).

Visual Discovery

In Visual Discovery activities, students view, touch, interpret, and bring to life compelling images as they discover key social studies concepts. Seeing and interacting with an image in combination with reading and recording notes on the content help students remember salient ideas.

Here are some tips for Visual Discovery activities:

- Arrange your classroom so that projected images will be large and clear.
- Ask carefully sequenced questions that lead to discovery.
- Challenge students to read about each image and apply what they learn.
- Have students interact with each image to demonstrate learning.

Social Studies Skill Builder

In Social Studies Skill Builders, students work in pairs or small groups on fast-paced, skill-oriented tasks such as mapping, graphing, analyzing artifacts, and forming hypotheses, to enhance their understanding of chapter content.

Here are some tips for Social Studies Skill Builders:

- Teach each skill through modeling and guided practice.
- Prepare students to work in pairs or small groups.
- Set clear expectations, allow students to practice each skill repeatedly, and give immediate feedback.
- Debrief the activity to help students make connections to key social studies concepts.

Experiential Exercise

In Experiential Exercises, participating in short, memorable experiences helps students grasp social studies concepts. Through the use of movement and introspection, students capture a moment or feeling that is central to understanding a particular concept, situation, or event.

Here are some tips for Experiential Exercises:

- Prepare students for a safe, successful experience by arranging the classroom appropriately, communicating clear behavioral and learning expectations, anticipating student reactions, and recognizing teachable moments.

- Bring authenticity to the experience by assuming an appropriate persona, hamming it up, and using simple props, costumes, music, and sound effects.
- Allow students to express their feelings immediately after the experience.
- Ask carefully sequenced questions to help students make connections between their experience and key concepts or events.

Writing for Understanding

Writing for Understanding activities give students a rich experience—such as viewing powerful images, role-playing, discussing complex issues, or acting out key events—to write about. Students develop ideas and form opinions during the experience, before beginning to write. The experience becomes a springboard for writing, challenging students to clarify ideas, organize information, and express what they have learned.

Here are some tips for Writing for Understanding activities:

- Have students record their ideas, thoughts, and feelings in prewriting activities.
- Guide students through the writing process.

Response Group

In Response Group activities, students work in small groups with thought-provoking resources to discuss critical thinking questions among themselves. A presenter then shares each group's findings with the class.

Here are some tips for Response Group activities:

- Create mixed-ability groups and a suitable classroom arrangement.
- Prepare students to answer provocative critical thinking questions.
- Allow groups time to prepare their responses.
- Facilitate a lively class discussion.

Problem Solving Groupwork

In Problem Solving Groupwork activities, students work in heterogeneous groups to create projects that require multiple abilities so that every student can contribute. Within a group, each student takes a defined role. After completing their task, groups present their projects to the class.

Here are some tips for Problem Solving Groupwork activities:

- Review ground rules for working cooperatively in groups.
- Give group members clearly defined roles and requirements.
- Give groups autonomy and time to prepare high-quality projects.
- After groups present their work, debrief each presentation for deeper meaning and accuracy.

Program Components

The components of *History Alive! The Ancient World* work together to maximize your time and creativity. Everything you need to provide insightful and stimulating classroom experiences is included in the program. There are also plenty of opportunities to add your own resources.

Lesson Guide

"Command central" for the program includes detailed, step-by-step procedures for implementing the classroom activities, as well as the following resources:

- Planning Guides detailing materials and timing for each part of the lesson guides
- social studies and language arts objectives
- Key Content Terms and academic vocabulary
- mini lesson guides for writing assignments tied to each Reading Further case study
- listings of online resources and literature recommendations
- recommendations for differentiating instruction for English language learners, students reading and writing below grade level, special education students, and advanced learners
- Guide to Reading Notes
- answers and rubrics for assessments

Student Edition

To help students focus their learning, each chapter of the text is organized around an Essential Question. In the Student Edition, you will find

- considerate text that is uncluttered and easy to navigate.
- powerful graphic elements that support visual learning, spark student interest, and foster comprehension.
- key concepts and vocabulary terms that are highlighted in the text and defined in the Glossary.
- Setting the Stage unit introductions that provide background on how the geography of the region affected its history. Each spread includes detailed maps that students use to complete Geography Challenge lessons.
- unit timelines that appear at the end of every unit and capture the most important events of the region's history at a glance.
- High-interest Reading Further case studies that explore the chapter concepts in depth.

Interactive Student Notebook

The Interactive Student Notebook is each student's personal repository of learning, all in one place. The Interactive Student Notebook includes

- Preview activities
- graphically organized Reading Notes
- Processing activities
- Reading Further writing activities

For more information, see "Using the Interactive Student Notebook" on pages xx–xxi.

Lesson Masters

Reproducible pages support classroom activities. Follow the materials list in the Lesson Guide to know how many copies of each master to prepare before class.

- Student Handouts and Information Masters
- Station Materials and Station Directions
- chapter assessments
- sets of cards containing images for the unit timelines

Visuals and Placards

Visual support for chapter activities, including

- maps, graphs, diagrams, and tables
- photographs

Sounds of History

Audio tracks, including dramatic readings, musical recordings, and sound effects, enhance the drama and realism of many of the activities.

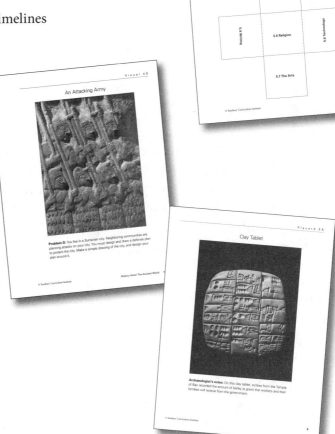

Chapter Essentials

While students look forward to the wide variety of activities they will experience in a TCI classroom, they also reap the benefits of TCI's consistent organization of learning in the chapters. Following sound pedagogical practices, each lesson begins with a Preview activity to spark interest and connect to prior learning, progresses to visually engaging Reading Notes, and concludes with a Processing activity that asks students to apply what they have learned.

Preview

The Preview activity is a short, engaging task that foreshadows upcoming content. The goal is to ignite interest, activate prior knowledge, tap a wide range of intelligences, and prepare students to tackle new concepts. Students complete most of the Preview activities in their Interactive Student Notebooks.

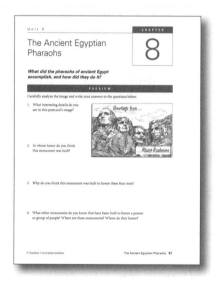

Types of Preview activities include

- connecting personal experiences with key concepts
- predicting
- analyzing artifacts, maps, photographs, paintings, drawings, political cartoons, song lyrics, and music
- responding to hypothetical scenarios
- depicting and explaining historical information
- examining the contributions of historical figures

Reading Notes

One of the most powerful ways to improve students' comprehension and retention is to have them complete graphically organized Reading Notes for each chapter. Using this format helps students see the underlying logic of and interconnections among events, facts, and concepts. When students record information in engaging, visual ways, they are better able to recall content months and even years later. Students complete the Reading Notes in their Interactive Student Notebooks.

Types of graphically organized Reading Notes include

- T-charts
- labeled and annotated maps, charts, diagrams, and illustrations
- flowcharts
- spoke diagrams
- time lines
- Venn diagrams
- speech bubbles

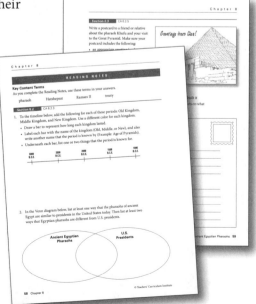

Reading Further

For each Reading Further, students complete a two-part writing activity about what they've read. The first part prepares them to write while the second part provides them with a guiding rubric for their work. Types of writing activities include

- business letters
- diary entries
- point-of-view statements
- comparing and contrasting

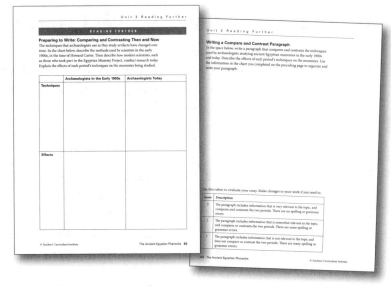

Processing

Processing activities challenge students to synthesize the information in a chapter to demonstrate their understanding of it. The intent is to allow students to actively apply what they have learned so that you—and they—can assess their comprehension. Students complete the Processing activities in their Interactive Student Notebooks or on separate sheets of paper.

Products of Processing activities include

- song and poem verses
- magazine covers
- posters
- Web page designs
- storyboards
- journal entries
- interviews
- collages

- advertisements
- illustrated timelines
- T-charts
- parables
- letters
- spoke diagrams
- dialogues
- annotated maps

Using the Interactive Student Notebook

In the Interactive Student Notebook, all parts of the integrated lesson come together as students create a dynamic repository for their learning. Students should store their notebooks in a three-ring binder. Because the pages are perforated, it is easy for you to collect only selected chapters to grade a one time, rather than whole binders.

Interactive Student Notebook Guidelines for Students

One of the most important steps for helping students to create successful notebooks is establishing clear guidelines. Decide ahead of time what you expect your students to produce in their notebooks. Clearly communicate your expectations on a single sheet of paper that students can glue into the inside front cover of their notebooks. Here are example guidelines that you might adapt for your own students.

Purpose   Your Interactive Student Notebook will help you to become a creative, independent thinker and writer. You will use your notebook in class for completing all chapter Preview, Reading Notes, Reading Further, and Processing activities. It will also help you study for tests.

Materials   You will need colored pencils, a glue stick, highlighters, scissors, tape, and a zipper pouch.

Grading   To earn an A– or higher grade, you must keep a complete, neat notebook, produce quality work, and consistently take the time to extend your learning beyond classroom assignments. Notebooks will be checked for completeness periodically—usually every three to four weeks, except during the first few weeks of class, when they will be checked more regularly. You must keep an updated assignment sheet listing all class assignments, due dates, and point values. Also include columns for recording self-assessment points and teacher-assessment points.

Absence   If you are absent, check the class assignment sheet the teacher has placed in the large envelope in the front of the class. It will list all assignments that are due.

Managing Assessment of Interactive Student Notebooks

If you teach four or five classes a day, you could have 150 or more student notebooks to monitor. Because so much of students' work appears in these notebooks, you will need an efficient and accurate system for assessing them.

Informal Assessment   Monitor student notebooks aggressively in the first few weeks of the course. Look at notebooks as you walk around, making positive comments and helpful suggestions. Here are some additional ideas:

- While students work on another assignment, conduct a quick review of the previous night's homework, giving students checks or special stamps to denote completed assignments.

- Provide a model of outstanding work for an assignment or set of class notes.

- Allow students to use their notebooks on a quiz or test. This will come as a pleasant surprise and reward for students with well-organized notebooks.

Formal Assessment   At the beginning of the course, clearly explain the criteria on which notebooks will be assessed, such as quality and completeness of assignments, visual appearance, neatness, higher-order thinking, and organization. Here are some additional ideas for assessing student work:

- Create a simple rubric that identifies the criteria you feel are most important.

- Stagger notebook collection so that you correct only one class set at a time.

- Grade selectively. Don't feel compelled to grade every notebook entry.

- Create an evaluation sheet like the one below to support your expectations of student work.

Notebook Assignment	Due Date	Possible Points	Student Assessment	Teacher Assessment
Chapter 6 Preview	11/8	5	3	4
Chapter 6 Reading Notes	11/9	20	19	17
Chapter 6 Processing	11/10	10	8	10
Chapter 9 Reading Notes	11/15	20	18	19
Chapter 9 Processing	11/16	10	9	8
Totals		65	57	58
Student Comments: I'm not used to these kinds of assignments, but I'm trying my best.				
Teacher Comments: Your work is solid. Think about creating some of your excellent visuals for extra credit.				

Organizing a TCI Classroom

Most of the activities in *History Alive! The Ancient World* require students to move into small groups of two, three, or four. With a brief training exercise, you can teach them how to do so quickly without wasting valuable time.

Moving Your Classroom Furniture

Tell students that they will be working in small groups of different sizes throughout the course. They must know how to move into each grouping quickly and efficiently with all their materials. When working in pairs, they should place their desks either side by side or face to face, with the edges touching. For groups of three or more, the front corners of the desks must touch.

With these expectations clear, allow students to practice moving into groups. Randomly assign students to groups and indicate where they should meet. Then say "Go!" and time them. If necessary, allow the class to discuss what went wrong and brainstorm ideas for getting into groups more efficiently. Have students repeat the process until they can do it in "record time."

Be prepared for students to think this exercise is silly. However, if you spend 20 minutes at the beginning of the course teaching this skill, you will save hours of instructional time. Your goal should be for students to be able to form various group configurations in less than one minute, without your needing to touch any student furniture.

Organizing Your Teacher Resources

History Alive! The Ancient World comes with all of the materials you need to excite your students about the history and legacy of the the ancient world. It will be up to you, however, to gather the materials for each chapter and organize them in a way that makes it fast and easy to conduct activities year after year. Here are some tips to save you time and make running your classroom much easier:

1. Begin preparation for each activity by gathering everything on the materials list, such as placards, visuals, and the audio tracks.

2. Make all the copies you will need of classroom masters, such as Student Handouts, Information Masters, and Station Materials. Consider creating these copies from the online resources at TeachTCI.

3. When you finish each activity, place all the printed materials in a clear, resealable plastic bag (an ideal size is 10 by 12 in. and 4 mm thick) with the Lesson Guide on top as a "label." This will keep the many individual activity pieces together and will ensure that next year's preparation takes virtually no time.

4. Prepare the equipment you will use, including projectors and computers.

Creating a Cooperative, Tolerant Classroom

The interactive, experiential, and stimulating learning at the heart of the TCI Approach can happen only when students feel comfortable sharing ideas, taking risks, working cooperatively, tolerating differences, and disagreeing honestly and respectfully with you and their classmates. Thus you need to take purposeful steps to develop a "safe" community in your classroom.

Here are some tips for creating a cooperative, tolerant classroom:

- Greet your students at the door every day to make a personal connection with them as they enter your classroom.

- Explain your expectations for classroom behavior, using specific examples. You may also involve students in shaping class rules.

- Stage an icebreaker at the beginning of the course to help students feel more comfortable with their new classmates. For example, make a list of descriptions (likes to dance, speaks another language, and the like), give each student a copy, and ask the class to get the autograph of one person who fits each profile.

- Convince students that learning to work effectively with others will benefit them throughout their lives.

- Teach students how to move efficiently into groups of various sizes.

- Use role-playing activities to teach students cooperative skills.

- Form mixed-ability groups.

- Allow newly formed groups to engage in team-building activities to promote group cohesion.

- Allow students to engage in groupwork activities without unnecessary interventions by you.

Assessing Learning

Effective assessment requires many approaches—individual and group, informal and formal—to create a well-rounded understanding of student performance. Here are some tips for evaluating student work.

Informal Assessment

Assessment of day-to-day activities benefits both you and your students. You send the message that every activity is important. And by identifying what works and what doesn't, you are able to adjust your instructional plans. Try these methods:

- Make your expectations known in advance so students will know how they will be rated.
- Note students' answers to questions, both oral and written.
- Evaluate participation in act-it-outs and class discussions.
- Look for students' level of cooperation in pairs and small groups.
- Ask students to assess their own work.
- Skim Interactive Student Notebooks as students work in class.

Groupwork Assessment

Evaluating groupwork presents a lot of questions: Should you rate the product or the process? The individual or the group? The amount of effort or the quality of the result? Here are five steps that will help you assess groupwork equitably:

1. Set clear criteria for evaluation.
2. Make both individuals and groups accountable.
3. Record notes as groups work and while they present their final products.
4. Have students complete self-assessments to evaluate their individual contributions as well as the group's performance.
5. Determine group and individual grades.

Formal Assessment

In addition to classroom observations and evaluation of student notebooks, you will need formal measurements of how much your students have learned. Research has shown that the TCI Approach improves student comprehension and retention. (For research results, visit www.teachtci.com.)

History Alive! The Ancient World provides an assessment for each chapter. You will find reproducible test pages in the Lesson Masters and answers in the Lesson Guide. Each chapter assessment has three parts.

Mastering the Content The first part contains multiple-choice questions that check students' understanding of the main concepts and content introduced in the chapter. These questions range from simple comprehension to application, analysis, and evaluation. They use the wording and formats most commonly found on standardized tests.

Applying Social Studies Skills The second part has short-answer tasks designed to assess how well students have mastered a wide range of history skills. Students are asked to read, compare, and analyze selected passages as well as a great variety of graphic elements, including maps, diagrams, illustrations, graphs, and tables of data. These skill assessments are scaffolded to guide students from simple tasks, such as identifying data, to more complex critical thinking tasks.

Exploring the Essential Question The third part returns to the Essential Question, asking students to apply what they have learned to a constructed-response task. Each writing task is accompanied by a prompt that provides information for students to draw upon and is carefully scaffolded to help students gather and organize the information they will need to complete the task. The final work product may be a written piece or a visual representation of information, similar to those called for in state assessments that include constructed-response tasks.

You will find digital versions of the assessments online at TeachTCI (see page xxvi). You can use the tests as they are, randomize the order of questions, edit questions, or add your own questions.

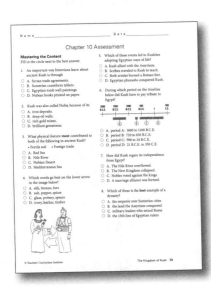

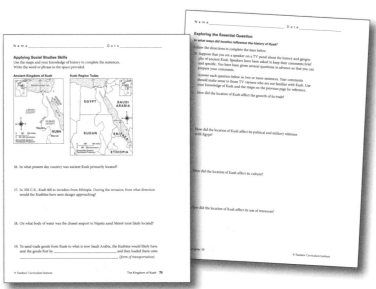

Enhancing Instruction with TeachTCI

Support for *History Alive! The Ancient World* extends beyond the box of print and audiovisual materials to a wealth of technology components. With a subscription to TeachTCI providing access to exclusive online resources, you will have the following tools to help you plan and extend lessons and customize assessments.

Teacher Resources Materials Online

Access digital versions of components—such as the Lesson Guide, Lesson Masters, and Interactive Student Notebook—all organized by chapter. Preview, print, and project items as needed.

Classroom Presenter

Project a digital lesson guide for each classroom activity from your internet-connected computer. Hidden teaching notes pop up for your eyes only, while animated visuals show students what to do.

Student Edition

You and your students can view the Student Edition text and images online. You'll see what your students are reading as you assign them chapters and Reading Challenges.

Reading Challenges Scoring Manager

Assign Reading Challenges to your class and track results of both individual students and entire classes. You'll know how much your students understand and which topics need reinforcement.

Assessment Creator

Build customized assessments for your class. This tool lets you add, delete, edit, and sort questions and answers.

Lesson Tips from the TCI Community

Get ideas, engage in professional exchanges with teachers around the country, and share your own best practices. Our discussion groups are organized by program and chapter.

Enrichment Resources

Enhance student learning with chapter-related Web links and in-depth essays on selected topics.

Customized State Correlations

See how the content you are teaching aligns to your state standards in easy-to-read chart form.

Enhancing Engagement with LearnTCI

LearnTCI allows students to interact with *History Alive! The Ancient World* on any computer with Internet access. With a LearnTCI subscription, students have access to the following online tools and resources.

Student Edition Text and Images

Students can read their Student Edition anywhere they have access to a computer with an Internet connection. They can zoom in on any image and sharpen their reading skills with a wealth of features.

Text-to-Audio Tool for Accessibility

Students can highlight the text and have it read to them. You decide which students have access to this feature, which is geared primarily toward English language learners and students reading below grade level.

Text Highlighting Tool

Students can highlight what they think are the main ideas of each section.

Main Idea Viewer

After using the Text Highlighting Tool, students can compare their answers to the main ideas identified by the program. Again, you decide which students have access to this feature. It is especially helpful for English language learners and students reading below grade level.

Reading Challenges

In Reading Challenges, students analyze videos, visuals, or primary sources related to the text and then respond to questions. To answer correctly, they need to read and understand the text as well as the multimedia element. Students receive immediate feedback, so if they didn't answer a question correctly, they can reread the passage to discover the correct answer.

Enrichment Resources

Students can gain deeper understanding by exploring links to other chapter-related Web sites and reading in-depth essays on selected topics.

Learn more about TeachTCI and LearnTCI at **www.teachtci.com/tech-demo**.

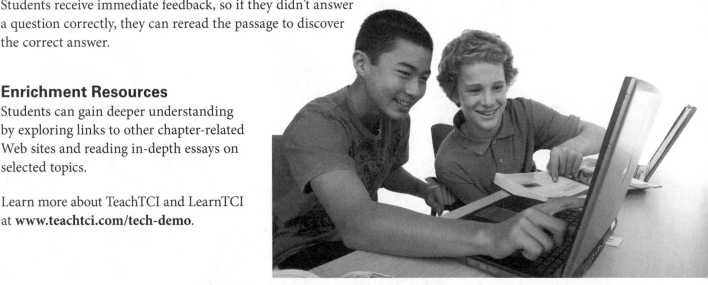

Growing Professionally

There is much, much more to learn about igniting students' interest in history and creating insightful and memorable classroom experiences. For a complete explanation of the TCI Approach, the Interactive Student Notebook, and how to create a cooperative, tolerant classroom, we encourage you to read *Bring Learning Alive!* This book covers every aspect of TCI's methodology for the middle and high school social studies classroom. Please visit **www.teachtci.com** or call Customer Service at **800-497-6138** for more information or to order.

TCI Academy Training

After you have taught a few TCI lessons and seen your students' active interest in learning about history, you may find that they have reignited your passion for teaching. Help your colleagues remember why they went into teaching by bringing TCI Academy training to your school or district.

Trainings are built around immersion lessons, in which teachers become students to experience the power of active, student-centered instruction. TCI Academy trainers are classroom teachers themselves and debrief activities to provide immediate feedback. You can mix and match TCI Academy sessions to build a course that best meets your needs. Please visit **www.tciacademy.com** or call us at **800-840-2698** to get started.

Early Humans and the Rise of Civilization

Overview

This activity introduces the geographic information essential to Unit 1. Students read and interpret maps to learn about key features that led to the development and settlement patterns of early humans. They annotate a map of Africa and the Middle East, answer questions in their Interactive Student Notebooks, and then discuss critical thinking questions. Students' comprehension of content and proficiency in map-reading and higher-order thinking skills will help you gauge their readiness for the unit. The pages that follow include a completed map, answers to questions, a scoring guide to inform your teaching, and suggestions for modifications to meet specific student needs.

Essential Geographic Understandings

1. Location of Africa and the Middle East

2. Key physical features including the Nile River, Great Rift Valley, Mediterranean Sea, Tigris River, and Euphrates River

3. Location of the Fertile Crescent and the Nile River valley

4. Impact of physical geography on the rise of civilization

Procedures

1 **Introduce the unit.** Tell students they will learn about the five types of early humans that developed over millions of years, the development of these early human ancestors over time, the gradual change from hunting-and-gathering societies to farming societies, and the resulting rise of civilization. (**Note:** In Chapter 2, students will be introduced to the term *hominid,* meaning "an early ancestor of humans.")

2 **Create a KWL chart.** Ask students to identify what they already know about early humans and what they want to learn. Use their responses to gauge how much additional background information they will need as you progress through the unit. Students will return to the KWL chart at the end of the unit and add the key information they have learned.

3 **Have students read Unit 1 "Setting the Stage" in the Student Edition.**

4 **Have students complete the Geography Challenge.** Monitor students as they work. You may wish to project the map from the Interactive Student Notebook and have students annotate it as the class works through the map-reading questions. Make sure students have grasped Essential Geographic Understandings 1 to 3.

5 **Discuss the "Critical Thinking" questions.** Help students understand the geographic relationships described in Essential Geographic Understanding 4.

Africa and the Middle East

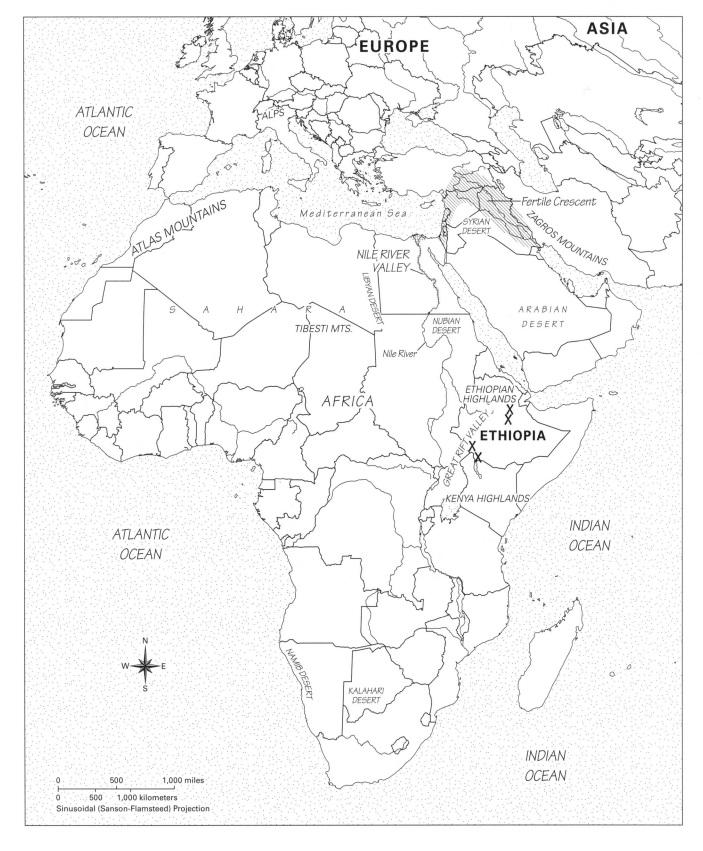

ASIA

EUROPE

ATLANTIC
OCEAN

ALPS

ATLAS MOUNTAINS

Mediterranean Sea

Fertile Crescent

SYRIAN
DESERT

ZAGROS MOUNTAINS

NILE RIVER
VALLEY

LIBYAN DESERT

S A H A R A

TIBESTI MTS.

NUBIAN
DESERT

A R A B I A N
D E S E R T

Nile River

AFRICA

ETHIOPIAN
HIGHLANDS

ETHIOPIA

GREAT RIFT VALLEY

KENYA HIGHLANDS

ATLANTIC
OCEAN

INDIAN
OCEAN

N
W   E
S

NAMIB DESERT

KALAHARI
DESERT

INDIAN
OCEAN

0   500   1,000 miles
0   500   1,000 kilometers
Sinusoidal (Sanson-Flamsteed) Projection

Geography Skills

Score 1 point for each correct answer. Use the map on the previous page to check shading and labeling.

1. Use the annotated map to check students' label for Africa. Europe lies to the north of Africa. Asia lies to the northeast of Africa.

2. Use the annotated map to check students' label for the Nile River. The Nile River flows into the Mediterranean Sea.

3. Use the annotated map to check students' shading and labeling of the Nile River valley.

4. The Fertile Crescent is the curved region in the Middle East, extending from the Persian Gulf to the Mediterranean Sea. The Tigris and the Euphrates rivers run through the Fertile Crescent. Use the annotated map to check students' shading and labeling of the Fertile Crescent.

5. Students should label the Atlantic Ocean, the Mediterranean Sea, and the Indian Ocean.

6. Check students' placement of an X in the Great Rift Valley region to mark the location of the fossil discovery. The annotated map has four; accept any one or any X in the Great Rift Valley region.

7. Students should label the Sahara, Arabian Desert, Syrian Desert, Kalahari Desert, Namib Desert, Nubian Desert, Libyan Desert.

8. Because the desert is dry, it is inhospitable to human life. Thus, early people avoided settling in the desert. Rather, they chose areas near rivers, which provided fresh water and fish, allowed them to grow crops, and later became the means of transport for trading.

Critical Thinking

Questions may have more than one correct answer. Score 1 to 3 points for each reasonable answer, depending on the strength of students' geographic reasoning.

9. Students should note that migration to the north would have required early humans to cross the Mediterranean Sea, in which case early humans would have needed the technology and resources to build some sort of seagoing vessel. It might have been easier for these people to migrate over land, making their way around the desert, to the Fertile Crescent.

10. Mesopotamia lies between the Tigris and the Euphrates rivers in the Fertile Crescent.

11. Without resources such as stone, wood, and metal, the people of the Fertile Crescent would have few materials with which to build shelters. In addition, it would have been difficult to craft any type of tools.

12. People need water to survive. They need fresh water for drinking and irrigating their crops. Fish and other sources of food live in water, as well, and waterways provide a method of transportation. For these reasons, early peoples naturally settled in those areas that had a reliable water supply.

Using Scores to Inform Instruction

Geography Skills A score of 6 out of 8 or better indicates that students have acquired sufficient geographic information to proceed with the unit.

Critical Thinking A score of 8 out of 12 or better indicates that students are beginning to understand the relationships between physical geography and the different ways in which people live.

Modifying Instruction

ELL or Learners with Special Education Needs Consider focusing on map-reading questions or limiting the number of "Critical Thinking" questions.

Students with Weak Map or Critical Thinking Skills Assign appropriate pages from the Social Studies Skills Toolkit in the back of the Lesson Masters.

Investigating the Past

How do social scientists interpret the past?

Overview

In a Social Studies Skill Builder, students learn how social scientists reconstruct the lives of prehistoric humans by examining images of cave paintings and other artifacts.

Objectives

In the course of reading this chapter and participating in the classroom activity, students will

Social Studies

- explain how social scientists such as archaeologists, historians, and geographers investigate the past.
- hypothesize about the lives of prehistoric humans and compare ideas with those of social scientists.
- interpret a cave painting by using the methodology of social scientists.

Language Arts

- clarify an understanding of texts by creating logical notes.
- write expository compositions that offer persuasive eveidence to validate arguments and conclusions.

Social Studies Vocabulary

Key Content Terms archaeologist, historian, geographer, artifact, prehistoric, ritual

Academic Vocabulary feature, environment, geometric, researcher, texture

Materials

*History Alive!
The Ancient World*

Interactive Student Notebooks

Visuals 1A and 1B

Placards 1A–1E (5 sets of 5; create additional sets of placards)

CD Track 1 (optional)

Lesson Masters
- Information Master 1 (1 transparency)
- Vocabulary Development handout (1 per student, on colored paper)

Activity	Suggested Time	Materials
Preview	10 minutes	• Interactive Student Notebooks
Vocabulary Development	30–40 minutes	• *History Alive! The Ancient World* • Interactive Student Notebooks • Vocabulary Development handout
Social Studies Skill Builder	60 minutes (1–2 regular periods) (1 block period)	• *History Alive! The Ancient World* • Interactive Student Notebooks • Visual 1A • Placards 1A–1E (5 sets of 5) • CD Track 1 (optional) • Information Master 1 (1 transparency)
Processing	15 minutes	• Interactive Student Notebooks • Visual 1B
Assessment	40 minutes	• Chapter 1 Assessment

Preview

1 **Have students complete the Preview activity in their Interactive Student Notebooks.** Students sketch a personal object and analyze it from the perspective of a social scientist living 20,000 years from now.

2 **Have volunteers share their answers.** Ask several students to share the object they drew and to explain what it might reveal about our lives today.

3 **Facilitate a brief discussion.** Ask,

- Will people living tens of thousands of years from now find it difficult to tell a complete story about our lives today? Why or why not?

- Do you think people in the future might reach conclusions that are incorrect or only partly true? Explain.

4 **Explain the connection between the Preview activity and Chapter 1.** Tell students that their objects will be considered "artifacts" by social scientists living 20,000 years from now, because the objects will provide clues about our current way of life. Likewise, prehistoric humans have left artifacts that give us clues about how they once lived. Social scientists act like detectives by carefully examining ancient art and artifacts and then drawing conclusions about these early humans. As each new clue is discovered, social scientists may need to change their interpretations. In this chapter, students will learn about the work of social scientists and emulate the "detective" process by making observations and hypotheses about cave art and artifacts.

> **Writing: Oral and Written Conventions**
>
> To write and talk about history, students should be using not just the simple past, present, and future tenses but also the perfect tenses. Review the past perfect tense, which is formed with *had* and used for the earlier of two past actions. Give examples such as, "The people *had grown* [past perfect] crops there before the river *flooded* [past]." Be sure students can identify the use of the past perfect in the text and use it correctly in their own formal presentations and writing.

Vocabulary Development

1 **Introduce the Key Content Terms.** Have students locate the Key Content Terms for the chapter in their Interactive Student Notebooks. These are important terms that will help them understand the main ideas of the chapter. Ask volunteers to identify any familiar terms and how they might be used in a sentence.

2 **Have students complete a Vocabulary Development handout.** Give each student a copy of the Vocabulary Development handout of your choice from the Reading Toolkit at the back of the Lesson Masters. These handouts provide extra Key Content Term practice and support, depending on your students' needs. Review the completed handout by asking volunteers to share one answer for each term.

Reading

1 **Introduce the Essential Question and have students read Section 1.1.** Afterward, have students use information from the section and from the chapter opener image to propose some possible answers to the Essential Question: *How do social scientists interpret the past?*

2 **Have students complete the Reading Notes for Chapter 1.** Before conducting the Social Studies Skill Builder, assign Sections 1.2 and 1.3. Use Guide to Reading Notes 1 to review these sections as a class and answer any questions students may have. Assign Sections 1.4 to 1.9 during the activity, as indicated in the procedures that follow. Remind students to use the Key Content Terms where appropriate as they complete their Reading Notes.

Social Studies Skill Builder

1 **Prepare the classroom.** Set up five stations around the room as shown at right. At each station, post the corresponding set of Placards 1A–1E on the wall. (**Note:** Create additional sets of placards.) Consider making a fun, cave-like environment. Turn on just one or two desk lamps, and turn off the overhead lights. Provide or have students bring in flashlights to help them explore the "cave" stations. Place the placards along the wall or on the floor underneath the sets of desks. Play CD Track 1, "Cave Sound Effects," while students are working.

2 **Place students in pairs and introduce the activity.** Tell students that they will be interpreting photographs of paintings and artifacts found in caves once inhabited by prehistoric humans. Students will play the role of detectives of the past to discover and interpret clues about how prehistoric humans lived.

3 **Review the directions for the activity.** Project a transparency of *Information Master 1: Directions for Interpreting Cave Art* and review the steps with the class.

4 **Model the activity.**

- Project *Visual 1A: Cave Painting of a Human* and tell students that this is a photograph of cave art.

- Have students turn to Reading Notes 1 in their Interactive Student Notebooks and find the image in their notes that matches the photograph on the transparency.

- As a class, complete the section of the Reading Notes that corresponds to this photograph (Section 1.4).

- Answer any questions students may have.

5 **Conduct the activity.** Project Information Master 1 again and leave it projected for students' use during the activity. Use Guide to Reading Notes 1 to check students' work. Continue this process until most pairs have had a chance to examine all the images.

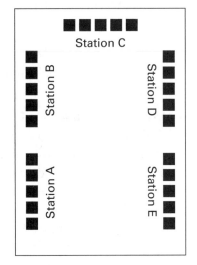

Placards 1A–1E

Information Master 1

6 **Wrap up the activity.** Ask students,

- From the evidence you gathered, what do we know for certain about the prehistoric humans who left their marks on these caves? (For example, we know something about the tools and materials cave artists used.)

- How did your interpretations of prehistoric humans change as you uncovered new information?

- What are some questions about prehistoric humans that social scientists still need to answer? (For example, why did cave artists paint? How did cave artists learn to paint?)

Visual 1A

Processing

1 **Have students use the skills of social scientists in analyzing a rock painting to complete the Processing activity.** Project *Visual 1B: Rock Painting.* Have students turn to the Processing activity for Chapter 1 in their Interactive Student Notebooks. Students will "discover" a rock painting in Africa and use the "detective" skills of social scientists to analyze it.

2 **Ask volunteers to share their answers.** Encourage students to defend their hypotheses by presenting evidence from the rock painting. As students present different hypotheses, reiterate that our interpretations of the past may be wrong and subject to change.

Visual 1B

3 **Reveal what social scientists think about the painting.** This is a rock painting from Pahi, Tanzania, showing a slender figure playing a flute or pipe. Social scientists have made the following hypotheses about this painting:

- A slender figure is playing a flute or pipe. Musical notes may drip from the end of the flute.

- The tail-like attachment may be a back apron, a garment still worn by men in southern Africa. For this reason, the musician is most likely a male.

- The figure does not have a face. Scholars think prehistoric humans feared that showing a person's face in works of art would lessen that person's power.

- The musician may be wearing a headdress.

- Prehistoric humans may have created this rock painting for use in a secret ritual in which they used music to contact spirits.

Quicker Coverage

Eliminate Stations To give students a quicker sampling of cave art and artifacts, set up only Stations A, C, and E. Before the activity, place students in groups of three.

Deeper Coverage

Enhance the Preview Activity After students have completed the Preview activity, read aloud selected excerpts from David Macaulay's *Motel of the Mysteries*. In this illustrated story, an archaeologist in the 41st century finds a 20th-century motel and mistakenly determines that it is a ceremonial burial chamber. Emphasize to students that historical interpretations may be incorrect and subject to change, as new evidence is discovered.

Analyze a List of Trash To give students practice in both their observation and hypothesis skills, present the following scenario and critical thinking questions:

"You have just arrived at a campsite. You see an ordinary can of trash and are suddenly overcome by a strong desire to sift through it to learn about the people who were here before you. The following list contains all the items you find in the trash can, in order, from the top to the bottom of the barrel."

1. diaper
2. broken sunglasses
3. soda cans
4. paper plates, plastic forks
5. foil
6. chicken bones
7. corn cobs
8. cherry fruit-drink bottles
9. broken necklace
10. red-stained clothes
11. size 16 boy's shirt, sleeve ripped
12. diaper
13. suntan lotion
14. soda cans
15. fishing line, old hooks
16. diaper
17. paper plates, plastic forks
18. bread bag wrapper
19. orange-juice container
20. egg shells
21. empty can of camping fuel
22. gum wrappers
23. diaper
24. toy doll dress
25. paper plates, plastic forks
26. soda cans
27. hot dog package
28. marshmallow bag

Use the evidence found in the trash to answer the following questions:

1. How many meals did the campers eat? What did they eat at each meal?

2. How many people do you think were at the campsite? What were their ages?

3. What are three activities the people did while camping? Give evidence to support you answer.

4. What other hypotheses can you make about who was camping or what happened while camping?

5. Explain how the following circumstances would change your conclusions:

   a The garbage list is *not* in any order.

   b. Some garbage is missing.

   c. Many different groups of campers had been to this campsite.

Assessment

Mastering the Content

1. C	5. D	9. A	13. A
2. B	6. B	10. D	14. B
3. B	7. A	11. C	15. B
4. A	8. D	12. C	

Applying Social Studies Skills

16. clay

17. The cracks may have happened soon after the sculptures were made, while the clay was drying.

18. Geographers would most likely be interested in the information describing the discovery of an artifact deep in a cave formed by an underground river in southern France.

19. The bisons' location, deep inside the cave, in a part of the cave that is hard to get to, may be the most likely reason why the bison sculptures were not found until modern times.

Exploring the Essential Question

20. Answers should include all of the elements requested in the prompt.

Scoring Rubric

Score	Description
3	Student poses three questions appropriate to the expertise of the three professions: archaeologist, historian, and geographer. (Sample questions: [archaeologist] What kinds of tools did the people at the site use? [historian] What events appear to have happened at the site? [geographer] Where is the site, and how did the people living there use their environment to survive?)
2	Student poses two questions appropriate to the respective professions. The third question is inappropriate or missing.
1	Student poses one question appropriate to one of the professions. The other two questions are inappropriate or missing.
0	Response does not match the task or is incorrect.

English Language Learners

Introduce the Term *Hypothesis* Before students complete the Reading Notes, help them understand what a hypothesis is. Give students concrete scenarios to show them that they make hypotheses every day. Below are some suggestions:

- A friend comes over to your house, and his or her hair is all wet. What hypotheses can you make about why your friend's hair is wet? *(It is raining outside, the friend just got out of the shower, someone threw a water balloon at your friend, etc.)*

- You wake up one morning in February and do not hear the usual sounds of traffic moving up and down the street. Hypothesize reasons why this might be the case. *(Cars cannot get through the deep snow that fell overnight, there is less traffic on weekend days, you set your alarm clock too early by mistake, etc.)*

Alternatively, place a "mystery" item in a bag or box. Have students examine the bag or reach in the box. They should then hypothesize what the mystery item might be. Make sure that students give evidence to back up their hypotheses.

Support the Class Discussion To prepare students to participate in the class discussion at the end of the Social Studies Skill Builder, provide them with a typed version of the three wrap-up questions. Have students think about or even write their responses to these questions while completing the activity.

Learners Reading and Writing Below Grade Level

Support the Reading Notes Conduct a prereading session before students read Section 1.2. Ask, *What is the title of this section? What are the headings in this section? What do you see in the image? Which subsection corresponds to the image? What do you already know about the people mentioned in the headings? What do you want to know about these people?* Then have students read and complete the corresponding Reading Notes for this section. Review the answers as a class. Before students read Section 1.3, ask, *What is the title of this section? What do you see in the image? Why do you think social scientists care about cave*

paintings? Then have students read and complete the corresponding Reading Notes for this section. Review the answers as a class.

Learners with Special Education Needs

Modify Activity Requirements To help students complete the Social Studies Skill Builder, reduce the number of placards they must examine. Or have students examine all five placards and label the significant details, but then read only three or four sections of the text. For the remaining sections, provide students with a copy of Guide to Reading Notes 1, from the Lesson Guide, to read and highlight.

Scaffold the Processing Activity Make the following modifications:

- As you project Visual 1B, ask students, *What interesting details do you see in this image? What colors, shapes, and materials are used in this artwork? What emotion does this artwork communicate to you? What do you think this person is doing?*

- Tell students that this is a rock painting from Pahi, Tanzania, showing a slender figure playing a flute or pipe. Then have students complete the Processing activity in their Interactive Student Notebooks.

- Before sharing their hypotheses as a class, students should share with a partner to brainstorm additional ideas and evidence.

Advanced Learners

Take a Virtual Tour Encourage students to write a paper based on a virtual tour of the cave at Lascaux (available on the Internet). As students progress through the tour, have them take notes for a one-page narrative. Their paper should describe their "walk" through the cave and include

- a short paragraph to set the scene.
- descriptions of three or four specific paintings in the cave.
- an analysis of what the paintings indicate about the lives of these ancient people.

Enrichment Resources

Find out more about the study of ancient history by exploring the following Enrichment Resources for *History Alive! The Ancient World* at www.teachtci.com.

Enrichment Readings These in-depth readings encourage students to explore selected topics related to the chapter. You may also find readings that relate the chapter's content directly to your state's curriculum.

Internet Connections The recommended Web sites provide useful and engaging content that reinforces skills development and mastery of subjects within the chapter.

Literature Recommendations

The following books offer opportunities to extend the content in this chapter.

Boy of the Painted Cave by Justin F. Denzel (New York: Putnam, 1996)

The Cave Painter of Lascaux by Roberta Angeletti (Berkeley, CA: Crystal Publications, 2004)

Dawn of Art: The Chauvet Cave by Jean-Marie Chauvet (New York: Harry N. Abrams, 1996)

Section 1.2

1.

Type of Social Scientist	What do they do?	What questions do they ask?	Symbol that represents their work
Archaeologists	Study the past by examining artifacts such as tools and coins.	Who lived in this place? When did they live here? What were they like?	Answers will vary.
Historians	Record the past. Study artifacts and documents.	What happened in the past? Why did events happen the way they did?	Answers will vary.
Geographers	Study natural and human features of the Earth. Create maps.	Where did people live? How did they use their environment to survive?	Answers will vary.

2. Social scientists are like detectives because they examine clues, ask questions, make observations, and come up with theories about how humans came to be.

Section 1.3

1. From cave paintings, social scientists can learn what kinds of animals roamed the Earth, what methods people used to hunt them, and what people believed.

2. Sketches will vary but may include bits of rope, lamps, and tools for painting and engraving.

Section 1.4

1,2. Labels and hypotheses will vary.

3. Additional important items students may label: mammoth or bison, spear, insides of the animal, birdlike mask, long stick with bird on top (spear thrower).

4. Many social scientists think that this painting was created as part of a hunting ritual. The artist may have been either asking for a successful hunt or recording something that actually happened.

Section 1.5

1,2. Labels and hypotheses will vary.

3. Additional important items students may label: bulls, bison, horses, ledge.

4. Social scientists' ideas include that the artist may have been trying to either capture the animals' "magical powers" or honor or please spirits. This painting may have also been used in a religious ceremony.

Section 1.6

1,2. Labels and hypotheses will vary.

3. Additional important items students may label: circular shape, sticklike animal, handprints.

4. Many social scientists think that the handprints were a way for artists to sign their paintings. The geometric shapes may have had special meanings in rituals.

Section 1.7

1,2. Labels and hypotheses will vary.

3. Additional important items students may label: leaping horse carved into the top, hundreds of tiny dashes in horse's head.

4. Some social scientists think that this tool was created for hunting. The horse carving may have been a good-luck symbol. It may have had some relation to the hunter's name or clan. Or it may have just been a decoration.

Section 1.8

1,2. Labels and hypotheses will vary.

3. Additional important items students may label: bison, gold-colored clay, carved lines for animal faces, coat markings, and fur.

4. Social scientists think these sculptures may have been created to show that the cave belonged to a certain clan or that an important coming-of-age ceremony took place there.

Section 1.9

1,2. Labels and hypotheses will vary.

3. Additional important items students may label: two piles of colored, rock-hard minerals; grindstone; sculptor's pick; engraving tool.

4. Social scientists think that the grindstone was used for grinding minerals into powder to make paints. The sharpened stone might have been used for sculpting and engraving.

Early Hominids

What capabilities helped hominids survive?

Overview

Students learn about the physical and cultural development of early hominid groups. In a Visual Discovery activity, students analyze images of various hominid groups and explore how physical and cultural adaptations gave later hominid groups advantages over earlier groups.

Objectives

In the course of reading this chapter and participating in the classroom activity, students will

Social Studies

- identify when and where various hominid groups lived.
- describe the physical and cultural adaptations of each hominid group.
- analyze how the capabilities of each hominid group—development of tools, use of fire, and living in groups—helped them survive.

Language Arts

- analyze text that uses the compare-and-contrast organizational pattern.
- use effective coordination and subordination of ideas to express complete thoughts.

Social Studies Vocabulary

Key Content Terms anthropologist, hominid, capability, migrate

Academic Terms skeleton, trait, intelligence, community, contribute

Materials

History Alive!
The Ancient World

Interactive Student Notebooks

Visuals 2A–2D

Lesson Masters

- Student Handout 2 (1 per group of 4)
- Vocabulary Development handout (1 per student, on colored paper)

Activity	Suggested Time	Materials
Preview	10 minutes	• Interactive Student Notebooks
Vocabulary Development	30–40 minutes	• *History Alive! The Ancient World* • Interactive Student Notebooks • Vocabulary Development handout
Visual Discovery	80 minutes (3 regular periods) (2 block periods)	• *History Alive! The Ancient World* • Interactive Student Notebooks • Visuals 2A–2D • Student Handout 2 (1 per group of 4)
Processing	15 minutes	• Interactive Student Notebooks
Assessment	40 minutes	• Chapter 2 Assessment

Preview

1 **Have students complete the Preview activity in their Interactive Student Notebooks.** Students describe the capabilities, or skills, of their favorite superhero and explain why these capabilities are important.

2 **Have students share their answers in pairs or as a class.**

3 **Explain the connection between the Preview activity and Chapter 2.** Tell students that, in the Preview activity, we call those characters superheroes because they have capabilities that we consider "superhuman," or beyond our capabilities today. In this chapter, students will learn about groups of prehistoric humans called hominids. Each hominid group developed new capabilities that gave them survival advantages over earlier hominid groups. In a way, each group could be considered a "super" version of the group that preceded it.

Vocabulary Development

1 **Introduce the Key Content Terms.** Have students locate the Key Content Terms for the chapter in their Interactive Student Notebooks. These are important terms that will help them understand the main ideas of the chapter. Ask volunteers to identify any familiar terms and how they might be used in a sentence.

2 **Have students complete a Vocabulary Development handout.** Give each student a copy of the Vocabulary Development handout of your choice from the Reading Toolkit at the back of the Lesson Masters. These handouts provide extra Key Content Term practice and support, depending on your students' needs. Review the completed handout by asking volunteers to share one answer for each term.

Reading

1 **Introduce the Essential Question and have students read Section 2.1.** Have students identify the Essential Question on the first page of the chapter. *What capabilities helped hominids survive?* Next have them read Section 2.1 and review the timeline in Section 2.2. Then ask students,

- What are hominids, and what kind of social scientist studies them?

- According to the timeline in Section 2.2, what are the names of the hominid groups you will learn about in this chapter?

- Which is the earliest hominid group? Which is the most recent?

- Which hominid group lived on Earth for the longest time period? For the shortest?

- What else would you like to know about hominid groups?

Reading: Expository Critique

As students read, have them consider how well the text presents the topic of hominids and the main idea that certain capabilities helped each hominid survive. Require students to support their assessment by citing specific text features, as well as specific phrases and sentences, that clearly describe and explain hominids and their capabilities.

2 **Have students complete the Reading Notes for Chapter 2.** Before conducting the Visual Discovery activity, have students read Section 2.2 in WRAP ("Whisper Read Alternating Paragraphs") pairs. Use the Guide to Reading Notes to help the class complete the Reading Notes for this section. Assign Sections 2.3 to 2.6 during the activity, as indicated in the procedures that follow. Remind students to use the Key Content Terms where appropriate as they complete their Reading Notes.

Visual Discovery

1 **Project *Visual 2A: Homo Habilis* and guide students in examining the image.** Have students carefully analyze the image and answer these questions:

- What interesting details do you see in this image?

- Which details give us clues about the location of this image?

- What activities are these hominids doing?

- What is significant about the way the hominids are removing the zebra skin, especially when compared with what most animals might do after killing prey?

- What does this image tell us about the capabilities of these hominids?

2 **Have students read Section 2.3 and complete the corresponding Reading Notes.** Have students work in pairs to complete their notes. Afterward, review the answers as a class.

3 **Project *Visual 2B: Homo Erectus* and guide students in examining the image.** Have students carefully analyze the image and answer these questions:

- What interesting details do you see in this image?

- Is the location of this image the same as the one in the first image? How can you tell?

- What activities are these hominids doing that are similar to the first group?

- What activities are different?

- Why might their different capabilities give this hominid group some advantages over the first group?

4 **Have students read Section 2.4 and complete the corresponding Reading Notes with their partners.** Review the answers as a class.

5 **Have students prepare to bring the image in Visual 2B to life by conducting an act-it-out.**

- Place students in groups of four and give each group a copy of *Student Handout 2: Early Hominid Act-It-Out Directions*.

- Assign each group a character in the image of *Homo Erectus*.

Visual 2A

Visual 2B

Student Handout 2

Group members will use that character's perspective to complete the steps on the handout. (**Note:** There is room below each question for students to write notes on the handout during the act-it-out preparation.)

- Give groups several minutes to prepare.

6 **Conduct the act-it-out.** Do the following:

- Call up one actor from each group to stand in front of the appropriate character in the projection of Visual 2B, taking on the body posture and facial expression of that character.

- Acting as the on-scene reporter, ask the different characters some of the questions from the handout.

- After the act-it-out, have the audience give the actors a round of applause.

7 **Project *Visual 2C: Homo Sapiens Neanderthalensis* and guide students in examining the image.** Have students carefully analyze the image and answer these questions:

- What interesting details do you see in this image?

- What activities are these hominids doing that are similar to the previous group? What activities are different?

- Why might their different capabilities give this hominid group some advantages over the previous group?

Visual 2C

8 **Have students read Section 2.5 and complete the corresponding Reading Notes with their partners.** Review the answers as a class. (**Note:** The word *Neanderthal* may also be spelled *Neandertal*.)

9 **Project *Visual 2D: Homo Sapiens Sapiens* and guide students in examining the image.** Have students carefully analyze the image and answer these questions:

- What interesting details do you see in this image?

- What do you think they are doing?

- What kinds of tools would help them do this?

- Why do you think they are doing this?

- How might this activity benefit their whole group, or clan?

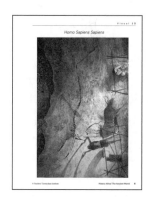

Visual 2D

10 **Have students read Section 2.6 and complete the corresponding Reading Notes with their partners.** Review the answers as a class.

11 **Have students prepare to bring the image in Visual 2D to life by conducting an act-it-out.**

- Have students get into their original groups of four and take out their copy of Student Handout 2.

- Assign each group a character in the image of *Homo Sapiens Sapiens*.

- Give groups several minutes to complete the steps on the handout, from their character's perspective.

12 Conduct the act-it-out. Do the following:

- Call up one actor from each group to stand in front of the appropriate character in the projection of Visual 2D, taking on the body posture and facial expression of that character. (**Note:** You may want to include more students by calling up two or three actors for each character in the image.)

- Acting as the on-scene reporter, ask the different characters some of the questions from the handout.

- After the act-it-out, have the audience give the actors a round of applause.

13 Wrap up the activity. Ask students,

- What interesting things did you learn in this chapter?

- What capabilities helped hominids survive?

Processing

Have students complete the Processing activity on a separate sheet of paper in their notebooks. Students will create a poster highlighting the capabilities of one of the hominid groups.

Quicker Coverage

Simplify the Act-It-Outs Rather than organize group act-it-outs, conduct "talking statue" act-it-outs. Follow these steps:

- After students have analyzed one of the images, assign pairs to a character in the image.

- Have each pair use information from the image and from their Reading Notes to complete the following sentence: "I feel _____ because . . ."

- Have one partner from each pair come up to the image and freeze in the position of their character.

- Tell students that when you tap them on the shoulder, they will "come to life," read their statement, and then freeze back into position.

- Quickly move through the statues, bringing them to life to hear their statements.

- After the act-it-out, have the audience give the actors a round of applause.

Divide and Conquer To reduce the amount of reading, divide the class into groups and assign each group one of the early hominids from Sections 2.3 to 2.6. (**Note:** You may need to assign more than one group to each hominid.) Give each group the corresponding Visual Discovery questions listed in this Lesson Guide for examining each visual. Give groups time to answer the questions, using the image in their textbook, and then give them time to complete the Reading Notes in their Interactive Student Notebooks. Project Visual 2A and have the *Homo habilis* group come to the front of the room. Ask them to share their answers to the Visual Discovery questions and Reading Notes. Allow the class to ask questions to ensure that all students complete their Reading Notes.

Repeat this process for the remaining hominid groups, emphasizing that each successive group was more physically and culturally advanced than preceding groups.

Deeper Coverage

Enhance the Processing Activity Rather than have students create a poster that highlights a single hominid group, have them create "Early Hominid Trading Cards" for three or four of the hominid groups. The trading cards can be modeled after popular game cards, such as Pokémon or Yu-Gi-Oh!, or sports cards, such as those for baseball or basketball players. Require the following items on each card:

- the scientific name and nickname of the hominid group
- a drawing of the hominid group doing something in its natural environment
- three descriptive facts about the hominid group's capabilities
- an icon representing the hominid group's most important "power" or capability
- a student-generated quotation that pays tribute to the hominid group
- any other creative touches to make the trading cards look more realistic

Research Hominid Migration Ask students to research and map the migration of *Homo erectus* and *Homo sapiens sapiens* from Africa to the rest of the world.

Assessment

Mastering the Content

1. D	5. B	9. B	13. C
2. A	6. B	10. D	14. D
3. A	7. A	11. C	15. C
4. D	8. C	12. A	16. B

Applying Social Studies Skills

17. the National Geographic Society

18. proved that early hominids walked on two feet, about 3.6 million years ago

19. early interpretations were completely wrong

Exploring the Essential Question

20. Answers should include all of the elements requested in the prompt.

Scoring Rubric

Score	Description
3	Student writes a short story that meets all four bulleted points.
2	Student writes a story that meets two or three of the bulleted points.
1	Student writes a story that meets only one of the bulleted points.
0	Response does not match the task or is incorrect.

English Language Learners

Preteach the Term *Capability* Before class, display images of various superheroes. On the board, write the statement: "One capability of _____ is that s/he can _____." For each superhero, ask, *What is one capability of this superhero?* Have volunteers answer t by filling in the statement. Model an example for students: "One capability of <u>Superman</u> is that he can <u>fly</u>." Then have students complete the Preview activity in their Interactive Student Notebooks.

Support the Act-It-Outs Provide groups with a copy of Student Handout 2 for each act-it-out that you do in class. Allow groups time to write their answers on the handout, rehearse what they are going to say, and use the handout during the act-it-out.

Learners Reading and Writing Below Grade Level

Scaffold the Reading Notes Use Guide to Reading Notes 2 to model the note taking for each section.

- For Section 2.3, provide all answers.

- For Section 2.4, provide the answer to Question 4, omitting key words for students to fill in: "Because Upright Man had _____, they were able to walk long distances. This allowed them to _____ from Africa to Asia and Europe. They used _____ to cook animal meat, survive the cold, and protect themselves from _____. They created shelters with tools like the _____. Shelters allowed Upright Man to live in _____ climates and in areas without caves or other natural *shelters*."

- For Section 2.5, have students complete the following sentence openers from Question 4: "Because Neanderthals lived in *groups*, they . . . With their *spears*, they . . . Neanderthals showed a sense of *community* because . . . This capability would have given them the benefit of . . ."

- Students complete Section 2.6 on their own.

Color Code the Reading Notes For the Reading Notes, show students how color can enhance memory. By choosing a different color for each hominid group to color in the timeline and the relevant parts of the image, students may be better able to recall associations between each hominid group and its capabilities.

Learners with Special Education Needs

Modify the Act-It-Outs Consider doing the following:

- Before students leave for the day, assign as homework the roles of the characters in the act-it-outs. Provide the questions you will ask, as well as a copy of the visual on which each act-it-out is based. Tell students to rehearse what they will say and do.

- During each act-it-out, involve these students in the role of "on-scene reporter." Guide the reporter to ask each actor the questions from Student Handout 2.

Provide a Processing Template Create a template for the Processing activity that students can fill in without referring back to the instructions. For example, draw a line at the top of the paper and label it "Name of hominid group," or draw a box in the center of the page and label it "Sketch of your hominid group doing something in their natural environment."

Advanced Learners

Enhance the Act-It-Outs Consider the following suggestions to involve the audience during the act-it-outs:

- In the first act-it-out, identify two or three sound effects that would fit with the scene, and have the audience practice them. Explain that audience members can perform the sound effects only when you signal to start—such as pointing to them. They must stop immediately at your signal to do so.

- For the second act-it-out, give audience groups two minutes to brainstorm serious questions for the characters. Then have them question the characters.

Create a Hominid Flowchart Have students create an illustrated flowchart to show the progression of advancements from one early hominid group to the next. Have students make their chart on poster board or large sheets of construction paper. The flowchart should include

- the name of each group of early hominids.

- the approximate time period in which these hominids lived.

- an explanation in both words and pictures of the specific advancements that distinguish each group from the one that preceded it.

Enrichment Resources

Find out more about early hominids by exploring the following Enrichment Resources for *History Alive! The Ancient World* at www.teachtci.com.

Enrichment Readings These in-depth readings encourage students to explore selected topics related to the chapter. You may also find readings that relate the chapter's content directly to your state's curriculum.

Internet Connections The recommended Web sites provide useful and engaging content that reinforces skills development and mastery of subjects within the chapter.

Literature Recommendations

The following books offer opportunities to extend the content in this chapter.

Exploring History: Prehistoric Peoples by Philip Brooks (London: Southwater, 2008)

Neandertals: a prehistoric puzzle by Yvette La Pierre (Minneapolis, MN: Twenty-First Century Books, 2008)

The Wisdom of the Bones: In Search of Human Origins by Pat Shipman and Alan Walker (New York: Vintage Books, 1997)

Section 2.2

1. *Australopithecus afarensis*, Lucy

2. Students should color the first rectangle on the timeline.

3. Students may color and label the hominids standing on two legs.

4. Because Lucy and her relatives were *bipeds* (walked on two feet), they could gather and carry food more easily, and could use their hands for defense.

Section 2.3

1. *Homo habilis*, Handy Man

2. Students should color the second rectangle on the timeline.

3. Students may color and label groups of hominids sitting together, as well as simple tools (rocks) that the hominids are using to skin the zebra.

4. Because Handy Man lived in *groups*, they were better able to hunt and protect themselves. Because they used simple tools, they were able to dig or make traps to catch small animals, tear the meat from dead animals, and crush bones for the marrow inside.

Section 2.4

1. *Homo erectus*, Upright Man

2. Students should color the third rectangle on the timeline.

3. Students may color and label the hominids walking upright, using fire, and using tools to skin the animals. Students may draw and label a simple shelter (oval hut covered by tree branches).

4. Because Upright Man had *strong bones*, they were able to walk long distances. This allowed them to migrate from Africa to Asia and Europe. They used *fire* to cook animal meat, survive the cold, and protect themselves from predators. They created *shelters* with tools like the hand ax. *Shelters* allowed Upright Man to live in colder climates and in areas without caves or other natural *shelters*.

Section 2.5

1. *Homo sapiens neanderthalensis*, Neanderthal Man

2. Students should color the fourth rectangle on the timeline.

3. Students may color and label the hominids living in groups, taking care of each other, and carrying flowers. Students may draw and label tools such as knives, scrapers, and spear points.

4. Because Neanderthals lived in *groups*, they were better able to travel and hunt together. With their *spears*, they could better hunt and trap animals. Neanderthals showed a sense of *community* because they cared for their sick and injured. This capability brought them the benefit of learning from the experience of older members of the *group*.

Section 2.6

1. *Homo sapiens sapiens*, Doubly Wise Man, Early Modern Humans

2. Students should color the last (fifth) rectangle on the timeline.

3. Students may color and label clothing and artwork. Students may draw and label tools such as needles and sculpting blades, or weapons such as bows and arrows, hooks, and spears.

4. Because early modern humans created complex *tools* like needles, they could sew animal skins together to make *clothing* that protected them from the cold. They made *weapons* such as spears and bows and arrows, which allowed early humans to hunt from a safer distance. Their *artwork* such as cave paintings and sculptures shows that early humans had feelings about the world and could communicate their thoughts to others.

From Hunters and Gatherers to Farmers

How did the development of agriculture change daily life in the Neolithic Age?

Overview

In a Writing for Understanding activity, students learn how the Neolithic development of agriculture led to a stable food supply, permanent shelters, larger communities, specialized jobs, and trade. Students use this knowledge to create a comic book about two Stone Age characters.

Objectives

In the course of reading this chapter and participating in the classroom activity, students will

Social Studies

- identify Neolithic settlements and explain the reason for their location.
- compare the lives of hunters and gatherers during the Paleolithic Age with the lives of people during the Neolithic Age.
- explain how the domestication of plants and animals created a stable food supply and led to important changes in shelter, communities, jobs, and trade.

Language Arts

- read aloud expository text fluently and accurately, with appropriate pacing, intonation, and expression.
- write expository compositions that follow an appropriate organizational pattern.

Social Studies Vocabulary

Key Content Terms Paleolithic Age, Neolithic Age, Fertile Crescent, Catal Hoyuk, domesticate, agriculture, nomad, trade, resource

Academic Vocabulary enable, temporary, rectangular, efficiently, major

Materials

History Alive! The Ancient World

Interactive Student Notebooks

Visual 3

Lesson Masters

- Student Handouts 3A, 3B, and 3D (1 per pair)
- Student Handout 3C (3 per pair)
- Vocabulary Development handout (1 per each student, on colored paper)

scissors

glue

colored pencils or markers

Activity	Suggested Time	Materials
Preview	10 minutes	• Interactive Student Notebooks
Vocabulary Development	30–40 minutes	• *History Alive! The Ancient World* • Interactive Student Notebooks • Vocabulary Development handout
Writing for Understanding	100–150 minutes (3 regular periods) (2 block periods)	• *History Alive! The Ancient World* • Interactive Student Notebooks • Visual 3 • Student Handouts 3A, 3B, and 3D (1 per pair) • Student Handout 3C (3 per pair) • scissors • glue • colored pencils or markers
Processing (optional)	20 minutes	• Interactive Student Notebooks
Assessment	40 minutes	• Chapter 3 Assessment

Preview

1   **Have students complete the Preview activity in their Interactive Student Notebooks.** Students sketch a simple cartoon strip showing one way that the invention of the computer has changed people's lives.

2   **Have students share their answers in pairs or as a class.**

3   **Explain the connection between the Preview activity and Chapter 3.** Tell students that there are many inventions, such as the computer, that have greatly changed people's lives. For people living in the Stone Age, one of the most important developments of their time was agriculture—the growing of crops and the domestication of animals. In this chapter, students will learn how agriculture led to a stable food supply, and what effects this major development had on life in the Stone Age.

Vocabulary Development

1   **Introduce the Key Content Terms.** Have students locate the Key Content Terms for the chapter in their Interactive Student Notebooks. These are important terms that will help them understand the main ideas of the chapter. Ask volunteers to identify any familiar terms and how they might be used in a sentence.

2   **Have students complete a Vocabulary Development handout.** Give each student a copy of the Vocabulary Development handout of your choice from the Reading Toolkit at the back of the Lesson Masters. These handouts provide extra Key Content Term practice and support, depending on your students' needs. Review the completed handout by asking volunteers to share one answer for each term.

Reading

1   **Introduce the Essential Question and have students read Section 3.1.** Afterward, have students use information from the section and from the chapter opener image to propose some possible answers to the Essential Question: *How did the development of agriculture change daily life in the Neolithic Age?*

2   **Have students complete the Reading Notes for Chapter 3.** Assign Sections 3.2 to 3.7 during the activity, as indicated in the procedures that follow. Remind students to use the Key Content Terms where appropriate as they complete their Reading Notes.

Writing for Understanding

1   **Have students read Section 3.2 and complete the corresponding Reading Notes.** Tell students that the chapter will focus on how life changed during the Stone Age. This section will introduce them to the Old Stone (Paleolithic) Age and the New Stone (Neolithic) Age. Call on students to read the section aloud, one paragraph at a time. Use Guide to Reading Notes 3 to help the class complete the Reading Notes for this section.

2   **Introduce the activity.** Tell students that they will be working in pairs to create a comic book about the exciting changes during the Neolithic Age. Partners will write their comic books through the eyes of two cartoon characters, Neolithic Nel and Neolithic Nick. However, before pairs can begin their comic books, they must first learn the various ways in which life changed during the Neolithic Age.

3   **Place students in pairs and preview the structure of the Reading Notes.** Have students turn to Section 3.3 in their Interactive Student Notebooks. Review the following procedures:

   • First, students will read Section 3.3 about creating a stable food supply.

   • Then, they will answer the first question to summarize how people obtained food during the Paleolithic Age.

   • Finally, they will answer the remaining three questions about the Neolithic Age by filling in the speech bubbles for Neolithic Nel. Students' answers should be written from Neolithic Nel's perspective. Review the sample thought bubble, and answer any questions students may have.

4   **Have students read Section 3.3 and then work with their partners to complete the corresponding page of the Reading Notes.** After all pairs have completed the Reading Notes, have a few volunteers share their answers with the class.

5   **Have students read and take notes for the remaining Sections 3.4 to 3.7.** Review students' work after every one or two pages of completed Reading Notes. Alternatively, have students stop after each section to allow volunteers to share their answers with the class.

6   **Give instructions for the writing assignment.** Distribute a copy of *Student Handout 3A: Creating a Comic Book* to each pair. Review the instructions with students, and answer any questions. Remind students that the information in their Reading Notes serves as prewriting for the comic book. Have pairs review their notes to identify information and statements they may be able to include in their comic book.

7   **Project *Visual 3: Sample Comic-Book Story Page* and have students evaluate the sample page.** Ask students to carefully evaluate the sample story page to see if it meets the requirements listed on Student Handout 3A. Then challenge students to suggest ideas for how this page might be improved.

Student Handout 3A

Visual 3

8   **Have pairs write and revise their comic books.** Distribute the following materials to each pair:

- one copy of *Student Handout 3B: Comic-Book Cover Template*
- three copies of *Student Handout 3C: Comic-Book Story Page Template*
- one copy of *Student Handout 3D: Comic-Book Characters*

Give pairs adequate time—one to two class periods—to write and revise their comic books. Emphasize that each pair should create a unique comic book.

9   **Conduct a peer read-around.**

- Write the following topics in a column on the board: food supply, shelter, communities, jobs, and trade.
- Have each pair trade their comic book with another pair. Allow students time to read their classmates' comic book.
- Tell students to discuss specific things they found effective in the comic book they read.
- Then have a volunteer from each pair come to the board and place a tally mark next to the topics that were covered in the comic book.
- Have students repeat this process by exchanging their comic books with a new pair.

10 **Wrap up the activity.** Ask students,

- Which topics were included in the greatest number of comic books?
- Do you think these topics represent the most important changes that occurred in people's lives from the Paleolithic Age to the Neolithic Age? Why or why not?
- How did the development of agriculture change daily life in the Neolithic Age?

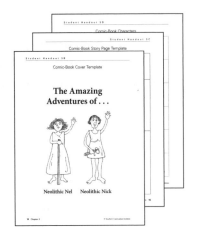

Student Handouts
3B–3D

Processing (optional)

1   **Understand the intent of the Processing activity.** The comic-book writing activity serves as this chapter's Processing activity. Should you choose not to have students do the writing activity, you might use the optional Processing activity in the Interactive Student Notebook.

2   **Have students complete the Processing activity.**

3   **Have students share their answers with their partners or with the class.**

Quicker Coverage

Replace the Writing Assignment Rather than have students create a comic book, have them create an illustrated flowchart. Tell them to fold a sheet of paper into six equal boxes and add arrows to connect the boxes, as shown below. Model the diagram on the board. Write a large title in the first box, and the headings as shown in the remaining boxes. Have students do the same on their charts. In each of their five boxes, have students do the following:

- In one or two complete sentences, explain how daily life changed from the Paleolithic Age to the Neolithic Age.

- Draw a simple illustration to show what life was like in the Neolithic Age.

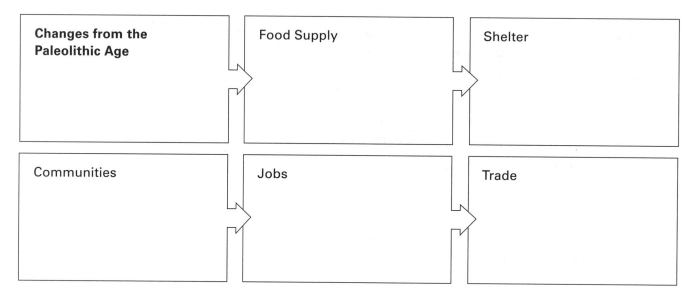

Deeper Coverage

Analyze *The Flintstones* After students have completed the activity, show a video clip from an episode of the TV show *The Flintstones*. Have students analyze the clip from the point of view of a paleoanthropologist. Instruct them to compare the cartoon with information from their Reading Notes. Have students write one paragraph about how the cartoon falsely represents the Neolithic Age, and one paragraph about how it correctly depicts this time period. Suggest that students use the Key Content Terms in their paragraphs.

Assessment

Mastering the Content

1. A	5. D	9. B	13. C
2. C	6. A	10. D	14. D
3. A	7. C	11. B	15. A
4. B	8. D	12. D	

Applying Social Studies Skills

16. corn

17. rice

18. barley or wheat or lentils or peas (accept any one of these, but not corn or rice)

19. D

Exploring the Essential Question

20. Answers should include all of the elements requested in the prompt.

Scoring Rubric

Score	Description
3	Student writes one or two appropriate sentences in each of the five circles. Sentences are clearly stated, include main ideas and/or significant details, and demonstrate command of standard English conventions.
2	Student responds to most or all parts of the task, but sentences may lack details or not be clearly stated.
1	Student responds to at least one part of the task. Sentences may contain factual and/or grammatical errors, or answers may not be written in full sentences.
0	Response does not match the task or is incorrect.

English Language Learners

Provide Sample Cartoons For the Preview activity, prepare a sample cartoon strip to show as a model. Your example might be student work saved from the previous year. You might also show samples of comic strips from the newspaper to demonstrate the use of speech bubbles.

Support the Reading Notes Use Guide to Reading Notes 3 to provide fill-in-the-blank notes. For example, for Section 3.2, you might provide students with the following:

During the _____Age, humans were hunters and _____. They were always looking for _____ and lived in temporary _____.
During the _____ Age, humans produced their own _____ and settled down in _____ place. Neolithic settlements were located _____ because the land was _____.

Learners Reading and Writing Below Grade Level

Complete the Reading Notes as a Class Rather than have pairs read and take notes on Sections 3.3 to 3.7 at one time, do the following for each section to guide the class to complete the Reading Notes:

- Ask, *What is the title of this section? What do you see in the image? What do you think this section will talk about?*

- Have students read the first paragraph in the section and fill in the first Reading Notes question about the Paleolithic Age. Review the answer as a class.

- Then ask, *How do you think daily life will change in the Neolithic Age?* Tell students to read the rest of that section to see if their guesses are correct. Then have students complete their Reading Notes.

- Have volunteers read their speech bubbles about Neolithic changes.

Learners with Special Education Needs

Modify the Preview Activity If students struggle to come up with ways in which the computer has changed our lives, use the invention of the airplane instead. Students may find it easier to create cartoons about transportation, as it is a more concrete concept. Alternatively, keep the computer example but provide the following sentences. Have students copy the sentences and then draw their cartoons: "In the past, it took a long time to write a letter and mail it at the post office." "But today, we can quickly type an e-mail and send it anywhere in the world."

Support the Reading Notes Provide a Word Bank for each section of notes. Tell students that they should include the following terms or phrases in their answers:

Section 3.2: hunter-gatherer, food, shelter, fertile

Section 3.3: dangerous, food supply, milk, meat, crops

Section 3.4: tents, wild animals, mud, cooking pit, protection

Section 3.5: settle, communities, defend

Section 3.6: food, specialized skills, beautiful, variety

Section 3.7: nearby, trade, travel, resources, spread ideas

Support the Writing Assignment Allow students to focus on one or two, rather than three, topics for the story pages of their comic books. Provide intermittent due dates for completing portions of this assignment. For example, you might have separate due dates for the cover page and each story page. Suggest that students first complete a draft of each page and then show it to you before writing their final drafts.

Advanced Learners

Enhance the Writing Assignment Add the following item to the directions on Student Handout 3A:

Include one additional story page on which you explain how one of the key changes from Paleolithic to Neolithic life paved the way for modern society. For example, Modern Maria might explain that because Neolithic Nel and Nick began to specialize in one job, people in our modern society attend college or technical schools to learn specific skills.

Enrichment Resources

Find out more about the Neolithic Age by exploring the following Enrichment Resources for *History Alive! The Ancient World* at www.teachtci.com.

Enrichment Readings This in-depth reading encourages students to explore selected topics related to the chapter. You may also find readings that relate the chapter's content directly to your state's curriculum.

Internet Connections The recommended Web sites provide useful and engaging content that reinforces skills development and mastery of subjects within the chapter.

Literature Recommendations

The following books offer opportunities to extend the content in this chapter.

Anooka's Answer by Marjorie Cowley (Boston: Clarion Books, 1996)

The Stone Age by Patricia D. Netzley (San Diego: Lucent Books, 1998)

Stone Age Farmers Beside the Sea: Scotland's Prehistoric Village of Skara Brae by Caroline Arnold (Boston: Houghton Mifflin, 1997)

Section 3.2

1. During the Paleolithic Age, humans were hunter-gatherers. They were always looking for food and took shelter in places such as caves. During the Neolithic Age, humans grew their own food, built permanent shelters, and settled down in one place. Symbols will vary.

2. Neolithic settlements were located east of the Mediterranean Sea because the land was fertile.

Section 3.3

1. During the Paleolithic Age, people obtained food by hunting animals and gathering plants. Some of the problems were that hunting was dangerous and the food supply was not dependable.

2. Possible student answers:

   "We learned that we could grow our own food by collecting and planting the seeds of plants."

   "We learned how to raise animals for their milk and meat. We also used animals to carry heavy loads and plow fields."

   "Agriculture means that we grow our own crops and domesticate animals. Agriculture was important because it gave us a stable food supply."

Section 3.4

1. During the Paleolithic Age, people lived in tents or caves. Shelters were temporary because people were nomads who moved around to follow wild animal herds and find new plants to eat.

2. Possible student answers:

   "Our houses were made of mud mixed with stones and tree branches."

   "We stored food in the floor of our houses. We dug a cooking pit in the floor."

   "Our permanent shelters protected us from weather and animals, made life more comfortable, allowed new ways to cook food, and let us form larger communities."

Section 3.5

1. During the Paleolithic Age, people lived in small bands of 20 to 60 people because they were always moving from place to place in search of food.

2. Possible student answers:

   "Because we lived in larger communities, we could divide up the work."

   "Working together allowed us to finish tasks faster."

   "In communities, we had more time to make our lives more comfortable and much safer. We could defend ourselves more easily. Our population increased."

Section 3.6

1. During the Paleolithic Age, people's most important job was to find food for survival.

2. Possible student answers:

   "Our specialized jobs included weaving, basket making, toolmaking, and trading."

   "We had more time to decorate pottery and polish stones to make our lives more beautiful."

   "The development of different jobs helped us focus on finding ways to do these jobs better. Different jobs added more variety to community life."

Section 3.7

1. During the Paleolithic Age, people used only the resources found nearby.

2. Possible student answers:

   "We traded to get resources that we did not have in our own area."

   "Our traders had to travel hundreds of miles—walking on foot, riding donkeys, or sailing on ships."

   "The growth of trade allowed us to make use of more resources. Because traders met new people, ideas and knowledge spread throughout the world."

The Rise of Sumerian City-States

How did geographic challenges lead to the rise of city-states in Mesopotamia?

Overview

In a Response Group activity, students learn how responses to geographic challenges resulted in the formation of complex Sumerian city-states.

Objectives

In the course of reading this chapter and participating in the classroom activity, students will

Social Studies

- describe the location and physical setting of Mesopotamia, including the Tigris and Euphrates river system.
- analyze geographic problems affecting ancient Mesopotamians and evaluate potential solutions.
- describe how Mesopotamians modified their physical environment to solve geographic problems.
- explain how the development of agricultural techniques, such as irrigation systems, led to the emergence of Sumerian city-states.

Language Arts

- support opinions with detailed evidence and with visual or media displays that use apporpriate technology.
- deliver presentations on problems and solutions that establish connections between the defined problem and at least one solution and that offer persuasive evidence to validate the proposed solution(s).

Social Studies Vocabulary

Key Content Terms Mesopotamia, Tigris River, Euphrates River, Sumer, irrigation, levee, silt, city-state

Academic Vocabulary complex, material, maintain, layer, dispute

Materials

History Alive! The Ancient World

Interactive Student Notebooks

Visuals 4A–4D

CD Tracks 2–5

Lesson Masters

- Vocabulary Development handout (1 per student, on colored paper)

poster paper (2 sheets per group of 3)

colored pencils or markers

Activity	Suggested Time	Materials
Preview	10 minutes	• Interactive Student Notebooks
Vocabulary Development	30–40 minutes	• *History Alive! The Ancient World* • Interactive Student Notebooks • Vocabulary Development handout
Response Group	140 minutes (2–3 regular periods) (1.5 block periods)	• *History Alive! The Ancient World* • Interactive Student Notebooks • Visuals 4A–4D • CD Tracks 2–5 • poster paper (2 sheets per group of 3) • colored pencils or markers
Processing	20 minutes	• Interactive Student Notebooks
Assessment	40 minutes	• Chapter 4 Assessment

Preview

1   **Have students complete the Preview activity for Chapter 4 in their Interactive Student Notebooks.** Students think of a problem or challenge they faced, and describe what they did to solve it.

2   **Have students share their answers in pairs or as a class.**

3   **Explain the connection between the Preview activity and Chapter 4.** Tell students that the people of ancient Mesopotamia also faced challenges. Just as students had to come up with ways to solve their problems in the Preview, the people of Mesopotamia had to come up with solutions for their problems. In this chapter, students will learn about four geographic challenges that Mesopotamians faced and discover how the solutions to these problems transformed Neolithic farming villages into complex Sumerian city-states.

Vocabulary Development

1   **Introduce the Key Content Terms.** Have students locate the Key Content Terms for the chapter in their Interactive Student Notebooks. These are important terms that will help them understand the main ideas of the chapter. Ask volunteers to identify any familiar terms and how they might be used in a sentence.

2   **Have students complete a Vocabulary Development handout.** Give each student a copy of the Vocabulary Development handout of your choice from the Reading Toolkit at the back of the Lesson Masters. These handouts provide extra Key Content Term practice and support, depending on your students' needs. Review the completed handout by asking volunteers to share one answer for each term.

Reading

1   **Introduce the Essential Question and have students read Section 4.1.** Afterward, have students use information from the section and from the chapter opener image to propose some possible answers to the Essential Question: *How did geographic challenges lead to the rise of city-states in Mesopotamia?*

2   **Have students complete the Reading Notes for Chapter 4.** Assign Sections 4.2 to 4.7 during the activity, as indicated in the procedures that follow. Remind students to use the Key Content Terms where appropriate as they complete their Reading Notes.

> **Vocabulary Development: Foreign Words in English**
>
> Remind students that English contains many words from foreign languages, and note that *levee* is one of them. Have students use a dictionary to find the language that gave us *levee* (Old French) and its meaning in that language ("to raise"). Help them relate the original meaning of the word to the meaning used in this chapter.

Response Group

1   Place students in groups of three and introduce the activity. Tell students that they will take on the roles of ancient Mesopotamians facing a series of problems. For each problem, students will learn about the issue, propose a solution, and then read to find out how Mesopotamians responded to the problem.

2   Have students read Section 4.2 and complete the corresponding Reading Notes in their Interactive Student Notebooks. Tell students that they will learn important information about the environment of Mesopotamia that will help them in their roles as ancient Mesopotamians. Use Guide to Reading Notes 4 to review the answers as a class. (**Note:** Students may struggle with the various proper names for this region. Consider using the map in Section 4.2 to explain the relative locations of the Fertile Crescent, Mesopotamia, Sumer, and Ur.)

3   Have students take on roles as Neolithic farmers. Project *Visual 4A: Zagros Mountains* and play CD Track 2, "Problem A: Food Shortages in the Hills." Tell students to take the roles of members of Neolithic farm families sitting around the dinner table. Their stomachs are growling, and it has just been announced that dinner has been canceled. Have students listen to the recording. Then review the details of the problem as described on the transparency.

Visual 4A

4   Have groups discuss possible solutions to Problem A. Encourage students to examine the image closely and use the information from the recording to discuss the four options listed. Group members should choose the option they think will best solve the food shortage and prepare to justify their choice with two reasons. Allow groups adequate time to discuss and jot down their ideas.

5   Appoint a Presenter for each group, and have groups share their answers. Ask Presenters to share with the class their group's solution to Problem A. Encourage them to point out details from Visual 4A that support their group's answers. (**Note:** If groups choose a variety of different solutions, consider holding a class debate and then a vote to decide what to do. If all groups choose the same solution, encourage each group to come up with a unique reason for either why group members chose that option or why they rejected another option.)

6   Have students read Section 4.3 and complete the corresponding Reading Notes. Clarify any questions students may have about the reading.

7   Repeat Steps 3–6 for Problems B–D. Make these modifications:

Problem B: Uncontrolled Water Supply in the River Valley

- Project *Visual 4B: Euphrates River* and play CD Track 3, "Problem B: Uncontrolled Water Supply in the River Valley." While students listen to the recording, have them picture themselves standing ankle deep in water and staring out at flooded fields.

Visual 4B

- Have groups discuss possible solutions to Problem B. Distribute poster paper on which student groups will draw their water-control systems. Give groups a limited amount of time, about 5 to 15 minutes, to complete their designs.

- Rotate the role of Presenter to a new student.

- Ask the first group's Presenter to share the group's plan for a water-control system. Ask all subsequent groups to share one aspect of their design that is similar to or different from that of any previous group.

- After the discussion, have students read Section 4.4 and complete the corresponding Reading Notes.

Problem C: Building and Maintaining a Complex Irrigation System

- Project *Visual 4C: Irrigation Canal near the Euphrates River* and play CD Track 4, "Problem C: Building and Maintaining a Complex Irrigation System." While students listen to the recording, have them picture themselves standing in an irrigation canal, holding shovels, under the hot sun.

- Follow the procedure for Problem A, having students conclude by reading Section 4.5 and completing the corresponding Reading Notes.

Problem D: Attacks by Neighboring Communities

- Project *Visual 4D: An Attacking Army* and play CD Track 5, "Problem D: Attacks by Neighboring Communities." While students listen to the recording, have them picture themselves holding weapons (spears or swords) and peering out the windows of their homes.

- Follow the procedure for Problem B, having students conclude by reading Section 4.6 and completing the corresponding Reading Notes.

8 **Have students read Section 4.7 and complete the corresponding Reading Notes.** Tell students to first complete the flowchart on their own, and then check with their group to verify that their answers are correct.

9 **Wrap up the activity with a class discussion.** Ask students,

- What major problems did Mesopotamians face?

- How did Mesopotamians modify their environment to solve these problems?

- How did geographic challenges eventually lead to the rise of city-states?

Visual 4C

Visual 4D

Processing

Have students complete the Processing activity on a separate sheet of paper. Students create a real estate advertisement encouraging people to move to one of the Sumerian city-states.

Quicker Coverage

Simplify the Preview Activity Require that students write about their problems and solutions, but forgo the illustration part of the activity.

Omit the Response Group for Problem C After students have completed their Reading Notes for Section 4.4, talk students through Problem C, rather than have groups discuss and present. Ask, *What problems might occur when irrigation systems pass through many different villages?* Have students read the first two paragraphs of Section 4.5 and then complete the "Problem" box of their Reading Notes. Tell students that Sumerian villages now had to work together. Use Guide to Reading Notes 4 to complete the "Solution" box as a class.

Change the Processing Rather than have students create real estate advertisements, have students answer the following question in a well-written paragraph: *How did geographic challenges lead to the rise of city-states in Mesopotamia?* Before students begin writing their responses, encourage them to review their Reading Notes, especially the flowchart for Section 4.7.

Deeper Coverage

Create an "Irrigation Treaty" After students have read Section 4.5, have the class work together to create a treaty that clearly explains the following:

- why different villages must cooperate to maintain the irrigation system
- two specific actions that all villages will take to maintain the system

Have a representative from each of the groups of three students that are working on the activity together sign the treaty and then lead the class in a round of applause for successfully drafting a treaty to solve this problem.

Enhance the Processing Challenge students to tailor their advertisements to entice people to move to one specific Sumerian city-state. Have students research one of the city-states on the map in Chapter 4. Then tell them to include in their advertisements at least two pieces of information unique to their city-state.

Assessment

Mastering the Content

1. A	5. C	9. C	13. A
2. D	6. B	10. C	14. B
3. A	7. C	11. D	15. A
4. B	8. D	12. B	

Applying Social Studies Skills

16. Kish, Ur (either order)

17. 1,700 miles (accept any answer between 1,200 and 2,000 miles)

18. southeast; Persian Gulf

19. Zagros Mountains

Exploring the Essential Question

20. Answers should include all of the elements requested in the prompt.

Scoring Rubric

Score	Description
3	Student completes the diagram with all required features and writes explanations of three features as responses to geographic challenges. Explanations are clearly stated and demonstrate command of standard English conventions.
2	Student responds to most or all parts of the task, but diagram may show some confusion, or explanations may not be clearly stated.
1	Student responds to at least one part of the task. Explanations may contain factual and/or grammatical errors and may lack details. Diagram may show a lack of understanding of the chapter material.
0	Response does not match the task or is incorrect.

Detecting the Past: Clues from Archaeology

1 **Discuss why archaeologists study artifacts.** Remind students that artifacts are objects made and used by people in the past. Archaeologists can learn about a society by examining artifacts.

2 **Draw a three-column chart on the board to show the three stages of an archaeologist's work.** Write these headings at the top of the columns: "Learn and Plan"; "Dig and Discover"; and "Preserve, Reconstruct, and Interpret." Say, *These are three general stages archaeologists use to do their work. First, they learn about the history of a site and then plan their own excavation. Next, they carefully dig, following their plan. Finally, they preserve, reconstruct, and interpret the artifacts.* Title the chart, "Woolley's Work at Ur."

3 **Have students read the Chapter 4 Reading Further in the Student Edition.** Ask, *What had Woolley already learned by the time he arrived at the site?* (Woolley had learned about the construction of a temple at the site, in what was once a part of the ancient city of Ur.) Have a volunteer enter this information in the first column of the chart.

4 **Have student groups copy and complete the chart about Woolley's work at Ur.** Form student groups of three to four members. Have each group choose a Recorder and a Spokesperson. The Recorder should copy the chart from the board. Then group members should work together to complete the chart, using information they learned from Reading Further 4. The Recorder should enter the information in the appropriate column.

5 **When groups have completed their charts, have each Spokesperson share his or her group's chart entries.** Begin with the first stage, "Learn and Plan." Have each Spokesperson share what his or her group placed in this column of their chart. A volunteer from each group should add this information under "Learn and Plan" on the board chart. Compare and contrast all groups' answers as a class. Repeat this process for the columns titled "Dig and Discover" and "Preserve, Reconstruct, and Interpret."

6 **Have students complete the Chapter 4 Reading Further in their Interactive Student Notebooks.** Have volunteers share their ideas about what an archaeologist in the future might conclude about our society and about the lives of students from artifacts the scientists might uncover. Ask the class to discuss how accurate each volunteer's conclusions are. Discuss how artifacts can answer questions, and also how these answers can change when new information is discovered.

English Language Learners

Scaffold the Activity After students listen to the CD track for each Mesopotamian problem, allow groups time to choose a solution, write down reasons for their choice, and rehearse their explanations. Then have each group stand and share their reasons. After the presentations, explain the solutions Mesopotamians came up with, showing visuals if possible. Allow students to ask clarifying questions, and then have them read and complete their Reading Notes.

Provide Sample Real Estate Advertisements Before students complete the Processing activity, show them an example of a real estate advertisement. Have students compare the example with the Processing instructions. Ask students whether the sample contains all the assignment requirements. Encourage students to brainstorm ways the sample could be improved.

Learners Reading and Writing Below Grade Level

Break Up the Reading For Section 4.2, have students read the first two paragraphs and complete the corresponding Reading Notes. Debrief as a class. Summarize aloud the bullet points in the third paragraph of Section 4.2. Then tell students that, during the activity, they will learn more about the problems Mesopotamians faced. For Sections 4.3 to 4.6, have students read the first few paragraphs in each section and then turn to the Reading Notes to complete the prompts in the "Problem" boxes. Debrief as a class. Have students finish reading each section in their books and then turn to the Reading Notes to complete the prompts in the "Solution" boxes. For Section 4.7, create an overhead transparency of the flowchart and model the Reading Notes. Read aloud the first paragraph of Section 4.7 in the student book. Tell students that the flowchart will help answer the Essential Question: *How did geographic challenges lead to the rise of city-states in Mesopotamia?* Read aloud the first two sentences of the second paragraph and fill in the first two boxes of the flowchart as a class. Then tell students to finish reading Section 4.7 and complete the rest of the flowchart.

Learners with Special Education Needs

Support the Response Group Activity Consider creating a transcript of CD Tracks 2–5, which present the Mesopotamian problems. Give students the transcript to study before brainstorming their solutions. For Problems B and D, display starting images that can be embellished as students create their irrigation system and defense system. For Problem B, provide a sketch of a simple village, with fields and a river running along one side of the village. Students will then determine how to transport water from the river to all the fields. For Problem D, provide a sketch of a group of houses, with a number of farms circling the houses. Students will then determine how best to defend their city-state. Consider allowing two students to share the role of Presenter.

Provide Reading Notes Assistance Use Guide to Reading Notes 4 to give students the answers to the written questions for Sections 4.2 to 4.6. For Section 4.2, students will circle and explain the geographic characteristic that might pose the biggest challenge to people living in Mesopotamia. For Sections 4.3 to 4.6, students will create pictures for each problem and solution, using the provided summaries for guidance. For Section 4.7, create an overhead transparency of the Reading Notes and fill in the flowchart as a class.

Advanced Learners

Offer an Alternative Processing Offer a written essay activity as an alternative to the Processing activity. Ask students to suppose that a group of Sumerian citizens is very upset by the decision to build walls and moats around their cities. The group feels that this system will be too costly to build and maintain. Also, these citizens do not like the idea of being isolated from the nearby farms and animals. Have students write an essay in which they argue for the necessity of these walls. In their essay, they should define the problem clearly (give the reasons the walls are needed) and propose a solution.

Enrichment Resources

Find out more about the rise of Sumerian city-states by exploring the following Enrichment Resources for *History Alive! The Ancient World* at www.teachtci.com.

Enrichment Readings These in-depth readings encourage students to explore selected topics related to the chapter. You may also find readings that relate the chapter's content directly to your state's curriculum.

Internet Connections The recommended Web sites provide useful and engaging content that reinforces skills development and mastery of subjects within the chapter.

Literature Recommendations

The following books offer opportunities to extend the content in this chapter.

Sumer: Cities of Eden by the editors of Time-Life Books (Alexandria, VA: Time-Life, 1993)

The Sumerians (History Opens Windows) by Jane Shuter (Chicago, IL: Heinemann Library, 2008)

Ancient Agriculture: From Foraging to Farming by Michael Woods and Mary B. Woods (Minneapolis, MN: Runestone Press, 2000)

Section 4.2

Possible answers: hilly and received rain (northern part), low plains with little rain (southern part), rivers sometimes flood, soil was hard and dry most of the year, few trees, few stones, few natural barriers.

Answers will vary, but students should justify the characteristic they circle by explaining why it would pose a challenge to people living in Mesopotamia.

Section 4.3

Problem

1. The advantages of living in the foothills included mild weather, plentiful rains, wood for shelters, and stones for toolmaking.

2. Pictures will vary but should show that there were food shortages in the foothills caused by increasing populations.

Solution

1. Farmers moved from the foothills to the plains of Sumer, near the Tigris and Euphrates rivers.

2. Pictures will vary but should show Mesopotamians moving south from the mountains to the plains.

3. The Sumerians were an ancient people who lived in Sumer, the plains region of southern Mesopotamia.

Section 4.4

Problem

1. During the spring, the Tigris and Euphrates rivers flooded the plains. For the rest of the year, Sumer was hot, dry, and windy.

2. Farmers had either too much water or not enough. They had no way to control the water supply.

3. Pictures will vary but should show frustrated farmers with their fields either flooded or too dry.

Solution

1. The Sumerians controlled the water supply by building an irrigation system.

2. Pictures will vary but should show levees preventing flooding and holes in the levees allowing water to flow to the fields.

3. The Sumerians also controlled the water supply by digging canals and constructing dams and reservoirs.

Section 4.5

Problem

1. Sumerian farmers had to maintain the irrigation system across village boundaries.

2. Pictures will vary but should show canals becoming clogged with silt.

Solution

1. Sumerian farmers had to work together for the common good to maintain the irrigation system.

2. Pictures will vary but should show workers clearing silt from canals and balancing reservoir water levels.

3. The Sumerians began to live in larger towns and cities.

Section 4.6

Problem

1. Pictures will vary but should show Sumerian cities fighting over the right to use water.

2. There were no natural geographic barriers (such as mountains and rivers) in the plains of Sumer.

Solution

1. The Sumerians built walls and moats around their cities.

2. Pictures will vary but should show a walled city of houses, surrounded by a moat, with farms outside the city.

3. The cities of Sumer are called city-states because they were like independent countries.

Section 4.7

Possible answer:

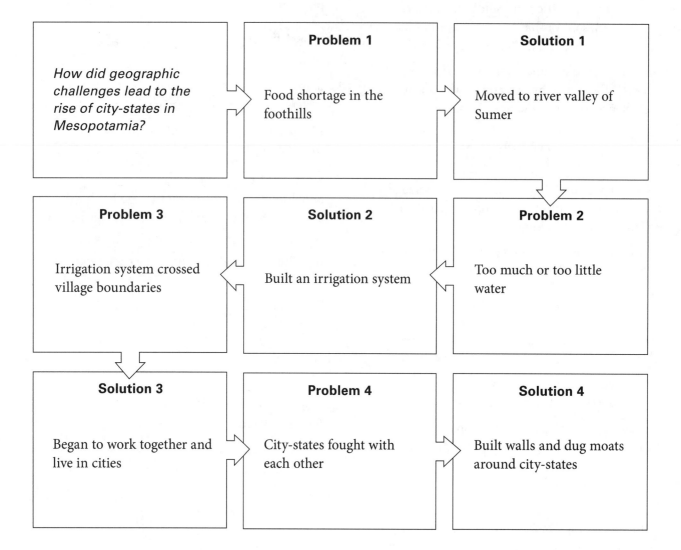

Ancient Sumer

Why do historians classify ancient Sumer as a civilization?

Overview

In a Social Studies Skill Builder, students learn about the characteristics of civilization and analyze artifacts to determine how each characteristic was exhibited in ancient Sumer.

Objectives

In the course of reading this chapter and participating in the classroom activity, students will

Social Studies

- analyze artifacts from ancient Sumer and explain how they are examples of the characteristics of civilization.
- identify agricultural inventions that allowed Sumerian city-states to create a stable food supply and a complex society.
- explain the relationship between religion and the social and political order in Sumer.
- explain the evolution of Sumerian written language, from pictographs to cuneiform.
- apply the characteristics of civilization to modern-day society.

Language Arts

- offer persuasive evidence to validate conclusions.
- support opinions with detailed evidence.

Social Studies Vocabulary

Key Content Terms civilization, social structure, technology, merchant, artisan, scribe, ziggurat, culture, cuneiform, pictograph

Academic Vocabulary challenge, create, network, luxury, professional

Materials

*History Alive!
The Ancient World*

Interactive Student Notebooks

Placards 5A–5H
(2 sets; print additional placards from TeachTCI)

Lesson Masters

- Information Master 5A
  (several copies on card stock)
- Information Master 5B
  (1 transparency)
- Vocabulary Development handout (1 per student, on colored paper)

transparent tape

Activity	Time	Materials
Preview	10 minutes	• Interactive Student Notebooks
Vocabulary Development	30–40 minutes	• *History Alive! The Ancient World* • Interactive Student Notebooks • Vocabulary Development handout
Social Studies Skill Builder	80 minutes	• *History Alive! The Ancient World* • Interactive Student Notebooks • Placards 5A–5H (2 sets–original set and 1 set of copies) • Information Master 5A (several copies on card stock) • Information Master 5B (1 transparency) • transparent tape
Processing	20 minutes	• Interactive Student Notebooks
Assessment	40 minutes	• Chapter 5 Assessment

Preview

1   **Have students discuss characteristics of a civilized society to complete the Preview activity for Chapter 5 in their Interactive Student Notebooks.** Students hypothesize what it means to be a "highly civilized" society.

2   **Have students share their answers in pairs or as a class.**

3   **Explain the connection between the Preview activity and Chapter 5.** Tell students that although they may have different opinions about what it means to be "civilized," historians use specific characteristics to determine whether a society is "civilized." In this chapter, students will learn about the characteristics of civilization and then examine how these characteristics determine why historians consider ancient Sumer a "civilization."

Vocabulary Development

1   Introduce the Key Content Terms. Have students locate the Key Content Terms for the chapter in their Interactive Student Notebooks. These are important terms that will help them understand the main ideas of the chapter. Ask volunteers to identify any familiar terms and how they might be used in a sentence.

2   **Have students complete a Vocabulary Development handout.** Give each student a copy of the Vocabulary Development handout of your choice from the Reading Toolkit at the back of the Lesson Masters. These handouts provide extra Key Content Term practice and support, depending on your students' needs. Review the completed handout by asking volunteers to share one answer for each term.

Reading

1   **Introduce the Essential Question and have students read Section 5.1.** Have students locate the Essential Question: *Why do historians classify ancient Sumer as a civilization?* Then have them read Section 5.1. Afterward, have students carefully analyze the chapter opener image. Then ask them to find words, phrases, or sentences in the text of Section 5.1 that connect to visual details in the chapter opener image. Have several volunteers share with the class the connections they found.

2   **Have students complete the Reading Notes for Chapter 5.** Assign Sections 5.2 to 5.9 during the activity, as indicated in the procedures that follow. Remind students to use the Key Content Terms where appropriate as they complete their Reading Notes.

Social Studies Skill Builder

1 **Prepare your classroom for the activity.** Follow these steps:

- Print one set of additional Placards 5A–5H from TeachTCI .

- Post the two sets (original and copies) of Placards 5A–5G on the walls along opposite sides of the room, as shown in the diagram.

- Post the two copies (original and copy) of *Placard 5H: Lyre* together.

- Create several dice for the activity, using the instructions and template on *Information Master 5A: Die Template*. Place the dice in a central location.

2 **Place students in pairs and introduce the activity in which students will examine basic characteristics of civilization.** Tell students that in this activity, they will determine whether ancient Sumer had each characteristic of civilization, by analyzing and drawing conclusions from artifacts unearthed by archaeologists.

3 **Have students read Section 5.2 and complete the corresponding Reading Notes in their Interactive Student Notebooks.** When they have finished, ask,

- What characteristics of civilization will we learn about in this chapter?

- What pictures or symbols did you use to represent these characteristics?

- What kinds of things might ancient Sumerians have left behind that could be examples of these characteristics?

4 **Explain the procedures for the activity.** Project a transparency of *Information Master 5B: Steps for Analyzing Artifacts* and review the steps for completing the activity. Answer any questions students may have. (**Note:** You may want to review the definition of primary and secondary sources by having students identify which type of source the artifacts represent, and which type of source the information in their text represents. You might also briefly discuss the credibility of these sources in learning about ancient Sumer.)

5 **Model the activity in which students will analyze ancient Sumerian artifacts.** As a class, practice the steps for completing the Reading Notes and analyzing ancient Sumerian artifacts. Do the following:

- Tell students to read Section 5.3 about creating a stable food supply.

- Have pairs complete the flowchart in the Reading Notes for Section 5.3. For now, have students leave the final activity in the section blank.

- Give pairs time to examine the placards and list *all* the artifacts that show evidence of a stable food supply in Sumer. Have volunteers share the artifacts they listed.

- Then tell students to choose *one* artifact and write a sentence explaining how the artifact relates to this characteristic of civilization.

- Have volunteers share their sentences, and answer any questions students may have about the activity steps.

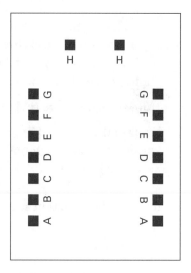

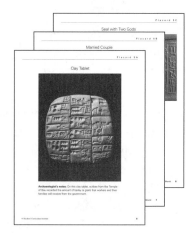

Placards 5A–5H

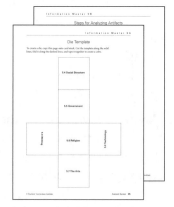

Information Masters 5A and 5B

6 **Conduct the Social Studies Skill Builder.** Have students follow the steps on Information Master 5B to complete the Skill Builder. Have pairs come to you to have their completed work checked, for the first two sections of the Reading Notes. If students are following directions accurately, consider circulating around the room to spot-check work rather than check the work of every pair for each section of the Reading Notes.

7 **Debrief the placards by having students share their ideas.** This activity will emphasize that a single artifact can provide evidence for more than one characteristic of civilization. After most pairs have learned about most of the characteristics of civilization, follow these steps to conduct *Last Pair Standing!*:

- Show the class one of the artifact placards.

- Have pairs check their Reading Notes to review which characteristics of civilization this artifact relates to.

- Tell pairs to stand up if they used this artifact as evidence for *one or more* characteristics of civilization.

- Then tell pairs to remain standing if they used this artifact as evidence for *two or more* characteristics, whereas the other pairs sit down.

- Continue this process until one pair is the "last pair standing." Ask this pair to list which characteristics of civilization this artifact relates to, and to explain one or two of the connections.

- Select a new placard and repeat the activity. (**Note:** It is sufficient to only do a few of the eight placards.)

8 **Wrap up the activity. Hold a short class discussion.** Ask,

- How can artifacts help us learn about ancient peoples?

- Why do historians classify ancient Sumer as a civilization? What evidence do you have to support your answer?

- What other primary or secondary sources might help historians determine characteristics that classify ancient Sumer as a civilization?

Processing

Have students complete the Processing activity on a separate sheet of paper. Students find, or draw, contemporary artifacts as evidence of civilization today. When students have finished their spoke diagrams, have them share some of their modern examples of civilization.

Quicker Coverage

Use Fewer Placards Post only Placards 5A, 5C, 5F, and 5G. Consider printing more than one set of additional placards from TeachTCI so that students have more viewing stations. The activity and placard debrief will run more quickly with less artifacts for students to analyze and discuss.

Simplify the Processing Activity Provide students with a premade copy of the spoke diagram to write on. Rather than have students find or draw modern artifacts that are examples of civilization, require only that students list two contemporary examples of each characteristic of civilization. Debrief as a class and have students add to their spoke diagrams as other students share examples of modern artifacts.

Deeper Coverage

Enhance the Preview Activity Try an inductive method of teaching the characteristics of civilization. Give each pair of students a penny. Tell students to suppose that they are archaeologists who have just unearthed this "artifact" (the penny) and know nothing about it. Have pairs list all the things they observe about this artifact, and then share with the class. On the board, list student observations, grouping them by the seven characteristics of civilization listed in Section 5.2; however, do *not* write the titles of the characteristics on the board at this time. After all student observations are listed, have students brainstorm possible titles for each grouping. Then reveal the "official" characteristics used in Chapter 5. Tell students that they will be learning about these characteristics of civilization and then looking at artifacts to determine why historians classify ancient Sumer as a civilization.

Modify the Processing Activity Offer a visual presentation activity as an alternative to Processing 5. Have students use PowerPoint, poster board, or some other visual display to show in what ways their community qualifies as a "civilization," on the basis of the requirements listed in this chapter. Their presentations should include

- each of the seven characteristics discussed in the lesson.
- at least one example for each characteristic, labeled and represented with some kind of image (drawing, magazine cutout, computer graphic, and so forth).
- a sentence or two for each example, telling why this particular example fits the given characteristic.

Assessment

Mastering the Content

1. A	5. D	9. C	13. C
2. B	6. A	10. C	14. D
3. B	7. A	11. D	15. B
4. C	8. B	12. A	16. B

Applying Social Studies Skills

17. Possible answers: arts (musician playing lyre); social structure (wealthy people banqueting); or stable food supply (enough food for a banquet)

18. Possible answers: social structure (workers bringing food for others to eat); stable food supply (fish, meat)

19. Possible answers: technology (wheel on the chariot, possibly metal weapons); government (kings led armies, city-states fought each other)

Exploring the Essential Question

20. Answers should include all of the elements requested in the prompt.

Scoring Rubric

Score	Description
3	Student completes accurate, specific sentences for all seven characteristics. Sentences are clearly stated, provide relevant details, and demonstrate command of standard English conventions.
2	Student responds to most or all parts of the task, but sentences may lack details or not be clearly stated.
1	Student responds to at least one part of the task. Sentences may
0	Response does not match the task or is incorrect.

English Language Learners

Preteach the Characteristics of Civilization Rather than use the current Preview activity, asking students to hypothesize about the meaning of "civilized," use the penny activity in Deeper Coverage instead. On seven pieces of poster paper, write the titles of the characteristics of civilization. Discuss each characteristic as a class. Under each title, write a definition of the characteristic and have students brainstorm one or two visuals that will help them remember this characteristic. While you create the posters, have students complete their Reading Notes for Section 5.2. Hang the posters around the classroom so that students can refer to them during the activity.

Modify the Processing Require less written work. Ask students to complete the first step (finding or drawing pictures for each of the seven characteristics of civilization), but for the sentence-completion step, allow them to choose just three of the characteristics.

Learners Reading and Writing Below Grade Level

Color Code the Reading Notes Encourage students to use colored pencils or pens to complete their Reading Notes. Suggest that they use a different color for each characteristic in the spoke diagram for Section 5.2. For each subsequent section of the Reading Notes, tell students to use the same color that corresponds to the one they used for that characteristic on the spoke diagram. Color coding can help students group their thoughts and see the relationship between the sections.

Review the Text Structure Before students complete the Social Studies Skill Builder, review the Essential Question and explicitly tell students that the goal of the activity is to determine the ways in which ancient Sumer can be classified as a civilization. Have students look at only the first paragraph of Sections 5.3 to 5.9. Ask, *What does the first paragraph of each section do?* (It explains one of the characteristics of civilization.) Ask, *What do you think the remaining paragraphs of each section will do?* (They will describe the ways in which life in ancient Sumer reflects that characteristic of civilization.)

Learners with Special Education Needs

Emphasize Vocabulary Before students read the chapter, have them create a set of vocabulary cards. On each card, students write one of the seven characteristics of civilization, define it, and draw a picture to depict the meaning.

Structure the Activity Further Rather than have students complete the Social Studies Skill Builder in pairs, guide students through each task by using the bulleted instructions in the activity about modeling the activity for every section. Make an overhead transparency of the Reading Notes and complete the notes together.

Advanced Learners

Write a Dialogue After students have completed the Processing activity, have pairs write and perform a dialogue between a Sumerian and a person living in the United States today. Their dialogue should include the following:

- two lines of dialogue in which the characters introduce themselves and the society they represent
- four lines of dialogue in which the characters discuss characteristics of civilization that illustrate similarities between Sumer and the United States
- four lines of dialogue in which the characters discuss characteristics of civilization that illustrate differences between Sumer and the United States
- two lines of dialogue concluding whether Sumer and the United States can be categorized as civilizations

Have students rehearse their dialogues, and then allow volunteers to present them before the class.

Enrichment Resources

Find out more about civilization in Sumer by exploring the following Enrichment Resources for *History Alive! The Ancient World* at www.teachtci.com.

Enrichment Readings These in-depth readings encourage students to explore selected topics related to the chapter. You may also find readings that relate the chapter's content directly to your state's curriculum.

Internet Connections These recommended Web sites provide useful and engaging content that reinforces skills development and mastery of subjects within the chapter.

Literature Recommendations

The following books offer opportunities to extend the content in this chapter.

Ancient Machines: From Wedges to Waterwheels by author (Minneapolis: Runestone Press, 2000)

The Usborne Introduction to Archaeology: Internet-linked by Abigail Wheatley and Struan Reid (Tulsa, OK: EDC Pub., 2005)

The Usborne Story of Music by Eileen O'Brien (Tulsa, OK: EDC Pub., 2006)

Section 5.2

Spoke diagrams will vary but should have the title for Section 5.2, "Characteristics of Civilization," in the large center oval, and the seven characteristics of civilization in the small ovals: stable food supply, social structure, government, religion, the arts (culture), technology, and language. Next to each oval, students should draw a picture that represents the characteristic.

Section 5.3

Invention #1: Irrigation System. System of canals and reservoirs allowed Sumerian farmers to regularly water their crops.

Invention #2: Plow. The plow helped farmers prepare the soil for planting, making farming faster and producing more food.

Possible artifacts for "stable food supply":

The *Clay Tablet* relates to this characteristic of civilization because it tells that the Sumerians raised barley.

The *Seal with Two Gods* relates to this characteristic of civilization because it shows one of the Sumerian gods using a plow to prepare a field for planting.

Section 5.4

Top: Priests, landowners, and government officials had the nicest homes and lived in the center of the city.

Middle: Merchants and artisans made and sold tools and luxury items. Farmers and fishers lived in small houses at the edge of the city, and farmers served in the army.

Bottom: Slaves had no property and lived with their owners.

Possible artifacts for "social structure":

The *Clay Tablet* relates to this characteristic of civilization because it indicates that there were classes of scribes and workers.

The *Seal of King* relates to this characteristic of civilization because it shows a class of government workers.

The *Chariot* relates to this characteristic of civilization because it shows a military class.

The *Gold Cup* relates to this characteristic of civilization because it indicates that there were artisans and an upper class.

Section 5.5

Religious beliefs made the government more powerful because the Sumerian people obeyed the will of their gods, and the gods chose the kings.

Government duties include recording and enforcing laws, collecting taxes, building temples, maintaining and patrolling irrigation canals, and leading the army. Students should circle and justify the duty they think was the most important.

Possible artifacts for "government":

The *Clay Tablet* relates to this characteristic of civilization because it shows that government officials distributed grain.

The *Seal of King* relates to this characteristic of civilization because it indicates that there were governors and a king.

The *Chariot* relates to this characteristic of civilization because it shows that there was an army.

The *King with Basket* relates to this characteristic of civilization because it illustrates that there was a king.

The *Lyre* relates to this characteristic of civilization because it indicates that there was a queen.

Section 5.6

A religious system includes worship practices and a set of beliefs.

Religion was important in Sumer because it influenced every part of daily life.

Pictures will vary but should show ways Sumerians expressed their religious beliefs, such as building temples and ziggurats, creating statues, or participating in religious ceremonies.

Possible artifacts for "religion":

The *Married Couple* relates to this characteristic of civilization because it was found in a shrine and may have been a gift to the gods.

The *Seal with Two Gods* relates to this characteristic of civilization because it shows two Sumerian gods.

The *King with Basket* relates to this characteristic of civilization because it indicates that one of the king's duties was to build temples.

Section 5.7

Metalworkers created practical objects and decorative items. Architects designed temples and ziggurats. Musicians played instruments and sang during ceremonies.

Music was an important art in Sumer because the Sumerians believed that it brought joy to the people and to the gods.

Possible artifacts for "the arts":

The *Married Couple* relates to this characteristic of civilization because it shows that there were sculptors.

The *Gold Cup* relates to this characteristic of civilization because it shows that there were skilled metalworkers.

The *King with Basket* relates to this characteristic of civilization because it shows that there were metalworkers, and architects for the temples.

The *Lyre* relates to this characteristic of civilization because it shows that the Sumerians had music.

Section 5.8

Pictures will vary but should show life in Sumer before the wheel, when people had to move goods in sledges, and after the wheel, when people used wheeled carts to carry heavier loads over longer distances.

Pictures will vary but should show an arch above a doorway and explain that arches added strength and beauty to Sumerian buildings.

Possible artifacts for "technology":

The *Seal with Two Gods* relates to this characteristic of civilization because it shows the invention of the plow.

The *Seal of King* relates to this characteristic of civilization because it shows that the Sumerians used the cylinder seal as a tool to create the image on clay.

The *Chariot* relates to this characteristic of civilization because it shows that the Sumerians had developed the wheel.

The *Gold Cup* relates to this characteristic of civilization because it shows artisans' use of technology and resources.

Section 5.9

Flowcharts will vary but should explain how the Sumerians developed the written language of cuneiform from an earlier form of writing using pictographs. Cuneiform was a better method of communication because the Sumerians could exchange more detailed information with each other.

Possible artifacts for "writing":

The *Clay Tablet* relates to this characteristic of civilization because it has writing on it.

The *Seal with Two Gods* relates to this characteristic of civilization because it has writing on it.

The *Seal of King* relates to this characteristic of civilization because it has writing on it.

The *King with Basket* relates to this characteristic of civilization because it has writing on it.

Exploring Four Empires of Mesopotamia

What were the most important achievements of the Mesopotamian empires?

Overview

In a Problem Solving Groupwork activity, students create "mechanical dioramas" that illustrate major achievements of the Akkadian, Babylonian, Assyrian, and Neo-Babylonian empires that ruled Mesopotamia from approximately 2300 to 539 B.C.E.

Objectives

In the course of reading this chapter and participating in the classroom activity, students will

Social Studies

- identify the location of the Akkadian, Babylonian, Assyrian, and Neo-Babylonian Empires.
- describe the military, economic, and cultural achievements of early Mesopotamian empires, such as Hammurabi's Code.
- evaluate the importance of Mesopotamian achievements.

Language Arts

- relate the speaker's verbal communication to the nonverbal message.
- use effective rate, volume, pitch, tone, and nonverbal elements to capture audience interest.

Social Studies Vocabulary

Key Content Terms empire, capital, tribute, code of laws, economy, siege

Academic Vocabulary strategy, assemble, technique, invader, unify

Materials

History Alive!
The Ancient World

Interactive Student Notebooks

Lesson Masters

- Information Master 6 (1 transparency)
- Student Handout 6 (1 per group of 4)
- Vocabulary Development handout (1 per student, on colored paper)

4 pieces of red construction paper, cut into 3-inch circles

masking tape

materials for making props and costumes, such as construction paper and scissors

Activity	Suggested Time	Materials
Preview	10 minutes	• Interactive Student Notebooks
Vocabulary Development	30–40 minutes	• *History Alive! The Ancient World* • Interactive Student Notebooks • Vocabulary Development handout
Problem Solving Groupwork	90–120 minutes (3 regular periods) (1.5 block periods)	• *History Alive! The Ancient World* • Interactive Student Notebooks • Information Master 6 (1 transparency) • Student Handout 6 (1 per group of 4) • 4 pieces of red construction paper, cut into 3-inch circles • masking tape • materials for making props and costumes, such as construction paper and scissors
Processing	15 minutes	• Interactive Student Notebooks
Assessment	40 minutes	• Chapter 6 Assessment

Preview

1 **Have students complete the Preview activity for Chapter 6 in their Interactive Student Notebooks.** Explain that much of what we know about ancient Mesopotamia comes from reliefs on stone slabs called steles (STEE-leez). A relief is a sculpture that is partially carved out of a stone. Tell students to design steles celebrating their most important personal achievements.

2 **Have students share their answers in pairs or as a class.**

3 **Explain the connection between the Preview activity and Chapter 6.** Tell students that the achievements on their steles are important because they represent accomplishments in the students' lives. Ancient civilizations also accomplished great things that we should remember. In this chapter, students will learn about the major achievements of four early empires in Mesopotamia.

Vocabulary Development

1 **Introduce the Key Content Terms.** Have students locate the Key Content Terms for the chapter in their Interactive Student Notebooks. These are important terms that will help them understand the main ideas of the chapter. Ask volunteers to identify any familiar terms and how they might be used in a sentence.

2 **Have students complete a Vocabulary Development handout.** Give each student a copy of the Vocabulary Development handout of your choice from the Reading Toolkit at the back of the Lesson Masters. These handouts provide extra Key Content Term practice and support, depending on your students' needs. Review the completed handout by asking volunteers to share one answer for each term.

Reading

1 **Introduce the Essential Question and have students read Section 6.1.** Afterward, have students respond to these questions:

- Why were other groups able to conquer the city-states of Sumer?

- In your own words, how would you define an empire?

Have students examine the timeline and preview and compare the maps in Chapter 6. Then ask,

- What general statement can be made about the size of an empire compared with the size of a city-state?

- Which of the empires in this chapter ruled Mesopotamia the earliest? The latest?

- Which of the empires controlled the largest amount of territory? What kinds of achievements might have helped this empire gain so much land?

> **Vocabulary Development: Multiple-Meaning Words**
>
> Remind students that many words have more than one meaning. Have students identify the meaning of *tribute* as it is used in this chapter and then use the dictionary to find the more common meaning of the word today. Challenge students to use both words in sentences, supplying as much context as possible to show how the meanings vary. Then discuss how the meanings overlap.

2 **Have students complete the Reading Notes for Chapter 6.** Assign Sections 6.2 to 6.9 during the activity, as indicated in the procedures for the Problem Solving Groupwork. Remind students to use the Key Content Terms where appropriate as they complete their Reading Notes.

Problem Solving Groupwork

1 **Introduce the activity in which students will create mechanical dioramas.** Tell students that some museums have mechanical dioramas that come to life when a museum visitor pushes a button. In this activity, students will work in groups, using their bodies and simple props and costumes, to design their own mechanical dioramas. Each group will create and present a diorama that represents one of the empires that ruled Mesopotamia.

2 **Model a mechanical diorama about ancient Sumer.** Project a transparency of *Information Master 6: Model Mechanical Diorama*, covering all but the introduction. Read aloud the introduction paragraph and select two volunteers to model the diorama. Reveal the preparation steps for the Scribe and the Trader and help the volunteers get into the proper position. Tape a red circle on the Scribe's sleeve and tell the class that this represents the "Start" button for the diorama. Then reveal the remaining instructions and have each student come to life by reading the appropriate speech. Afterward, ask the class,

Information Master 6

- What Sumerian achievement did the mechanical diorama represent?

- What information did each person in the diorama present? (the first person described the achievement; the second person explained its importance)

- How could the props be improved? How could the dialogue be improved?

3 **Arrange students in groups of four and assign each group an empire.** You might prepare a transparency that shows group assignments and seating arrangements. (**Note:** Depending on class size, you may have two groups assigned to each empire.)

4 **Assign roles and review the steps for creating a mechanical diorama.** Give each group a copy of *Student Handout 6: Steps for Creating a Mechanical Diorama.* Assign each student a role: Historian, Set Designer, Props Manager, or Director. Explain that, to prepare the diorama, each student will be responsible for leading their group through one or two of the steps. Then review Steps 2–7 on the handout.

5 **Monitor groups as they create their dioramas.** Allow students adequate time to prepare and rehearse their dioramas. Monitor the progress of groups by checking their work and initialing steps completed on Student Handout 6.

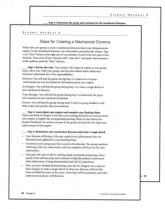

Student Handout 6

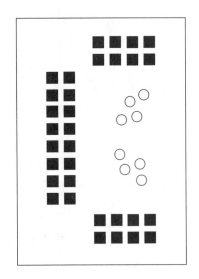

6   Arrange the classroom for presentations. After groups have prepared and rehearsed their dioramas, have students arrange their desks as shown in the diagram.

7   Have the Akkadian groups prepare to present their dioramas as the class reads about the Akkadian Empire.

- Assign each Akkadian group a part of the classroom in which to set up, and have group members review Step 7 of Student Handout 6. Tell students to tape a red "Start" button to the arm of the first speaker in each pair in the group, and then freeze in their starting positions.

- As groups prepare to present, have the rest of the class read Sections 6.2 and 6.3 to learn about the Akkadian Empire. Before the presentations begin, tell students to complete the *first* prompt of the Reading Notes for Section 6.2.

8   Have groups present their mechanical dioramas. Have the first Akkadian group present its diorama. But first point to one pair in the group, and ask audience members what Akkadian achievement they think this pair represents. After students have made their guesses, choose one member of the audience to discover the answer by pushing the "Start" button for that pair. Do the same for the second pair. Repeat the process with the other Akkadian group.

9   Have students complete their Reading Notes for the Akkadian Empire.

- Ask the members of both groups to return to their original diorama positions.

- Have audience members quickly draw and label sketches in their Reading Notes of one military (Section 6.2) and one cultural (Section 6.3) achievement of the Akkadian Empire. Suggest that students may want to draw the props or the costumes from the dioramas.

- Then have students complete the sentences to explain why they think each achievement was important.

- Tell the class that students may push any of the "Start" buttons if they need information repeated.

- As a class, complete the last prompt of the Reading Notes for Section 6.3. Answer any questions students may have about the Akkadian Empire.

10   Repeat Steps 7–9 for the remaining empires.

11   Hold a class discussion after the group presentations. Ask,

- What were the most important achievements of each civilization?

- Compare and contrast large empires ruled from a capital city with small, independent city-states. What are the advantages and disadvantages of each?

- Some rulers tried governing their large empires by force; some rulers, by law. Which type of government do you think would be most effective in controlling the different peoples of an empire? Why?

Processing

Have students do the Processing activity in their Interactive Student Notebooks. Students complete a report card evaluating the achievements of four Mesopotamian empires.

Quicker Coverage

Substitute Posters for Presentations To save time, have students use poster paper to draw a stationary version of their dioramas, rather than prepare and present live dioramas. Display the posters and conduct a gallery walk so that students can complete their Reading Notes by examining the posters. Edit Student Handout 6 by doing the following:

- Change the title to "Steps for Drawing a Poster Version of a Diorama." Revise the introduction to read, "Work with your group to create a poster version of a diorama."

- In Step 1, change the last two roles (Props Manager and Director) to Artist and Writer. Insert this text. **Artist:** You will lead the group during Step 4 to create the visuals on the poster of your diorama. **Writer:** You will lead the group during Step 4 to write speech bubbles on the poster of your diorama.

- In Step 3, change the first sentence in the second bullet to read, "Everyone in your group must take part in the planning and drawing of the poster version of your diorama. Delete the third bullet.

- Replace the current Steps 4–7 with the following text:

  _____ **Step 4: Create a poster version of the mechanical diorama.**

  Using your sketch as a rough draft, draw the mechanical diorama on poster paper. It should show two pairs of students, each positioned in a way that demonstrates their empire's achievements.

  Next to each pair, write speech bubbles explaining what the characters would say if a museum visitor pushed their "Start" button. One person should have 2–4 sentences explaining the achievement, and the other person should have 2–4 sentences explaining the importance of the achievement.

  _____ **Step 5: Place your mechanical diorama poster on the wall.** Then, when instructed, examine the posters to learn about the achievements of the other Mesopotamian empires. Complete the corresponding Reading Notes for each empire.

Deeper Coverage

Modify the Processing Offer a formal writing assignment as an alternative to the report card. Give students the instructions that follow. Then have several volunteers dress up as distinguished historians and orally present their papers to the class. Make sure these volunteers represent different positions on the question, *Which empire had the most important achievements?*

Instructions for students: Suppose that you are a world-famous historian. You have been asked to present a report at an important historical conference. The topic to be addressed will answer this question: *Which empire had the most important achievements?*

On a separate sheet of paper, prepare a report that follows the structure outlined below. Your report should have

- an introductory paragraph in which you (1) explain why you are an expert on this topic (you can make this information up), and (2) clearly state your position on the topic question.

- one paragraph in which you describe at least two specific examples to support your position.

- one paragraph in which you anticipate at least one argument from an audience member who may favor a different empire. In this paragraph, write an argument in response.

- a concluding paragraph in which you restate your position and briefly summarize your main supporting points.

Writing: Revision

Have students evaluate their persuasive compositions by making sure that each sentence and each paragraph lead smoothly to the next. Suggest these revisions:

- adding or improving transitional words or phrases to link paragraphs and sentences

- moving ideas to create a more effective and logical order

- deleting or rewriting inconsistent or contradictory ideas

Assessment

Mastering the Content

1. D	5. B	9. C	13. D
2. A	6. C	10. D	14. B
3. B	7. A	11. D	15. A
4. A	8. B	12. A	16. C

Applying Social Studies Skills

17. 2125–2000 B.C.E. (accept any dates that correspond to the period between the Akkadian and the Babylonian empires, as shown on the timeline)

18. Students should add the Hittites to the timeline between 1600 and 1100 B.C.E.; Babylonian, Assyrian

19. Assyrian; Neo-Babylonian

Exploring the Essential Question

20. Answers should include all of the elements requested in the prompt.

Scoring Rubric

Score	Description
3	Student completes all four parts of the task. Sentences on plaques are accurate, clearly stated, focused on an important achievement, and supported by details; and demonstrate command of standard English conventions.
2	Student responds to most or all parts of the task, but sentences on plaques may lack details or not be clearly stated.
1	Student responds to at least one part of the task. Sentences on plaques may contain factual and/or grammatical errors and may lack details.
0	Response does not match the task or is incorrect.

English Language Learners

Preteach *Empire* Present the term *empire* before students begin the activity. Show a picture of the Empire State Building and ask students to describe it. (Tall, impressive, etc.) Tell students that it is fitting that this building has the term *empire* in its name because an empire is also large. Then have students read Section 6.1 to find out how we define *empire* in social studies.

Create Silent Roles Allow some students to have a nonspeaking role in the diorama, perhaps as the fifth member in a group of four. They should make appropriate gestures when the "Start" button is pushed.

Learners Reading and Writing Below Grade Level

Review Social Studies Terms Before students read, list these terms on the board: *Military, Political, Cultural, Economic*. Explain that the reading applies these categories to the achievements of each empire. Have students define the terms and list on the board types of achievements that might fit in each category. For example, students may connect *Political* to politics and the president. Brainstorm other items students should look for in the reading, such as leaders, capital cities, or government activities. Allow students to refer to this list as they complete their Reading Notes.

Modify the Reading Notes To help students organize the Reading Notes, have them create a fun study guide. Give each student a square sheet of paper, 8.5 inches by 8.5 inches. Have students fold each corner so that the four points meet in the center. Tell students to write the name of one of the four empires on each of the four triangles. Next, have students open the triangles and use the inside of each triangle to take notes about the corresponding empire. Afterward, students should fold each triangle in again, trace its outline on the central square, and use the outlined space to add a simple drawing for the corresponding empire.

Learners with Special Education Needs

Support the Reading Notes Prepare a hint sheet to help students complete Reading Notes 6. Randomly list the answers in Guide to Reading Notes 6. Students can refer to the hint sheet and match each empire with a particular achievement and its importance.

Support the Performance Give students a copy of Information Master 6 to help them brainstorm their own props and speeches. As needed, allow some students to write their lines on note cards. When their "Start" button is pushed, students should read their lines loudly and clearly.

Modify the Processing Activity Tell students to evaluate the achievements of only two of the empires. Either assign empires or allow students to choose.

Advanced Learners

Enhance the Processing Activity Do the following:

- Rather than give students the criteria to evaluate the Mesopotamian empires, have students choose two of the following or come up with their own: Fair, Creative, Aggressive, Unique, Inventive, Useful, Appreciative of the Arts, or Ruthless.

- After students evaluate the empires, have them write a one-paragraph response to the prompt: *Which of the Mesopotamian empires had the most important achievements?*

- Conduct a quick wrap-up activity. Post an empire in each of the four corners of the room. Have students stand near the empire they think had the most important achievements. Allow students to present their arguments for choosing their empire. Have volunteers take part in a short class debate.

Research the Persian Empire The end of Chapter 6 refers to the Persian Empire conquering the Neo-Babylonians. Have students research and report on:

- Where was the Persian Empire?

- When did the Persian Empire rule Mesopotamia? How did it rise and fall?

- Who were the major leaders of the Persian Empire?

- What were the military, political, economic, and cultural achievements of the Persian Empire?

Enrichment Resources

Find out more about ancient Mesopotamian empires by exploring the following Enrichment Resources for *History Alive! The Ancient World* at www.teachtci.com.

Enrichment Readings These in-depth readings encourage students to explore selected topics related to the chapter. You may also find readings that relate the chapter's content directly to your state's curriculum.

Internet Connections The recommended Web sites provide useful and engaging content that reinforces skills development and mastery of subjects within the chapter.

Literature Recommendations

The following books offer opportunities to extend the content in this chapter.

Babylonians: Cradle of Civilization by Eleaine Landau (Brookfield, CT: Millbrook Press, 1997)

Empires of Mesopotamia by Don Nardo (San Diego, CA: Gale Group, 2001)

Mesopotamia: The Mighty Kings edited by Dale E. Brown (Alexandria, VA: Time Life, 1995)

Section 6.2

1. Sargon led the Akkadians to conquer the Sumerian city-states around 2300 B.C.E.

2. Pictures on the stele will vary.

   This stele represents the Akkadian military achievement of . . . creating an empire through military strategies and smart political strategies.

   This achievement was important because . . . it ended the fighting between small city-states, and it helped create the world's first empire.

Section 6.3

1. Pictures on the stele will vary.

   This stele represents the Akkadian cultural achievement of . . . sculpting steles.

   This achievement was important because . . . it has given us some glimpses of the history of the Akkadian Empire.

2. The Akkadian empire lasted for about 200 years and fell because its kings could not rule such a large empire.

Section 6.4

1. After the Akkadian empire fell, Hammurabi was the next king to unite Mesopotamia. His capital city was Babylon.

2. Pictures on the stele will vary.

   This stele represents the Babylonian political achievement of . . . developing a code of laws.

   This achievement was important because . . . it was the first code of laws to apply to everyone.

Section 6.5

1. Pictures on the stele will vary.

   This stele represents the Babylonian economic achievement of . . . developing Babylon as a trading center.

   This achievement was important because . . . it enriched people's lives and brought new ideas to Babylon.

2. Slaves and women and could own property and keep money of their own.

Section 6.6

1. Assyria was located north of Babylon. The Assyrians conquered the land around the Tigris and Euphrates rivers, as well as Syria, Phoenicia, and Egypt.

2. Pictures on the stele will vary.

   This stele represents the Assyrian military achievement of . . . new weapons and war strategies, especially siege warfare.

   This achievement was important because . . . it allowed the Assyrians to create and expand a great empire.

Section 6.7

1. Pictures on the stele will vary.

   This stele represents the Assyrian cultural achievement of . . . bas-reliefs.

   This achievement was important because . . . realism was introduced into sculpture.

2. The Assyrian Empire lasted for about 300 years and fell because the territory was too large to control.

Section 6.8

1. After the Assyrians, the Babylonians regained control of Mesopotamia. Their most famous king was Nebuchadrezzar II.

2. Pictures on the stele will vary.

   This stele represents the Neo-Babylonian military achievement of . . . building protective walls and a moat around Babylon.

   This achievement was important because . . . it kept Babylonians safe.

Section 6.9

1. Pictures on the stele will vary. This stele represents the Neo-Babylonian cultural achievement of . . . building the Hanging Gardens of Babylon.

   This achievement was important because . . . the gardens were an engineering masterpiece.

2. The Neo-Babylonian Empire lasted only 75 years before it fell to the Persian Empire led by Cyrus.

Early Humans and the Rise of Civilization

Unit 1 Timeline Challenge

Early Humans and the Rise of Civilization

About 1.8 million B.C.E.–200,000 B.C.E.
Homo Erectus, Upright Man
Homo erectus hominids in the Paleolithic Age discover how to use fire.

About 230,000–30,000 B.C.E.
Homo Sapiens Neanderthalensis, Neanderthal Man
Homo sapiens neanderthalensis hominids make tools and live in groups.

About 3500–3000 B.C.E.
Sumerians Create City-States
Sumerians use irrigation to provide a stable food supply, enabling villages to grow into powerful city-states.

About 2400 B.C.E.
Cuneiform
Sumerians develop a written language, called cuneiform, to record information about trade.

About 4000 B.C.E.
First Cities
Ancient Mesopotamians establish the city of Ur along the Euphrates River.

About 2300–2100 B.C.E.
Akkadian Empire
Akkadians build the world's first empire in the Fertile Crescent region.

2,000,000 B.C.E.   1,500,000 B.C.E.   1,000,000 B.C.E.   500,000 B.C.E.   10,000 B.C.E.   Today

About 150,000 B.C.E.–Today
Homo Sapiens Sapiens, Doubly Wise Man
Homo sapiens sapiens create complex tools and art.

About 8000–3000 B.C.E.
Neolithic Age
People learn how to domesticate animals and grow crops for food.

Homo Sapiens Sapiens

10,000 B.C.E.   8000 B.C.E.   6000 B.C.E.   4000 B.C.E.   2000 B.C.E.   Today

About 1752–1750 B.C.E.
Code of Hammurabi
King Hammurabi creates a code of laws to unify and preserve order in the Babylonian Empire.

About 900–612 B.C.E.
Assyrian Empire
Under Assyrian rule, the citizens of Mesopotamia obey their kings and gods.

About 605–539 B.C.E.
Neo-Babylonian Empire
The Neo-Babylonians make advances in the fields of mathematics and astronomy.

64   Unit 1   Early Humans and the Rise of Civilization   65

Overview

This Timeline Challenge helps students review the main events and ideas of this unit while providing practice in reading and interpreting timelines. You can vary and expand the activity according to students' needs and the amount of time available.

Basic Procedure

1 **Introduce the timeline in the Student Edition.** Direct students to the Early Humans and the Rise of Civilization Timeline at the end of Unit 1 in the Student Edition. You may wish to have students read aloud and discuss the timeline entries.

2 **Introduce the Timeline Challenge in the Interactive Student Notebook.** Direct students to the Unit 1 Timeline Challenge in their notebooks. Point out the two types of questions, "Timeline Skills" and "Critical Thinking," and model how to answer each type.

3 **Have students complete the Timeline Challenge.** Monitor students as they work. Use the Guide to Unit 1 Timeline Challenge to check their answers. You may wish to project a transparency of the Timeline Challenge as you work through the questions with the class and conduct a discussion of the "Critical Thinking" questions.

4 **Complete the KWL chart.** Return to the KWL chart created at the beginning of the unit, and ask students to list the key information they have learned.

Classroom Timeline

1 **Prepare the Timeline Challenge Cards.** Copy and cut the cards from *Student Handout TC1: Unit 1 Timeline Challenge Cards.* You may wish to laminate the cards for future use.

2 **Create a timeline on a classroom wall.** On an empty wall or a large bulletin board, make a timeline with masking tape or colored paper. Mark off the time intervals in advance, or ask students to do so in class.

3 **Have students place the Timeline Challenge Cards.** Distribute cards to individual students or pairs and have them tape the cards to the timeline in the correct locations. Call on students to provide more information on the timeline topics to review main events and issues.

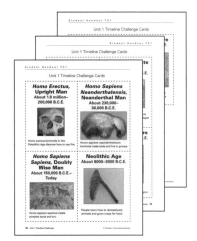

Student Handout TC1

Internet Research

1 **Review students' suggestions for additional timeline entries.** Have students share their answers to the last question of the Timeline Challenge.

2 **Have students conduct Internet research.** Ask students to choose and research one of their suggested events.

3 **Have students create additional Timeline Challenge Cards.** Direct students to research an appropriate image for their cards and then use the computer to create an illustrated card, complete with timeline entry.

Timeline Skills

Score 1 point for each correct answer.

1. *Homo sapiens neanderthalensis* hominids lived side by side with prehistoric humans.

2. *Homo erectus* hominids discovered how to use fire.

3. The Neolithic Age lasted for about 5,000 years. It was important because the gradual shift from hunting and gathering to domesticating animals and growing crops enabled people to settle down in one place.

4. The world's first cities were located in Mesopotamia and were established about 4000 B.C.E.

5. City-states developed in Sumer from about 3500 to 3000 B.C.E.

6. The Sumerians developed cuneiform about 2400 B.C.E., and it was used to record information about trade.

7. The world's first empire was the Akkadian Empire.

8. The Assyrians established their empire about 850 years after King Hammurabi's reign.

9. The Neo-Babylonian Empire rose to power in Mesopotamia after the Assyrian Empire.

Critical Thinking

Score 1 to 3 points for each answer, depending on the thoroughness of the response.

10. One important difference between life in the Paleolithic Age and life in the Neolithic Age was in how people got food. During the Paleolithic Age, people obtained food by hunting animals and gathering plants. In the Neolithic Age, people raised animals and grew crops, which provided a stable food supply. Another difference is that people lived in temporary shelters during the Paleolithic Age, but lived in permanent shelters during the Neolithic Age. Finally, trade grew during the Neolithic Age. During the Paleolithic Age, people rarely traded with other groups.

11. a. Archaeologists and historians study the past by examining artifacts and documents that people have left behind. We may know more about recent events than earlier ones because there is more evidence available to social scientists. Written records, for example, could not have been left behind by cultures that had yet to develop writing.
    b. The development of cuneiform helps explain why we know more about recent events, because cuneiform is a system of writing that was used to record information about trade.

12. According to the timeline, four different empires ruled Mesopotamia between about 2300 and 539 B.C.E. The empires were the Akkadian, Babylonian, Assyrian, and Neo-Babylonian. Geography was one reason why this region was desirable to conquerors. Mesopotamia is located between the Tigris and the Euphrates rivers. With complex irrigation systems, cities were able to grow and thrive. An empire that controlled these resources could also grow and thrive.

13. Answers will vary. Students must explain why the events they chose merit inclusion.

Using Scores to Inform Instruction

Timeline Skills A score of 6 out of 9 indicates that students understand most of the key events of this unit.

Critical Thinking A score of 8 out of 12 indicates that students are able to think critically about most of the key issues of this unit.

If students score below these levels, consider reviewing timeline and critical thinking skills.

UNIT **2**

Ancient Egypt and the Middle East

Ancient Egypt and the Middle East

Overview

This activity introduces the geographic information essential to Unit 2. Students read and interpret maps to learn about the ways in which geography affected the early settlement of ancient Egypt and the Middle East. They annotate an outline map, answer questions in their Interactive Student Notebooks, and then discuss critical thinking questions. Students' comprehension of content and proficiency in map-reading and higher-order thinking skills will help you gauge their readiness for the unit. The pages that follow include a completed map, answers to questions, a scoring guide to inform your teaching, and suggestions for modifications to meet specific student needs.

Essential Geographic Understandings

1. Location of ancient Egypt and the Middle East

2. Key physical features: Arabian Peninsula, Nile River, Mediterranean Sea, Red Sea, Gulf of Aden, Persian Gulf, Nubian Desert, Libyan Desert

3. Location of the Nile River valley and the Nile River delta

4. Impact of physical geography on the early settlement of the ancient kingdoms of Egypt and the Middle East

5. Relationships between the ancient kingdoms of Egypt, Kush, and Israel

Procedures

1. **Introduce the unit.** Tell students they will learn about three civilizations in ancient Egypt and the Middle East—the Egyptian, Kushite, and Israelite civilizations. They will also learn about the development of one of the world's major religions, Judaism.

2. **Create a KWL chart.** Ask students to identify what they already know about these civilizations and what they want to learn. Use their responses to gauge how much additional background information they will need as you progress through the unit. Students will return to the KWL chart at the end of the unit and add the key information they have learned.

3. **Have students read Unit 2 "Setting the Stage" in the Student Edition.**

4. **Have students complete the Geography Challenge.** Monitor students as they work. You may wish to project the map from the Interactive Student Notebook and have students annotate it as the class works through the map-reading questions. Make sure students have grasped Essential Geographic Understandings 1 to 3.

5. **Discuss the "Critical Thinking" questions.** Help students understand the geographic relationships described in Essential Geographic Understandings 4 and 5.

Ancient Egypt, Kush, and Israel

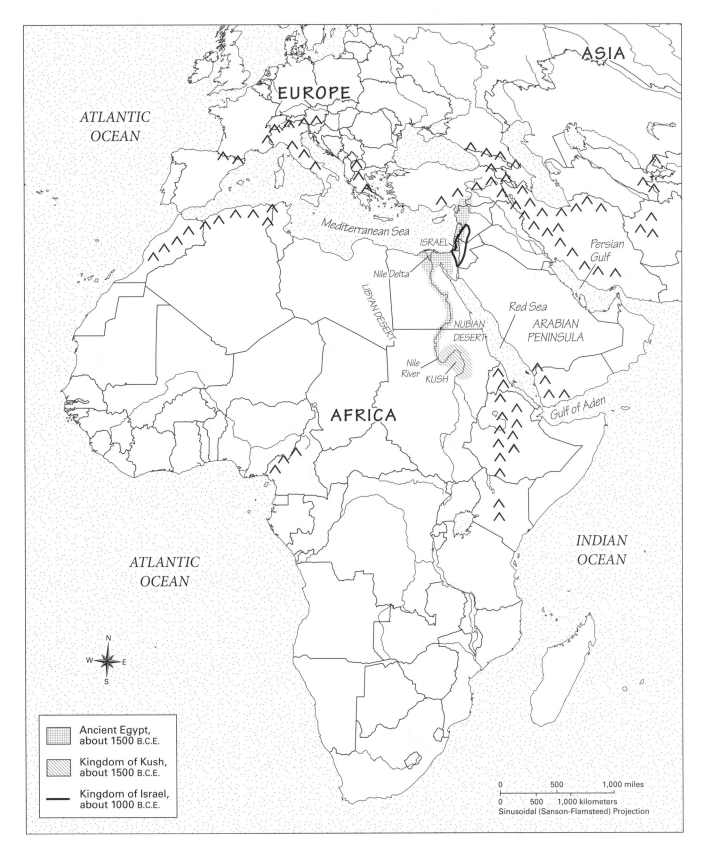

ASIA

EUROPE

ATLANTIC OCEAN

Mediterranean Sea

ISRAEL

Nile Delta

LIBYAN DESERT

Persian Gulf

Red Sea

ARABIAN PENINSULA

NUBIAN DESERT

Nile River

KUSH

AFRICA

Gulf of Aden

ATLANTIC OCEAN

INDIAN OCEAN

N
W   E
S

Ancient Egypt, about 1500 B.C.E.

Kingdom of Kush, about 1500 B.C.E.

Kingdom of Israel, about 1000 B.C.E.

0   500   1,000 miles
0   500   1,000 kilometers
Sinusoidal (Sanson-Flamsteed) Projection

Geography Skills

Score 1 point for each correct answer. Use the map on the previous page to check shading and labeling.

1. Students should label the Arabian Peninsula on the map. The Arabian Peninsula is part of Asia.

2. Students should shade ancient Egypt on the map and key. Egypt is part of Africa.

3. Use the annotated map to check student labels for the Nile River and the Nile River delta.

4. Use the annotated map to check student labels for the Mediterranean Sea, the Red Sea, the Gulf of Aden, and the Persian Gulf.

5. Students should label Israel and Kush on their maps.

6. Students should label the Nubian Desert and the Libyan Desert.

7. The two major vegetation zones in both ancient Egypt and the Middle East are desert and desert scrub.

8. Egypt was by far the largest of the ancient kingdoms. Israel and Kush were similar to one another in size.

Critical Thinking

Questions may have more than one correct answer. Score 1 to 3 points for each reasonable answer, depending on the strength of students' geographic reasoning.

9. Students should note that the land to the west of Egypt, in central North Africa, is entirely desert. There is no body of water that would support life in this region.

10. Early people were not likely to settle in a desert region. Rather, they would likely choose land near rivers or seas, which would provide drinking water, a means of transportation, and a source of food such as fish.

11. Kush was located on the Nile River between Egypt and both central and southern Africa. This location enabled people from all three regions to bring goods to Kush to trade.

12. Students should realize that flat land provides a natural area for farming and herding.

13. The deserts provided protection from attack by invading armies that did not want to risk crossing these harsh areas. To do so would have meant carrying enough water and food to last for the long trip across the desert.

14. The Nile River had a great impact on the lives of the ancient Egyptians. Its life-giving water and yearly floods allowed people to survive and prosper. It might have been natural for them to consider the river as a sort of god bestowing blessings on its people.

Using Scores to Inform Instruction

Geography Skills A score of 6 out of 8 or better indicates that students have acquired sufficient geographic information to proceed with the unit.

Critical Thinking A score of 12 out of 18 or better indicates that students are beginning to understand the relationships between physical geography and the different ways in which people live.

Modifying Instruction

ELL or Learners with Special Education Needs Consider focusing on map-reading questions or limiting the number of "Critical Thinking" questions.

Students with Weak Map or Critical Thinking Skills Assign appropriate pages from the Social Studies Skills Toolkit in the back of the Lesson Masters.

Geography and the Early Settlement of Egypt, Kush, and Canaan

How did geography affect early settlement in Egypt, Kush, and Canaan?

Overview

In an Experiential Exercise, students use their bodies to model the physical geography of ancient Egypt, Kush, and Canaan to learn about how environmental factors influenced early settlement in these areas.

Objectives

In the course of reading this chapter and participating in the classroom activity, students will

Social Studies

- model the physical geography, including major river systems, of ancient Egypt, Kush, and Canaan.

- recognize locations of early human settlement in these areas.

- describe how environmental factors supported permanent settlement and the development of civilization in these areas.

Language Arts

- write a short expository composition that states a thesis and offers persuasive evidence to validate arguments and conclusions.

Social Studies Vocabulary

Key Content Terms topography, vegetation, Nile River, Egypt, Kush, Mediterranean Sea, Canaan, Jordan River

Academic Vocabulary factor, physical, geography, aspect, diverse

Materials

History Alive! The Ancient World

Interactive Student Notebooks

Visuals 7A–7C

Lesson Masters

- Vocabulary Development handout (1 per student, on colored paper)

- colored pencils (blue, brown, green)

Activity	Suggested Time	Materials
Preview	15 minutes	• Interactive Student Notebooks • Visual 7A
Vocabulary Development	30–40 minutes	• *History Alive! The Ancient World* • Interactive Student Notebooks • Vocabulary Development handout
Experiential Exercise	60–90 minutes (2 regular periods) (1 block period)	• *History Alive! The Ancient World* • Interactive Student Notebooks • Visuals 7B and 7C • colored pencils (blue, brown, green)
Processing	30 minutes	• Interactive Student Notebooks
Assessment	40 minutes	• Chapter 7 Assessment

Preview

1   **Introduce students to environmental factors in a landscape.** Explain that these factors might include bodies of water, landforms, plant life, and weather. Project *Visual 7A: A Landscape* and tell students that they will use this drawing of a landscape to identify environmental factors that would affect their choices of where to settle.

2   **Have students identify environmental factors to complete the Preview activity in their Interactive Student Notebooks.** Students will identify and explain the importance of three factors in the image.

3   **Have students share their responses in pairs or as a class.**

4   **Connect the Preview activity to Chapter 7.** Tell students that there are many environmental factors that affect people's choices of where to settle. In ancient Mesopotamia, for example, people settled near the rivers. There, farmers could build irrigation systems to store floodwater for later use. In this chapter, students will learn about three important environmental factors and their effect on early settlement in ancient Egypt, Kush, and Canaan.

Visual 7A

Vocabulary Development

1   **Introduce the Key Content Terms.** Have students locate the Key Content Terms for the chapter in their Interactive Student Notebooks. These are important terms that will help them understand the main ideas of the chapter. Ask volunteers to identify any familiar terms and how they might be used in a sentence.

2   **Have students complete a Vocabulary Development handout.** Give each student a copy of the Vocabulary Development handout of your choice from the Reading Toolkit at the back of the Lesson Masters. These handouts provide extra Key Content Term practice and support, depending on your students' needs. Review the completed handout by asking volunteers to share one answer for each term.

Reading

1   **Introduce the Essential Question and have students read Section 7.1.** Have students identify the Essential Question on the first page of the chapter: *How did geography affect early settlement in Egypt, Kush, and Canaan?* Then have students read section 7.1. Afterward, have students use information from Section 7.1 and from the chapter opener image to propose some possible answers to the Essential Question.

2   **Have students complete the Reading Notes for Chapter 7.** Assign Sections 7.2 to 7.4 during the activity, as indicated in the procedures for the Experiential Exercise. Remind students to use the Key Content Terms where appropriate as they complete their Reading Notes.

> **Vocabulary Development: Unknown Words**
>
> Have students identify any embedded definitions, restatements, examples, contrasts, or other context clues in the text that help reveal the meanings of the key terms as well as other unknown words or words with novel meanings. Point out that context clues can take the form of single words, complete sentences, and sometimes even entire paragraphs.

Experiential Exercise

1 **Introduce the activity about environmental factors that affected three ancient civilizations.** Tell students that they are going to learn about three important environmental factors that affected settlement in ancient Egypt, Kush, and Canaan. Students will use their bodies to create a "map" of the physical geography of these areas. Then they will use this "map" to determine the best place for humans to settle, considering the environmental factors of these areas. (**Note:** The day before the activity, tell students that they will be participating in an exercise that will require them to sit or lie on the floor. Encourage them to wear clothes that are appropriate for this activity.)

2 **Have students annotate a landscape drawing to complete the Reading Notes for Section 7.2.** Have students read Section 7.2 and complete the Reading Notes in their Interactive Student Notebooks. Students will write sentences about water, topography, and vegetation, on or near the landscape drawing provided. (**Note:** To assist students, you may project *Visual 7A: A Landscape.*) Use Guide to Reading Notes 7 to review students' responses.

3 **Arrange the classroom.** Have students move chairs and desks to the edges of the room to create a large open space in the center.

4 **Have students model the physical geography of ancient Egypt and Kush.** Project *Visual 7B: Physical Features of Egypt and Kush.* Select half the class (about 15 students) to model the physical geography of ancient Egypt and Kush. Use these guidelines and the figures on the visual to help students position themselves:

Visual 7B

Group 1: Mediterranean Sea Have four or five students sit in a circle on the floor, with their knees touching. Have students extend and move their arms to represent waves.

Group 2: Nile River Have four or five students lie on their backs, end to end. Make sure the student closest to Group 1 has his or her feet touching the "Mediterranean Sea." Have students in Group 2 slowly move their arms toward Group 1 to show that the Nile River flows into the Mediterranean Sea.

Group 3: Red Sea Have two or three students sit cross-legged on the floor. Have them extend and move their arms to represent waves.

Group 4: Libyan, Nubian, and Arabian Deserts Have three or more students lie on the floor, with their legs and arms outstretched. These students can stage-whisper the words "hot and dry."

5 **Have "settlers" move into the map of ancient Egypt and Kush.** Divide the remaining students into groups of four or five. Give groups a minute to discuss which area they think is the best place to settle. Remind them to think about the environmental factors of water, topography, and vegetation. Select one group at a time to settle in ancient Egypt and Kush. Tell group members to be very careful *not* to touch any of the physical features or other settlers as groups move to stand in the area they have selected. (**Note:** If space is limited, have each group select a representative to settle in ancient Egypt and Kush.)

6 **Debrief the ancient Egypt and Kush experience.** Ask "settlers" these questions:

- Why did you choose to settle in the place you selected?
- What are the positive aspects of this site? The negative aspects?
- If you had to move from your site, where would you go and why?
- Why do you think this area is sometimes called the "gift of the Nile"?
- Do you think ancient Egyptians and Kushites had to worry much about foreign invaders? Why or why not?

After debriefing, have students sit on the floor for the next part of the activity, or have them return the desks and chairs to their original positions.

7 **Have students complete the Reading Notes for Section 7.3.** Have students read Section 7.3 and complete the corresponding Reading Notes in their Interactive Student Notebooks. Afterward, use Guide to Reading Notes 7 to review students' responses.

8 **Have students model the physical geography of Canaan.** Project *Visual 7C: Physical Features of Canaan*. Select the other half of the class (about 15 students) to model the physical geography of Canaan. Use these guidelines and the figures on the visual to help students position themselves:

Visual 7C

Group 1: Mediterranean Sea Have four or five students sit in a circle on the floor, with their knees touching. Have students extend and move their arms to represent waves.

Group 2: Dead Sea and Sea of Galilee For the Dead Sea, have two students sit on the floor, with their knees touching. For the Sea of Galilee, have one student sit cross-legged on the floor. Have students extend and move their arms to represent waves.

Group 3: Jordan River Have two students lie sideways on the floor to represent the relatively narrow nature of this river. Have both students slowly move their arms toward the Dead Sea to show in which direction the Jordan River flows.

Group 4: Syrian and Negev Deserts Have two to four students lie on the floor, with their legs and arms outstretched. These students can stage-whisper the words "hot and dry."

Group 5: Lebanon Mountains Have two or three students stand with their feet apart and arms hooked together. These students can stage-whisper the words "rocky and grassy."

9 **Have "settlers" move into the map of ancient Canaan.** Divide the remaining students into groups of four or five. Give groups a minute to discuss which area they think is the best place to settle. Remind them to think about the environmental factors of water, topography, and vegetation. Select one group at a time to settle in ancient Canaan. Tell group members to be very careful *not* to touch any of the physical features or other settlers as groups move to stand in the area they have selected. (**Note:** If space is limited, have each group select a representative to settle in ancient Canaan.)

10 Debrief the ancient Canaan experience. Ask "settlers" these questions:

- Why did you choose to settle in the place you selected?

- What are the positive aspects of this site? The negative aspects?

- If you had to move from your site, where would you go and why?

- Do you think this area was able to support large-scale farming? Why or why not?

- How else might people have supported themselves in this region?

After debriefing, have students sit on the floor for the next part of the activity, or have them move the desks and chairs back to their original positions.

11 Have students complete the Reading Notes for Section 7.4. Have students read Section 7.4 and complete the corresponding Reading Notes in their Interactive Student Notebooks. Afterward, use Guide to Reading Notes 7 to review students' responses.

12 Wrap up the activity. Hold a class discussion. Ask,

- Which environmental factor (water, topography, or vegetation) had the greatest effect on people's choices of where to settle in ancient Egypt and Kush? Why?

- Which environmental factor (water, topography, or vegetation) had the greatest effect on people's choices of where to settle in ancient Canaan? Why?

- How might environmental factors have contributed to the rise of civilizations in these areas?

Processing

Have students complete the Processing activity on a separate sheet of paper. Students draw and label a map of their state and write a paragraph explaining how water, topography, and vegetation likely affected settlement in their state.

Quicker Coverage

Conduct a Mini-Activity Rather than have individual students complete the Reading Notes for Section 7.2, conduct a short activity as a class. Before class, use Guide to Reading Notes 7 and the reading to create a list of statements explaining how each environmental factor affects settlement. For example, for *water*, you might include, *Farmers could divert river water for irrigation*. Write each statement on an index card. In class, write the terms *water, topography,* and *vegetation* on the board. Pair students and give each pair an index card. Have pairs match up their index cards with the appropriate environmental factor.

Skip Map Creation As an alternative to the Experiential Exercise, in which students model the physical geography of ancient Egypt, Kush, and Canaan, project the visual of each region and have small groups of students discuss where to settle. Give each group a sticky note with a different color or number. Have each group place its sticky note on the projected map. Use the debrief questions to discuss each group's placement.

Deeper Coverage

Research Settlement As an extension to the Processing activity, have students research the actual locations of the first settlements in their state. Have students label these early settlements on a state map for display in the classroom. Other students can use this map for reference, to see how close they came to pinpointing the areas of early human settlement.

Assessment

Mastering the Content

1. C	5. A	9. C	13. C
2. A	6. B	10. A	14. C
3. B	7. C	11. A	15. B
4. D	8. D	12. D	

Applying Social Studies Skills

Possible answers:

16. by providing fresh water from the Nile River to drink; by allowing people to fish; by providing water for farming; by leaving silt on the fields after a flood, improving the soil; by providing an easy way to travel by boat (any one)

17. by protecting people in the Nile Valley from invasion; by keeping settlement within the Nile Valley because the desert was too dry to farm (any one)

18. by providing fresh water from the Sea of Galilee for farming; by providing fresh water to drink; by enabling people to fish for food (any one)

19. by providing fresh water from the Jordan River for farming; by providing fresh water to drink; by enabling people to fish for food (any one)

Exploring the Essential Question

20. Answers should include all of the elements requested in the prompt.

Scoring Rubric

Score	Description
3	Student completes an advertisement that includes all five bulleted points. The advertisement is clearly stated, persuasive, supported by accurate details, and demonstrates command of standard English conventions.
2	Student responds to most or all parts of the task, but the advertisement may lack details, lack a persuasive approach, or not be clearly stated.
1	Student responds to at least one part of the task. The advertisement may contain factual and/or grammatical errors and may lack details.
0	Response does not match the task or is incorrect.

English Language Learners

Substitute Sentences for Paragraphs Rather than have students write paragraphs for the Reading Notes and Processing activity, have them write their three most important ideas in complete sentences.

Provide Resources For the Processing activity, provide simple physical feature and vegetation maps of your state. Allow students to reference these maps as they drawn their own.

Learners Reading and Writing Below Grade Level

Support Comprehension Provide photocopies of the book pages for Section 7.2. As students read these pages, have them highlight or underline, in color, the significance of each environmental factor discussed. Suggest that they use *blue* for water, *brown* for topography, and *green* for vegetation. Later, as students complete their Reading Notes, encourage them to use the highlighted information and to record their notes for each factor in the same three colors.

Conduct a Prewriting Activity For the Processing activity, have students first complete their maps. Then, pair students to discuss their ideas for the paragraph response. Encourage students to use these ideas as they write their paragraphs.

Learners with Special Education Needs

Use Representatives During the Experiential Exercise, use name tags to represent the presence of group members during the settlement part of the activity. Have students write their names on pieces of construction paper. They can ask a peer to place their names in the specific areas where they would choose to settle.

Provide an Outline Map For the Processing activity, provide a simple outline map of your state. Also consider labeling one or more important physical features to serve as a clue to identifying other features.

Advanced Learners

Use Thematic Maps After students have modeled and settled the map of each area in the Experiential Exercise, give small groups of students copies of thematic maps to examine. Consider using a physical features map, including elevation; a vegetation map; and/or a climate map. Ask students, *Where would you settle? Did your location change from before? Why or why not? How did environmental factors affect your decision?*

Enrichment Resources

Find out more about the geography of ancient Egypt, Kush, and Canaan by exploring the following Enrichment Resources for *History Alive! The Ancient World* at www.teachtci.com.

Enrichment Readings These in-depth readings encourage students to explore selected topics related to the chapter. You may also find readings that relate the chapter's content directly to your state's curriculum.

Internet Connections These recommended Web sites provide useful and engaging content that reinforces skills development and mastery of subjects within the chapter.

Literature Recommendations

The following books offer opportunities to extend the content in this chapter.

Ancient Egypt by John Malam (New York: Enchanted Lion Books, 2004)

Egypt, Kush, Aksum: Northeast Africa by Kenny Mann (Parsippany, NJ: Dillon Press, 1997)

Farming & Food (The Ancient Egyptians) by Jane Shuter (Des Plaines, IL: Heinemann Library, 1999)

Section 7.2

The following statements are possible answers to each question. The locations of statements on the drawing will vary.

1. People needed fresh drinking water to live.

   - People bathed and washed things in fresh water.
   - People could fish and also hunt birds and animals that gathered near water.
   - Farmers needed water to grow their crops.
   - Farmers could divert river water for irrigation.
   - Rivers were used as highways for trade.

2. Farmers grew crops in large, flat areas.

   - Coastal plains and river valleys had rich soil.
   - Steep mountains were hard to cross.
   - The rocky land made farming difficult in the mountains.
   - Hot and dry deserts contained very little water for farming.
   - Intense heat in deserts made travel difficult.

3. Vegetation near rivers and lakes was usually green and lush.

   - Mountains were often covered with trees.
   - Deserts had little vegetation.
   - Plants were a source of food.
   - People made useful products out of plants.
   - Trees provided shade from the hot sun.

Section 7.3

1. The Mediterranean Sea, the Red Sea, the Nile River, and the Arabian, Libyan, and Nubian deserts should be labeled as shown on the map below.

2. Student symbols (*H* or other) that indicate human settlements should be located as shown on the map below.

Ancient Egypt and Kush

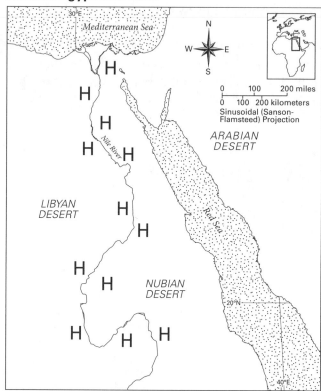

3. Paragraphs will vary but should include at least five words or phrases from the Word Bank. A sample paragraph is provided below.

   Geography affected the choices made by the Egyptians and the Kushites to settle near the Nile River. The Nile River was a source of fresh water in an area that was mostly desert. The Libyan Desert, the Arabian Desert, and the Nubian Desert were too hot and dry. But in the Nile River valley, the river provided natural irrigation and fertilization. The topography included wide, flat areas of land that were good for farming. Vegetation was rare in the dry deserts, but it was plentiful near the Nile River.

Section 7.4

1. The Mediterranean Sea, the Sea of Galilee, the Dead Sea, the Jordan River, the Lebanon Mountains, and the Negev and Syrian deserts should be labeled as shown on the map below.

2. Student symbols (*H* or other) that indicate human settlements should be located as shown on the map below.

Ancient Canaan

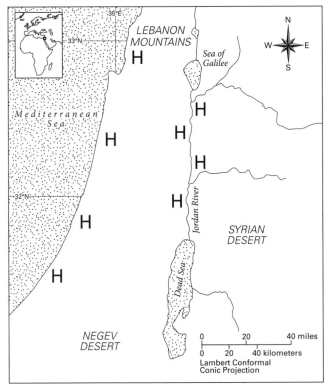

3. Paragraphs will vary but should include at least five words or phrases from the Word Bank. A sample paragraph is provided below.

Geography affected people's choices of where to settle in ancient Canaan. Some people settled near the Mediterranean Sea. The wet, fertile plains were good for farming. The sea allowed traders from many lands to visit Canaan. Other people settled near the Jordan River. This river was the most important source of fresh water in the area. Vegetation was most plentiful near the Jordan River. The hilly topography and dry soil caused many people to become herders. Herders were nomads, and some tried herding cattle and camels in the Negev and Syrian deserts.

The Ancient Egyptian Pharaohs

What did the pharaohs of ancient Egypt accomplish, and how did they do it?

Overview

In a Writing for Understanding activity, students board an Egyptian sailing boat and "visit" monuments along the Nile River to learn about four ancient Egyptian pharaohs and their important accomplishments. After completing their journey, they write a letter about what they have seen and learned on their tour.

Objectives

In the course of reading this chapter and participating in the classroom activity, students will

Social Studies

- identify the accomplishments of four key pharaohs from ancient Egypt: Khufu, Senusret I, Hatshepsut, and Ramses the Great.

- analyze ancient Egyptian art and architecture to better understand the accomplishments of the pharaohs.

- hypothesize some ways in which Egyptian pharaohs achieved their most impressive accomplishments, and the effects of those accomplishments on ancient Egypt.

Language Arts

- create a multi-paragraph personal letter with expository text that engages the interest of the reader and states a clear purpose.

- revise writing to improve the organization and consistency of ideas within and between paragraphs.

Social Studies Vocabulary

Key Content Terms pharaoh, Hatshepsut, Ramses II, treaty

Academic Vocabulary period, accomplish, structure, authority, reign

Materials

History Alive! The Ancient World

Interactive Student Notebooks

Visuals 8A–8G

CD Tracks 6–14

Lesson Masters

- Station Directions 8A and 8B (1 per every 4 students)
- Station Materials 8A (1 per pair, cut apart and placed in an envelope)
- Station Materials 8B (1 per pair)
- Information Masters 8A–8C (1 transparency of each)
- Vocabulary Development handout (1 per student, on colored paper)

masking tape

Activity	Suggested Time	Materials
Preview	10 minutes	• *History Alive! The Ancient World* • Interactive Student Notebooks • Visual 8A
Vocabulary Development	30–40 minutes	• *History Alive! The Ancient World* • Interactive Student Notebooks • Vocabulary Development handout

Writing for Understanding	140 minutes
	(3 regular periods)
	(1.5 block periods)
		• *History Alive! The Ancient World*
		• Interactive Student Notebooks
		• Visuals 8B–8G
		• CD Tracks 6–14
		• Station Directions 8A and 8B
		  (1 per every 4 students)
		• Station Materials 8A (1 per pair, cut
		  apart and placed in an envelope)
		• Station Materials 8B (1 per pair)
		• Information Masters 8A–8C
		  (1 transparency for each)

Processing (optional)	20 minutes	• Interactive Student Notebooks
Assessment	40 minutes	• Chapter 8 Assessment

Preview

1   **Invite students to examine a famous American monument and think about why it was created.** Project *Visual 8A: Postcard of Mount Rushmore* and reveal the first question on the visual. Review the directions for the Preview activity and have students write the answer to the first question in their Interactive Student Notebooks. After students record their answers, have a few volunteers share their responses. Repeat for each of the questions on the visual.

2   **Have students share their responses in pairs or as a class.**

3   **Connect the Preview activity to Chapter 8.** Explain to students that Mount Rushmore was built to honor American presidents George Washington, Thomas Jefferson, Abraham Lincoln, and Franklin Roosevelt and to commemorate their achievements. Similarly, in ancient Egypt, great monuments, such as pyramids and temples, were built to honor the pharaohs and to commemorate their achievements, although typically the pharaohs themselves had their monuments built. Tell students that in this chapter, they will "sail" the Nile River and visit four of these monuments to learn about some ancient Egyptian pharaohs and their accomplishments. Then students will write a letter describing what they learned.

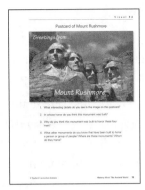

Visual 8A

Vocabulary Development

1   **Introduce the Key Content Terms.** Have students locate the Key Content Terms for the chapter in their Interactive Student Notebooks. These are important terms that will help them understand the main ideas of the chapter. Ask volunteers to identify any familiar terms and how they might be used in a sentence.

2   **Have students complete a Vocabulary Development handout.** Give each student a copy of the Vocabulary Development handout of your choice from the Reading Toolkit at the back of the Lesson Masters. These handouts provide extra Key Content Term practice and support, depending on your students' needs. Review the completed handout by asking volunteers to share one answer for each term.

Reading

1 **Introduce the Essential Question and have students read Section 8.1.** After students have finished reading, have them use information from the section and from the chapter opener image to respond to these questions:

- What items were found in the tomb of King Tutankhaten? (three nested coffins, the smallest in solid gold; a mummy; a golden mask; jewelry; good luck charms; statues; weapons; furniture; a chariot)
- What do these items tell us about this pharaoh and ancient Egypt?
- Why do you think the pharaohs of ancient Egypt built great monuments to themselves?
- What might be some of the great accomplishments of these pharaohs, and how might the pharaohs have achieved them?

2 **Have students complete the Reading Notes for Chapter 8.** Assign Sections 8.2 to 8.6 during the activity, as indicated in the procedures for the Writing for Understanding activity. Remind students to use the Key Content Terms where appropriate as they complete their Reading Notes.

Writing for Understanding

Phase 1: Taking a felucca tour of ancient Egyptian monuments

1 **Before class, prepare materials and the classroom for the activity.** Follow these steps:

- Move desks to the edges of the room.
- Create "tourist stations" by taping copies of *Station Directions 8A: The White Chapel: What Does It Tell Us?* to the wall or on desks throughout the room. Create at least one station for every four students.
- Create an envelope for each pair of students that contains the cut-apart pieces of *Station Materials 8A: Carving from the White Chapel*. Place two envelopes at each tourist station.

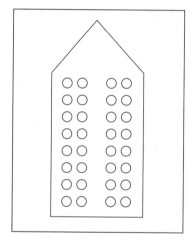

Classroom Map

Station Directions 8A

Station Materials 8A

- Have copies of *Station Directions 8B: Hatshepsut's Temple: What Does It Tell Us?* (one for each station) and *Station Materials 8B: Carving from Hatshepsut's Temple* (one for each pair) prepared and ready to place at each tourist station halfway through the activity.

- Use masking tape to create a large outline of a felucca (an Egyptian sailing boat) on the floor as shown on the classroom map on the preceding page. Students will sit inside the outline, either on the floor or on chairs.

- Pair students and prepare a seating chart that shows pair assignments and seating arrangements.

- Create a transparency of each Information Master.

Station Directions 8B

2 **Project the seating chart and have students "board" the felucca and sit in their assigned places.**

3 **Begin the felucca tour.** Project *Visual 8B: Our Tour Guide* and play CD Track 6, "Welcome to the Tour." Then have pairs read Section 8.2 and complete the Reading Notes for this section.

4 **Sail to the first site at Giza.** Project *Visual 8C: The Great Pyramid at Giza* and play CD Track 7, "Giza." Then have pairs read Section 8.3. Students should not yet complete the Reading Notes for this section.

Station Materials 8B

5 **Discuss how the Great Pyramid was built.** Project and review *Information Master 8A: How Was the Great Pyramid Built?* Give student pairs several minutes to discuss which hypothesis they think best explains how the Great Pyramid was built. Students should be prepared to give reasons for their choice. Then have volunteers share their choice of hypothesis, and their reasons. After most pairs have shared their ideas, play CD Track 8, "How Khufu Built the Great Pyramid at Giza," to hear what the tour guide says.

6 **Have students complete the Reading Notes for Section 8.3.** Afterward, have several volunteers share their postcards with the class.

7 **Sail to the next site at Karnak.** Project *Visual 8D: The White Chapel at Karnak* and play CD Track 9, "Karnak." Then have students read Section 8.4. Students should not yet complete the Reading Notes for this section.

Visual 8B

Visual 8C

Information Master 8A

Visual 8D

8 **Have students visit the White Chapel.** Tell students to step off the felucca and go to one of the "tourist stations" around the room. Make sure there are no more than two pairs per station. Have students do the following at their tourist station:

- Read Station Directions 8A and reassemble the broken carving from the White Chapel.

- Share with another pair a hypothesis about what the carving might represent.

- Put the carving pieces back in the envelopes and reboard the felucca.

9 **Debrief the visit to the White Chapel and have students complete the Reading Notes for Section 8.4.** Ask several volunteers to share what they think the carving represents. Then play CD Track 10, "Reconstructing the White Chapel at Karnak." Finally, have students complete the Reading Notes for Section 8.4. Afterward, have several volunteers share their postcards with the class.

10 **Sail to the next site at Dayr al-Bahri.** Project *Visual 8E: Hatshepsut's Temple at Dayr al-Bahri* and play CD Track 11, "Dayr al-Bahri." Then have students read Section 8.5. While students are reading, place at each tourist station one copy of Station Directions 8B and two copies of Station Materials 8B.

11 **Have students visit Hatshepsut's temple.** Tell pairs to step off the felucca and go to one of the "tourist stations" around the room. Make sure there are no more than two pairs per station. Have students do the following at their tourist station:

Visual 8E

- Read Station Directions 8B and create their list of items from the carving.

- Share their list of items with another pair and explain how these items might have been used by the ancient Egyptians.

- Reboard the felucca.

12 **Debrief the visit to Hatshepsut's temple and have students complete the Reading Notes for Section 8.5.** Ask several volunteers to share their list of items and how those items might have been used by the ancient Egyptians. Then project *Visual 8F: Carving from Hatshepsut's Temple* and play CD Track 12, "Hatshepsut's Expedition to Punt." Finally, have students complete the Reading Notes for Section 8.5. Afterward, have several volunteers share their postcards with the class.

Visual 8F

13 Sail to the final site at Abu Simbel. Project *Visual 8G: The Great Temple of Ramses II at Abu Simbel* and play CD Track 13, "Abu Simbel." Then have students read Section 8.6. Students should not yet complete the Reading Notes for this section.

14 Discuss what happened to the Great Temple of Ramses II. Project and review *Information Master 8B: What Happened to the Great Temple of Ramses II?* Give pairs several minutes to discuss the option they would have recommended to the Egyptian government and why. Then have volunteers share which option they selected and why. After most pairs have shared their ideas, play CD Track 14, "The Great Temple of Ramses," to hear what the tour guide says.

15 Have students complete the Reading Notes for Section 8.6. Afterward, have several volunteers share their postcards with the class. Finally, return the class to its regular configuration.

Visual 8G

Phase 2: Writing a letter about your felucca tour

16 Have students write a first draft of their letter. Project a transparency of *Information Master 8C: Writing a Letter About Your Tour of Ancient Egypt.* Review the directions and answer any questions. Have students write their first drafts neatly, in pencil, using every other line, to facilitate the peer-checking activity to follow. (**Note:** Depending on your class, or particular students, you may want to add to, delete, or revise some of the required elements listed on Information Master 8C.)

Information Master 8B

17 Have pairs peer-check the first drafts. Project Information Master 8C and have each student create a checklist by writing down each of the bulleted items for the writing assignment. Alternatively, you can make a copy of Information Master 8C for each student. Review the directions for the following peer-checking activity, and then have pairs complete it. (**Note:** You may want to make a transparency of a sample draft you have written, or one from a previous year, and practice the steps as a class.)

- Exchange letters with your partner. Carefully read through your partner's letter and look for each of the items from the checklist.

- For each item you find in the draft, check off that item on the checklist and circle that item in the letter. If you cannot find an item in the draft, then leave that item blank on the checklist.

- When you are both done, review the checklist with your partner. Point out the items you found and those that are missing. Return the checklist and the letter to the author.

Information Master 8C

18 Give students time to write their final drafts. Remind students to use the results of the peer-checking activity to help them revise their letters by including any required items that were missing or unclear. (**Note:** Consider collecting the first drafts, checklists, and final drafts to verify that students incorporated the feedback.)

Processing (optional)

1 **Understand the intent of the Processing activity.** The letter writing activity serves as this chapter's Processing activity. Should you choose not to have students do the writing activity, you might use the optional Processing activity in the Interactive Student Notebook.

2 **Have students complete the Processing activity.**

3 **Have students share their answers with their partners or with the class.**

Quicker Coverage

Reduce the Number of Sites Skip the tour stops at Giza and the Great Pyramid, and at Karnak and the White Chapel (Steps 4–9). Instead, have students read and complete the Reading Notes for Sections 8.3 and 8.4. Then have students visit Hatshepsut's temple and the temple of Ramses the Great (Steps 10–15).

Deeper Coverage

Add an Additional Egyptian Site Have students use the Internet or books from a library to identify one additional site from ancient Egypt. Students should research information to learn about the site and about the accomplishments of the pharaoh who had it built. You might suggest these sites to students: The Sphinx at Giza; The Step Pyramid at Saqqara; the Temple of Horus at Edfu; Luxor Temple; the Temple of Seti I at Abydos.

Assessment

Mastering the Content

1. B	5. C	9. D	13. C
2. B	6. A	10. D	14. C
3. D	7. D	11. D	15. A
4. A	8. C	12. D	16. B

Applying Social Studies Skills

17. writing on monuments; letters on cuneiform tablets

18. movement or expansion toward the south

19. warfare; diplomacy; trade; exchange of letters (any three)

Exploring the Essential Question

20. Answers should include all of the elements requested in the prompt.

Scoring Rubric

Score	Description
3	Student completes a two paragraph article that matches all six bulleted points. The article is clearly stated and demonstrates command of standard English conventions.
2	Student responds to most or all parts of the task, but article may lack details or not be clearly stated.
1	Student responds to at least one part of the task. Article may contain factual and/or grammatical errors and may lack details.
0	Response does not match the task or is incorrect.

The Egyptian Mummy Project

1   **Introduce the idea that tools and techniques that people use in their lives and in scientific study change over time.** Ask students to think about how some of the things they use and the ways they do things have changed over the last hundred years. Have students look around the classroom and point out what might be similar and what might be different if this were a classroom in the early 1900s.

2   **Have students look at the photograph on the second page of the Chapter 8 Reading Further.** Ask students, *What do you think might be happening in this photograph?* Explain that scientists have recently begun to use new technologies to examine ancient Egyptian mummies and other artifacts. Tell students that they will be reading about how scientists made interesting discoveries while taking part in the Egyptian Mummy Project.

3   **Have students read the Chapter 8 Reading Further.** After students finish reading, discuss how techniques used by archaeologists have changed over time, from Howard Carter's methods in the 1900s to those used in the modern-day Egyptian Mummy Project. How did the techniques of each period affect the mummies being studied?

4   **Have students complete the first page of the Reading Further activity in their Interactive Student Notebooks.** Invite students to share their ideas about the techniques that archaeologists have used in their study of mummies and other artifacts of ancient Egypt. How have new technologies changed the way artifacts are studied?

5   **Introduce the writing activity.** Tell students that they will write a compare and contrast paragraph based on the information in the chart they completed on the first page of the Reading Further activity in their Interactive Student Notebooks.

6   **Review the features of a Compare and Contrast paragraph.** Remind students to begin with an introductory sentence. They should then include two to three sentences about how archaeologists examined mummies a century ago. Next, they should write two to three sentences comparing and contrasting modern techniques with the methods used in the early 1900s. Explain that students should include information about the effects of the techniques of each time period on the mummies. Students should end their paragraphs with a concluding sentence that summarizes their information, rephrases their introductory sentence, or states a conclusion.

7   **Have students complete the Reading Further in their Interactive Student Notebooks.** Have each student write a paragraph, using the notes in his or her chart, to compare and contrast how archaeologists studied mummies and how the mummies were affected "Then and Now." Invite volunteers to share their paragraphs.

English Language Learners

Modify the Letter-Writing Activity Modify the letter-writing activity so that students choose only one site to describe in a single paragraph. You might also provide a template that illustrates the proper format for writing a letter.

Modify and Model the Peer-Checking Activity For the peer-checking activity, consider scaling back the number of items that students must look for in the draft letters. Then, before students begin the peer-checking activity, model the process by making a transparency of a draft letter and going through it together, as a class.

Learners Reading and Writing Below Grade Level

Prepare a Hint Sheet Prepare a hint sheet to help students complete the Reading Notes for Chapter 8. It should list in random order all the answers provided in the Guide to Reading Notes 8 in the Lesson Guide. Give students this sheet before they begin the "felucca tour." As students read each section of text, they can refer to the hint sheet to complete their postcards.

Learners with Special Education Needs

Create a "Portable Tourist Site" If you have students who may find the physical aspects of the tour challenging, create a "portable tourist site" by taping the station directions and materials on a large cardboard box or easel. Slide each portable tourist site up to the edge of the "boat" for students to visit without having to move around the classroom.

Highlight Key Words on Each Copy of the Station Directions For example, you might highlight direction words such as *examine*, *list*, and *discuss*. You might also highlight specific factual information needed to complete the Reading Notes or to do the station's activity.

Provide a Copy of Guide to Reading Notes 8 from the Lesson Guide As students visit each site on the tour, have them highlight the important facts that they find in the given answers for that site.

Advanced Learners

Have Students Research Additional Information for Their Postcards For each of the sites students visit on their felucca tour, have them do additional research on the Internet or in a library about the pharaoh (Khufu, Senusret I, Hatshepsut, Ramses the Great) and/or the monument (the Great Pyramid, the White Chapel, the temple at Dayr al-Bahri, the temple at Abu Simbel). Have students incorporate this information into their Reading Notes postcards and into their final writing assignment.

Have Students Create a Journal of Their Felucca Tour Use these directions for an alternative or additional writing assignment:

Create a four-page journal describing your felucca tour of ancient Egyptian monuments. Use your Reading Notes to help you complete the journal. Be sure to use correct grammar and spelling. Each page of your journal should be about your visit to a different site and must include these parts:

- A short paragraph describing each new destination, including the direction and approximate distance from the previous location.

- A paragraph describing the site you visited, including some description of the art or architecture of the monument at that site, and any other interesting information or facts about the site or monument.

- A paragraph discussing the pharaoh who built the monument at that site, including when he or she ruled, what kind of ruler he or she was, and what some of his or her most important or interesting accomplishments were.

- At least two photographs, artifacts, or souvenirs from your visit to the site. These items should relate to something you wrote about in your journal. Write a short caption describing each item.

Enrichment Resources

Find out more about Egyptian pharaohs by exploring the following Enrichment Resources for *History Alive! The Ancient World* at www.teachtci.com.

Enrichment Readings These in-depth readings encourage students to explore selected topics related to the chapter. You may also find readings that relate the chapter's content directly to your state's curriculum.

Internet Connections These recommended Web sites provide useful and engaging content that reinforces skills development and mastery of subjects within the chapter.

Literature Recommendations

The following books offer opportunities to extend the content in this chapter.

Hatshepsut, His Majesty, Herself by Catherine M. Andronik (New York: Atheneum, 2001)

Pyramid (Eyewitness Books) by James Putnam (London; New York: Dorling Kindersley Children, 2004)

The Tomb of King Tutankhamen (Unearthing Ancient Worlds) by Michael Woods and Mary B. Woods (Minneapolis, MN: Twenty-First Century Books, 2008)

Section 8.2

1.

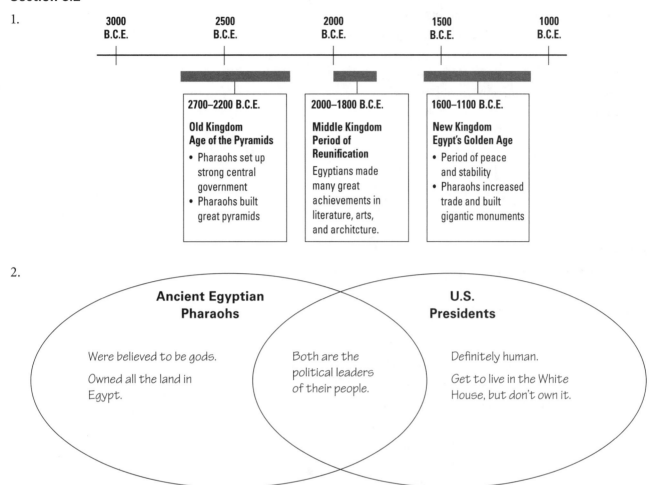

| 3000 B.C.E. | 2500 B.C.E. | 2000 B.C.E. | 1500 B.C.E. | 1000 B.C.E. |

2700–2200 B.C.E.

Old Kingdom
Age of the Pyramids
- Pharaohs set up strong central government
- Pharaohs built great pyramids

2000–1800 B.C.E.

Middle Kingdom
Period of Reunification

Egyptians made many great achievements in literature, arts, and architcture.

1600–1100 B.C.E.

New Kingdom
Egypt's Golden Age
- Period of peace and stability
- Pharaohs increased trade and built gigantic monuments

2.

Ancient Egyptian Pharaohs

Were believed to be gods.

Owned all the land in Egypt.

Both are the political leaders of their people.

U.S. Presidents

Definitely human.

Get to live in the White House, but don't own it.

Section 8.3

Postcards may include the following information:

- Khufu ruled from about 2551 to 2528 B.C.E., during the Old Kingdom. Some stories describe Khufu as a cruel leader. Others say that he was kind.

- Khufu established the pharaoh as the central authority; he kept strict control over Egypt's food supply and declared himself a god. And he built the Great Pyramid.

- The Great Pyramid is over 450 feet tall and made of more than 2 million stone blocks. It took about 20 years to build.

- There are different theories about how the Great Pyramid was built, but most Egyptologists think that thousands of workers cut stone blocks, dragged them to the site, pulled them up ramps, and put them into place to create the pyramid.

Section 8.4

Postcards may include the following information:

- Senusret I ruled from about 1971 to 1926 B.C.E., during the Middle Kingdom. \He was a strong ruler who governed a stable, unified Egypt.

- During Senusret's rule, some of Egypt's greatest works of literature were written, including "The Story of Sinuhe." Senusret also built and improved religious buildings, including the White Chapel.

- The White Chapel was made of alabaster, a white stone. Detailed carvings decorated the pillars of the chapel. The chapel may have been originally covered in gold.

- Archaeologists discovered the ruins of the White Chapel inside another monument. They were able to put the broken pieces together, like a giant puzzle, and reconstruct the White Chapel.

Section 8.5

Postcards may include the following information:

- Hatshepsut ruled from about 1473 to 1458 B.C.E., during the New Kingdom. She was Egypt's first female ruler. She stayed in power by appointing loyal advisers to government positions and by demanding the same respect that a male ruler would be given.

- Hatshepsut was known for promoting trade with other countries, including an expedition, undertaken by over 200 men, to the African kingdom of Punt.

- Hatshepsut also constructed the stunning temple at Dayr al-Bahri, which was built directly into a cliff.

- Outside the temple were 200 sphinx statues. Inside were carvings of scenes from Hatshepsut's reign, including the expedition to Punt.

Section 8.6

Postcards may include the following information:

- Ramses II ruled for more than 60 years, from 1290 to 1224 B.C.E., during the New Kingdom. He was known as Ramses the Great.

- At the age of ten, Ramses was a captain in Egypt's army. In his lifetime, he had over 100 wives, and more than 100 children. He built the temple at Abu Simbel.

- At the front of the temple are four giant sculptures of Ramses. The temple was built so that, twice a year, the sun would line up with the entrance and shine down three halls to fall on another giant statue of Ramses.

- In the 1960s, the entire temple was cut from the cliff side, moved to a higher location, and reassembled to save it from floods created by the dam built by the Egyptian government in the 1940s.

Daily Life in Ancient Egypt

How did social class affect daily life in ancient Egypt?

Overview

In a Problem Solving Groupwork activity, students create and perform interactive dramatizations to learn about the social structure of ancient Egypt and its effect on daily life for members of each social class.

Objectives

In the course of reading this chapter and participating in the classroom activity, students will

Social Studies

- explain why the social structure of ancient Egypt is organized like a pyramid, and how religion affects that organization
- identify the key aspects of daily life for five social classes in ancient Egypt.
- discuss the role of written language and various art forms in ancient Egypt.

Language Arts

- read aloud expository text fluently and accurately and with appropriate pacing, intonation, and expression.
- deliver informative presentations using facts, details, examples, and explanations developed from written and visual sources.

Social Studies Vocabulary

Key Content Terms social pyramid, social class, status, noble, peasant, afterlife, hieroglyph

Academic Vocabulary supreme, occupy, rigid, role, neutral

Materials

History Alive! The Ancient World

Interactive Student Notebooks

Visuals 9A–9E

CD Track 15

Lesson Masters

- Student Handouts 9A–9E (1 per group of 4)
- Vocabulary Development handout (1 per student, on colored paper)

Activity	Suggested Time	Materials
Preview	15 minutes	• Interactive Student Notebooks
Vocabulary Development	30–40 minutes	• *History Alive! The Ancient World* • Interactive Student Notebooks • Vocabulary Development handout
Problem Solving Groupwork	150–180 minutes (3–4 regular periods) (1.5–2 block periods)	• *History Alive! The Ancient World* • Interactive Student Notebooks • Visuals 9A–9E • CD Track 15 • Student Handouts 9A–9E (2 copies of each handout; 1 handout per group of 4)
Processing	15 minutes	• Interactive Student Notebooks
Assessment	40 minutes	• Chapter 9 Assessment

Preview

1   **Have students complete the Preview activity for Chapter 9 in their Interactive Student Notebooks.** Tell students that they will determine where various people belong on the social pyramid of their school.

2   **Have students share their responses in pairs or as a class.** Then ask,

   • How did you decide where to place each individual or group on the social pyramid?

   • Why are the levels at the top of the social pyramid smaller than those at the bottom?

   • How might your school benefit from having a social pyramid?

   • How might the level on a social pyramid affect the everyday life of an individual or group?

3   **Connect the Preview activity to Chapter 9.** Tell students that society in ancient Egypt was also structured like a social pyramid. Similar to the principal, the pharaoh enjoyed the highest status. Pharaohs were all-powerful, and their word was law. Similar to students, peasants made up the largest social class. They were at the bottom of the social pyramid. Tell students that in this chapter, they will learn about the social structure of ancient Egypt and its effect on daily life for the members of each social class.

Vocabulary Development

1   **Introduce the Key Content Terms.** Have students locate the Key Content Terms for the chapter in their Interactive Student Notebooks. These are important terms that will help them understand the main ideas of the chapter. Ask volunteers to identify any familiar terms and how they might be used in a sentence.

2   **Have students complete a Vocabulary Development handout.** Give each student a copy of the Vocabulary Development handout of your choice from the Reading Toolkit at the back of the Lesson Masters. These handouts provide extra Key Content Term practice and support, depending on your students' needs. Review the completed handout by asking volunteers to share one answer for each term.

Reading

1   **Introduce the Essential Question and have students read Section 9.1.** Have students identify the Essential Question on the first page of the chapter: *How did social class affect daily life in ancient Egypt?* Then have students read Section 9.1. Afterward, have students use information from Section 9.1 and from the chapter opener image to propose some possible answers to the Essential Question.

2 **Have students complete the Reading Notes for Chapter 9.** Assign Sections 9.2 to 9.7 during the activity, as indicated in the procedures for the Problem Solving Groupwork. Remind students to use the Key Content Terms where appropriate as they complete their Reading Notes.

Problem Solving Groupwork

1 **Put students in groups of four.** You may want to create a transparency that shows assigned groups and seating arrangements.

2 **Introduce the activity—preparing an interactive dramatization of one social class in ancient Egypt.** Explain to groups that in this activity, they will become experts on one social class in ancient Egypt. They will work together to create an interactive dramatization that brings to life a typical scene from the daily lives of members of that social class. The dramatization will have props and costumes and must involve members of the audience.

3 **Have students complete the Reading Notes for Section 9.2 about the social classes in ancient Egypt.** Tell students that this section introduces them to six social classes in ancient Egypt. Have them read Section 9.2 and complete the corresponding Reading Notes in their Interactive Student Notebooks. Afterward, use Guide to Reading Notes 9 in the Lesson Guide to review their responses.

4 **Assign one of five social classes lower than the pharaoh to each group of students.** Assign one of these social classes—government officials, priests, scribes, artisans, and peasants—to a group of students. In larger classes, you will need to assign the same social class to more than one group.

5 **Distribute and review materials for creating an interactive dramatization.** Be prepared to display Visuals 9A–9E. Pass out one copy of the related *Student Handouts 9A–9E: Preparing an Interactive Dramatization* to each group according to their assigned social group. Briefly review the steps for creating an interactive dramatization. Encourage students to sound out the Egyptian greetings as best as they can.

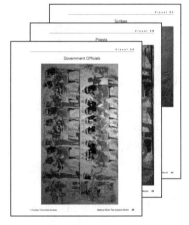

Visuals 9A–9E

6 **Monitor groups as they create their interactive dramatizations.** Allow adequate time—at least two class periods—for preparation. Have groups obtain your initials as they complete each step on Student Handout 9. Pay special attention to Step 3 on the handout, making sure groups incorporate all six items into their dramatizations. The groups representing peasants will need access to CD Track 15, "Peasants' Harvesting Chant."

7 **Arrange the classroom for presentations.** When groups are ready, create a stage area in the front of the room, with the projector centrally located. Set up the CD player for groups to play their music and sound effects.

8 **Have the first group perform.** Project *Visual 9A: Government Officials* and have the corresponding group invite four audience members to participate in its dramatization. Remind performers to speak loudly and clearly.

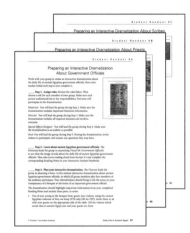

Student Handouts 9A–9E

Encourage all students to be supportive, respectful, and attentive. (**Note:** The six items listed in Step 3 on *Student Handout 9A: Preparing an Interactive Dramatization About Government Officials* provide an easy and useful evaluation checklist for each presentation. Also consider evaluating for these two items: all actors can be seen and heard clearly; costumes and props are creative and appropriate.)

9 **Have students complete the Reading Notes for Section 9.3.** After each dramatization, have students in the audience complete their Reading Notes by recording key information from the performance. Then have them read the relevant section in their books and fill in the section of their Reading Notes.

10 **Repeat Steps 8 and 9 for the remaining groups.** Project the appropriate visual for each group and use the checklists on Student Handouts 9B–9E to evaluate the groups.

11 **Wrap up the activity.** Hold a class discussion using the following questions:

- How would you describe daily life in ancient Egypt?

- If you had lived in ancient Egypt, in which social class would you have wanted to be and why?

- In what ways was daily life in ancient Egypt similar to today? In what ways was it different?

Processing

Have students complete the Processing activity for Chapter 9 in their Interactive Student Notebooks. Have students compare and contrast the social pyramid of ancient Egypt with a social pyramid of their school. Afterward, consider having students share their responses with a partner, or invite volunteers to share with the class.

Quicker Coverage

Streamline the Activity Assign each group a section and the corresponding visual from the list below:

- Section 9.3, Visual 9A

- Section 9.4, Visual 9B

- Section 9.5, Visual 9C

- Section 9.6, Visual 9D

- Section 9.7, Visual 9E

With their groups, students should read their assigned section and complete the corresponding Reading Notes. Then have groups annotate their visuals with information from their reading, making sure to focus on information needed to complete the Reading Notes for that section. Have each group select a presenter to lead the class through an examination of the visual as well as share the information that the class needs to complete their Reading Notes.

> **Listening and Speaking: Oral Communication**
>
> Remind students that they can convey social class, as well as create interest, not only through words, costumes, and props, but also through choices they make about their rate, volume, pitch, and tone. Students should also consider the posture and likely gestures that would most accurately convey social standing and hold the audience's attention.

Create Posters Assign one of the five social classes to each group. Have groups read the appropriate section and complete the corresponding Reading Notes for their assigned social class. Afterward, have each group make a poster that includes all the information needed to complete the Reading Notes. Have groups display their posters on the walls of the classroom, and conduct a gallery walk to allow students to complete the Reading Notes for other sections.

Deeper Coverage

Have Groups Research Social Classes Have groups use the Internet or books from a library to learn more about their assigned social class. Groups can then augment their presentations with what they learn.

Assessment

Mastering the Content

1. B	5. C	9. B	13. B
2. C	6. B	10. B	14. C
3. C	7. A	11. A	15. D
4. D	8. C	12. C	16. A

Applying Social Studies Skills

17. a statue of a seated man wearing long hair and a beard

18. Answers will vary. Possible answers: They worked together as a team. They used tools to chip the hard stone.

19. Answers will vary. Possible answers: What did stone carvers wear? How did stone carvers reach high places on the statue? How did stone carvers wear their hair?

Exploring the Essential Question

20. Answers should include all of the elements requested in the prompt.

Scoring Rubric

Score	Description
3	Student completes a narrative that matches all five bulleted points. The narrative has a clear, appropriate point of view, includes details, and demonstrates command of standard English conventions.
2	Student responds to most or all parts of the task, but narrative may be unclear or lack details.
1	Student responds to at least one part of the task. Narrative may contain factual and/or grammatical errors and may lack details.
0	Response does not match the task or is incorrect.

English Language Learners

Pair Students For the Preview and Processing activities, pair proficient English speakers with less proficient English speakers. Also consider providing specific names for the individuals and groups in the Preview activity to help students better identify where each one belongs on the social pyramid.

Rehearse Dramatizations Before Another Group Pair two groups to give students an opportunity to rehearse their dramatizations for an audience. After each group has rehearsed its dramatization, have students discuss each other's dramatizations and offer suggestions.

Share Information Verbally For Sections 9.3–9.7, have students identify and share with a partner at least three important details about the daily lives of the social class in each section.

Learners Reading and Writing Below Grade Level

Color-code the Reading Notes Have students select one color for each of the social classes. Beginning with the Reading Notes for Section 9.2, students should write their notes in the selected color for each social class.

Provide Copies of the Reading As students complete their Reading Notes, consider providing a copy of the reading for Sections 9.3–9.7. Students can complete the second task for each of these sections by highlighting the appropriate facts for that social class. Students can complete the third task for each of these sections by underlining statements that answer the question.

Cut Apart Student Handouts Rather than give groups a copy of both pages of the Student Handout 9 for their assigned social class, cut apart the handout by step. Give each group member the corresponding step for his or her assigned role in a dramatization. With less to read, students can be more focused on the task at hand.

Learners with Special Education Needs

Have Students Share a Role Create groups of five students to allow two of the group members to share a role during the activity. Alternatively, review the responsibilities of the roles with students ahead of time and have them select a role in which they feel most comfortable.

Offer Sentence Starters For the Processing activity, give students these sentence starters to compare each level on the social pyramids.

Government officials in ancient Egypt are similar to the assistant principal in my school because . . .

Government officials are different from the assistant principal because . . .

Priests in ancient Egypt are similar to the teachers in my school because . . .

Priests are different from the teachers because . . .

Scribes in ancient Egypt are similar to the office staff in my school because . . .

Scribes are different from the office staff because . . .

Artisans in ancient Egypt are similar to the student council in my school because . . .

Artisans are different from the student council because . . .

Peasants in ancient Egypt are similar to the students in my school because . . .

Peasants are different from the students because . . .

Advanced Learners

Have Students Write a Dialogue In place of the Processing activity, have students create at least two characters from two different social levels and write a one-page dialogue between the characters that highlights the similarities and differences in their lives. The dialogues should include the following:

- a description of the main role of each character in Egyptian society
- two differences that set the social classes apart from each other
- one thing that each character would have in common with the other

Enrichment Resources

Find out more about daily life in ancient Egypt by exploring the following Enrichment Resources for *History Alive! The Ancient World* at www.teachtci.com.

Enrichment Readings These in-depth readings encourage students to explore selected topics related to the chapter. You may also find readings that relate the chapter's content directly to your state's curriculum.

Internet Connections These recommended Web sites provide useful and engaging content that reinforces skills development and mastery of subjects within the chapter.

Literature Recommendations

The following books offer opportunities to extend the content in this chapter.

Growing Up in Ancient Egypt by Rosalie David (Mahwah, NJ: Troll Associates, 1997)

The Mystery of the Hieroglyphs by Carol Donoughue (New York: Oxford University Press, 2002)

Secrets of the Mummies: Uncovering the Bodies of Ancient Egyptians by Shelley Tanaka (New York: Scholastic, 2000)

Section 9.2

Students' completed social pyramids should resemble the pyramid diagram in Section 9.2 of their books. Students' symbols and captions will vary but should accurately reflect the members of the six social classes in the pyramid diagram.

1. Ancient Egyptian society was structured like a pyramid because there were six distinct levels of social classes. The classes near the top of the pyramid had fewer people and enjoyed higher status. The classes near the bottom of the pyramid had more people but lower status.

2. At the top of the social pyramid was the pharaoh, who had the most power. Religion strengthened the pharaoh's authority. Pharaohs were regarded as gods, and their word was law. Priests were also a powerful group because they were in charge of religious rituals, and religion touched every part of people's daily lives.

3. Egyptian women enjoyed greater freedom and more rights than most women in the ancient world. They could own land and run businesses. They could ask for divorces and represent themselves in legal matters. Some women in the middle and upper classes worked as doctors, government officials, or priestesses.

4. The social pyramid in ancient Egypt was rigid because there was little chance to move up to a higher class. People usually stayed in the same class as their parents. Each group had its own role to play. The Egyptians believed that their class system created a stable, well-ordered society. For example, if peasants stopped farming, then there would be no one else to provide a dependable food supply.

Section 9.3

1. Students should shade in the second-highest level on the social pyramid and label it "government officials."

2. Facts will vary but might include the following:
   - The vizier advised the pharaoh, appointed and supervised other officials, and served as chief judge.

- The chief treasurer collected taxes in the form of such things as grain, cows, cloth, and silver.

- The general of the armies advised the pharaoh in matters of war and national security, such as protecting Egypt from invaders, and he also helped make alliances with other kingdoms.

3. Government officials led lives of luxury. Most were nobles who had great wealth, fine homes, and plenty of time to socialize. They attended lavish banquets and dressed in fine clothing and jewelry.

Section 9.4

1. Students should shade in the third-highest level on the social pyramid and label it "priests."

2. Facts will vary but might include the following:
   - The High Priest advised the pharaoh and oversaw all religious ceremonies.
   - Temple priests were in charge of the many temples throughout Egypt.
   - Other priests handled the more common concerns and requests, such as giving advice and performing healings.
   - Women priestesses oversaw temples that were devoted to music and dancing.

3. Priests had to purify themselves because they were the only ones who could enter the sanctuaries. To purify themselves, they had to avoid certain foods, cleanse their bodies, shave off body hair, and wear clothes made of linen cloth.

Section 9.5

1. Students should shade in the fourth-highest level on the social pyramid and label it "scribes."

2. Facts will vary but might include the following:

   - Boys started at around the age of five and spent 12 years or more at scribe schools.

   - Life in scribe schools was difficult; students studied for many hours, and teachers were strict.

   - There were different kinds of scribes, such as legal and military scribes.

   - Scribes kept records of the grain and food supply.

   - Some scribes calculated taxes and some recorded census results.

3. Scribes were Egypt's official writers and record keepers, so they were highly respected and well paid. Only men were allowed to be scribes. Becoming a scribe was one of the few ways that men could rise above their parents' social class.

Section 9.6

1. Students should shade in the fifth-highest level on the social pyramid and label it "artisans."

2. Facts will vary but might include the following:

   - Egyptian artisans included carpenters, jewelers, leather- and metalworkers, painters, potters, sculptors, and weavers.

   - Artisans made beautiful objects such as jewelry and furniture.

   - The most skilled artisans were the stone carvers who produced the statues, engravings, and reliefs found in ancient Egyptian temples, tombs, and monuments.

3. Though artisans were highly skilled, they were seen by the upper classes as common laborers. Therefore, artisans rarely received recognition for their work. Artisans lived in modest, rectangular homes that were barely 10 yards long. They worked side by side in large workshops for 10 days at a stretch. Workers depended entirely on their employers for food.

Section 9.7

1. Students should shade in the bottom level on the social pyramid and label it "peasants."

2. Facts will vary but might include the following:

   - During the flooding season, while waiting for the river water to go down, farmers labored on royal projects.

   - During the planting season, farmers sowed their fields with seeds and irrigated the land. The main crops were wheat and barley.

   - During the harvest season, farmers and their families worked together. Men cut down the plants, and women and children gathered the tall stocks of grain.

3. Peasants were the lowest and largest social class in ancient Egypt. Although society depended on their work, they were seen as unskilled laborers. They had the fewest comforts. They lived in plain houses of mud bricks and had little furniture. Their diet was simple, and they spent most of their lives working.

The Kingdom of Kush

In what ways did location influence the history of Kush?

Overview

In a Visual Discovery activity, students analyze images of significant events and leaders from four periods in the history of ancient Kush to learn about the development of the independent kingdom of Kush and its changing relationship with ancient Egypt.

Objectives

In the course of reading this chapter and participating in the classroom activity, students will

Social Studies

- identify the location of the civilization of Kush.

- analyze and describe images that show the commercial, cultural, and political relationship between Kush and Egypt, and the development in Kush of an independent economy, government, and culture.

- explain how location influenced the history of Kush during four different time periods.

Language Arts

- emphasize salient points to assist listeners' understanding of main ideas and concepts.

- use a timeline to effectively and coherently organize main ideas.

Social Studies Vocabulary

Key Content Terms Meroë, dynasty, kandake

Academic Vocabulary complicate, unique, establish, superior

Materials

History Alive! The Ancient World

Interactive Student Notebooks

Visuals 10A–10D

Lesson Masters

- Student Handouts 10A–10B (1 per group of 4)

- Vocabulary Development handout (1 per student, on colored paper)

colored pencils

Activity	Suggested Time	Materials
Preview	15 minutes	• Interactive Student Notebooks
Vocabulary Development	30–40 minutes	• *History Alive! The Ancient World* • Interactive Student Notebooks • Vocabulary Development handout
Visual Discovery	100 minutes (2–3 regular periods) (1–1.5 block periods)	• *History Alive! The Ancient World* • Interactive Student Notebooks • Visuals 10A–10D • Student Handouts 10A and 10B (1 per group of 4) • colored pencils
Processing	20 minutes	• Interactive Student Notebooks
Assessment	40 minutes	• Chapter 10 Assessment

Preview

1 **Have students complete the Preview activity in their Interactive Student Notebooks.** Students create a sensory figure of a famous person to illustrate what that individual experienced and felt during his or her lifetime.

2 **Have students share their responses in pairs or as a class.**

3 **Connect the Preview activity to Chapter 10.** Tell students that in this chapter, they will be creating sensory figures for leaders of the ancient kingdom of Kush. Similar to the famous people in students' sensory figure illustrations, the leaders of ancient Kush saw, heard, touched, and felt many different things during their lifetime. In this chapter, students will learn about the development of the independent kingdom of Kush and examine its changing relationship with ancient Egypt.

Vocabulary Development

1 **Introduce the Key Content Terms.** Have students locate the Key Content Terms for the chapter in their Interactive Student Notebooks. These are important terms that will help them understand the main ideas of the chapter. Ask volunteers to identify any familiar terms and how they might be used in a sentence.

2 **Have students complete a Vocabulary Development handout.** Give each student a copy of the Vocabulary Development handout of your choice from the Reading Toolkit at the back of the Lesson Masters. These handouts provide extra Key Content Term practice and support, depending on your students' needs. Review the completed handout by asking volunteers to share one answer for each term.

Reading

1 **Introduce the Essential Question and have students read Section 10.1.** Have students identify the Essential Question on the first page of the chapter: *In what ways did location influence the history of Kush?* Then have students read Section 10.1. Afterward, have students use information from Section 10.1 and from the chapter opener image to propose some possible answers to the Essential Question.

2 **Have students complete the Reading Notes for Chapter 10.** Assign Sections 10.2 to 10.5 during the activity, as indicated in the procedures for the Visual Discovery. Remind students to use the Key Content Terms where appropriate as they complete their Reading Notes.

Visual Discovery

1 **Place students in pairs.** You may want to create a transparency that shows student partners and seating arrangements.

2 **Introduce the activity and the concept of an act-it-out.** Explain to students that in this activity, they will analyze images representing four key periods in the history of the kingdom of Kush. They will read more about these time periods in which location greatly influenced events in Kush. For two of these time periods, students will work in groups to prepare characters for act-it-outs, in which actors will "step into" images to bring them to life.

3 **Examine Time Period 1: The Egyptianization of Kush.** Project *Visual 10A: Kushites Bringing Tribute to Egyptian Governor.* Help students analyze the image by asking,

Visual 10A

- What interesting details do you see in this image?
- How would you describe the appearance of the large figure seated to the right? Who might this person be?
- How would you describe the appearance of the smaller figures to the left? What do they seem to be doing?
- If the figures to the left are from Kush and the figure to the right is from Egypt, what do you think the relationship is between these two civilizations during this time period?

4 **Have pairs complete the sensory figure of the Kushite leader in the Reading Notes for Section 10.2.** Have pairs read Section 10.2 and complete the corresponding Reading Notes in their Interactive Student Notebooks. Then, as a class, review their entries for the sensory figure of the Kushite king. Encourage students to add details to their sensory figures. (**Note:** Alternatively, you may want to complete the Reading Notes together as a class until you are confident that pairs can do so on their own.)

5 **Have pairs reexamine Visual 10A.** Encourage them to use information from the reading to answer these questions:

- What is happening in this image and why?
- In what ways did location influence Kush during this time period?

6 **Examine Time Period 2: Kush Conquers Egypt.** Project *Visual 10B: King Piye Receiving Gifts from Egyptian Princes.* Ask,

Visual 10B

- What interesting details do you see in this image?
- How would you describe the appearance of the figure standing on the platform to the left? Who might this person be?
- What are the figures in front of him doing? Why might they be doing this?
- If the figure to the left is from Kush and the figures kneeling in front of him are from Egypt, what do you think the relationship is between these two civilizations during this time period?

7   **Have pairs complete the sensory figure of the Kushite leader in the Reading Notes for Section 10.3.** Have pairs read Section 10.3 and complete the corresponding Reading Notes in their Interactive Student Notebooks. Review their responses as a class.

8   **Have students prepare to bring the image to life.** Place two student pairs together to form groups of four. Give each group a copy of *Student Handout 10A: Bringing to Life the Payment of Tribute to Kush*. Assign each group a character from the list on the handout. There may be more than one group assigned to a character. Give groups several minutes to complete the steps on their handout, from their characters' perspectives.

9   **Conduct the act-it-out.** Choose one or more volunteers as actors for each character in the act-it-out. Have actors step into the image and take on the body postures and facial expressions of their characters. Acting as a historian, ask the characters the questions from the handout. Afterward, have the audience give the actors a round of applause. (**Note:** Consider involving the audience by allowing audience members to ask appropriate questions. You may need to give audience groups a minute to brainstorm questions.)

10   **Examine Time Period 3: The Kushite Capital of Meroë.** Project *Visual 10C: Kushite Ironworkers.* Ask,

- What interesting details do you see in this image?
- What tools and materials are these men using? What do they seem to be making?
- What natural resources might be available to these men for this work?
- If these men are making iron weapons, how might this skill be helpful to Kush?

11   **Have pairs complete the sensory figure of the Kushite leader in the Reading Notes for Section 10.4.** Have pairs read Section 10.4 and complete the corresponding Reading Notes in their Interactive Student Notebooks. Review their responses as a class.

12   **Have pairs reexamine Visual 10C.** Encourage them to use information from the reading to answer these questions:

- How did Kush benefit from moving its capital to Meroë?
- In what ways did location influence Kush during this time period?

13   **Examine Time Period 4: Kush Returns to Its African Roots.** Project *Visual 10D: Kandake Amanirenas and Prince Akinidad.* Ask,

- What interesting details do you see in this image?
- How would you describe the appearance of the two figures standing to the right? Who might these people be?
- What seems to be happening in the background?
- If the woman to the right is the leader of Kush and this event is taking place along its northern border, what challenges might be facing Kush?

Student Handout 10A

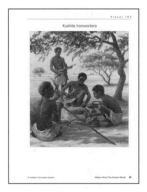

Visual 10C

Visual 10D

14 Have pairs complete the sensory figure of a Kushite leader in the Reading Notes for Section 10.5. Have pairs read Section 10.5 and complete the corresponding Reading Notes in their Interactive Student Notebooks. Review their responses as a class.

15 Have students prepare to bring the image to life. Place two student pairs together to form groups of four. Give each group a copy of *Student Handout 10B: Bringing to Life the War Between Kush and Rome.* Assign each group a character from the list on the handout. There may be more than one group assigned to a character. Give groups several minutes to complete the steps on their handout, from their characters' perspectives.

16 Conduct the act-it-out. Choose one or more volunteers as actors for each character in the act-it-out. Have actors step into the image and take on the body postures and facial expressions of their characters. Acting as a historian, ask the characters the questions from the handout. Afterward, have the audience give the actors a round of applause. (**Note:** Consider involving the audience by allowing audience members to ask appropriate questions. You may need to give audience groups a minute to brainstorm questions.)

Student Handout 10B

Processing

Have students complete an illustrated timeline as the Processing activity for Chapter 10 in their Interactive Student Notebooks. On a separate sheet of paper, students copy a timeline of four periods in the history of Kush. Then they annotate and illustrate each boxed date on the timeline and evaluate the influence of location on the history of Kush.

Quicker Coverage

Skip Act-It-Outs In place of the act-it-outs for Visuals 10B and 10D, have pairs reexamine the images. For Visual 10B, ask the class these questions: *What is happening in this image and why? In what ways did location influence Kush during this time period?* For Visual 10D, ask the class these questions: *What challenges faced Kush, and how did Kushites deal with them? In what ways did location influence Kush during this time period?*

Deeper Coverage

Create a Storybook In place of the Processing activity, have students work in pairs or small groups to create a children's storybook showing how location influenced the history of Kush. Consider requiring these elements for the storybook:

- a cover page with a title and an illustration that will attract readers
- a page with a description of the setting (Kush) and an appropriate illustration
- one or more pages on each of the four main time periods in the history of Kush
- a narrative that uses sensory detail, such as what characters saw, heard, touched, and felt (emotions)
- illustrations, dialogue, or other clever and creative touches

Assessment

Mastering the Content

1. C	5. D	9. A	13. D
2. C	6. A	10. C	14. B
3. B	7. B	11. C	15. B
4. D	8. D	12. A	

Applying Social Studies Skills

16. Sudan

17. from the south or southeast

18. Red Sea

19. caravan (camels, wagons—accept any reasonable overland means of transportation); boats (ships, barges—accept any reasonable water transportation)

Exploring the Essential Question

20. Answers should include all of the elements requested in the prompt.

Scoring Rubric

Score	Description
3	Student completes all four parts of the task. Comments are clearly stated, supported by details, and demonstrate command of standard English conventions.
2	Student responds to most or all parts of the task, but comments may lack details or not be clearly stated.
1	Student responds to at least one part of the task. Comment(s) may contain factual and/or grammatical errors and may lack details.
0	Response does not match the task or is incorrect.

English Language Learners

Provide a Model Prepare a sample sensory figure to present on a transparency as you explain each step of the Preview activity. Consider using a figure that is familiar to students, such as a student eating in the cafeteria. As you point to the figure's eyes, ask students what this figure might see. Write some responses on the transparency. Repeat for the ears (hear), hands (touch), and heart (feel). When students complete their own sensory figure, you may want to give them the choice to use a figure from their native country.

Support the Essential Question After students read Section 10.1 and propose possible answers to the Essential Question, consider some other examples in which the location of a country has influenced its history. Have students describe the location of a familiar place, such as Mesopotamia or their native country, and then propose ways that its location influenced its history.

Prepare a Hint Sheet To help students complete the sensory figures in the Reading Notes for Chapter 10, prepare a hint sheet for students to reference. On this sheet, list in random order all the "possible answer" statements provided for the sensory figures in Guide to Reading Notes 10. As students read each section, they can refer to the hint sheet as they complete their Reading Notes.

Learners Reading and Writing Below Grade Level

Provide Model Reading Notes Use Guide to Reading Notes 10 to give students more support for completing the sensory figures. Create a model transparency for each section, with information that allows students to work progressively toward independence. Include the following information for the sensory figures:

- For Section 10.2, omit from each statement any words that appear in the Word Bank, and have students fill in the blanks.

- For Sections 10.3 and 10.4, write in each box the correct word from the Word Bank and tell students to use these words in their statements.

- Have students complete Section 10.5 without assistance.

Learners with Special Education Needs

Give Examples Before students begin the Preview activity, identify specific examples of individuals for them to use. Give students some names of historical figures they are familiar with (e.g., George Washington, Abraham Lincoln, Martin Luther King Jr.), current political leaders (e.g., the president, their governor), or a sports figure from a local team.

Review the Location of Kush Have students complete the map and the two corresponding questions in the Reading Notes for Section 10.2. Before students move on to the sensory figure and its corresponding question, use Guide to Reading Notes 10 to review the important information about the location of Kush.

Have Groups Use Note Cards As groups prepare their character for the act-it-outs, have students use note cards to write down possible responses to the discussion questions. Encourage actors to use their note cards as they participate in the act-it-outs.

Advanced Learners

Add to Sensory Figures Include additional requirements for completing the sensory figures in the Reading Notes for Sections 10.2–10.5. Have students write an additional statement about what each Kushite leader is thinking and saying. Then students should draw leader lines from the statements to the figure's head and mouth, respectively.

Research and Map Kush In addition to or instead of the illustrated timeline in the Processing activity, have students work in pairs or small groups to research information about the location of Kush. For each of the four main time periods explored in the chapter, students should create a political map of Kush that shows its borders and at least one major city.

Enrichment Resources

Find out more about the kingdom of Kush by exploring the following Enrichment Resources for *History Alive! The Ancient World* at www.teachtci.com.

Enrichment Readings These in-depth readings encourage students to explore selected topics related to the chapter. You may also find readings that relate the chapter's content directly to your state's curriculum.

Internet Connections These recommended Web sites provide useful and engaging content that reinforces skills development and mastery of subjects within the chapter.

Literature Recommendations

The following books offer opportunities to extend the content in this chapter.

Ancient African Kingdom of Kush by Pamela F. Service (New York: Benchmark Books, 1998)

The Ancient Kushites (People of the Ancient World) by Liz Sonneborn (New York: Franklin Watts/Scholastic, 2005)

Lost Cities of the Ancient World by Joel Levy (London: New Holland Publishers Ltd., 2008)

Section 10.2

Students' completed maps should resemble the map of Egypt and Kush in Section 10.2 of their books. Egypt and Kush should appear as two different colors.

1. Location and natural resources made Kush an important trading hub. Because the kingdom was located on the Nile River, Kush linked central and southern Africa to Egypt.

2. Kush traded gold, ivory, leather, and timber for Egypt's grain and linen. Kush also sold slaves to the Egyptians.

Possible sensory statements follow:

With my eyes, I see . . . the valuable gold that comes from our mines.

With my ears, I hear . . . the languages of the many people who use our kingdom as a trading hub.

With my hands, I touch . . . the piles of goods we had to pay in tribute to Egypt before we regained our independence.

With my heart, I feel . . . sad that my kingdom of Kush has become totally Egyptianized. We speak their language, worship their gods, and wear their style of clothing.

Responses to the question will vary, but students might discuss how the kingdom's location on the Nile River and its rich natural resources made Kush an important trading hub. Also, Kush's location as Egypt's neighbor made Kush a likely conquest of the more powerful Egypt. Kush's society became Egyptianized while under Egyptian control.

Section 10.3

Possible sensory statements follow:

With my eyes, I see . . . the beauty of the temple we built at Jebel Barkal.

With my ears, I hear . . . the joyous shouts of my armies as we take control of Egypt.

With my hands, I touch . . . the trembling ground as the armies of the Assyrians drive us out of Egypt.

With my heart, I feel . . . proud that the Kushite pharaohs are the dynasty that revived the past glory of Egypt.

Responses to the question will vary, but students might discuss how Kush conquered nearby Egypt, when Egypt fell into political chaos and became weak and unstable. King Piye of Kush declared himself pharaoh, and the kingdom of Kush extended from the southern Nile to the Mediterranean Sea. During this time, Kushite pharaohs built new temples and pyramids in both Egypt and Kush.

Section 10.4

Possible sensory statements follow:

With my eyes, I see . . . our new capital of Meroë, safely out of reach of the Egyptians.

With my ears, I hear . . . the voices of people who come from as far away as Rome to trade with us.

With my hands, I touch . . . the weapons and tools that our ironworkers have made from our rich natural resources.

With my heart, I feel . . . hopeful that our ability to produce iron will make us a stronger, wealthier kingdom.

Responses to the question will vary, but students might discuss how Kush moved their capital to Meroë to keep it safe from Egypt. Because of its location, Meroë helped Kush remain an important center of trade. Most routes took traders through Kush, and Kush traded with neighbors and distant lands. Also, Meroë had everything it needed to produce iron and became well known for its ironworking. Meroë became a large and wealthy city.

Section 10.5

Possible sensory statements follow:

> With my eyes, I see . . . artwork, clothing, and buildings that all represent a return to our <u>African</u> roots.

> With my ears, I hear . . . the people of Kush speaking <u>Meroitic</u>, our new, native language.

> With my hands, I touch . . . the peace <u>treaty</u> that the Roman general and I, <u>Kandake</u> Amanirenas, have signed.

> With my heart, I feel . . . anger at the <u>Romans</u> for intruding on our land.

Responses to the question will vary, but students might discuss how Kush was able to return to its African roots after its separation from Egypt. Kushite society no longer imitated Egyptian styles, and Kushite culture flourished. Kush revived its practice of female leadership. Location again put Kush at risk, however, when the Romans conquered Egypt. Romans built forts on Kush's borders and demanded tribute from Kush. Kush attacked Roman forts and signed a peace treaty after three years of fighting.

The Origins of Judaism

How did Judaism originate and develop?

Overview

In a Writing for Understanding activity, students identify key historical leaders of the ancient Israelites and explain their role in the development of Judaism.

Objectives

In the course of reading this chapter and participating in the classroom activity, students will

Social Studies

- describe the origins of Judaism as the first monotheistic religion.
- identify the Torah as the source of the basic teachings of Judaism and as a source of information on the history of the Israelites, also called Hebrews.
- explain the significance of Abraham, Moses, David, and Solomon in the history of the Israelites and in the development of Judaism.
- document on a timeline the locations and movements of the ancient Israelites, including the Exodus from Egypt.

Language Arts

- write expository compositions with persuasive evidence to validate arguments and conclusions.
- revise writing to improve the organization and consistency of ideas within paragraphs.

Social Studies Vocabulary

Key Content Terms Torah, Israelite, Judaism, tradition, Israel, slavery, Jerusalem, covenant, Exodus, Ten Commandments

Academic Vocabulary eventually, fundamental, foundation, symbol

Materials

History Alive! The Ancient World

Interactive Student Notebooks

Lesson Masters

- Information Master 11 (1 transparency)
- Vocabulary Development handout (1 per student, on colored paper)

11" × 17" paper (1 sheet per student)

cardboard tubes or wooden dowels (2 for every 3 students)

colored markers or pencils

transparent tape

Activity	Suggested Time	Materials
Preview	15 minutes	• Interactive Student Notebooks
Vocabulary Development	30–40 minutes	• *History Alive! The Ancient World* • Interactive Student Notebooks • Vocabulary Development handout
Writing for Understanding	120 minutes (3 regular periods) (1.5 block period)	• *History Alive! The Ancient World* • Interactive Student Notebooks • Information Master 11 (1 transparency) • 11" × 17" paper (1 sheet per student) • cardboard tubes or wooden dowels (2 for every 3 students) • colored markers or pencils • transparent tape
Processing (optional)	20 minutes	• Interactive Student Notebooks
Assessment	40 minutes	• Chapter 11 Assessment

Preview

1 **Invite students to think about people who have made important contributions to the United States throughout its history.** Have students complete the Preview activity for Chapter 11 in their Interactive Student Notebooks. Students identify two important historical figures who contributed to the development of the United States.

2 **Have students share their responses in pairs or as a class.**

3 **Connect the Preview activity to Chapter 11.** Tell students that many important historical figures contributed to the development of the United States. We remember the ideas and actions of these individuals because of their notable impact on this country. In this chapter, students will learn about four key figures in the history of the ancient Israelites and in the development of Judaism.

Vocabulary Development

1 **Introduce the Key Content Terms.** Have students locate the Key Content Terms for the chapter in their Interactive Student Notebooks. These are important terms that will help them understand the main ideas of the chapter. Ask volunteers to identify any familiar terms and how they might be used in a sentence.

2 **Have students complete a Vocabulary Development handout.** Give each student a copy of the Vocabulary Development handout of your choice from the Reading Toolkit at the back of the Lesson Masters. These handouts provide extra Key Content Term practice and support, depending on your students' needs. Review the completed handout by asking volunteers to share one answer for each term.

Reading

1 **Introduce the Essential Question and have students read Section 11.1.** Have students identify the Essential Question on the first page of the chapter: *How did Judaism originate and develop?* Then have students read Section 11.1. Afterward, have students respond to these questions:

   - When did the Jewish civilization develop, and where was it located?
   - Which religion was founded by the Israelites?
   - What is the Torah, and what information does it record?

2 **Have students complete the Reading Notes for Chapter 11.** Assign Sections 11.2 to 11.6 during the activity, as indicated in the procedures for the Writing for Understanding activity. Remind students to use the Key Content Terms where appropriate as they complete their Reading Notes.

> **Writing: Written English Language Conventions**
>
> Use the chapter vocabulary and other key terms to teach or review some rules of capitalization:
>
> 1. Capitalize geographical names (Israel, Jerusalem);
>
> 2. Capitalize the names of religions and peoples (Judaism, Israelite);
>
> 3. Capitalize the names of sacred books (Torah);
>
> 4. Capitalize words used in a special sense (not just any ten commandments but the Ten Commandments; not just an exodus, but the Exodus).

Writing for Understanding

1 **Place students in groups of three.** You may want to prepare a transparency before class that shows group assignments and seating arrangements.

2 **Introduce the activity in which students will create ancient scrolls about four Jewish leaders.** Explain to students that in this activity, they will become experts on four key figures—Abraham, Moses, David, and Solomon—in the history of the ancient Israelites and in the development of Judaism. As experts, students will contribute their part of an ancient scroll by writing and illustrating a page about their assigned leaders. Students will use their page to teach other group members about their leaders. Then pages from all students will be joined together to create the ancient scrolls.

3 **Have groups read about the four Jewish leaders to complete the Reading Notes for Sections 11.2 and 11.3.** Tell students that Section 11.2 introduces them to the Torah, and other parts of the Hebrew Bible, as one historical source of information about the early history of the Israelites. Section 11.3 introduces them to four key historical figures and their contributions to the development of Judaism. Have students read both sections and complete the corresponding Reading Notes in their Interactive Student Notebooks. Afterward, use Guide to Reading Notes 11 to review their responses.

4 **Assign groups to their historical figures.** Assign one-third of the groups to each of the following ancient Jewish leaders and the corresponding sections of Chapter 11.

   • Abraham: Section 11.4

   • Moses: Section 11.5

   • David and Solomon: Section 11.6

5 **Have groups complete the Reading Notes for their assigned section and Jewish leader.** Have group members take turns reading aloud their assigned section of Chapter 11. Afterward, students in each group should work together to complete the corresponding Reading Notes for their assigned section in their Interactive Student Notebooks.

6 **Review the directions for designing ancient scroll pages.** Project *Information Master 11: Designing a Page for an Ancient Scroll.* Review the orientation of the scroll page and the list of required elements, and answer any questions students may have.

7 **Have students write and illustrate their ancient scroll pages.** Distribute a sheet of 11-by-17–inch paper to each student. Give students time to write and illustrate their scroll pages. Remind them to orient the page horizontally and to leave at least a 1-inch margin along the left- and right-hand sides of their scroll pages. Encourage students to share and discuss their ideas with other group members.

Information Master 11

8 **Have groups review their ancient scroll pages.** After all group members have completed their ancient scroll pages, have them exchange and check one another's scroll pages. Each group member should make sure the scroll page reviewed has all the required elements on the handout.

9 **Form new groups of three.** Create new groups of three that include one student with a completed scroll page for Abraham, another student with a page for Moses, and a third student with a page for David and Solomon. (**Note:** Extra students may be partnered with another student who researched the same figure, thus creating some groups of four.)

10 **Have group members teach each other about the figure they researched.** Have group members take turns using their scroll page to teach one another about the figure they researched. During the presentations, the other members should complete the corresponding sections of their Reading Notes.

11 **Have groups assemble ancient scrolls.** Have each group tape together their pages, horizontally, by section, to form a scroll. Then groups can carefully attach the two ends of the scroll to cardboard tubes and roll each end toward the middle, similar to an ancient scroll. (**Note:** You may want to tell students that Torah scrolls are read from right to left, and not left to right like students' scrolls.)

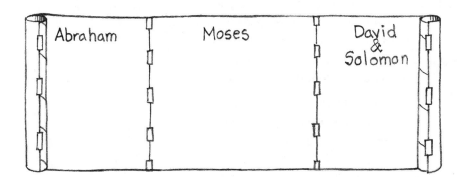

12 **Conduct a read-around and wrap-up.** Have each group exchange their scroll with that of another group and read the other group's scroll. Ask groups to look for two similarities and two differences between their scroll and the one they read. Afterward, have students respond to these questions:

- Which ancient Jewish figure do you find most interesting and why?
- In what ways did your scrolls help you learn about these figures?
- Why do you think sources like the Torah are helpful to historians?
- How did Judaism originate and develop?
- Why were the contributions of Abraham, Moses, David, and Solomon significant?

Processing (optional)

1 **Understand the intent of the Processing activity.** The ancient scroll page serves as this chapter's Processing activity. Should you choose not to have students do this writing activity, you might use the optional Processing activity in the Interactive Student Notebook.

2 **Have students complete the Processing activity.**

3 **Have students share their answers with their partners or with the class.**

Quicker Coverage

Skip the Scroll Creation Follow the groupings and procedures to complete the Reading Notes as outlined in the activity. Then create new groups of three and have students use their Reading Notes to teach one another about their assigned historical figures.

Deeper Coverage

Add Scroll Pages Have students create two separate scroll pages for David and Solomon, rather than the one page for both figures. Begin the Writing for Understanding activity by pairing students. Assign one-quarter of the pairs to each of the four key historical figures and corresponding sections of reading. Pairs assigned to David or Solomon may want to conduct additional research to complete their scroll pages. After pairs have completed and checked their scroll pages, form groups of four for the teaching and assembling of the ancient scrolls.

Assign Research Have students in groups research information about the Passover Seder meal. Assign each group to a general topic (e.g., the Seder Plate, traditional foods) or to a specific part of the ceremony. Have groups create a poster or use presentation software to illustrate what they have learned. After groups have shared their research, ask the following questions: *How does this meal commemorate the Exodus from Egypt? What does this tradition reveal about the development of Judaism?*

Assessment

Mastering the Content

1. B	5. C	9. C	13. A
2. B	6. D	10. B	14. D
3. A	7. C	11. B	15. C
4. D	8. A	12. D	16. D

Applying Social Studies Skills

17. stone; gold

18. Lebanon; that was an area where these types of trees grew best, there were not a lot of cedar and cypress trees growing near Jerusalem, etc.

19. wall (also accept other items visible in the picture and built of stone)

Exploring the Essential Question

20. Answers should include all of the elements requested in the prompt.

Scoring Rubric

Score	Description
3	Student completes all three postcards. Postcards are clearly stated, reflect the viewpoint of the individual indicated, and demonstrate command of standard English conventions.
2	Student responds to most or all parts of the task, but postcards may not be clearly stated or may not reflect distinctive viewpoints.
1	Student responds to at least one part of the task. Postcards may contain factual and/or grammatical errors and may lack details.
0	Response does not match the task or is incorrect.

English Language Learners

Brainstorm Examples Before students complete the Preview activity, brainstorm as a class a list of historical figures who have been important in the development of the United States. Briefly discuss the contributions made by each one.

Utilize Technology As students draft their paragraphs to complete their ancient scroll pages, encourage them to use a word processing program that checks grammar, spelling, and punctuation. Students can print out their edited paragraphs to paste onto their scroll pages.

Learners Reading and Writing Below Grade Level

Conduct a Guided Review of the Reading Rather than have groups read Sections 11.2 and 11.3, review the content as a class. Make a transparency of the appropriate sections in Guide to Reading Notes 11. Use the transparency to guide students through the main ideas of each section.

Prepare a Hint Sheet Use Guide to Reading Notes 11 to prepare a hint sheet to help students complete their Reading Notes for Sections 11.4–11.6. For the first three prompts in each section, list in random order the possible responses provided in the Guide. Omit the names and use pronouns so that students have to match the correct actions, contributions, and quotations to the correct historical figure. As students read their assigned section and later listen to other students' presentations, they should find the appropriate statements to copy into their Reading Notes.

Learners with Special Education Needs

Pair Students At the beginning of the Writing for Understanding activity, place students in pairs instead of groups of three. Assign one-third of the pairs to each historical figures. Rather than have students create individual pages, have each pair create one scroll page on their assigned figure. When you form new groups to share information and create the scrolls, place three pairs together to create groups of six.

Provide a Copy of the Guidelines Give each student a copy of Information Master 11 to serve as a checklist for the required elements on the ancient scroll page. Students can also use this as a reference when they exchange and review other students' scroll pages later in the Writing for Understanding activity. Also consider having students draft their pages in pencil and check with you before finalizing their pages. Initial their copy of Information Master 11 once you have checked their drafts.

Provide Guide to Reading Notes 11 Give students a copy of Guide to Reading Notes 11 for Sections 11.4 to 11.6. As group members share their ancient scroll pages in presentations to one another, have students highlight the important facts presented by their peers, to help them complete their Reading Notes.

Advanced Learners

Add a Question to the Wrap-Up Add a discussion question to the wrap-up of the Writing for Understanding activity. Ask students, *What do the lives of these historical figures reveal about the values of the ancient Israelites?* Consider expanding the discussion by having students research information about the influence of religion on the daily life of the ancient Israelites.

Compare Ancient Religions Compare and contrast the religious teachings of the ancient Egyptians with those of the ancient Israelites. Have students work in pairs or groups and complete an appropriate graphic organizer (e.g., Venn diagram, T-chart) summarizing their main ideas. Review as a class, and consider discussing why similarities and differences might exist between the teachings of these two religions.

Enrichment Resources

Find out more about the origins of Judaism by exploring the following Enrichment Resources for *History Alive! The Ancient World* at www.teachtci.com.

Enrichment Readings These in-depth readings encourage students to explore selected topics related to the chapter. You may also find readings that relate the chapter's content directly to your state's curriculum.

Internet Connections The recommended Web sites provide useful and engaging content that reinforces skills development and mastery of subjects within the chapter.

Literature Recommendations

The following books offer opportunities to extend the content in this chapter.

Bible Lands (Eyewitness Books) by Jonathon Tubb (New York: Dorling Kindersley Children, 2000)

David by Barbara Cohen (New York: Clarion Books, 1995)

Exodus by Brian Wildsmith (Grand Rapids, MI: Eerdmans Books for Young Readers, 1998)

Section 11.2

1. Historians rely on a variety of sources to learn about the ancient Israelites, such as archaeological artifacts and written records. The Torah is likely the most useful source because it was passed down orally from ancient times and then written down.

2. 1950 B.C.E.: Abraham, the ancestor of the Jews, migrated with his family from Ur in Mesopotamia to Canaan.

   1800 B.C.E.: Many Israelites fled from Canaan to Egypt because of famine.

   1000 B.C.E.: After escaping from Egypt and wandering in the desert, the Israelites settled in Canaan and set up the kingdom of Israel.

Timeline titles will vary.

Section 11.3

Possible answers:

Jewish Leader	Action as Leader	Contribution to Judaism
Abraham	led his people to Canaan	introduced the idea of one God was a model of faith and obedience
Moses	led Israelites out of Egypt	gave Judaism its fundamental laws, the Ten Commandments
David	created a united kingdom of Israelites established Jerusalem as a holy city	made Jerusalem a powerful symbol of the Jews' faith in God
Solomon	built Jerusalem's first great temple	the temple was a powerful symbol of the Jews' faith in God

Section 11.4

Possible answers:

1. Abraham left his own country to go to the land of Canaan, which became the Jews' "promised land."

2. Abraham was the ancestor of the Jewish people.

   Abraham introduced the belief in a single God and then made a pact of faith and obedience with God.

3. "I [God] will make a covenant between myself and you [Abraham]."

4. Sketches of artifacts will vary.

Section 11.5

Possible answers:

1. Moses helped the Israelites escape from Egypt.

2. Moses led the Exodus of Israelites out of slavery in Egypt.

   Moses gave Judaism God's fundamental laws and teachings, the Ten Commandments.

3. "I [God] will send you [Moses] to the pharaoh, and you shall free my people.'"

4. Sketches of artifacts will vary.

Section 11.6

Possible answers:

1. David led the Israelites to defeat the Philistines. Solomon built the great First Temple of Jerusalem.

2. David united Israel and Judah into a strong Israelite kingdom. The Torah says he defeated the Philistine giant, Goliath, with a slingshot and a stone. Some of the Psalms in the Hebrew Bible are attributed to David, a poet and musician.

   Solomon built Jerusalem's great First Temple of Jerusalem. Solomon was a poet and is credited as the author of several books, including the Book of Proverbs and Ecclesiastes, in the part of the Hebrew Bible called Writings.

3. "The Israelite kingdom will remain with him [David] and with his children [Solomon] and his children's children forever."

4. Sketches of artifacts will vary.

Learning About World Religions: Judaism

What are the central teachings of Judaism, and why did they survive to modern day?

Overview

In an Experiential Exercise, students identify the central teachings of Judaism as they explore ways in which these traditions have survived throughout history.

Objectives

In the course of reading this chapter and participating in the classroom activity, students will

Social Studies

- describe the central laws and teachings of Judaism.

- summarize the ways in which the laws and teachings of Judaism remain influential today.

- explain why and how Judaism survived and developed despite the Jewish Diaspora.

Language Arts

- select and use an appropriate tone and strategy to restate, teach, and execute multi-step instructions and directions.

- make reasonable assertions about a news article, through accurate and supporting citations.

Social Studies Vocabulary

Key Content Terms polytheism, monotheism, Talmud, ethics, exile, Jewish Diaspora, Yavneh

Academic Vocabulary capture, survive, source, instruct, disperse

Materials

History Alive! The Ancient World

Interactive Student Notebooks

Lesson Masters

- Student Handout 12A (4 copies, each on different-colored paper; 1 additional copy on white paper)

- Student Handout 12B (4 copies, each in the same colors used above)

- blank sheets of colored paper (1 for each color used for student handouts)

- Information Master 12 (1 transparency)

- Vocabulary Development handout (1 per student, on colored paper)

Activity	Suggested Time	Materials
Preview	15 minutes	• Interactive Student Notebooks
Vocabulary Development	30–40 minutes	• *History Alive! The Ancient World* • Interactive Student Notebooks • Vocabulary Development handout
Experiential Exercise	60 minutes (1–2 regular periods) (1 block period)	• *History Alive! The Ancient World* • Interactive Student Notebooks • Student Handout 12A (4 copies, each on different-colored paper; 1 additional copy on white paper) • Student Handout 12B (4 copies, each in the same colors used above) • blank sheets of colored paper (1 for each color used for student handouts) • Information Master 12 (1 transparency)
Processing	30 minutes	• Interactive Student Notebooks
Assessment	40 minutes	• Chapter 12 Assessment

Preview

1 **Have students describe a family tradition to complete the Chapter 12 Preview activity in their Interactive Student Notebooks.** Students reflect on a tradition that is shared and preserved in their family.

2 **Have students share their responses in pairs or as a class.**

3 **Connect the Preview activity to Chapter 12.** Tell students that there are many different types of traditions that are passed down over time. In their families, one of these traditions may have been a favorite recipe or a bedtime story. Religious traditions are also passed down. The teachings and traditions of Judaism were preserved and passed down from ancient times, despite many serious challenges. In this chapter, students will learn about the central teachings of Judaism and the reasons why these traditions have survived throughout history.

Vocabulary Development

1 **Introduce the Key Content Terms.** Have students locate the Key Content Terms for the chapter in their Interactive Student Notebooks. These are important terms that will help them understand the main ideas of the chapter. Ask volunteers to identify any familiar terms and how they might be used in a sentence.

2 **Have students complete a Vocabulary Development handout.** Give each student a copy of the Vocabulary Development handout of your choice from the Reading Toolkit at the back of the Lesson Masters. These handouts provide extra Key Content Term practice and support, depending on your students' needs. Review the completed handout by asking volunteers to share one answer for each term.

Reading

1 **Introduce the Essential Question and have students read Section 12.1.** Have students identify the Essential Question on the first page of the chapter: *What are the central teachings of Judaism, and why did they survive to modern day?* Then have students read Section 12.1. Afterward, have students respond to these questions:

- What happened to the kingdom of Israel after it split into two nations?
- What does the word *diaspora* mean?
- What event marked the beginning of the Jewish Diaspora?
- What did the Jewish Diaspora signify for Judaism and its followers?

2 **Have students complete the Reading Notes for Chapter 12.** Assign Sections 12.2 to 12.4 during the activity, as indicated in the procedures for the Experiential Exercise. Remind students to use the Key Content Terms where appropriate as they complete their Reading Notes.

> **Writing: Narratives**
>
> To help students build a more personal sense of the Jewish Diaspora, have them write a personal narrative from the point of view of someone forced into exile. Work as a class to develop a story map or other organizer, including the time and place, and a sequence of events. Elicit ideas for how dialogue, suspense or rising action, and resolution could be developed, and then have students draft and revise on their own.

Experiential Exercise

1 Understand that the intent of the activity is to explore how Jews passed on the central teachings of Judaism through the centuries. In this activity, students will learn four simple classroom truths that are analogous to the central teachings and traditions of Judaism. Five students, acting as "teachers," will learn these classroom truths and a set of corresponding body movements. Four of the teachers will be dispersed to the corners of the classroom to teach these truths, and the fifth teacher will remain in the center of the classroom as a resource. Similar to one generation of Jews passing along traditions to the next generation, teachers will teach a group of students who will then teach another group of students. Additional connections between the activity and history are noted in seven of the procedural steps that follow. If possible, it is ideal to start this activity at the beginning of a class.

2 Prepare the materials. Before class, prepare the following materials:

- Make four copies of *Student Handout 12A: Classroom Truths and Movements,* each on a different-colored (not white) sheet of paper. Make a fifth copy on white paper.
- Make four copies of *Student Handout 12B: Tokens,* using the same four colors used for Student Handout 12A. Cut apart the tokens and create a separate pile for each number to make eight piles.
- Make a transparency of *Information Master 12: The "Preserve and Pass Along" Activity.*

3 Arrange the classroom. Create an open workspace in each corner of the room by arranging the desks as shown. Place a single desk or table in the center of the room. Color code the corners by posting in each corner a blank sheet of the colored paper used for Student Handout 12A. Have students sit at any desk but the single one in the center.

4 Begin the activity by projecting Information Master 12 and revealing *only* the objective. Tell students that they are going to participate in the "Preserve and Pass Along" activity. Review *only* the objective on Information Master 12. To increase motivation for the activity, consider offering a reward to the class for successfully completing the activity.

5 Choose and prepare five "teachers." Select five volunteers who will act as "teachers" and teach the simple "classroom truths" and corresponding movements to their "students." Give the five copies (four on colored paper and one on white paper) of Student Handout 12A to teachers and have them stand together in one corner to study the handouts. Make sure teachers clearly understand the classroom truths and corresponding movements. Meanwhile, have the remaining students take out their Interactive Student Notebooks and *History Alive! The Ancient World.* (**Note:** The "classroom truths" are analogous to the central teachings and traditions of Judaism. The student "teachers" are analogous to rabbis who preserve and pass down these teachings.)

Student Handout 12A

Student Handout 12B

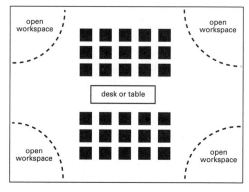

Classroom Map

Information Master 12

6 **Distribute tokens to "students."** Tell the remaining class members that they are the "students" who will learn the simple classroom truths and movements. Quickly distribute the tokens, cut apart, from Student Handout 12B. Pass out all the 1s, then the 2s, and so on, until all remaining students have tokens. Tell students that it is very important that they hold on to these tokens for the entire activity.

7 **Reveal the guidelines on Information Master 12.** Explain that there are additional guidelines for the activity. Reveal and review the guidelines.

8 **Disperse four teachers to the corners of the room.** Send the four teachers with colored handouts to the corresponding corners of the classroom by saying: *According to the guidelines of this activity, these four "teachers of the classroom truths" are no longer allowed to stay together. Instead, they are being dispersed to the four corners of the room.* (**Note:** This action is analogous to many Jews being expelled from Israel by the Romans in 70 C.E.)

9 **Permit one teacher to stay.** Have the teacher with the white handout sit at the center desk. Say to students: *This one "teacher of the classroom truths," and this one only, will be allowed to stay here among you.* Explain that this teacher will act as a resource for the four teachers at the corners. (**Note:** This action is analogous to the Romans allowing Yohanan ben Zaccai and a group of rabbis to remain in Israel after the fall of Jerusalem.)

10 **Conduct the "Preserve and Pass Along" activity.** Follow these steps:

- Tell students seated at desks to read Sections 12.2 to 12.4 and complete the corresponding Reading Notes in their Interactive Student Notebooks.

- Have the four students with Token 1 go to the corner that matches the color of their token. Remind them that they will have two minutes to learn the four classroom truths and movements. (**Note:** This group of students—and each successive group—are analogous to the generations of Jews who lived dispersed throughout the world.)

- Give the teachers in the corners two minutes to teach the four classroom truths and movements to their students. (**Note:** This part of the activity is analogous to one generation of Jews passing down the central teachings of Judaism to the next. The corners are roughly analogous to the synagogues where this kind of teaching took place.)

- Have the four teachers return to seats in the middle of the classroom and begin their Reading Notes. Tell the students in each corner that they are now the teachers. To help maintain silence, consider keeping the returning teachers segregated from those students who have yet to learn the classroom truths or movements.

- Repeat the above steps for the four students holding Token 2, then Token 3, and so on, until the entire class has learned the four classroom truths and movements.

11 Select four students to present the classroom truths and movements. Ask the last four students who learned the classroom truths and movements to come to the front of the room. Remind the class that these students need to accurately present the four classroom truths and movements to assure that the entire class has successfully "passed" this activity. Give these students a minute to confer among themselves to make sure they know the classroom truths and movements. (**Note:** This part of the activity is analogous to modern-day Jews from around the world returning to the modern nation of Israel.)

12 Have the four students present the classroom truths and movements. Have each student present one rule and its corresponding movement. Consider allowing the fifth teacher—the student who was at the center desk—to join you as a judge. The goal of the activity is for students to fairly accurately present the classroom truths. (**Note:** The presentations are analogous to Jews successfully preserving and passing along the central beliefs and teachings of Judaism through the centuries.)

13 Debrief the experience. Ask,

- What emotions did you feel during this activity?
- What factors made it difficult to teach or learn the classroom truths and movements?
- What techniques or strategies did you use to make sure you taught or learned the classroom truths and movements accurately and quickly?
- In what ways might this activity be similar to what you read about in Chapter 12?

14 Connect the experience to the chapter. Give students time, if needed, to finish reading Sections 12.2 to 12.4 and complete the corresponding Reading Notes. Then have students work in pairs or small groups to fill in the T-chart on the last page of their Reading Notes for Chapter 12. Students use the chart to identify similarities between their experience in the activity and the information they learned in the chapter. Afterward, have volunteers share their responses with the class.

Processing

Have students complete the research activity about Judaism as the Processing activity for Chapter 12 in their Interactive Student Notebooks. Students do research to find a current article illustrating a central teaching of Judaism.

Quicker Coverage

Create More Teaching Areas Make one or more additional teaching areas for the activity. Clear space along one or more walls of the classroom, or consider using the hallway outside the classroom. For each additional teaching area you create, make one more copy of Student Handout 12A and Student Handout 12B on another color paper (not white). Be sure to color code the additional teaching areas with a blank sheet of colored paper that corresponds to these copies.

Hold a Class Discussion Rather than have students complete the T-chart in the Reading Notes in the final step of the activity, hold a brief class discussion. Ask the Essential Question, *What are the central teachings of Judaism, and why did they survive to modern day?* Encourage students to draw upon both their experience in the classroom activity and the information they learned in Chapter 12.

Deeper Coverage

Assign a Timeline Activity Have students work in pairs or small groups to make annotated timelines of Jewish history during the Jewish Diaspora. Begin with the destruction of Jerusalem by the Babylonians in 586 B.C.E., and end with the creation of modern Israel in 1948. Students should include key events in Chapter 12, as well as additional events that they find through research.

Assessment

Mastering the Content

1. C	5. A	9. C	13. B
2. B	6. D	10. A	14. C
3. A	7. C	11. D	15. D
4. D	8. B	12. B	16. A

Applying Social Studies Skills

17. Judah

18. Babylon

19. Romans

Exploring the Essential Question

20. Answers should inclued all of the elements requested in the prompt.

Scoring Rubric

Score	Description
3	Student completes all three scrolls as appropriate. Writing on scrolls fits together into a coherent narrative that is clearly stated, well-reasoned, and demonstrates command of standard English conventions.
2	Student responds to most or all parts of the task, but writing on scrolls may not be clearly stated or may not fit together.
1	Student responds to at least one part of the task. Writing on scrolls may contain factual and/or grammatical errors and may lack details.
0	Response does not match the task or is incorrect.

English Language Learners

Provide Copies of Guidelines Provide a copy of Information Master 12 when you review the activity guidelines in the Experiential Exercise. Allow students to discuss the activity with a peer and ask any questions they might have. Ask students to explain in their own words what is expected of them in this activity.

Pair Students For the Experiential Exercise, pair a less proficient English speaker with a more proficient English speaker. Have the pair go to the teaching area to learn the classroom truths together. After they have learned the truths, have partners review them for each other to check for understanding. Consider allotting extra time for this. Have the pair remain together to teach the truths to the next student(s).

Offer an Alternative Processing Activity Rather than have students write about an article illustrating a teaching of Judaism, have them identify examples they are familiar with. For instance, you might ask students to identify examples of practicing equality and social justice.

Learners Reading and Writing Below Grade Level

Complete a Prereading Exercise During the Experiential Exercise, have students complete a prereading exercise rather than the Reading Notes sections 12.2 to 12.4. Then, after debriefing the activity experience, have students work in pairs to complete their Reading Notes together.

Provide a Word Bank For the Reading Notes for Sections 12.3 and 12.4, provide a Word Bank to help students write the rabbi's responses. Include the following terms for each of these student questions:

How did the Jewish Diaspora begin, and why was it difficult for followers of Judaism? Babylonians, scattered, alive

Which foreign powers ruled Judah, and how did they treat the Jews? Persians, Greeks, Romans

What happened after the Jews rose up against the Romans in 66 C.E.? Romans, Temple, homeland

Where did the Jews live during the Jewish Diaspora? scattered, gentile

Who was Yohannan ben Zaccai, and why was he significant? Romans, Yavneh, school

What new practices developed over time that helped Judaism survive? rabbi, synagogue, service

Provide Articles For the Processing activity, find two or more appropriate articles to give to students. Also consider highlighting for students the key portions of each article.

Learners with Special Education Needs

Offer an Alternative Activity The day before you conduct the Experiential Exercise, review the activity with students. Allow them to choose the role of observer. Give these students a copy of the T-chart from the Reading Notes, with the "Classroom Activity" column already completed. During the activity, observers mark those statements that they see happening. You might also provide partial answers in the "Teachings and History of Judaism" column, asking students to fill in omitted words or phrases as they do the reading for each section.

Provide a Partially Completed T-Chart Use Guide to Reading Notes 12 to partially fill in the T-chart for the final step of the Experiential Exercise. Include the statements on the right-hand side of the chart, under "Teachings and History of Judaism." Have students fill in the left-hand side of the chart. Consider giving this chart to students at the start of the activity so that they may complete it as they participate.

Advanced Learners

Offer a Research Assignment Have students further research the Torah and the Talmud and their importance to modern Jews. If possible, students might visit a local synagogue to interview a rabbi. Before they conduct their interviews, have them prepare a list of questions for you to review. Encourage them to include a few questions about key aspects of this period in Jewish history, such as the Diaspora and Yohanan ben Zaccai.

Enrichment Resources

Find out more about the main beliefs and teachings of Judaism by exploring the following Enrichment Resources for *History Alive! The Ancient World* at www.teachtci.com.

Enrichment Readings These in-depth readings encourage students to explore selected topics related to the chapter. You may also find readings that relate the chapter's content directly to your state's curriculum.

Internet Connections These recommended Web sites provide useful and engaging content that reinforces skills development and mastery of subjects within the chapter.

Literature Recommendations

The following books offer opportunities to extend the content in this chapter.

Judaism (Eyewitness Books) edited by Shaila Awan (New York: Dorling Kindersley Children, 2003)

Judaism by Michael Keene (Milwaukee, WI : World Almanac Library, 2006)

Judaism by Geoff Teece (North Mankato, MN: Smart Apple Media, 2005)

Section 12.2

Central Beliefs and Teachings of Judaism		
Teaching	**Description**	**Influence Today**
monotheism	belief in one God who is the source of standards of morality (right and wrong)	Judaism is the world's oldest monotheistic religion. Through study of sacred texts, and through prayer, many Jews feel that God is close to them in their daily lives.
following Jewish teachings	laws like the Ten Commandments instruct Jews on how to lead upright and honorable lives	A larger set of laws and practices developed over time, such as loving your neighbors, keeping a Sabbath, and the celebration of Passover. Jews observe these rules and practices in different ways.
equality and social justice	belief that God considers all people equal, and that treating people fairly and caring for less fortunate people are important	Stories and sayings teach about treating everyone fairly. Caring for those less fortunate in society is a basic value in Judaism.
importance of study	studying the Hebrew Bible, the Talmud, and other writings	Jews value study and learning. Many Jews learn about Jewish history, law, and traditions through reading and discussion. They also pass on their knowledge to other members of the faith.

Section 12.3

Answers will vary. Possible answers:

Student: How did the Jewish Diaspora begin, and why was it difficult for followers of Judaism?

Rabbi: The Jewish Diaspora began in 597 B.C.E., when the Babylonians conquered Judah. Thousands of Jews entered captivity in Babylon. From this time on, the followers of Judaism were scattered in many lands or were dominated by foreign rulers. It would not be easy to keep Judaism alive.

Student: Which foreign powers ruled Judah, and how did they treat the Jews?

Rabbi: The Babylonians were conquered in 539 B.C.E. by the Persians. The Persian king Cyrus ended the exile of the Jews, and many of them returned to Judah. For nearly 400 years, Judah was ruled by foreigners. Most rulers were harsh. The Greek ruler Antiochus tried to force the Jews to worship idols of Greek gods, but the Jews rebelled and drove the Greeks out. The Romans conquered Judah in 63 B.C.E.

While they did allow Jews to practice their religion and govern some affairs, the Romans were quick to act against any sign of rebellion. They executed more than 50,000 Jews.

Student: What happened after the Jews rose up against the Romans in 66 C.E.? in 135 C.E.?

Rabbi: The Jews kept the Romans out of Jerusalem for three years, but in 70 C.E., Titus led a Roman army against the Jews. The Jews were outnumbered, and the Romans destroyed Jerusalem and the Second Temple. In 135 C.E. the Romans ended another Jewish revolt and forced most Jews to move away. This began the final exile of the Jewish people from their homeland.

Section 12.4

Answers will vary. Possible answers:

Student: Where did the Jews live during the Jewish Diaspora?

Rabbi: After losing control of their homeland, Jews were exiled throughout many gentile, or non-Jewish, lands.

Student: Who was Yohannan ben Zaccai, and why was he significant?

Rabbi: Yohannan ben Zaccai was a rabbi who gained permission from the Romans to start a Jewish school in the town of Yavneh. He was afraid that Judaism would not survive because of the fighting with the Romans. When Jerusalem fell, Yavneh became the center of Jewish learning. Ben Zaccai's rabbis trained teachers and rabbis, who returned home to share what they had learned. The rabbis at Yavneh made sure that Jews still had leaders to guide them.

Student: What new practices developed over time that helped Judaism survive?

Rabbi: New practices were introduced to ensure that the teachings of Judaism would be passed on. The rabbis at Yavneh made the synagogue more important. They also created a religious service for use in the synagogue.

Chapter 12 T-Chart

Answers will vary. Possible answers:

Classroom Activity	Teachings and History of Judaism
• The first classroom truth we learned was that our class has only one true teacher.	• The first central teaching of Judaism—monotheism—is that there is only one God.
• The second classroom truth we learned was to respect and follow the classroom truths.	• Another central belief of Judaism is to follow Jewish teachings.
• The third classroom truth we learned was to help other students if they are having trouble.	• Another central belief of Judaism is equality and social justice.
• The fourth classroom truth we learned was to complete all assignments creatively and thoughtfully.	• A final central belief of Judaism is the importance of study.
• Four teachers were forced to leave the center of the room and were dispersed to different corners of the room.	• When the kingdom of Judah fell to the Babylonians, the Jewish Diaspora began. Hundreds of years later, the Romans also forced many Jews to leave their homeland.
• The classroom teacher could impose a penalty on the entire class if some students did not follow the strict rules about how the four classroom truths could be taught.	• Foreigners—like Greeks and Romans—were often harsh rulers, quick to act against any sign of rebellion among Jews.
• One of the original teachers was allowed to stay in the center of the room.	• The Romans allowed Rabbi Yohanan ben Zaccai to start a Jewish school in Yavneh.
• Teachers from the four corners of the room could consult with the teacher in the center.	• Rabbis came from many places to study at the school in Yavneh, and then they returned to their communities to share what they had learned.
• Teachers and students had specific areas in each corner of the room where they could learn the classroom truths.	• Jews built synagogues as places to worship, study, and hold meetings.
• The last group of students came back to the center of the room to share the classroom truths.	• Starting in 1948, Jews from around the world came back to settle in the new Jewish state of Israel.

Ancient Egypt and the Middle East

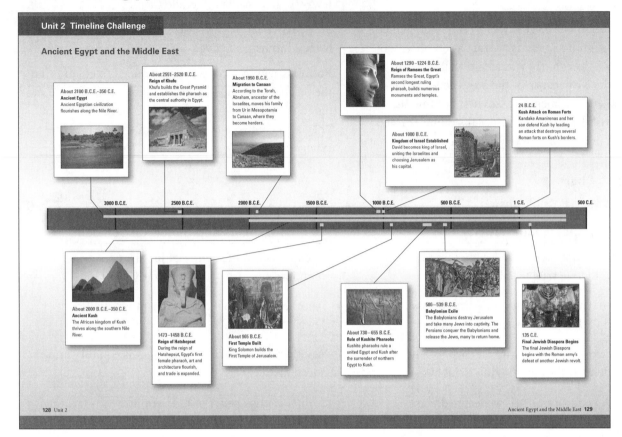

About 3100 B.C.E.–350 C.E.
Ancient Egypt
Ancient Egyptian civilization flourishes along the Nile River.

About 2551–2528 B.C.E.
Reign of Khufu
Khufu builds the Great Pyramid and establishes the pharaoh as the central authority in Egypt.

About 1950 B.C.E.
Migration to Canaan
According to the Torah, Abraham, ancestor of the Israelites, moves his family from Ur in Mesopotamia to Canaan, where they become herders.

About 1290–1224 B.C.E.
Reign of Ramses the Great
Ramses the Great, Egypt's second longest ruling pharaoh, builds numerous monuments and temples.

24 B.C.E.
Kush Attack on Roman Forts
Kandake Amanirenas and her son defend Kush by leading an attack that destroys several Roman forts on Kush's borders.

About 1000 B.C.E.
Kingdom of Israel Established
David becomes king of Israel, uniting the Israelites and choosing Jerusalem as his capital.

3000 B.C.E. 2500 B.C.E. 2000 B.C.E. 1500 B.C.E. 1000 B.C.E. 500 B.C.E. 1 C.E. 500 C.E.

About 2000 B.C.E.–350 C.E.
Ancient Kush
The African kingdom of Kush thrives along the southern Nile River.

1473–1458 B.C.E.
Reign of Hatshepsut
During the reign of Hatshepsut, Egypt's first female pharaoh, art and architecture flourish, and trade is expanded.

About 965 B.C.E.
First Temple Built
King Solomon builds the First Temple of Jerusalem.

About 730–655 B.C.E.
Rule of Kushite Pharaohs
Kushite pharaohs rule a united Egypt and Kush after the surrender of northern Egypt to Kush.

586–539 B.C.E.
Babylonian Exile
The Babylonians destroy Jerusalem and take many Jews into captivity. The Persians conquer the Babylonians and release the Jews, many to return home.

135 C.E.
Final Jewish Diaspora Begins
The final Jewish Diaspora begins with the Roman army's defeat of another Jewish revolt.

Overview

This Timeline Challenge helps students review the main events and ideas of this unit while providing practice in reading and interpreting timelines. You can vary and expand the activity according to students' needs and the amount of time available.

Basic Procedure

1 **Introduce the timeline in the Student Edition.** Direct students to the Ancient Egypt and the Middle East Timeline at the end of Unit 2 in the Student Edition. You may wish to have students read aloud and discuss the timeline entries.

2 **Introduce the Timeline Challenge in the Interactive Student Notebook.** Direct students to the Unit 2 Timeline Challenge in their notebooks. Point out the two types of questions, "Timeline Skills" and "Critical Thinking," and model how to answer each type.

3 **Have students complete the Timeline Challenge.** Monitor students as they work. Use the Guide to Unit 2 Timeline Challenge to check their answers. You may wish to project a transparency of the Timeline Challenge as you work through the questions with the class and conduct a discussion of the "Critical Thinking" questions.

4 **Complete the KWL chart.** Return to the KWL chart created at the beginning of the unit, and ask students to list the key information they have learned.

Classroom Timeline

1 **Prepare the Timeline Challenge Cards.** Copy and cut the cards from *Student Handout TC2: Unit 2 Timeline Challenge Cards.* You may wish to laminate the cards for future use.

2 **Create a timeline on a classroom wall.** On an empty wall or a large bulletin board, make a timeline with masking tape or colored paper. Mark off the time intervals in advance, or ask students to do so in class.

3 **Have students place the Timeline Challenge Cards.** Distribute cards to individual students or pairs and have them tape the cards to the timeline in the correct locations. Call on students to provide more information on the timeline topics, to review main events and issues.

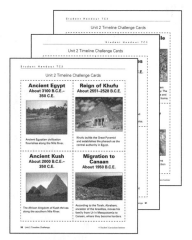

Student Handout TC2

Internet Research

1 **Review students' suggestions for additional timeline entries.** Have students share their answers to the last question of the Timeline Challenge.

2 **Have students conduct Internet research.** Ask students to choose and research one of their suggested events.

3 **Have students create additional Timeline Challenge Cards.** Direct students to research an appropriate image for their cards and then use the computer to create an illustrated card, complete with timeline entry.

Timeline Skills

Score 1 point for each correct answer.

1. Abraham's migration to Canaan happened first.

2. Khufu was responsible for building the Great Pyramid of Egypt.

3. Ramses the Great ruled Egypt about 1,200 years after the reign of Khufu.

4. The African kingdom of Kush existed for about 2,350 years, from about 2000 B.C.E. to 350 C.E.

5. Hatshepsut ruled Egypt from about 1473 to 1458 B.C.E. Her reign is significant because she was Egypt's first female pharaoh.

6. The Kushite pharaohs ruled Egypt after Ramses the Great.

7. The First Temple of Jerusalem was built during the reign of King Solomon.

8. The Jews were held in captivity in Babylon for 47 years.

9. Kush attacked and destroyed several Roman forts on its borders in 24 B.C.E. Kush signed a peace treaty with Rome, three years later, and no longer had to pay tribute to Rome.

10. In 7135 C.E., the Romans put down another Jewish revolt. This event began the final exile of the Jews from the region, known as the Jewish Diaspora.

Critical Thinking

Score 1 to 3 points for each answer, depending on the thoroughness of the response.

11. The Nile River created a long and fertile valley in which both Egypt and Kush could develop and thrive. The river provided natural irrigation and fertilization. Summer floods left silt that made the soil perfect for farming. The river was surrounded by deserts, which provided a natural barrier to invaders. The river also provided a waterway for trade.

12. Answers may vary. Possible answer: Egypt and Kush were trading partners, but sometimes one kingdom dominated the other. During the New Kingdom period (about 1600 to 1100 B.C.E.), Egypt conquered Kush and forced Kush to pay tribute.

Kush society became Egyptianized. When the New Kingdom collapsed, Kush became independent again. The relationship changed around 730 B.C.E., after Kush invaded and overtook Egypt. For the next 75 years, Kushite pharaohs ruled a united kingdom of Kush and Egypt.

13. a. Abraham's move with his family to Canaan about 1950 B.C.E. was significant to the development of Judaism because Canaan was believed to be the land promised by God as a reward for the people's devotion. The Torah states that God told Abraham that Abraham would be the father of a great nation of people if he moved to Canaan.
   b. According to the Torah, it was Abraham who introduced the Israelites to the belief in one god. At that time, most people worshipped many gods and goddesses.

14. Answers will vary. Students must explain why the events they chose merit inclusion.

Using Scores to Inform Instruction

Timeline Skills A score of 7 out of 10 indicates that students understand most of the key events of this unit.

Critical Thinking A score of 8 out of 12 indicates that students are able to think critically about most of the key issues of this unit.

If students score below these levels, consider reviewing timeline and critical thinking skills.

Ancient India

Geography Challenge

Timeline Challenge

Ancient India

Overview

This activity introduces the geographic information essential to Unit 3. Students read and interpret maps to learn about the ways in which geography affected settlement patterns in ancient India. Students annotate an outline map, answer questions in their Interactive Student Notebooks, and then discuss critical thinking questions. Students' comprehension of content and proficiency in map-reading and higher-order thinking skills will help you gauge their readiness for the unit. The pages that follow include a completed map, answers to questions, a scoring guide to inform your teaching, and suggestions for modifications to meet specific student needs.

Essential Geographic Understandings

1. Location of ancient India

2. Distinction between present-day India and ancient India

3. Key physical features: Arabian Sea, Bay of Bengal, Himalayas, Hindu Kush, Thar Desert, Deccan Plateau, Eastern and Western Ghats, Indus River, Ganges River, Brahmaputra River

4. Location of the Indus River valley

5. Impact of physical geography on the early settlement of ancient India

6. Impact of physical geography on the development of ancient Indian cultures

Procedures

1 **Introduce the unit.** Tell students they will learn about civilizations of ancient India and the development of Hinduism and Buddhism.

2 **Create a KWL chart.** Ask students to identify what they already know about ancient India and what they want to learn. Use their responses to gauge how much additional background information they will need as you progress through the unit. Students will return to the KWL chart at the end of the unit and add the key information they have learned.

3 **Have students read Unit 3 "Setting the Stage" in the Student Edition.**

4 **Have students complete the Geography Challenge.** Monitor students as they work. Use the guide on the next two pages to check their answers. You may wish to project the map from the Interactive Student Notebook and have students annotate it as the class works through the map-reading questions. Make sure students have grasped Essential Geographic Understandings 1 to 4.

5 **Discuss the "Critical Thinking questions."** Help students understand the geographic relationships described in Essential Geographic Understandings 5 and 6.

Ancient India

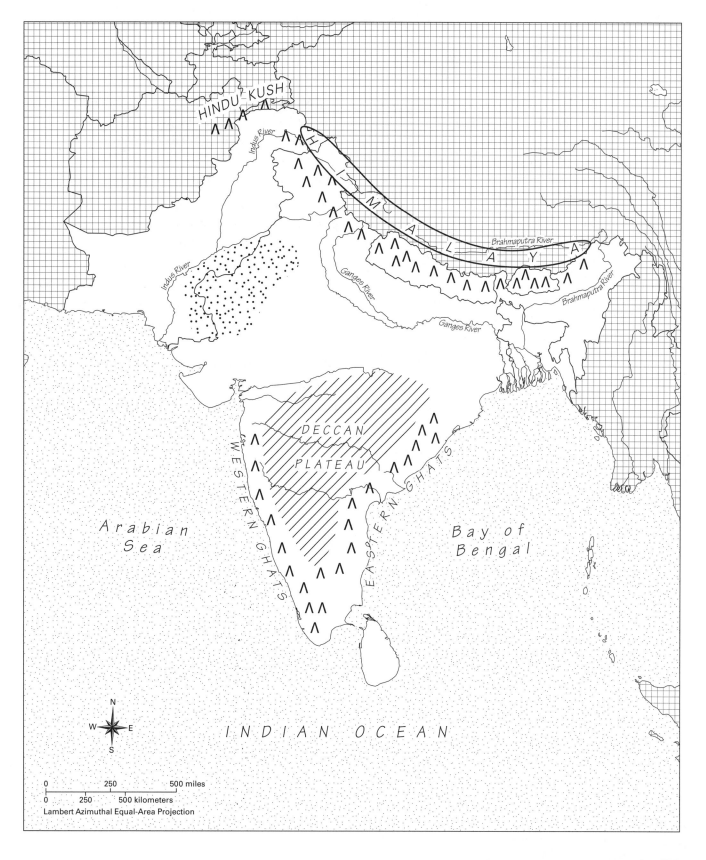

Geography Skills

Score 1 point for each correct answer. Use the map on the previous page to check shading and labeling.

1. Students' labels should show the southern part of ancient India as surrounded by the Arabian Sea to the west, the Indian Ocean to the south, and the Bay of Bengal to the east.

2. India is part of the continent of Asia.

3. Use the annotated map to check students' labels for the Indus, Ganges, and Brahmaputra rivers.

4. The Deccan Plateau is located between the Eastern Ghats and and the Western Ghats.

5. Students should circle the label for the Himalayas. The Himalayas are unique because they are the highest mountains in the world.

6. The Mauryan Empire was bordered in the north by the Himalayan and the Hindu Kush mountain ranges. Its northwestern border was located to the northwest of the Indus River. Its southern portion, comprising all of ancient India, with the exception of the southern tip of the subcontinent, was bordered by the Arabian Sea to the west and the Bay of Bengal to the east.

7. The Mauryan Empire was larger than the Gupta Empire.

8. The Indus empties into the Arabian Sea. The Ganges empties into the Bay of Bengal.

Critical Thinking

Questions may have more than one correct answer. Score 1 to 3 points for each reasonable answer, depending on the strength of students' geographic reasoning.

9. Land in the Indus River valley was fertile, and fresh water was readily available. These factors made it possible to produce food. The river also provided a route for travel and trade.

10. The location of the Himalayas, as well as their forbidding height, made them an extremely effective barrier between ancient India and the rest of Asia, allowing the cultures of ancient India to develop without influence from outsiders.

11. Living near the sea would have enabled settlers to have the added advantages of using the resources of the sea, as well as the land and river. Such resources would have included fish and shellfish, salt, and seaweed. Access to sea travel would have also provided a possible link to other cultures in faraway lands. Possible disadvantages might have included the vulnerability of a coastal settlement to attack from outsiders, as well as to potentially hazardous weather conditions.

Using Scores to Inform Instruction

Geography Skills A score of 6 out of 8 or better indicates that students have acquired sufficient geographic information to proceed with the unit.

Critical Thinking A score of 6 out of 9 or better indicates that students are beginning to understand the relationships between physical geography and the different ways in which people live.

Modifying Instruction

ELL or Learners with Special Education Needs Consider focusing on map-reading questions or limiting the number of "Critical Thinking" questions.

Students with Weak Map or Critical Thinking Skills Assign appropriate pages from the Social Studies Skills Toolkit in the back of the Lesson Masters.

Geography and the Early Settlement of India

How did geography affect early settlement in India?

Overview

In a Response Group activity, groups identify physical features of the Indian subcontinent and explain how geography influenced the location of early settlement in India.

Objectives

In the course of reading this chapter and participating in the classroom activity, students will

Social Studies

- locate and describe eight key physical features of the Indian subcontinent, including the major river systems.
- explain how geography affected the location of early settlement in India and supported the rise of civilization there.
- predict and map the location of early human settlement in India.

Language Arts

- deliver oral communications using detailed evidence.
- write an expository paragraph using persuasive evidence.

Social Studies Vocabulary

Key Content Terms subcontinent, monsoon, plateau

Academic Vocabulary fertile, elevate, brief, intense

Materials

History Alive!
The Ancient World

Interactive Student Notebooks

Visuals 13A–13I

Lesson Masters

- Student Handout 13A (1 per every 2 groups, cut in half)
- Student Handout 13B (1 per group)
- Student Handout 13C (1 copy of each page)
- Vocabulary Development handout (1 per student, on colored paper)

colored pencils

scissors

Activity	Suggested Time	Materials
Preview	15 minutes	• Interactive Student Notebooks
Vocabulary Development	30–40 minutes	• *History Alive! The Ancient World* • Interactive Student Notebooks • Vocabulary Development handout
Response Group	90 minutes (2 regular periods) (1 block period)	• *History Alive! The Ancient World* • Interactive Student Notebooks • Visuals 13A–13I • Student Handout 13A (1 per every 2 groups, cut in half) • Student Handout 13B (1 per group) • Student Handout 13C (1 copy of each page) • colored pencils • scissors
Processing	20 minutes	• Interactive Student Notebooks
Assessment	40 minutes	• Chapter 13 Assessment

Preview

1 **Have students identify geographic features as they complete the Preview activity in their Interactive Student Notebooks.** Students draw and label a picture identifying the geographic characteristics of the ideal place for people living in ancient times to settle.

2 **Have students share their responses in pairs or as a class.** Then ask, *What features and characteristics make a place ideal for settlement?*

3 **Connect the Preview activity to Chapter 13.** Tell students that in this chapter, they will learn about the physical features of ancient India. After mapping these features and learning about their characteristics, students will determine what place in ancient India made the ideal location for settlement.

Vocabulary Development

1 **Introduce the Key Content Terms.** Have students locate the Key Content Terms for the chapter in their Interactive Student Notebooks. These are important terms that will help them understand the main ideas of the chapter. Ask volunteers to identify any familiar terms and how they might be used in a sentence.

2 **Have students complete a Vocabulary Development handout.** Give each student a copy of the Vocabulary Development handout of your choice from the Reading Toolkit at the back of the Lesson Masters. These handouts provide extra Key Content Term practice and support, depending on your students' needs. Review the completed handout by asking volunteers to share one answer for each term.

Reading

1 **Introduce the Essential Question and have students read Section 13.1.** Have students identify the Essential Question on the first page of the chapter: *How did geography affect early settlement in India?* Then have students read Section 13.1. Afterward, have students use information from Section 13.1 and from the chapter opener image to propose some possible answers to the Essential Question.

2 **Have students complete the Reading Notes for Chapter 13.** Assign Sections 13.2 to 13.10 during the activity, as indicated in the procedures for the Response Group activity. Remind students to use the Key Content Terms where appropriate as they complete their Reading Notes.

> **Vocabulary Development: Shades of Meaning**
>
> Help students with Academic Vocabulary by exploring shades of meaning. For example, for *brief*, present related meanings such as *concise, instant, quick, short,* and *abrupt.* Work with students to create a context for each word by finding nouns to pair with each adjective, such as "concise speech" (not "concise run") and "abrupt ending" (not "abrupt book").

Response Group

1 Place students in groups of three. You may want to create a transparency that shows group assignments and seating arrangements.

2 Introduce the activity in which students will identify eight key physical features and their effect on early settlement of the Indian subcontinent. Tell students that they are going to learn about eight key physical features on the Indian subcontinent. After discussing each feature's suitability for human settlement, students will predict where they think the first settlements in India were located.

3 Have groups complete the Reading Notes for Sections 13.2–13.9. Tell students that they will learn about the eight key physical features of the Indian subcontinent. Follow these steps for Section 13.2:

- Project *Visual 13A: Brahmaputra River* and ask, *What type of physical feature do you see? How would you describe this feature?*

- Have groups read Section 13.2 and, in their Interactive Student Notebooks, complete the corresponding parts of the map and the matrix in the Reading Notes.

- Use the map on Visual 13A and Guide to Reading Notes 13 to review their responses.

Repeat these steps for the features in Sections 13.3–13.9, using Visuals 13B–13H.

4 Distribute materials. Give each group one set of physical features cards from *Student Handout 13A: Physical Features Cards* and one copy of *Student Handout 13B: Critical Thinking Questions.* Have groups cut apart the cards from Student Handout 13A.

5 Have groups discuss Critical Thinking Question A. Give groups several minutes to discuss Critical Thinking Question A on Student Handout 13B. Groups should arrange the physical features cards along the spectrum, from the most likely to the least likely.

6 Prepare for a class discussion of Critical Thinking Question A. On the board, draw or project the spectrum from Student Handout 13B. Have groups appoint a Spokesperson. Give each Spokesperson one of the physical features from *Student Handout 13C: Physical Features of India.* Allow Spokespersons one minute to create a "human spectrum" by arranging themselves in order, from the most likely to the least likely features that would produce a dependable food supply. There will be disagreement, but assure students that they will have the opportunity for discussion.

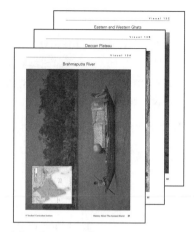

Visuals 13A–13H

Student Handout 13A

Student Handout 13B

Student Handout 13C

7 **Facilitate a class discussion of Critical Thinking Question A.** Tell Spokespersons to hold their physical features pages up so everyone can see them. Then invite Spokespersons and class members to make arguments for changing the order of features on the spectrum. Encourage lively debate by calling on students with differing opinions. Afterward, collect the pages of Student Handout 13C to redistribute for the class discussions of Critical Thinking Questions B and C.

8 **Repeat Steps 5–7 for Critical Thinking Questions B and C.**

9 **Reveal the locations of early settlements in India.** Project *Visual 13I: Geographic Influence on Early Settlements in India* to reveal the locations of the earliest settlements in India. Ask,

- Where were the earliest settlements in India located?
- What made these places ideal for settlement?

10 **Have groups complete the Reading Notes for Section 13.10.** Tell students that they will read more about the locations of early settlements in India. Have groups read Section 13.10 and complete the corresponding Reading Notes in their Interactive Student Notebooks.

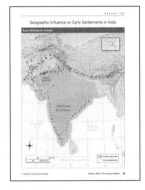

Visual 13I

Processing

Have students complete the Processing activity in their Interactive Student Notebooks. Students write a paragraph explaining why the Indus and Ganges rivers were ideal locations for settlement in ancient times.

Quicker Coverage

Use Critical Thinking Question C Rather than have groups discuss all three Critical Thinking Questions, discuss only Critical Thinking Question C. This question asks groups to predict which physical feature is likely to be the site of India's earliest settlement. In the ensuing discussion, encourage groups to consider which physical features are likely to produce a dependable food supply and to support quality trade.

Deeper Coverage

Research Monsoons Have groups research monsoons and their impact on the geography of the Indian subcontinent. Assign to each group one major city chosen from various regions throughout the subcontinent, such as Mumbai, India, and Dhaka, Bangladesh. Have groups locate two photographs—one from the summer months and one from the winter months. Also have groups find information about the average monthly precipitation. Ask groups to present their research to the class. Have the class discuss how this information might affect where people first settled on the Indian subcontinent.

Assessment

Mastering the Content

1. D	5. B	9. B	13. B
2. A	6. B	10. C	14. C
3. A	7. C	11. A	15. B
4. C	8. D	12. D	

Applying Social Studies Skills

16. Calcutta

17. Western Ghats, on the Arabian Sea

18. Jodhpur

19. near Allahabad in the northern plain

Exploring the Essential Question

20. Answers should include all of the elements requested in the prompt.

Scoring Rubric

Score	Description
3	Student completes a poster that complies with all three bulleted points. The poster is clearly stated, uses vivid and precise language, is supported by details, and demonstrates command of standard English conventions.
2	Student responds to most or all parts of the task, but poster may lack details or not be clearly stated.
1	Student responds to at least one part of the task. Poster may contain factual and/or grammatical errors and may lack details.
0	Response does not match the task or is incorrect.

Saving the Ganges

1 **Elicit students' prior knowledge about environmental pollution.** Ask students to name some of the environmental issues facing the planet and their local community. Ask what students know about (a) different types of pollution and their causes, (b) actions that individuals and communities can take to prevent or clean up environmental pollution, and (c) the different obstacles that might be encountered in trying to preserve a clean environment (e.g., costs, effects on businesses, lack of public awareness). Write students' ideas on the board.

2 **Have students read the first two pages of the Chapter 13 Reading Further in the Student Edition.** Have students recall facts about the pollution of the Ganges. Use information in the article to identify the causes of the pollution and the reasons why the problem has become so serious.

3 **Ask students to predict whether or not the Ganges can be saved.** Invite students to brainstorm ideas about what it would take to clean up the river. Have students make predictions about whether the Ganges can be cleaned up.

4 **Have students read the rest of the Reading Further.** Discuss whether the information in the last two pages has changed their predictions about whether the Ganges can be cleaned up.

5 **Point out that having accurate information is a good first step toward solving a problem.** Discuss the kinds of facts Dr. Veer Bhadra Mishra had to present to the Indian government in his efforts to obtain support for his campaign to clean up the Ganges. Have students complete the first page of the Reading Further in their Interactive Student Notebooks and share their lists of facts from the article and possible sources that could supply and verify this information.

6 **Have students complete the Reading Further activity in their Interactive Student Notebooks.** Ask students to share and compare their questions and their ideas about research sources for information about the water in their community.

English Language Learners

Explain Ratings Help students better understand the rating column in the matrix as they complete the Reading Notes for Sections 13.2 to 13.9. Conduct a brief class discussion in which students describe characteristics for the physical features at each rating. An example follows.

- 1 (unsuitable for settlement): dry, hot, cold, mountainous, rocky soil, no vegetation
- 5 (very suitable for settlement): plentiful water, normal rainfall, mild temperatures, flat land, good soil, ample vegetation

Support Spokespersons Allow appropriate Spokespersons to choose the physical feature for the class discussion of the Critical Thinking Questions. In discussion with his or her group, the Spokesperson should write notes on an index card explaining the reasons for the feature's placement on the spectrum. Encourage Spokespersons to practice their explanations with their groups.

Learners Reading and Writing Below Grade Level

Provide a Copy of the Sections Provide a copy of the text in Sections 13.2 through 13.9. As students read, encourage them to highlight words and phrases describing each physical feature. Have students use their highlighting to complete the "Description" column in the Reading Notes for these sections.

Offer a Prewriting Activity Before students write the paragraph for the Processing activity, offer them a prewriting activity to help them organize their ideas. Have students copy and complete the outline below.

I. Topic Sentence

II. Indus River valley (Why is it suitable for settlement?)
- Fact
- Fact

III. Ganges River valley (Why is it suitable for settlement?)
- Fact
- Fact

IV. First Physical Feature (Why is it unsuitable for settlement?)
- Fact
- Fact

V. Second Physical Feature (Why is it unsuitable for settlement?)
- Fact
- Fact

Learners with Special Education Needs

Provide Cloze Notes Use the Guide to Reading Notes to create cloze notes for the "Description" column in the Reading Notes for Sections 13.2 to 13.9. Make a copy of the Guide to Reading Notes and white-out key phrases and terms that students will fill in by doing the reading.

Use Discussion Prompts Use prompts during the class discussion of each Critical Thinking Question to help Spokespersons articulate and evaluate their reasons for the placement of the physical features on the spectrum. Consider the following:

- *[Name of physical feature] is most likely because . . .*
- *[Name of physical feature] is least likely because . . .*
- *[Name of physical feature] is more likely than [name of physical feature] because . . .*
- *[Name of physical feature] is less likely than [name of physical feature] because . . .*

Advanced Learners

Research Physical Features Have students do research to find two or more additional facts about each feature they have labeled on the map of the Indian subcontinent. Students could write these facts directly on the map, or they could a write them on another sheet of paper and use a key and place symbols on their maps. Research can be done in a library or on the Internet, where students might find a virtual tour of India. Encourage students to use the Internet Connections for Chapter 13.

Enrichment Resources

Find out more about the geography and early settlement of India by exploring the following Enrichment Resources for *History Alive! The Ancient World* at www.teachtci.com.

Enrichment Readings These in-depth readings encourage students to explore selected topics related to the chapter. You may also find readings that relate the chapter's content directly to your state's curriculum.

Internet Connections The recommended Web sites provide useful and engaging content that reinforces skills development and mastery of subjects within the chapter.

Literature Recommendations

The following books offer opportunities to extend the content in this chapter:

The Ganges by Rob Bowden (Chicago, IL: Raintree, 2004)

India: The Land by Bobbie Kalman (New York: Crabtree Publishing Company, 2001)

Welcome to India by Fiona Conboy and Sunandini Arora Lal (Milwaukee, WI: G. Stevens Publishing, 2000)

Sections 13.2 to 13.9

1. Use the map below to check students' maps.

Physical Features of India

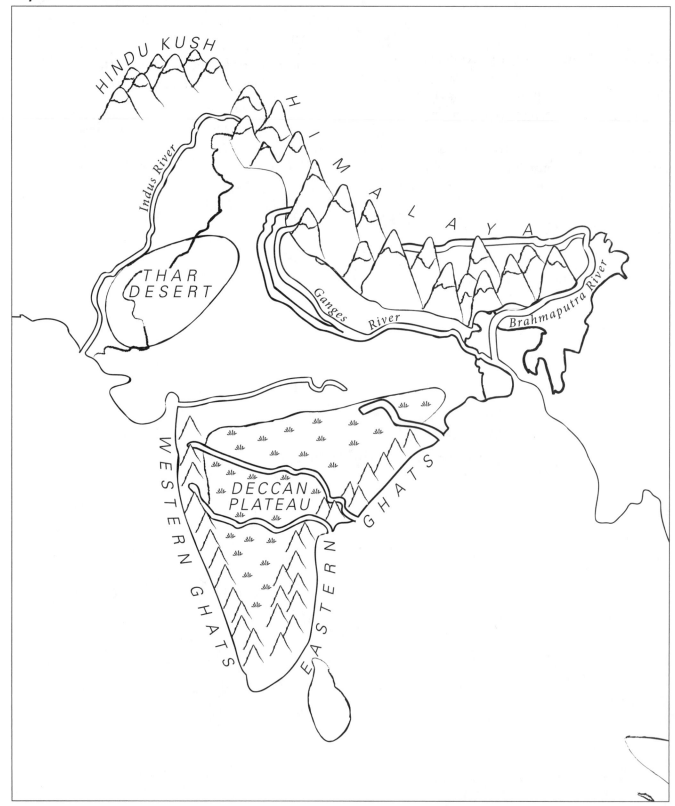

2. Use the completed matrix below to check students' answers. Ratings will vary but should be in the range indicated.

Physical Feature	Description	Rating
Brahmaputra River	The Brahmaputra River begins in the Himalayas. It joins the Ganges River, on the plains, and makes the land here very fertile.	4 or 5
Deccan Plateau	The Deccan Plateau is an elevated, flat area of land between two mountain ranges in southern India. The plateau is fairly dry but is watered by monsoons. Some of the land is fertile.	3
Eastern and Western Ghats	The Eastern and Western Ghats are long mountain ranges near India's coasts. The Western Ghats are high and very wet, whereas the Eastern Ghats are lower and not so wet.	3
Ganges River	The Ganges River begins in the Himalayas. It leaves sediment on the northern plains, making that area fertile. The river can flood its banks in the rainy season.	4 or 5
Himalaya Mountains	This mountain range is the highest in the world. The tallest peaks are always covered in snow and ice.	1 or 2
Hindu Kush Mountains	The Hindu Kush are high mountains that form a barrier between India and Afghanistan. The Khyber Pass through these mountains connects central Asia to India.	1 or 2
Indus River	The Indus River begins in the Himalayas and empties into the Arabian Sea. It deposits sediment in the Indus River valley. It is also a source of water for farming.	4 or 5
Thar Desert	The Thar Desert is a hot area of sand and stones, with little water. It is a home for lizards, snakes, gazelles, and birds.	1 or 2

Section 13.10

1. Use the map in Section 13.10 of *History Alive! The Ancient World* to check students' completed maps. Students should correctly show early settlements in both the Indus and Ganges river valleys.

2. The first people in India most likely chose to settle near rivers because the rivers provided plenty of water. The fertile soil was ideal for farming. The rivers could also be used for travel and trade.

Unlocking the Secrets of Mohenjodaro

What can artifacts tell us about daily life in Mohenjodaro?

Overview

In an Experiential Exercise, students act as archaeologists and examine artifacts from Mohenjodaro to learn about daily life in the Indus valley civilization.

Objectives

In the course of reading this chapter and participating in the classroom activity, students will

Social Studies

- form hypotheses about the function of artifacts and ruins from an ancient city in the Indus Valley.
- analyze artifacts to draw conclusions about daily life in the Indus valley civilization.
- explain why Mohenjodaro is an important archaeological site.

Language Arts

- demonstrate an understanding of text by creating logical notes.
- connect and clarify main ideas by using other sources.

Social Studies Vocabulary

Key Content Terms Mohenjodaro, citadel, Indus valley civilization, granary

Academic Vocabulary reveal, function, drain, channel, transport

Materials

*History Alive!
The Ancient World*

Interactive Student Notebooks

Visuals 14A and 14B

Placards 14A–14H

Lesson Masters

- Station Materials 14 (2 copies)
- Information Master 14 (1 transparency)
- Vocabulary Development handout (1 per student, on colored paper)

masking tape

scrap paper

books

Activity	Suggested Time	Materials
Preview	15 minutes	• Interactive Student Notebooks • Visual 14A
Vocabulary Development	30–40 minutes	• *History Alive! The Ancient World* • Interactive Student Notebooks • Vocabulary Development handout
Experiential Exercise	50–70 minutes (2 regular periods) (1 block period)	• *History Alive! The Ancient World* • Interactive Student Notebooks • Visual 14B • Placards 14A–14H • Station Materials 14 (2 copies) • Information Master 14 (1 transparency) • masking tape • scrap paper • books
Processing	20 minutes	• Interactive Student Notebooks
Assessment	40 minutes	• Chapter 14 Assessment

Preview

1 **Have students complete the Preview activity in their Interactive Student Notebooks.** Project *Visual 14A: Ancient Indian Artifact* and have students use the image to complete the Preview activity. They form hypotheses on the purpose of this unidentified object.

2 **Have students share their responses in pairs or as a class.** Afterward, reveal the object's true use. The artifact is a bangle or bracelet, similar to the ones people have been wearing in India since ancient times.

3 **Connect the Preview activity to Chapter 14.** Tell students that in this chapter, they will explore artifacts from Mohenjodaro, an ancient city in the Indus river valley. Like the bracelet, many of the objects and structures will be unfamiliar to them. Students will form hypotheses about how these artifacts may have been used and what that tells us about the daily life of the people in that civilization.

Visual 14A

Vocabulary Development

1 **Introduce the Key Content Terms.** Have students locate the Key Content Terms for the chapter in their Interactive Student Notebooks. These are important terms that will help them understand the main ideas of the chapter. Ask volunteers to identify any familiar terms and how they might be used in a sentence.

2 **Have students complete a Vocabulary Development handout.** Give each student a copy of the Vocabulary Development handout of your choice from the Reading Toolkit at the back of the Lesson Masters. These handouts provide extra Key Content Term practice and support, depending on your students' needs. Review the completed handout by asking volunteers to share one answer for each term.

Reading

1 **Introduce the Essential Question and have students read Section 14.1.** Have students identify the Essential Question on the first page of the chapter: *What can artifacts tell us about daily life in Mohenjodaro?* Then have students read Section 14.1. Afterward, have students use information from Section 14.1 and from the chapter opener image to propose some possible answers to the Essential Question.

2 **Have students complete the Reading Notes for Chapter 14.** Assign Sections 14.2 to 14.10 during the activity, as indicated in the procedures for the Experiential Exercise. Remind students to use the Key Content Terms where appropriate as they complete their Reading Notes.

Experiential Exercise

1 **Understand the intent of the activity.** In this activity, students assume the role of archaeologists and "excavate" the ruins of Mohenjodaro. Through the use of desks, the site is re-created as realistically as possible in a classroom setting. At the site are eight research stations where students excavate and analyze artifacts, which are represented by placards. (**Note:** If re-creating the site is not possible, consider the alternative options for conducting this activity, found in the Quicker Coverage section that follows these procedures.)

2 **Gather and prepare materials.** Before class, gather *Placards 14A–14H: Station (A–H)Artifacts*, masking tape, scrap paper, and some books. Make two copies of *Station Materials 14: Excavation Materials*. (**Note:** Two copies of Station Materials 14 will allow you to set up eight stations that accommodate two pairs at a time. You may also wish to create a second set of placards.) Cut apart the following items from Station Materials 14:

   - statue puzzle for Station C (Keep each copy of the puzzle separate.)
   - seals for Station D
   - game piece puzzle for Station G (Keep each copy of the puzzle separate.)

3 **Arrange the classroom.** Arrange desks to create Stations A–H, as indicated in the diagram. Use the diagram to place the placards on the desks or beneath the desks on the floor, with the image lying facedown. Arrange additional station materials as instructed by the Station Setup directions on the back of the placards. (**Note:** Alternatively, have students set up the stations at the beginning of class. Place the materials for each station in a large plastic bag and assign teams of students to set up each station.)

4 **Introduce the activity in which students role-play archaeologists examining artifacts.** Project *Visual 14B: The Citadel at Mohenjodaro*. Remind students that this image shows the ruins of the citadel at Mohenjodaro and that archaeologists first located these ruins in 1922. Tell students that they will visit eight research stations and role-play archaeologists as they examine artifacts to form ideas about daily life in this civilization. Afterward, they will read their books to learn the ideas that archaeologists have determined about these ancient objects and structures.

Placards 14A–14H

Station Materials 14

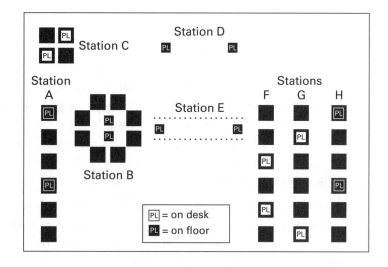

5 **Have students complete the Reading Notes for Section 14.2.** Tell students that this section provides background information about the ruins found at Mohenjodaro. Have them read Section 14.2 and complete the corresponding Reading Notes in their Interactive Student Notebooks. Afterward, use the Guide to Reading Notes to review their responses.

6 **Place student "archaeologists" in pairs and review steps for the excavation.** Project *Information Master 14: Excavating the Ruins of Mohenjodaro.* Together with pairs, review Steps 1–5. Emphasize to students that, during the excavation, for each section of Reading Notes, they will only complete the drawing and record their ideas. They will record the archaeologists' ideas after the excavation has been completed.

7 **Conduct the excavation.** Assign one or two pairs to each of the eight stations. Remind students to follow the steps on Information Master 14 and, when they are finished, to leave the station in its original condition so that subsequent pairs can excavate the artifact in the same way. Consider having pairs raise their hands for you to check their work before they move to the next station. Monitor pairs as they excavate, and continue the activity until most pairs have visited most of the stations.

8 **Have pairs share their ideas about the artifacts.** Once pairs have visited most of the stations, announce that each pair will become "experts" on the station where they are currently working. One station at a time, have pairs use the image on the placard to point out which part of the drawing in the Reading Notes they had to complete. Then have them share their ideas about what they think the object or structure may have been used for. Allow other pairs to add their own ideas.

9 **Have pairs complete the Reading Notes for Sections 14.3–14.10.** Tell students that these sections reveal what archaeologists think about these artifacts. Have pairs read Sections 14.3–14.10 and record in their Interactive Student Notebooks the archaeologists' ideas about the objects and structures. Use the Guide to Reading Notes to check their answers.

10 **Wrap up the activity.** Hold a class discussion, using the following questions.

   - Which of the artifacts most interested you? Most surprised you?

   - What can artifacts tell us about daily life in Mohenjodaro?

   - Why do you think it is difficult for us to know exactly what life was like in ancient civilizations?

   - What questions do you still have about daily life in ancient India?

Processing

Have students complete the Processing activity in their Interactive Student Notebooks. Students design a magazine cover highlighting the discoveries at Mohenjodaro and what they reveal about daily life in the Indus valley civilization.

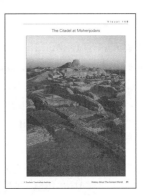

Visual 14B

Information Master 14

Reading: Informational Materials

Before students complete the Processing activity, you may wish to review structural features of magazines. Emphasize the contrast between the cover, with its persuasive and attention-grabbing purposes and the table of contents, with its organizational, informational, and high interest purposes. Also discuss elements of the cover, including the relative prominence of the type and illustration for the lead story over other text elements.

Quicker Coverage

Use Desks as Stations Rather than use desks to physically re-create the ruins at Mohenjodaro, use desks to create eight stations around the edges of the classroom. Create each station using two or three desks. Place the placards facedown on top of the desks and follow the directions to set up any additional materials. Alternatively, place the placards and station materials in large envelopes labeled by station. Have pairs "excavate" at their desks, using the envelopes.

Eliminate Excavation Assign one of the artifacts to each pair of students. Give each pair a placard and direct them to use the placard to complete the drawing and to record their ideas in the Reading Notes. Then have each pair share their drawing and their ideas with the rest of the class. As they listen, class members should use this information to complete the appropriate parts of their Reading Notes.

Deeper Coverage

Expand the Preview Activity Before students complete the Preview activity in their Interactive Student Notebooks, ask three volunteers to represent each of the object's potential uses. Give each volunteer a copy of one of the tasks below. Project Visual 14A and invite the volunteers to make their arguments.

Volunteer 1: Your task is to convince the class that the object is a petrified bagel. Use the following arguments and any of your own:

- The object is shaped like a bagel.
- When objects become petrified, they become reddish in color.
- Bagels are a very popular food.

Volunteer 2: Your task is to convince the class that the object is a heavy bracelet. Use the following arguments and any of your own:

- The object looks as though it would fit perfectly around someone's wrist.
- Even in ancient times, people were concerned with their appearance.
- Many ancient peoples made similar pieces of jewelry out of local resources, like clay or stone.

Volunteer 3: Your task is to convince the class that the object is a form of money. Use the following arguments and any of your own:

- Coins are often round in shape, and many countries put holes in the center of their coins.
- Ancient Indians needed money, just as people do today.
- Many ancient peoples made money out of local resources, like clay or stone, because metal was not available.

Play *Last One Standing* After pairs have read and completed the Reading Notes for Sections 14.3–14.10, play a game that will allow students to identify the characteristics of civilization represented by the artifacts on the placards. Give pairs time to prepare for the game. Have them write down which characteristic(s) of civilization is displayed by each artifact. You may want to review with students the seven characteristics: stable food supply; social structure; government; religion; the arts (culture); technology; and writing. Then follow these steps to play *Last One Standing*:

- Have each pair determine who will be their first "standee."
- Select at random one of the placards and show it to the class.
- Ask standees to rise if they identified one or more characteristics of civilization for this artifact.
- Ask standees to remain standing if they identified two or more characteristics. Standees who identified only one characteristic must sit down.
- Continue this process until one student is the "last one standing." Have this student name and explain the characteristics identified. Allow volunteers to help explain how each characteristic relates to the object.
- Select a new placard and repeat the activity for as many placards as time allows.

Assessment

Mastering the Content

1. C	5. D	9. A	13. C
2. A	6. D	10. B	14. C
3. B	7. B	11. B	15. A
4. C	8. A	12. D	16. B

Applying Social Studies Skills

17. 1922; 1965

18. it exposed them to damage from the weather

19. Answers will vary. Possible answers: new discoveries brought new information; he learned from their earlier research and added to it; he had the benefit of knowledge gained from
further excavations done in 1945

Exploring the Essential Question

20. Answers should include all of the elements requested in the prompt.

Scoring Rubric

Score	Description
3	Student completes all parts of the task. The two captions are clearly stated, identify or describe the artifact shown, draw a conclusion about daily life, and demonstrate command of standard English conventions.
2	Student responds to most or all parts of the task, but captions may lack conclusions about daily life, lack details, or not be clearly stated.
1	Student responds to at least one part of the task. Captions may contain factual and/or grammatical errors and may lack details.
0	Response does not match the task or is incorrect.

English Language Learners

Review the Preview Options Make sure all students understand the three options listed as descriptions for the unidentified artifact in the Preview activity. Review the options as a class or consider having students work in pairs to complete the Preview activity.

Highlight the Activity Directions On Information Master 14, highlight or underline key direction words (e.g., *locate, excavate, examine, discuss, record, return*). Next to each word, draw a simple symbol to help students understand what to do. For example, draw a simple shovel for *excavate*. Draw an eye for *examine*; draw a pencil for *record*. Explain these symbols as you review the steps with the class.

Create Multi-Language Magazine Covers For the Processing activity, encourage students to create the magazine cover in their native language, since news of Mohenjodaro's discovery would be shared in many countries. Have students show and explain their magazine covers to their classmates.

Learners Reading and Writing Below Grade Level

Conduct a Discussion for the Preview Activity Use the Preview activity directions in the Interactive Student Notebook to conduct a class discussion on the unidentified artifact. Have students vote on the options, and ask volunteers to share their reasoning.

Divide the Reading Notes When pairs are ready to complete the Reading Notes for Sections 14.3–14.10, assign one half of the pairs to read and record the archaeologists' ideas for only four of the eight artifacts. Assign the rest of the pairs to the remaining four artifacts. When pairs are finished, form groups of four by placing together two pairs who have each covered a different set of artifacts. While one pair shares what they learned about their assigned artifacts, the other pair should take notes. Then the pairs switch to cover the information about the rest of the artifacts.

Learners with Special Education Needs

Make Stations Accessible When setting up the stations, make sure materials are accessible to all students. Place materials for Stations B, D, and H on desks. Place materials for Station E on chairs rather than on the floor. Place materials for Stations F, G, and H at the desks on either end of the rows.

Model the Steps for Excavation As you review the steps for excavation on Information Master 14, use the materials at one station to model the process. Show students how to locate the placards at each station.

Provide a Template for the Processing Activity Provide a blank template on which students can create their magazine covers. Include the magazine title and a line beneath it for the subtitle. Divide the remaining space into three areas in which students can draw their visuals and write their captions. Consider providing art supplies that students can use to add colorful and creative touches to their covers.

Advanced Learners

Compare Civilizations Have students complete a Venn diagram to compare and contrast daily life in Mohenjodaro with daily life in ancient Egypt (or another civilization they have studied). In the outer parts of the diagram, labeled for each civilization, students should identify what is different or unique about them. In the center of the diagram, students should identify similarities between the two civilizations. Have students share their responses and discuss why these similarities and differences may exist.

Design Commercials As an alternative to or an expansion of the Processing activity, have students work in pairs or groups to design television commercials for a documentary program about the discoveries at Mohenjodaro. Students should create a title for their program. Commercials should include the following: an engaging script that encourages viewers to watch the documentary, one or more visuals, and any other touches that will make it more realistic (e.g., time, channel, date). Scripts should introduce the civilization of Mohenjodaro and give at least three details about daily life that viewers will learn more about in the documentary.

Enrichment Resources

Find out more about Mohenjodaro and the Indus valley civilization by exploring the following Enrichment Resources for *History Alive! The Ancient World* at www.teachtci.com.

Enrichment Readings These in-depth readings encourage students to explore selected topics related to the chapter. You may also find readings that relate the chapter's content directly to your state's curriculum.

Internet Connections The recommended Web sites provide useful and engaging content that reinforces skills development and mastery of subjects within the chapter.

Literature Recommendations

The following books offer opportunities to extend the content in this chapter:

Science in Ancient India by Melissa Stewart (New York: Franklin Watts, 1999)

The Token Gift by Hugh William McKibbon (Willowdale, ON; Buffalo, New York; distributed in the U.S.A. by Firefly Books Inc.: Annick Press Ltd., 1996)

Traditions from India by Shelby Mamdani (London: Hodder Wayland, 2000)

Section 14.2

1. By studying the ruins of Mohenjodaro, we see that the city was carefully planned. The citadel was on a platform of mud and brick. Below the citadel were nine streets that divided the city into blocks, like those of a modern city.

2. Scientists are not sure what happened to the Indus valley civilization. The civilization disappeared around 1900 B.C.E. Some scientists had believed that invaders destroyed the cities. Other scientists think that natural events, such as a flood or an earthquake, caused the decline.

Section 14.3

Station A

1. Completed drawings should resemble the photograph in Section 14.3 of the student book.

2. Students' ideas about the objects will vary.

3. These objects are weights and a scale found in the ruins of Mohenjodaro. These artifacts suggest that ancient Indians used standard weights as they traded goods. Some weights were found in jewelers' shops.

Section 14.4

Station B

1. Completed drawings should resemble the photograph in Section 14.4 of the student book.

2. Students' ideas about the structure will vary.

3. It seems likely that people in Mohenjodaro used the Great Bath as a pool to bathe in. One room had a well that supplied the bath with water, and a drain removed dirty water. Some scientists think that the Great Bath might have been used for religious rituals.

Section 14.5

Station C

1. Completed drawings should resemble the two photographs in Section 14.5 of the student book.

2. Students' ideas about the objects will vary.

3. The statue shows a man. He has a short beard and wears a patterned robe over his left shoulder. He might represent both a priest and a king. The beads show that people in this ancient city wore jewelry. Women may have worn beads in necklaces, bracelets, earrings, and rings.

Section 14.6

Station D

1. Completed drawings should resemble the photograph in Section 14.6 of the student book.

2. Students' ideas about the objects will vary.

3. People may have worn these seals as charms to keep away evil, because small loops were found on the backs of many of the seals. These seals may also have been pressed into wax to form tags, as a way to identify the owners of certain goods.

Section 14.7

Station E

1. Completed drawings should resemble the photograph in Section 14.7 of the student book.

2. Students' ideas about the structure will vary.

3. This structure was part of a sewer system that carried dirty water and waste out of homes and into the Indus River. A network of clay pipes connected the buildings and homes to the main sewer system, making it possible for all residents to have had indoor bathrooms. Deep wells allowed people to store water, including rainfall.

Section 14.8

Station F

1. Completed drawings should resemble the photograph in Section 14.8 of the student book.

2. Students' ideas about the structures will vary.

3. These structures are ruins of houses in Mohenjodaro. Such houses were made of mud bricks, stood two stories high, and faced narrow alleys. Homes had from one to a dozen rooms. Scientists believe that poorer people may have lived in the smaller homes, while richer people lived in the larger homes.

Section 14.9

Station G

1. Completed drawings should resemble the photograph in Section 14.9 of the student book.

2. Students' ideas about the objects will vary.

3. These objects are game pieces. Dice, stone balls, grooved clay tracks, and stone game boards have been uncovered. Scientists believe that the dice and pawns were used in an early form of chess, which may have originated in ancient India. Children might have played with stone balls rolled along clay tracks and mazes.

Section 14.10

Station H

1. Completed drawings should resemble the photograph in Section 14.10 of the student book.

2. Students' ideas about the object will vary.

3. This object is one of the many small clay models found in Mohenjodaro. The model might be a toy, but scientists believe that it also shows how people might have transported farm goods to market.

Learning About World Religions: Hinduism

What are the origins and beliefs of Hinduism?

Overview

In a Response Group activity, students analyze images representing important beliefs in Hinduism to discover the religion's origins in ancient traditions and discuss how these beliefs affect life in ancient India and today.

Objectives

In the course of reading this chapter and participating in the classroom activity, students will

Social Studies

- explain the relationship among Vedic religion, Brahmanism, and Hinduism.
- outline the social structure of the caste system.
- describe important beliefs in Hinduism and discuss their influence on daily life.
- assess the impact of ancient beliefs and practices on life in modern India.

Language Arts

- deliver oral communications using detailed evidence.
- compose an acrostic poem.

Social Studies Vocabulary

Key Content Terms Hinduism, Vedas, Sanskrit, Brahmanism, caste, dharma, karma, reincarnation, pilgrimage

Academic Vocabulary affect, specific, interpret, divine, cycle

Materials

*History Alive!
The Ancient World*

Interactive Student Notebooks

Visuals 15A–15E

Lesson Masters

- Vocabulary Development handout (1 per student, on colored paper)

Activity	Suggested Time	Materials
Preview	20 minutes	• Interactive Student Notebooks
Vocabulary Development	30–40 minutes	• *History Alive! The Ancient World* • Interactive Student Notebooks • Vocabulary Development handout
Response Group	100 minutes (2–3 regular periods) (1–1.5 block periods)	• *History Alive! The Ancient World* • Interactive Student Notebooks • Visuals 15A–15E
Processing	20 minutes	• Interactive Student Notebooks
Assessment	40 minutes	• Chapter 15 Assessment

Preview

1 **Have students complete the Preview activity in their Interactive Student Notebooks.** Once they have finished their drawings showing how religion influences life in the United States, ask students to circulate around the room, and share their work. Have them discuss their ideas with at least five other students.

2 **Lead a class discussion.** Ask, *In what ways does religion affect American society? What other nations can you think of that have religious traditons different from those commonly practiced in the United States? How might religion affect people in other countries?*

3 **Connect the Preview activity to Chapter 15.** Tell students that n this chapter, they will learn about the origins and beliefs of Hinduism, a religion that developed, over time, from ancient Indian traditions. Today, Hinduism is a complex religion, practiced by millions of people worldwide. Its followers have many beliefs, deities, and practices that differ from place to place. Hinduism affects modern India in multiple ways. It can be argued that Indian society has been influenced by religion more than American society has. A knowledge of Hinduism is essential to an understanding of the history and traditions of ancient and present-day India.

Vocabulary Development

1 **Introduce the Key Content Terms.** Have students locate the Key Content Terms for the chapter in their Interactive Student Notebooks. These are important terms that will help them understand the main ideas of the chapter. Ask volunteers to identify any familiar terms and how they might be used in a sentence.

2 **Have students complete a Vocabulary Development handout.** Give each student a copy of the Vocabulary Development handout of your choice from the Reading Toolkit at the back of the Lesson Masters. These handouts provide extra Key Content Term practice and support, depending on your students' needs. Review the completed handout by asking volunteers to share one answer for each term.

Reading

1   **Introduce the Essential Question and have students read Section 15.1.**
Have students identify the Essential Question on the first page of the chapter: *What are the origins and beliefs of Hinduism?* Then have students read Section 15.1. Afterward, have students use information from Section 15.1 and from the chapter opener image to propose some possible answers to the Essential Question.

2   **Have students complete the Reading Notes for Chapter 15.** Assign Sections 15.2 to 15.8 during the activity, as indicated in the procedures for the Response Group. Remind students to use the Key Content Terms where appropriate as they complete their Reading Notes.

Response Group

1   **Place students in groups of three.** You may want to create a transparency that shows group assignments and seating arrangements.

2   **Introduce the activity.** Tell students that they will analyze images related to important beliefs in Hinduism. They will read about these beliefs and the ways they have affected daily life in India. Then students will discuss which belief they think has most influenced life in India.

3   **Have groups complete the Reading Notes for Sections 15.2 and 15.3.** Tell students that these sections discuss the origins of Hinduism and the caste system. Have groups read Sections 15.2 and 15.3 and complete the corresponding Reading Notes in their Interactive Student Notebooks. Use Guide to Reading Notes 15 to review their responses.

4   **Introduce visuals of some Hindu Deities.** Project *Visual 15A: Hindu Deities.* To help students analyze the image, ask,

Visual 15A

- What do you see?
- In what ways are these figures similar to each other? Different from each other?
- What characteristics suggest that these figures are not human?
- What do you think these figures represent?

5   **Have groups complete the Reading Notes for Sections 15.4 and 15.5.**
Tell students that the image they examined illustrates Hindu beliefs about gods, or deities. Point out that Sections 15.4 and 15.5 discuss Hindu beliefs about Brahman and other deities. Have groups read Sections 15.4 and 15.5 and complete the corresponding Reading Notes in their Interactive Student Notebooks. Afterward, have students reexamine Visual 15A. Ask, *What do these figures represent? From your reading, what else in the image do you now understand more clearly?*

6   **Introduce the concept of dharma.** Project *Visual 15B: Dharma.* To help students analyze the image, ask,

- What do you see?

- What different roles are shown?

- How is the figure in the center different from the others? Who might the figure be?

- Why do you think the artist chose to arrange the parts of this image like a flower?

7   **Have groups complete the Reading Notes for Section 15.6.** Tell students that the image they examined illustrates Hindu beliefs about dharma. Have groups read Section 15.6 and complete the corresponding Reading Notes in their Interactive Student Notebooks. Afterward, have students reexamine Visual 15B. Ask, *Why did the artist choose to arrange the parts of this image like a flower? From your reading, what else in the image do you now understand more clearly?*

8   **Introduce the concept of karma.** Project *Visual 15C: Karma.* To help students analyze the image, ask,

- What do you see?

- What details indicate that this image is divided into three sections?

- How would you describe the actions of the figures in the middle section?

- What might the artist be trying to show about the effects of people's actions?

9   **Have groups complete the Reading Notes for Section 15.7.** Tell students that the image they examined illustrates Hindu beliefs about karma. Have groups read Section 15.7 and complete the corresponding Reading Notes in their Interactive Student Notebooks. Afterward, have students reexamine Visual 15C. Ask, *What was the artist likely trying to show about the effects of people's actions? From your reading, what else in the image do you now understand more clearly?*

10 **Introduce the concept of samsara.** Project *Visual 15D: Samsara.* To help students analyze the image, ask,

- What do you see?

- Which eight figures represent the same person?

- Where is the breath going as it rises from the figure on the lower left?

- What might the breath and the differently dressed figures represent?

11 **Have groups complete the Reading Notes for Section 15.8.** Tell students that the image they examined illustrates Hindu beliefs about reincarnation, or samsara. Have groups read Section 15.8 and complete the corresponding Reading Notes in their Interactive Student Notebooks. Afterward, have students reexamine Visual 15D. Ask, *What do the breath and the differently dressed figures represent? From your reading, what else in the image do you now understand more clearly?*

Visual 15B

Visual 15C

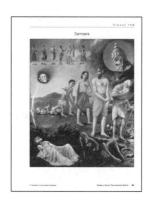

Visual 15D

12 Have groups discuss the Critical Thinking Question. Project *Visual 15E: Critical Thinking Question.* Tell students that they will now discuss in groups which of these four Hindu beliefs—deities, dharma, karma, or samsara—they think has most influenced life in India. Review the information that students have read about each belief and give groups several minutes to discuss the Critical Thinking Question.

13 Facilitate a class discussion. Follow these steps:

- Have each group appoint a Spokesperson.

- Have Spokespersons create a human bar graph by standing in front of the belief in the projection of Visual 15E that their group thinks has most influenced life in India. If there are multiple students for a belief, they should line up in front of each other as if creating a bar on a graph.

- Selecting one belief at a time, have Spokespersons standing in front of each belief give one reason for choosing this belief.

- After Spokespersons share reasons for all four beliefs, encourage students to challenge and discuss any of the reasons they heard.

- Finally, allow Spokespersons to briefly confer with their groups and then rearrange their positions on the bar graph if their opinions have changed.

Visual 15E

Processing

Have students complete the Processing activity in their Interactive Student Notebooks. Students compose an acrostic poem for the word *Hinduism*.

Quicker Coverage

Skip the Class Discussion Eliminate Steps 12 and 13 that outline procedures for a class discussion. Instead, wrap up the analysis of Visuals 15A–15D by asking students to identify at least one way each of these beliefs has influenced life in India.

Skip the Image Analysis Eliminate Steps 4, 6, 8, and 10 that guide students through a spiral set of questions used to help students analyze each image on Visuals 15A–15D. Instead, have groups read each section in the book and complete the corresponding Reading Notes. After groups have completed each section of Reading Notes, show the corresponding transparency and ask students to share ideas on how the image helps them understand what they read about that belief. Then proceed through the steps for the discussion of the Critical Thinking Question.

Deeper Coverage

Create Mandalas Have students work individually or in their groups to create a mandala reflecting Hindu beliefs about deities, dharma, karma, and samsara. Tell students that a mandala is a circular diagram used in Hinduism and Buddhism to increase spiritual awareness. Hindu mandalas usually consist of a combination of lines and triangles within a circle and a square, and designs range from simple to very complex. Then have students follow these steps:

1. Brainstorm a symbol to represent each of the four Hindu beliefs—deities, dharma, karma, and samsara. Students may use the visuals or symbols from their Reading Notes or create new ones.

2. Draw a mandala outline, such as the one below, onto a large piece of paper.

3. Place the symbols in the spaces in the circle, using whatever order students think makes the most sense.

4. Draw at least four additional symbols or illustrations around the circle to represent the ways that these beliefs have influenced life in India.

5. Use color and creative touches to make the mandala visually interesting.

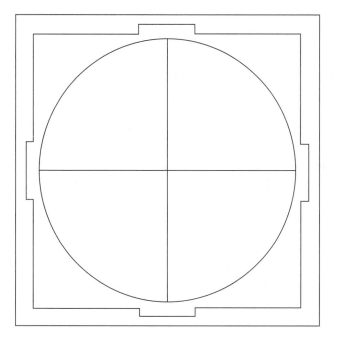

Assessment

Mastering the Content

1. A	5. B	9. C	13. A
2. C	6. B	10. A	14. B
3. A	7. D	11. D	15. D
4. C	8. D	12. B	16. C

Applying Social Studies Skills

17. be willing to give up riches and power

18. dharma, duty

19. Answers will vary. Possible answers: do their duty, put family first, follow the rules, obey their parents (accept all reasonable answers)

Exploring the Essential Question

20. Answers should include all of the elements requested in the prompt.

Scoring Rubric

Score	Description
3	Student completes all four parts of the graphic organizer, and satisfies the five bulleted guidelines. Reponses are clearly stated, are supported by examples or details from the story, and demonstrate command of standard English conventions.
2	Student responds to most or all parts of the task, but responses may not meet some of the guidelines, or may lack details or may not be clearly stated.
1	Student responds to at least one part of the task. Responses may contain factual and/or grammatical errors and may lack details.
0	Response does not match thetask or is incorrect.

English Language Learners

Support a Discussion Provide note cards and a copy of Visual 15E while students discuss the Critical Thinking Question. Have groups circle the belief they have chosen and write down three or more reasons. Have each group member select one reason to share, writing it down on his or her note card. Pair each group with a group that has chosen a different belief, and have groups share their reasons. Encourage the two paired groups to ask clarifying questions of each other. Then facilitate the class discussion as outlined in the activity procedures.

Provide Sample Sentences For the Processing activity, change the word *Hinduism* to *Hindu* and require only four Key Content Terms. Fill in a few letters of the acrostic poem ahead of time (see samples below). Leave blanks in place of the italicized words, for students to fill in the Key Content Terms.

Hindus built beautiful temples to express their love for (*their deities*).

I

Nonviolence is one effect of the Hindu belief in (*dharma*).

D

Under <u>Hinduism</u>, (*karma*) is made up of all the good and evil that a person has done.

Learners Reading and Writing Below Grade Level

Provide Sections of Guide to Reading Notes 15 For Sections 15.4 to 15.7, provide a partial Guide to Reading Notes as a model for taking notes. Make the following changes to have students work progressively more independently.

- For Section 15.4, omit key words from the answers, for students to fill in as they read.

- For Sections 15.5 and 15.6, provide one key point and one effect.

- For Section 15.8, ask students to provide two key points and two effects.

Learners with Special Education Needs

Provide Guide to Reading Notes 15 Provide a copy of Guide to Reading Notes 15 to students as they read about Hindu beliefs in Sections 15.4 to 15.8. White-out the section number and name of the belief. Have students match the Guide to the section as they read.

Conduct a Prewriting Activity Use the word *Hindu* as the base for the acrostic poem. Have students find and highlight words in their Reading Notes that begin with each of the letters in the word *Hindu*. Encourage students to write sentences, but allow them to use words or phrases. Provide students with a list of sample words and phrases to use in their acrostics. Examples are given below.

Hinduism began . . .

In ancient India, . . .

Not just one deity . . .

Dharma stands for . . .

Under the law of karma, . . .

Advanced Learners

Research Evidence Have groups research information to support their answers to the Critical Thinking Question. Encourage them to go beyond the information in the reading and find new examples of ways that these beliefs have influenced life in India.

Add Poem Requirements For the Processing activity, give students the following additional requirements for completing the acrostic poem.

- Add these terms to your poem: Sanskrit, *Ramayana,* nonviolence, reincarnation, pilgrimage, meditation.

- Try to add rhyme and/or rhythm to your lines.

Create Thematic Maps Have students work in pairs or small groups to research and create thematic maps about Hinduism. Consider one of the following ideas:

- spread of Hinduism over time

- location of Hindu temples in the region

- percentage of Hindus by state

- population of Hindus by country

Enrichment Resources

Find out more about Hinduism by exploring the following Enrichment Resources for History Alive! The Ancient World at www.teachtci.com.

Enrichment Readings These in-depth readings encourage students to explore selected topics related to the chapter. You may also find readings that relate the chapter's content directly to your state's curriculum.

Internet Connections The recommended Web sites provide useful and engaging content that reinforces skills development and mastery of subjects within the chapter.

Literature Recommendations

The following books offer opportunities to extend the content in this chapter:

Hindu by Anita Ganeri (Mankato, MN: Sea-to-Sea Publications, 2005)

Traditions from India by Shelby Mamdani (Austin, TX: Raintree Steck-Vaughn, 1999)

Hinduism by Madhu Bazaz Wangu (New York: Facts on File, 2001)

Section 15.2

1. No single person founded Hinduism. It developed slowly, over a long period of time, growing out of centuries of older traditions.

2. Answers will vary. Possible answers:

Vedic religion

- oldest roots of Hinduism
- named for the Vedas
- grew out of traditions brought to India by the Aryans
- honored a number of deities associated with nature and social order

Brahmanism

- more complex rituals
- named for Brahmin class of priests and religious scholars
- Brahmins interpreted the Vedas and performed required rituals

Hinduism

- modern-day religion that is very complex
- many beliefs, forms of worship, and deities exist, and often differ by region
- Vedas remain sacred to many Hindus today

3. The chart is organized from earliest form of religion that contributed to Hinduism to present day. Vedic religion grew into Brahmanism, which influenced modern-day Hinduism.

Section 15.3

1. *Brahmins*—priests and religious scholars

   Kshatriyas—rulers and warriors

   Vaishyas—herders and merchants

   Shudras—servants, farmers, laborers

2. Answers will vary, but students should show that the caste system changed over time by growing more complex. By medieval times, there were thousands of castes.

3. The caste system affected life in India because people were born into a caste and could not change it. They could only marry within their own caste.

Section 15.4

1. • supreme power that some Hindus believe is greater than all other deities
   - to these Hindus, only Brahman exists forever
   - to these Hindus, everything is part of Brahman, including the human soul

2. Followers of the ancient Vedic religion and Brahmanism communicated with their deities by holding elaborate rites and sacrifices outdoors.

3. • magnificent in size and design
   - doors often face east, toward the rising sun
   - building are covered with beautiful carvings and sculptures

4. Visuals will vary.

Section 15.5

Answers will vary. Possible answers:

1. • there are many deities in Hindu sacred texts and worship
   - in some Hindu traditions, there are three important deities
   - Brahma, Vishnu, and Shiva each control one aspect of the universe

2. One effect of this belief on life in India is that literature describes heroic deities battling evil.

3. Another effect of this belief on life in India is that sacred texts about deities have inspired religious holidays and festivals.

4. Visuals will vary.

Section 15.6

Answers will vary. Possible answers:

1. • dharma stands for law, obligation, and duty
   • each social class was said to have its own duties that involved a certain type of work
   • Hindus are also expected to follow a common dharma, or set of values

2. One effect of this belief on life in India is that many Hindus value nonviolence because they believe all life forms have a soul.

3. Another effect of this belief on life in India is that the cow is honored as the symbol of Hindus' respect for life.

4. Visuals will vary.

Section 15.7

Answers will vary. Possible answers:

1. • karma explains why Hindus should live according to dharma
   • the law of karma governs what happens to people's souls after death
   • karma is made up of all the good and evil that a person had done in past lives

2. One effect of this belief on life in India is that karma was used to explain why people had a certain status in society.

3. Another effect of this belief on life in India is that karma was used to justify the caste system until people started criticizing it.

4. Visuals will vary.

Section 15.8

Answers will vary. Possible answers:

1. • the continuous cycle of birth, death, and rebirth
   • samsara ends when the soul escapes from the cycle of reincarnation
   • it takes many lifetimes before a person can balance his or her karma and be released from samsara

2. One effect of this belief on life in India is that people would worship faithfully according to pre-scribed rules to free themselves.

3. Another effect of this belief on life in India is that ancient Hindus would make pilgrimages to sacred places to cleanse them of their sins.

4. Visuals will vary.

Learning About World Religions: Buddhism

What are the main beliefs and teachings of Buddhism?

Overview

In a Visual Discovery activity, students analyze images to learn about the life of Siddhartha Gautama and how his teachings became the basis of Buddhism.

Objectives

In the course of reading this chapter and participating in the classroom activity, students will

Social Studies

- describe the life of Siddhartha Gautama and explain how he became the Buddha.
- analyze paintings to clarify information presented in a historical narrative.
- summarize the main teachings of Buddhism.

Language Arts

- connect and clarify main ideas by using other sources.
- use verbal and nonverbal elements to sustain audience interest and attention.

Social Studies Vocabulary

Key Content Terms Buddha, ascetic, enlightenment, alms, nirvana, Buddhism, Four Noble Truths, Eightfold Path

Academic Vocabulary embrace, prediction, transform, deny, seek

Materials

*History Alive!
The Ancient World*

Interactive Student Notebooks

Visuals 16A–16E

Lesson Masters

- Student Handouts 16A and 16B (1 copy of each per pair)
- Vocabulary Development handout (1 per student, on colored paper)

Activity	Suggested Time	Materials
Preview	15 minutes	• Interactive Student Notebooks
Vocabulary Development	30–40 minutes	• *History Alive! The Ancient World* • Interactive Student Notebooks • Vocabulary Development handout
Visual Discovery	100–125 minutes (2–3 regular periods) (1.5 block periods)	• *History Alive! The Ancient World* • Interactive Student Notebooks • Visuals 16A–16E • Student Handouts 16A and 16B (1 copy of each per pair)
Processing	20 minutes	• Interactive Student Notebooks
Assessment	40 minutes	• Chapter 16 Assessment

Preview

1 **Have students complete the Preview activity in their Interactive Student Notebooks.** Students define what they think happiness is and how one achieves it.

2 **Have students share their responses in pairs or as a class.**

3 **Connect the Preview activity to Chapter 16.** Tell students that there are many ways to define happiness. In this chapter, students will learn about the life of Siddhartha Gautama, an Indian prince who was born around 563 B.C.E. He introduced a new way to achieve nirvana, or happiness, through enlightenment, or spiritual insight. He became known as the Buddha. The Buddha's teachings developed into the religion of Buddhism, which is now followed by millions of people around the world.

Vocabulary Development

1 **Introduce the Key Content Terms.** Have students locate the Key Content Terms for the chapter in their Interactive Student Notebooks. These are important terms that will help them understand the main ideas of the chapter. Ask volunteers to identify any familiar terms and how they might be used in a sentence.

2 **Have students complete a Vocabulary Development handout.** Give each student a copy of the Vocabulary Development handout of your choice from the Reading Toolkit at the back of the Lesson Masters. These handouts provide extra Key Content Term practice and support, depending on your students' needs. Review the completed handout by asking volunteers to share one answer for each term.

Reading

1 **Introduce the Essential Question and have students read Section 16.1.** Have students identify the Essential Question on the first page of the chapter: *What are the main beliefs and teachings of Buddhism?* Then have students read Section 16.1. Afterward, have students use information from Section 16.1 and from the chapter opener image to propose some possible answers to the Essential Question.

2 **Have students complete the Reading Notes for Chapter 16.** Assign Sections 16.2 to 16.7 during the activity, as indicated in the procedures for the Visual Discovery. Remind students to use the Key Content Terms where appropriate as they complete their Reading Notes.

Visual Discovery

1 **Place students in pairs and introduce the activity in which students will prepare act-it-outs about events in Buddha's life.** Explain to students that in this activity, they will analyze images related to the life of Buddha and his path to enlightenment. For two of these images, students will prepare characters for act-it-outs, in which actors will "step into" these images to bring them to life.

2 **Have students examine a visual of the details of Siddhartha's birth.** Project *Visual 16A: Siddhartha as a Baby.* Focus students' attention on the right-hand side of the image. Make sure students notice the image of a baby being held by a figure seated against a red background. To help students analyze the image, ask,

Visual 16A

- What do you see?

- How would you describe the setting?

- Why do you think the man in the palace is holding a baby? Who might this man be?

- What details in the scene suggest that this baby's birth is unique?

3 **Have pairs complete the Reading Notes for Section 16.2.** Have pairs read Section 16.2 and complete the corresponding Reading Notes in their Interactive Student Notebooks. (**Note:** Alternatively, you may want to complete the Reading Notes together as a class until you are confident pairs can do so on their own.)

4 **Have pairs prepare to bring the image on Visual 16A to life.** Give each pair a copy of *Student Handout 16A: Bringing to Life Siddhartha as a Baby.* Assign each pair a character from the list on the handout. There may be more than one pair assigned to a character. Give pairs several minutes to complete the steps on their handout to prepare the talking statue for their assigned character.

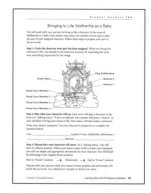

Student Handout 16A

5 **Conduct the act-it-out.** Choose volunteers as actors for each character in the act-it-out. Have actors step into the image and "freeze" in their starting positions as talking statues. One "statue" at a time, tap the actors' shoulders as if you were pressing a "button" to "unfreeze" them. Actors should say their lines, make their movements, and then "refreeze." Afterward, have the audience give the actors a round of applause.

6 **Have students examine a visual of Siddhartha's privileged early life.** Project *Visual 16B: Siddhartha's Princely Life.* Direct students' attention to the upper right-hand area of the image. To help students analyze the image, ask,

- What do you see?

- How would you describe the setting?

- Who is the young man holding the bow? Why do you think so?

- What do the details of this scene reveal about Siddhartha's early life?

Visual 16B

7 **Have pairs complete the Reading Notes for Section 16.3.** Have pairs read Section 16.3 and complete the corresponding Reading Notes in their Interactive Student Notebooks. Use Guide to Reading Notes 16 to review students' responses as a class.

8 **Have students examine a visual of Siddhartha seeing aging, sickness, and death.** Project *Visual 16C: Siddhartha Discovers Suffering*. Focus students' attention on the bottom center of the image, where a figure (Siddhartha) in a carriage is extending his arm. Make sure students can find the three figures just to the right of the figure holding a fan over his shoulder. To help students analyze the image, ask,

- What do you see?
- How would you describe the setting?
- Who is the man in the carriage? What is he (Siddhartha) pointing at?
- What do you think the three figures Siddhartha is pointing at represent? How might Siddhartha be affected by seeing these figures (old age, sickness, death)?

Visual 16C

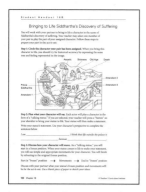

9 **Have pairs complete the Reading Notes for Section 16.4.** Have pairs read Section 16.4 and complete the corresponding Reading Notes in their Interactive Student Notebooks.

10 **Repeat Steps 4 and 5 to conduct an act-it-out for Visual 16C.** Give pairs a copy of *Student Handout 16B: Bringing to Life Siddhartha's Discovery of Suffering* to prepare for the act-it-out.

Student Handout 16B

11 **Have students examine a visual of Siddhartha becoming an ascetic.** Project *Visual 16D: Siddhartha Becomes an Ascetic*. Direct students' attention to the upper right-hand corner of the image. Make sure students see Siddhartha standing near the forest. To help students analyze the image, ask,

- What do you see?
- How would you describe the setting?
- Who is the man in the forest? How does this image contrast with earlier images of this man (Siddhartha)?
- Why do you think Siddhartha is alone?

12 **Have pairs complete the Reading Notes for Section 16.5.** Have pairs read Section 16.5 and complete the corresponding Reading Notes in their Interactive Student Notebooks. Use Guide to Reading Notes 16 to review students' responses as a class.

Visual 16D

13 Have students examine a visual of Siddhartha becoming the Buddha.
Project *Visual 16E: Siddhartha Becomes the Buddha*. Focus students' attention on the center of the image. To help students analyze the image, ask,

- What do you see?

- How would you describe the setting?

- Who is the man in the center of the image? How has his (Siddhartha's) appearance changed from when he first became an ascetic?

- Why do you think Siddhartha is sitting in this position? What might have happened to him while he was meditating?

Visual 16E

14 Have pairs complete the Reading Notes for Section 16.6. Have pairs read Section 16.6 and complete the corresponding Reading Notes in their Interactive Student Notebooks. Use Guide to Reading Notes 16 to review students' responses as a class.

15 Have pairs complete the Reading Notes for Section 16.7. Have pairs read Section 16.7 summarizing Buddha's teachings and then complete the corresponding Reading Notes in their Interactive Student Notebooks. Review responses as a class, using Guide to Reading Notes 16.

Processing

Have students complete the Processing activity in their Interactive Student Notebooks. Students write a mock interview with the Buddha, asking him questions about his life and teachings. (**Note:** Students might work in pairs to write their interviews and then perform them for the class.)

Quicker Coverage

Skip the Act-it-Outs Rather than conduct act-it-outs for Visuals 16A and 16C, use Guide to Reading Notes 16 to review the important details of the corresponding sections of Reading Notes.

Deeper Coverage

Write an Advice Column In place of, or in addition to, the Reading Notes for Section 16.7, have students, acting as the Buddha, write an advice column for teenagers. In the column, students should define the Buddha's meaning of happiness and the pathway he believes people can take to achieve it. Then students should provide specific advice that the Buddha might give to teenagers on how they should approach their schoolwork, how they should treat their friends and classmates, and how they should act at home with their families.

Create Sensory Figures Provide an image of the Buddha which students annotate by writing statements about what he might have thought, seen, heard, said, touched, and felt (feelings) during his lifetime. Students might also reasearch the meaning of specific details of the image, such as the Buddha's mudras (hand gestures) and signs of his princely life (e.g., extended earlobes).

> **Writing: Formatting**
>
> Consider requiring word-processed mock interviews to meet these formatting requirements: appropriate use of page orientation, margins, and spacing. Note how interviews use the same conventions that plays do to signal speakers. In both forms, the speaker's name begins a new line at the left margin, is often written in capital letters, and is followed by a colon and a space. An extra line of space separates one speaker from the next.

Assessment

Mastering the Content

1. B	5. A	9. B	13. A
2. C	6. C	10. C	14. C
3. D	7. A	11. B	15. D
4. B	8. D	12. A	16. D

Applying Social Studies Skills

17. stress

18. elephant's footprint, footprint of an elephant

19. Possible answers: useful practices, helpful qualities, smaller truths (accept all plausible answers)

Exploring the Essential Question

20. Answers should include all of the elements requested in the prompt.

Scoring Rubric

Score	Description
3	Student writes sentences in all six empty boxes. Sentences are clearly stated, correctly illustrate the principle on the Eightfold Path, and demonstrate command of standard English conventions.
2	Student responds to most or all parts of the task, but sentences may relate only partially to the principle on the path or may not be clearly stated.
1	Student responds to at least one part of the task. Sentences may not fit the principles they are supposed to illustrate and/or may contain grammatical errors.
0	Response does not match the task or is incorrect.

English Language Learners

Support the Reading Notes Provide additional structure as students complete the Reading Notes for Sections 16.2 to 16.6. Show an example of a headline and a caption from a newspaper. Then use Guide to Reading Notes 16 to do the following:

- For Sections 16.2 and 16.3, provide the headline and caption, but have students complete the labeling of details in the image.

- For Sections 16.4 and 16.5, provide the headline, but have students complete the labeling of details in the image and write the caption.

- For Section 16.6, have students complete the Reading Notes on their own.

Provide an Alternative Processing Activity As an alternative to writing a mock interview for the Processing activity, give students the option to make a historical marker to mark the Buddha's birthplace. Have students include information about his early life, his path to enlightenment, and his teachings. Students can write, or create visuals with captions, or both, on their historical markers.

Learners Reading and Writing Below Grade Level

Offer a Word Bank Provide a Word Bank to help students complete the Reading Notes for Sections 16.2 to 16.6. Have students use these words and phrases in their captions for each image. Also consider copying the student edition pages for these sections and having students highlight sentences using these words or phrases as they read. A suggested Word Bank is provided below:

- Section 16.2: King Suddhodana, Prince Siddhartha, Brahmins
- Section 16.3: servants, palaces, amusement, wealth
- Section 16.4: ascetic, sickness, death, aging, travel
- Section 16.5: forest, bowl, meditation, self-denial, extreme
- Section 16.6: the Buddha, Bodhi tree, enlightenment

Learners with Special Education Needs

Offer Choices for Act-it-Outs On the day preceding the act-it-outs for the Visual Discovery, explain the activity. Review the characters on Student Handouts 16A and 16B, and ask students to choose which character they would like to act out for the class. As pairs prepare act-it-outs, have them write their character's statement on a note card for reference.

Give Interview Questions Give students questions for the mock interview in the Processing activity. Remind students to answer these questions from the Buddha's point of view. Recommend that students choose three or more questions from the suggested ones below.

- What was your life like as you were growing up?
- When did you decide to leave this life behind?
- What happened to you after you left your family?
- When did you know that you were the Buddha?
- What do you think happiness is?
- How do you think people find happiness?

Advanced Learners

Interpret Stories Explain that the Buddha often shared his teachings through parables, or simple stories with a lesson. Have students work in small groups to research and select a parable to share with the class. Each group should provide a visual to illustrate the parable, summarize or read it aloud, and explain which Buddhist teachings are evident in the parable.

Compare Forms of Buddhism Have students find more information about the two main forms of Buddhism (Theravada and Mahayana) and complete a matrix to summarize what they learned. The matrix might include information on the main beliefs, the countries where practiced, the important religious texts, and common practices. After students complete the matrix, discuss as a class the similarities and differences between these two forms of Buddhism and the one from ancient India they learn about in their book. Have students speculate on the reasons why the similarities and differences might exist. (**Note:** You might also consider adding other forms of Buddhism to the matrix, such as Tibetan and Zen.)

Enrichment Resources

Find out more about Buddhism by exploring the following Enrichment Resources for History Alive! The Ancient World at www.teachtci.com.

Enrichment Readings These in-depth readings encourage students to explore selected topics related to the chapter. You may also find readings that relate the chapter's content directly to your state's curriculum.

Internet Connections The recommended Web sites provide useful and engaging content that reinforces skills development and mastery of subjects within the chapter.

Literature Recommendations

The following books offer opportunities to extend the content in this chapter:

The Buddha by Paul Mantell (New York: Aladdin Paperbacks, 2007)

Buddhism by Anita Ganeri (New York: Peter Bedrick Books, 2001)

Wisdom of the Crows and Other Buddhist Tales by Sherab Chodzin and Alexandra Kohn (Berkeley, CA: Tricycle Press, 2004)

Section 16.2

Students' responses will vary. Possible response:

Headline: A Prince or a Buddha?

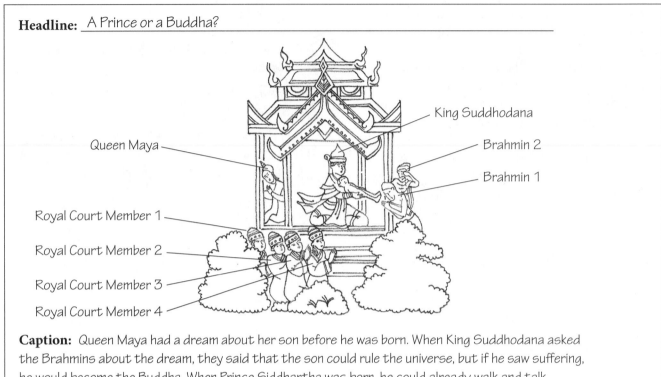

Queen Maya

King Suddhodana

Brahmin 2

Brahmin 1

Royal Court Member 1

Royal Court Member 2

Royal Court Member 3

Royal Court Member 4

Caption: Queen Maya had a dream about her son before he was born. When King Suddhodana asked the Brahmins about the dream, they said that the son could rule the universe, but if he saw suffering, he would become the Buddha. When Prince Siddhartha was born, he could already walk and talk.

Section 16.3

Students' responses will vary. Possible response:

Headline: Siddhartha Lives in Luxury

Siddhartha

fine house

entertainment

servants

Caption: King Suddhodana wanted his son to be a great ruler, so he used his wealth to provide Siddhartha with luxuries and amusements. Servants gave the prince everything he needed. At 16, Siddhartha married, and he and his wife spent their time enjoying the prince's many palaces.

Section 16.4

Students' responses will vary. Possible response:

Headline: Siddhartha Discovers Suffering

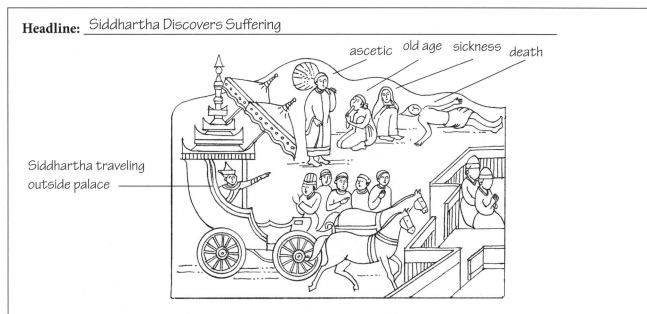

ascetic   old age   sickness   death

Siddhartha traveling outside palace

Caption: After Siddhartha became a father, he spent more time traveling outside his palace. On his first trip, he saw old age; on his second, he saw sickness; and on his third, he saw death. On his fourth trip, he met an ascetic who told him that one can only be free of suffering when one gives up worldly desires, pleasures, and comforts.

Section 16.5

Students' responses will vary. Possible response:

Headline: Siddhartha Leaves His Family

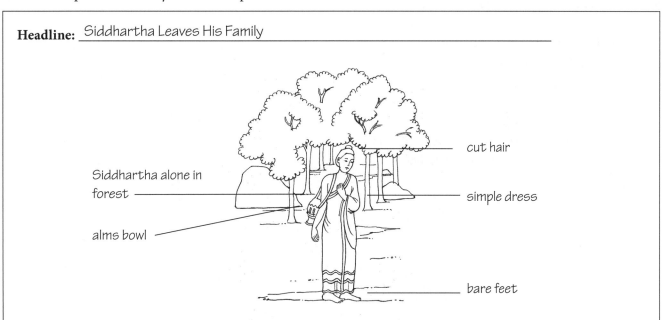

cut hair

Siddhartha alone in forest

simple dress

alms bowl

bare feet

Caption: Siddhartha gave up his life of luxury and went to live in the forest as an ascetic. There, he wore simple clothing, walked in bare feet, and carried only a bowl to use for begging. He did not find enlightenment while living in this way.

Section 16.6

Students' responses will vary. Possible response:

Headline: Siddhartha Becomes the Buddha

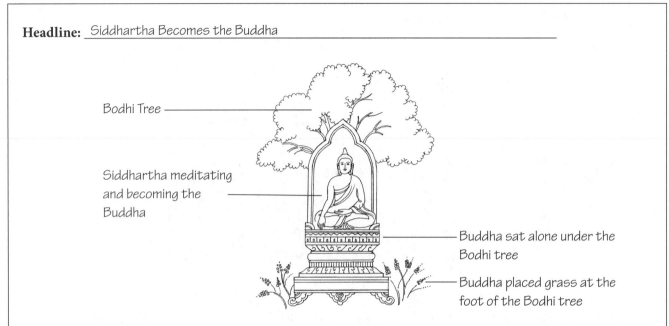

Bodhi Tree

Siddhartha meditating and becoming the Buddha

Buddha sat alone under the Bodhi tree

Buddha placed grass at the foot of the Bodhi tree

Caption: Siddhartha learned that an ascetic's way of life did not bring enlightenment. He decided to follow a "middle way" instead. On his 35th birthday, he vowed to meditate under the Bodhi tree until he finally achieved enlightenment. By morning, he had became the Buddha, the Awakened One.

Section 16.7

1. Students' drawings and captions will vary, but should illustrate that the idea behind the Four Noble Truths is that all things change. Even when one finds pleasure, it does not last forever.

2. Students' drawings and captions will vary, but should illustrate the Buddha's belief in the path on which people should travel to end their suffering—the Eightfold Path. This path follows the "middle way," a balance between pleasure and pain.

3. Answers will vary.

The First Unification of India

How did Ashoka unify the Mauryan Empire and spread Buddhist values?

Overview

In a Social Studies Skill Builder, students interpret excerpts from King Ashoka's edicts to analyze how he unified the Mauryan Empire during his rule.

Objectives

In the course of reading this chapter and participating in the classroom activity, students will

Social Studies

- describe the expansion of the Mauryan Empire and the political and moral achievements of King Ashoka.
- explain how King Ashoka and his edicts contributed to the spread of Buddhism in India, Ceylon, and Central Asia.
- interpret excerpts from Ashoka's edicts to create visual representations.
- classify Ashoka's edicts into categories representing various ways Ashoka promoted unity in India.

Language Arts

- determine meanings of words using word, sentence, and paragraph clues.
- identify and use structural features to communicate an understanding.

Social Studies Vocabulary

Key Content Terms Mauryan Empire, Ashoka, edict

Academic Vocabulary horror, vast, reject, execute, promote

Materials

History Alive!
The Ancient World

Interactive Student Notebooks

Lesson Masters

- Information Master 17 (1 transparency)
- Student Handout 17A (2 copies of the 8-page handout, 1 page per pair)
- Student Handout 17B (1 per student)
- Vocabulary Development handout (1 per student, on colored paper)

11" × 17" sheets of paper (1 per pair)

colored pencils or markers

Activity	Suggested Time	Materials
Preview	15 minutes	• Interactive Student Notebooks
Vocabulary Development	30–40 minutes	• *History Alive! The Ancient World* • Interactive Student Notebooks • Vocabulary Development handout
Social Studies Skill Builder	90 minutes (2 regular periods) (1 block period)	• *History Alive! The Ancient World* • Interactive Student Notebooks • Information Master 17 (1 transparency) • Student Handout 17A (2 copies of the 8-page handout, 1 page per pair) • Student Handout 17B (1 per student) • 11" × 17" sheets of paper (1 per pair) • colored pencils or markers
Processing	20 minutes	• Interactive Student Notebooks
Assessment	40 minutes	• Chapter 17 Assessment

Preview

1 **Have students complete the Preview activity in their Interactive Student Notebooks.** Students examine a modern-day billboard and evaluate its effectiveness.

2 **Have students share their responses in pairs or as a class.**

3 **Connect the Preview activity to Chapter 17.** Tell students that there were no billboards in ancient India. However, a leader named King Ashoka carved official messages to his people on walls, rocks, and tall pillars throughout his empire. Known as edicts, these messages were displayed in public places to tell people how to live. In this chapter, students will learn more about Ashoka and how he used edicts to unify his empire and spread Buddhist values.

Vocabulary Development

1 **Introduce the Key Content Terms.** Have students locate the Key Content Terms for the chapter in their Interactive Student Notebooks. These are important terms that will help them understand the main ideas of the chapter. Ask volunteers to identify any familiar terms and how they might be used in a sentence.

2 **Have students complete a Vocabulary Development handout.** Give each student a copy of the Vocabulary Development handout of your choice from the Reading Toolkit at the back of the Lesson Masters. These handouts provide extra Key Content Term practice and support, depending on your students' needs. Review the completed handout by asking volunteers to share one answer for each term.

Reading

1 **Introduce the Essential Question and have students read Section 17.1.** Have students identify the Essential Question on the first page of the chapter: *How did Ashoka unify the Mauryan Empire and spread Buddhist values?* Then have students read Section 17.1. Afterward, have students use information from Section 17.1 and from the chapter opener image to propose some possible answers to the Essential Question.

2 **Have students complete the Reading Notes for Chapter 17.** Assign Sections 17.2 to 17.4 during the activity, as indicated in the procedures for the Social Studies Skill Builder. Remind students to use the Key Content Terms where appropriate as they complete their Reading Notes.

Social Studies Skill Builder

1   **Place students in pairs.** You may want to prepare a transparency that shows pair assignments and seating arrangements.

2   **Have pairs complete the Reading Notes for Sections 17.2–17.4.** Tell students that this reading will introduce them to King Ashoka and the Mauryan Empire. Have pairs read Sections 17.2–17.4 and complete the corresponding Reading Notes in their Interactive Student Notebooks. Afterward, use Guide to Reading Notes 17 to review their responses.

3   **Introduce the activity in which students will examine excerpts from Ashoka's edicts.** Tell students that they will interpret excerpts from Ashoka's edicts and create modern-day billboards that represent the edicts' main ideas. Afterward, they will post the billboards, and their classmates will use them to identify which of Ashoka's four main goals is emphasized.

4   **Review steps for creating billboards.** Project the first page of *Information Master 17: Creating Billboards for Ashoka's Edicts* and review the steps with students.

Information Master 17

5   **Have students interpret a sample edict.** Project the sample edict on the second page of Information Master 17. Have students identify and define key words and phrases. Give pairs a minute to discuss what they think the edict means and which of Ashoka's four goals it best emphasizes. Ask volunteers to share their responses and offer suggestions on how they might represent the edict on a billboard.

6   **Have pairs create their billboards.** Distribute to each pair one of the nine pages of *Student Handout 17A: Ashoka's Edicts.* (**Note:** In classes larger than 18, more than one pair will be assigned to an edict). Monitor pairs as they interpret their edicts and sketch their billboard drafts. When pairs complete their drafts, check to make sure their sketches clearly and accurately represent the assigned edicts. Give each pair a piece of 11" × 17" paper for creating their billboard.

Student Handout 17A

7   **Have pairs post their billboards.** Designate areas along the classroom walls for each of the edicts. Have pairs post their assigned edicts and billboards in the appropriate areas.

8   **Have pairs examine the billboards.** Distribute to each student a copy of *Student Handout 17B: Interpreting Ashoka's Edicts* and review the directions. Have pairs begin with the billboard(s) for their assigned edict. Continue until most pairs have examined most of the edicts.

Student Handout 17B

9 **Wrap up the activity.** Have pairs share their responses to Student Handout 17B. Use Guide to Student Handout 17B as a reference. Then hold a class discussion. Ask,

- What are the main ideas expressed in Ashoka's edicts?
- What are some of the ways in which Ashoka's leadership promoted unity in India?
- In what ways did Ashoka's Buddhist beliefs contribute to unity in India?
- What happened to the Mauryan Empire after Ashoka died? Why do you think that happened?

Processing

Have students complete the Processing activity in their Interactive Student Notebooks. Students design the home page for a Web site that Ashoka might have used to communicate with the people in his empire.

Quicker Coverage

Eliminate Edicts Use four of the nine edicts from Student Handout 17A. Choose one edict to represent each goal. Make enough copies of the edicts so that you can assign one-quarter of the pairs to each edict. Once billboards are completed, designate one wall of the classroom for each edict and post the billboards there. Conduct a gallery walk to have pairs examine the billboards for each edict. The following edicts are recommended to represent Ashoka's four goals:

- Edict B for Buddhist Values
- Edict A for General Welfare
- Edict F for Justice
- Edict E for Security

Deeper Coverage

Compare the Goals of Leaders Compare the goals of Ashoka with those of contemporary leaders. Have students work in pairs or small groups to research the agendas of some of today's government officials to identify their goals. Consider focusing on the president, the state governor, or a local official. Have students find an appropriate quotation and then explain the goal it emphasizes. Ask volunteers to share their quotations and explanations. Then facilitate a class discussion by asking, *What are the main goals shared by today's leaders? In what ways are they similar to those of Ashoka? In what ways are they different? What might explain those similarities and differences?*

Assessment

Mastering the Content

1. A	5. D	9. A	13. C
2. B	6. D	10. D	14. B
3. B	7. B	11. B	15. A
4. C	8. B	12. D	

Applying Social Studies Skills

16. Indian Ocean

17. Answers will vary. Possible answers: Japan; Sumatra; Java

18. Burma; Siam

19. Himalayas

Exploring the Essential Question

20. Answers should include all of the elements requested in the prompt.

Scoring Rubric

Score	Description
3	Student completes three report cards with a letter grade and a comment. Teacher comments are clearly stated, supported by details, and demonstrate command of standard English conventions.
2	Student completes most or all parts of the report cards, but teacher comments may lack details or not be clearly stated.
1	Student responds to at least one part of the task. Teacher comment(s) may contain factual and/or grammatical errors and may lack details.
0	Response does not match the task or is incorrect.

English Language Learners

Provide Examples Find additional or alternative examples of billboards for the Preview activity. Conduct an image search on the Internet to locate a billboard in the native language(s) of students.

Support Comprehension of Edicts On each edict, provide definitions for any words that students may find challenging. Consider assigning students to create billboards on Edicts A or B, which are the most straightforward and succinct.

Learners Reading and Writing Below Grade Level

Offer an Oral Option In the Preview activity, after students have identified key words and visuals on the billboard, allow them the option of answering the questions orally.

Substitute Sentences for Paragraphs Rather than have students write paragraphs for the Reading Notes for Sections 17.2 and 17.3, allow them to write sentences to summarize the main ideas. Also, to support summarizing, consider providing copies of the book pages for these sections. Tell students to find and highlight the required words and phrases as they read.

Learners with Special Education Needs

Provide Partial Reading Notes Use Guide to Reading Notes 17 to provide students with partial notes for Sections 17.2 and 17.3. In the sample response for Section 17.2, delete all the underlined words. In the sample response for Section 17.3, delete all the underlined words and a few additional key terms. Students will use the reading to fill in the terms that are missing.

Provide Partial Activity Notes Use Guide to Student Handout 17B but without the terms in the "Goal" column circled. As students visit each edict, they should circle the goal they believe is best emphasized, and then highlight two to five key words in the given answer in the third column. Consider leaving one or more explanations blank for students to fill in on their own.

Offer Sample Home Pages During the Processing activity, show students one or more samples of Web site home pages. Consider showing the home page from a government institution or agency Web site that includes a variety of text and visual features, such as those from the White House (www.whitehouse.gov) and the National Park Service (www.nps.gov). You may want to provide students with additional support by giving them a blank home page template or by brainstorming features that typically appear on Web site home pages.

Advanced Learners

Give Processing Options Allow students to use the guidelines for the Processing activity to create another form of media that Ashoka might use to communicate with his people. Students might record a radio announcement, create a television commercial, write an editorial, or design a Web video.

Analyze Ashoka as a Candidate As an alternative to the Processing activity, have students think about how Ashoka would perform in a modern-day American election. Have students design a Web page that opposes or challenges Ashoka as a political candidate. The page should cite at least three of Ashoka's edicts as the reasons why voters should *not* support his candidacy.

Enrichment Resources

Find out more about Ashoka and the Mauryan Empire by exploring the following Enrichment Resources for *History Alive! The Ancient World* at www.teachtci.com.

Enrichment Readings These in-depth readings encourage students to explore selected topics related to the chapter. You may also find readings that relate the chapter's content directly to your state's curriculum.

Internet Connections The recommended Web sites provide useful and engaging content that reinforces skills development and mastery of subjects within the chapter.

Literature Recommendations

The following books offer opportunities to extend the content in this chapter:

Asoka and Indian Civilization by H. A. Kanitkar and Hemant Kanitkar (St. Paul, MN: Greenhaven Press, 1980)

Buddhist Temple by Angela Wood (Milwaukee, WI: Gareth Stevens, 2000)

Shower of Gold: Girls and Women in the Stories of India by Maniam Selvan (North Haven, CT: Linnet Books, 1999)

Section 17.2

1. Check students' maps by referring to the map of the Mauryan Empire in Section 17.2 of *History Alive! The Ancient World*.

2. Students' paragraphs will vary. Possible response:

Ancient India was divided into many small <u>kingdoms</u> that were weak from fighting each other. Chandragupta Maurya used his great army to <u>conquer</u> and <u>unite</u> all of northern India. He kept his empire strong by using <u>force</u> whenever necessary. He used his powerful army, a network of spies, and even torture. His rule was harsh, but it was successful in some ways. He created a strong <u>central government</u>. He made sure farmers had water for their crops. The empire continued to grow after he gave up power.

Section 17.3

Students' paragraphs will vary. Possible response:

Ashoka expanded the Mauryan Empire through a series of <u>wars</u>. After one especially brutal battle, he decided to <u>reject</u> violence and embrace Buddhism. He supported the <u>Buddhist</u> values of love, peace, and nonviolence. He gave up wars of conquest. He wanted his people to follow the Buddhist path and urged them to be kind, respectful, and moral. He <u>spread</u> Buddhism beyond India by sending his son to Ceylon. Ashoka was a <u>practical</u> ruler, though. He still allowed slavery, kept a strong army, and did not return any of the lands the Mauryas had conquered.

Section 17.4

1. Answers should describe the four main goals of Ashoka's edicts.

   - Buddhist Values. These edicts encouraged Buddhist teachings, such as being respectful, practicing nonviolence, not getting attached to worldly things and acting morally.

   - General Welfare. These edicts promoted people's well-being, such as making sure people had good health, shelter, clean water, and food.

   - Justice. These edicts were in regard to fair laws and described how people would be treated in court and in jail.

   - Security. These edicts were concerned with the enemies of the Mauryan Empire and noncitizens. They dealt with issues of peace and conquest.

2. Answers will vary. Sample answer: These edicts were carved into walls, rocks, and tall pillars in public places as a way to communicate with the greatest number of people. Spreading Ashoka's messages of Buddhist values helped more people to know and follow the same laws.

3. Answers will vary. Sample answer: Ashoka helped to spread Buddhism throughout his empire and beyond, by introducing it to his people and to Ceylon. Later, Buddhism spread from northwestern India to Central Asia. From there, it spread to China, Korea, and Japan.

The following are possible responses. An edict may represent more than one goal, and explanations will vary.

Edict	Goal	Why We Chose This Goal
Edict A: "On the roads, . . . trees have been planted for the enjoyment of animals and men. I have had ponds dug and shelters erected along the roads. Everywhere I have had wells dug."	Buddhist Values (General Welfare) Justice Security	This edict talks about improving the environment to promote the well-being of humans and animals.
Edict B: "It is good to be obedient to one's mother and father, friends, and relatives. It is good not only to spend little, but to own the minimum of property."	(Buddhist Values) General Welfare Justice Security	This edict tells people to obey their elders, and not to spend a lot of money or have a lot of possessions.
Edict C: "My officers have been appointed for the welfare [safety] and happiness of the . . . people. I have given them . . . authority in judgment and punishment. But it is desirable that there should be uniformity [sameness] in judicial [trial] procedure and punishment."	Buddhist Values General Welfare (Justice) Security	This edict says that the same rules should apply to everyone and that officers are appointed with the authority to judge and punish.
Edict D: "This world and the other [world after death] are hard to gain without great love of righteousness [correct behavior], great self-examination, great obedience, and great effort."	(Buddhist Values) General Welfare Justice Security	This edict says that to have a good life on Earth and life after death, one must be well-behaved, thoughtful, obedient, and hardworking.

Edict	Goal	Why We Chose This Goal
Edict E: "If the unconquered peoples on my border ask what is my will, they should understand this: I desire that they should trust me and should have only happiness in their dealings with me."	Buddhist Values General Welfare Justice (Security)	This edict tells unconquered people to trust Ashoka and know that he wants to have a good relationship with them.
Edict F: "This . . . has been engraved so that the officials of the city should always see to it that no one is ever imprisoned or tortured without good cause. To ensure this, officers who are not fierce or harsh shall be sent out every five years on a tour of inspection."	Buddhist Values General Welfare (Justice) Security	This edict says that Ashoka will send out officers to make sure that no one is put in prison or tortured without a good cause.
Edict G: "There is no gift comparable to the gift of dharma [righteousness, or correct behavior], which is good behavior toward slaves and servants; obedience to parents; generosity toward friends, acquaintances, and relatives; . . . and abstention [staying away] from killing living beings."	(Buddhist Values) General Welfare Justice Security	This edict tells people that there is no better way to live than by dharma (or correct behavior), the practice of being kind to servants and slaves, obeying parents, showing generosity to friends, and not killing living things.
Edict H: "Everywhere, I, Ashoka, King Priyadarsi, Beloved of the Gods, have arranged for two kinds of medical treatment: medical treatment for people and medical treatment for animals."	Buddhist Values (General Welfare) Justice Security	This edict tells people that medical treatment is available for people and animals.
Edict I: "Men who are sentenced to death are to be given three days' respite [waiting period before being put to death]. During this period, relatives may plead for the prisoners' lives, or the accused may make donations or undertake a fast [period of not eating] for a better rebirth in the next life."	Buddhist Values General Welfare (Justice) Security	This edict says that people who are sentenced to death can have a three-day period in which relatives can plead for them, or prisoners can pray and fast for a better existence in the next life.

The Achievements of the Gupta Empire

Why is the period during the Gupta Empire known as a "golden age"?

Overview

In a Writing for Understanding activity, students "visit" seven sites around the Gupta Empire that highlight important cultural and intellectual achievements and explain in writing why this period was a "golden age" in ancient India.

Objectives

In the course of reading this chapter and participating in the classroom activity, students will

Social Studies

- identify the Gupta Empire on a map and locate its key cities.

- define what characteristics classify a historical time period as a "golden age."

- describe the important aesthetic and intellectual traditions of ancient India, including literature, medicine, metallurgy, and mathematics.

- explain why the period during the Gupta Empire is known as a "golden age."

Language Arts

- create a multi-paragraph expository composition.

- revise writing to improve organization and clarity.

Social Studies Vocabulary

Key Content Terms Gupta Empire, alliance, province, golden age, philosophy

Academic Vocabulary prosperity, achievement, mathematics, astronomy, axis

Materials

*History Alive!
The Ancient World*

Interactive Student Notebooks

Lesson Masters

- Station Directions 18A– 18G (2 copies of each)

- Information Master 18 (1 transparency)

- Student Handout 18 (at least 1 copy per student)

- Vocabulary Development handout (1 per student, on colored paper)

sticky notes

colored markers or pencils

scissors

string

Activity	Suggested Time	Materials
Preview	15 minutes	• Interactive Student Notebooks
Vocabulary Development	30–40 minutes	• *History Alive! The Ancient World* • Interactive Student Notebooks • Vocabulary Development handout
Writing for Understanding	180 minutes (3–4 regular periods) (1.5–2 block periods)	• *History Alive! The Ancient World* • Interactive Student Notebooks • Station Directions 18A–18G (2 copies of each) • Information Master 18 (1 transparency) • Student Handout 18 (at least 1 copy per student) • sticky notes • colored markers or pencils • scissors • string
Processing (optional)	20 minutes	• Interactive Student Notebooks
Assessment	40 minutes	• Chapter 18 Assessment

Preview

1 **Have students complete the Preview activity in their Interactive Student Notebooks.** Students discuss what characteristics might classify a historical time period as a "golden age."

2 **Have students share their responses in pairs or as a class.**

3 **Connect the Preview activity to Chapter 18.** Tell students that a "golden age" is a period of great prosperity and achievement. Ancient India experienced a golden age during the Gupta Empire, which ruled India from 320 to 550 C.E. During this time, many innovative ideas in the arts and sciences improved Indian life and left a lasting mark on world civilization. In this chapter, students will learn about the Gupta Empire and the important accomplishments that defined this period as a "golden age."

Vocabulary Development

1 **Introduce the Key Content Terms.** Have students locate the Key Content Terms for the chapter in their Interactive Student Notebooks. These are important terms that will help them understand the main ideas of the chapter. Ask volunteers to identify any familiar terms and how they might be used in a sentence.

2 **Have students complete a Vocabulary Development handout.** Give each student a copy of the Vocabulary Development handout of your choice from the Reading Toolkit at the back of the Lesson Masters. These handouts provide extra Key Content Term practice and support, depending on your students' needs. Review the completed handout by asking volunteers to share one answer for each term.

Reading

1 **Introduce the Essential Question and have students read Section 18.1.** Have students identify the Essential Question on the first page of the chapter: *Why is the period during the Gupta Empire known as a "golden age"?* Then have students read Section 18.1. Afterward, have students respond to these questions:

- What is a "golden age"?

- What conditions allow for a "golden age" to develop?

- Why might the period during the Gupta Empire be known as a "golden age"?

2 **Have students complete the Reading Notes for Chapter 18.** Assign Sections 18.2 to 18.9 during the activity, as indicated in the procedures for the Writing for Understanding activity. Remind students to use the Key Content Terms where appropriate as they complete their Reading Notes.

Writing for Understanding

1 **Arrange the classroom.** Use desks to set up the station clusters as shown in the diagram. Post the corresponding copies of *Station Directions 18A–18G: Travel Sites* on the wall above the desks. Use sticky notes to create flaps that cover each square showing the achievement and section number on the Station Directions. Place at least two copies of the Student Edition, *History Alive! The Ancient World*, at each station. (**Note:** The station arrangement reflects the location of key sites in the Gupta Empire. You may want to use masking tape to create a compass rose on the floor in the center of the classroom. Also consider putting the materials for Station F beneath the desks at the station to simulate entering a cave.)

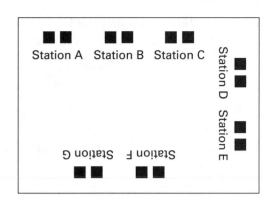

2 **Introduce the activity.** Tell students that they are going to assume the role of writers traveling through ancient India during the time of the Gupta Empire. They will "tour" different sites located throughout the empire to learn about the important achievements and discoveries that were made during this "golden age." They will then use their notes to write and illustrate a palm-leaf book about their travels.

3 **Have students complete the Reading Notes for Section 18.2.** Tell students that this section provides background information about the Gupta Empire. Have students read Section 18.2 and complete the corresponding Reading Notes in their Interactive Student Notebooks. Use Guide to Reading Notes 18 to review students' responses.

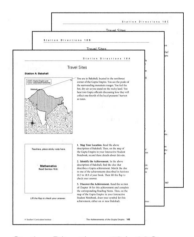

Station Directions 18A–18G

4 **Review steps for the tour.** Tell students that there are seven stations set up around the classroom. Each station represents a different site in the Gupta Empire. At each station, students will find instructions to do the following:

- Read a vivid description of the site and record details on the map of the Gupta Empire in their Interactive Student Notebooks.

- Find a clue in the description to help them identify the achievement they will discover at this site.

- Check their guesses for the achievement by lifting the flap on the Station Directions.

- Read the appropriate section of Chapter 18 for that achievement and complete the corresponding Reading Notes.

- Draw their achievement symbol, either on or near the site, on the map of the Gupta Empire in their Interactive Student Notebooks.

5   **Place students in pairs and conduct the tour.** Assign one or two pairs to each of the seven stations. Remind students to follow the steps at each station. Monitor pairs as they work, and use Guide to Reading Notes 18 to provide feedback.

6   **Introduce the palm-leaf book.** Tell students that they will now use their notes to write and illustrate palm-leaf books about the achievements of the Gupta Empire. Archaeologists have discovered palm-leaf books from India that date from around 550 C.E., near the end of the Gupta Empire. Ancient bookmakers carved writing into the leaf or bark and then rubbed ink on the carving to fill it in. Painters added illustrations. The books were held together by a string that ran through a hole in the center of the pages. To read palm-leaf books, people placed them on a flat surface and turned each page from top to bottom.

Information Master 18

7   **Review the directions for creating palm-leaf books.** Project a transparency of *Information Master 18: Creating a Palm-Leaf Book.* Review the instructions for creating a palm-leaf book, and answer any questions students may have.

8   **Have students write and illustrate their palm-leaf books.** Give students adequate time to draft, edit, and revise their palm-leaf books. Distribute copies of *Student Handout 18: Palm-Leaf Book Page* or give students paper on which to create their final palm-leaf books. Students will need at least six pages for their books. Afterward, have students punch or cut holes in the middle of the book and use string to join the pages together, as shown in the illustration on Information Master 18.

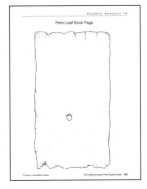

Student Handout 18

Processing (optional)

1   **Understand the intent of the Processing activity.** The palm-leaf book writing assignment serves as this chapter's Processing activity. Should you choose not to have students do the writing assignment, you might use the optional Processing activity in the Interactive Student Notebook.

2   **Have students complete the Processing activity.**

3   **Have students share their answers with their partners or with the class.**

Quicker Coverage

Skip the Travel Site Tour Rather than have students "tour" India to learn about the achievements, have them use the directions in the Interactive Student Notebook to complete the Reading Notes. When students write their palm-leaf books, eliminate the requirement to provide information about the places they visited.

Skip the Palm-Leaf Book After students complete their "tour" of India to learn about the achievements, wrap up the activity with a brief discussion. Use these questions:

- What was the most interesting place you visited?
- Which achievement or discovery did you find most impressive and why?
- How did the Guptas support and encourage these achievements?
- Why is the period during the Gutpa Empire known as a "golden age"?

Substitute an Essay for the Palm-Leaf Book In place of the palm-leaf book, have students write a multiparagraph essay that answers the Essential Question: *Why is the period during the Gupta Empire known as a "golden age"?* Use the guidelines on Information Master 18 to frame the essay. Students should include an introduction, two or three body paragraphs, and a conclusion.

Deeper Coverage

Add Stations Add stations to the "tour" of India. For example, add a station about architecture, such as the Mahabodhi Temple Complex located in Bodh Gaya, and a station about trade, located in Taxila in present-day Pakistan. Use the map in Section 17.2 in Chapter 17 of *History Alive! The Ancient World* or have students research the places to add the new locations to the map of the Gupta Empire. Rather than provide written information at these stations, have students use computers to visit selected Web sites to learn about these places and achievements. One useful site is the UNESCO World Heritage Centre Web site, where students can read more about each of these locations and their achievements, view recent news, and take a panoramic tour.

Conduct a Peer Read-Around Place students in small groups of three or four. Allow group members to exchange and read each other's palm-leaf books. Have students provide feedback to each other on what they liked best about the writing and illustrations and what one thing they learned from reading the palm-leaf books.

Assessment

Mastering the Content

1. C	5. B	9. D	13. A
2. B	6. D	10. A	14. D
3. D	7. C	11. B	15. C
4. A	8. B	12. D	16. C

Applying Social Studies Skills

17. Answers will vary. Possible answers: rippling waves; something that looks like a crocodile or a fish

18. Hinduism. Answers will vary. Possible answers: The Hindu religion had many deities; each god has different powers; this elaborate work of art shows one of many deities.

19. Answers will vary. Possible answers: The Buddha looks very calm and peaceful; his expression and posture suggest that he has reached enlightenment.

Exploring the Essential Question

20. Answers should include all of the elements requested in the prompt.

Scoring Rubric

Score	Description
3	Student completes a poster or booklet text that complies with all three bulleted points. Poster or text is clearly stated, persuasive, supported by details, and demonstrates command of standard English conventions. (**Note:** If you did not emphasize place names when teaching the chapter, you may choose to accept generic descriptions such as "a cave with cave paintings" instead of a specific place name.)
2	Student responds to most or all parts of the task, but poster or text may lack details or not be clearly stated.
1	Student responds to at least one part of the task. Poster or text may contain factual and/or grammatical errors and may lack details.
0	Response does not match the task or is incorrect.

English Language Learners

Apply a "Golden Age" to Students Give additional scaffolding for the Preview activity. Before students complete the prompts in the Interactive Student Notebook, ask them to reflect on a time of achievement in their own lives. Have students share their responses. Afterward, have students identify some common characteristics in their examples. Then provide a simple definition of a "golden age" and have students complete the Preview activity.

Highlight the Station Directions Underline or highlight key directional words to help students focus on the tasks required on Station Directions 18A–18G. Such words might include *read, record, find, match,* and *draw*. Also consider circling or highlighting (in a different color) the clue in the description to help students match the location to the achievement.

Utilize Technology As students complete their palm-leaf pages, encourage them to draft their writing, using a word processing program that checks grammar, spelling, and punctuation. Students can print out their edited paragraphs and paste them onto their palm-leaf book pages.

Learners Reading and Writing Below Grade Level

Share Reading Notes When students visit stations in their "tour" of ancient India, have partners work together to complete one set of Reading Notes for Sections 18.3–18.9. Then make a copy so that each partner has an individual set of Reading Notes to use for writing the palm-leaf book.

Learners with Special Education Needs

Model the Process for Stations Before pairs visit the stations to learn about the achievements, model the process. Choose one station and make a transparency of the Station Directions. Project the image and guide the class in completing the steps.

Eliminate Stations Consider reducing the number of stations—from seven to three or four—that students visit during the "tour" of ancient India. Have students choose the achievement in Chapter 18 they want to learn about, and have them visit the corresponding station. You may wish to have students complete the Reading Notes for the remaining achievements by following the directions in the Interactive Student Notebook. Alternatively, consider reducing the number of palm-leaf pages about achievements from three to two.

Advanced Learners

Add Primary Sources Include primary sources at each of the seven stations students visit on their "tour" of ancient India. At stations, post photographs, artwork, excerpts of literature, poetry, documents, and other resources for students to consider as they determine why this time period was a "golden age." Encourage students to use these primary sources to support their writing in the palm-leaf books. Some examples of primary sources might include a photograph of the ruins at Nalanda, a translated excerpt from the *Bhagavad Gita*, an image from the murals or carvings at the Ajanta or Ellora caves, or a photograph of the iron pillar at Meharauli.

Research the End of the Gupta Empire Have students work in pairs or small groups to learn about the end of the Gupta Empire. They should write or present a summary of the historical events, and explain what they think caused the empire to fall.

Enrichment Resources

Find out more about the Gupta Empire by exploring the following Enrichment Resources for *History Alive! The Ancient World* at www.teachtci.com.

Enrichment Readings These in-depth readings encourage students to explore selected topics related to the chapter. You may also find readings that relate the chapter's content directly to your state's curriculum.

Internet Connections The recommended Web sites provide useful and engaging content that reinforces skills development and mastery of subjects within the chapter.

Literature Recommendations

The following books offer opportunities to extend the content in this chapter.

Ancient India by Virginia Shomp (New York: Franklin Watts, 2005)

India's Gupta Dynasty by Kathryn Hinds (New York: Benchmark Books, 1996)

India: The Culture by Bobbie Kalman, Margaret Hoogeveen, and Christine Arthurs (Toronto: Crabtree Publishing Company, 2009)

Section 18.2

1. Check students' maps against the map in Section 18.2 of *History Alive! The Ancient World.*

2. The Gupta Empire began under Chandragupta I. The Guptas united the kingdoms in northern India by conquering them in war. They also formed alliances by arranging marriages between members of their family and the sons and daughters of other rulers.

3.

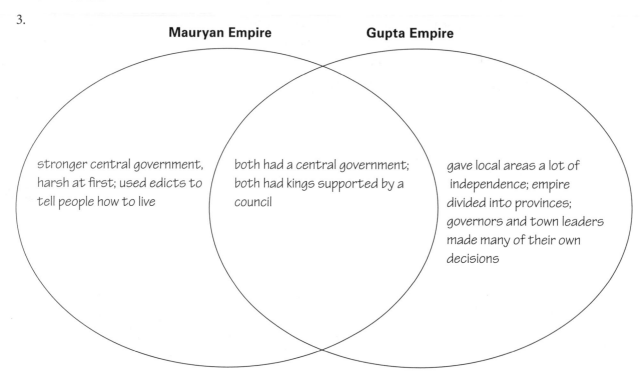

Mauryan Empire

stronger central government, harsh at first; used edicts to tell people how to live

both had a central government; both had kings supported by a council

Gupta Empire

gave local areas a lot of independence; empire divided into provinces; governors and town leaders made many of their own decisions

Sections 18.3–18.9

Use the completed matrix to check students' responses. Responses will vary.
The following are possible responses.

Section	Achievement and Symbol	Details About the Achievement	How does this achievement show that the Gupta Empire was a "golden age"?
18.3	Universities Symbols will vary.	• The Guptas built colleges and universities throughout the empire. Some were Hindu and some were Buddhist. • Only males and teachers' daughters could attend. • Universities trained students in religion, mathematics, astronomy, chemistry, Sanskrit, sculpture, painting, music, dancing, logic, grammar, and medicine.	Possible response: Universities promoted learning, which encouraged people's ability to make discoveries and advancements in other achievements.
18.4	Literature Symbols will vary.	• Gutpa writers wrote poetry, fables, folktales, and plays. • Another form of writing was Sanskrit literature. Texts that had been passed down orally for generations were written down. • One example is the *Bhagavad Gita,* which is a poem about Prince Arjuna and Krishna.	Possible response: Many types of writing flourished during this period, which shows that literature was important. Not only did writers have the time and support to be creative, but they were also recording beloved ancient texts.
18.5	Painting Symbols will vary.	• Painting was an important part of life for noble families. • Subjects included gods, religious stories, and rich or royal families and their lives of luxury. • The most famous Gupta paintings are the Ajanta cave murals. Various scenes show Buddhist values, royal subjects, and images in nature.	Possible response: During this time of peace and prosperity, artists and nobles had the time to create great artworks. The scenes in paintings reflected the prosperity of the times.

Section	Achievement and Symbol	Details About the Achievement	How does this achievement show that the Gupta Empire was a "golden age"?
18.6	Sculpture Symbols will vary.	• Statues were made out of bronze, wood, stone, and terra-cotta. • Buddha, Hindu gods, and famous people were subjects of sculptures. • Sculptures stood on their own foundations or were carved into the walls of caves and temples.	Possible response: Sculptures were skillfully made out of many types of materials, which shows that artists had the time, resources, and support to create these works.
18.7	Metalwork Symbols will vary.	• Metalworkers were famous for their engravings on gold and copper coins, often honoring Gupta rulers. • An iron pillar at Meharauli stands 25 feet tall and weighs about 13,000 pounds. The iron is nearly rust free. • No one knows how Gupta ironworkers acquired such advanced metalworking skills.	Possible response: Coins made by metalworkers often highlighted the wealth and achievements of Gupta rulers; ironworkers were able to develop highly advanced skills.
18.8	Mathematics Symbols will vary.	• The decimal system was developed and zero was first treated as a number during the Gupta period. • The famous mathematician Aryabhata used his knowledge of astronomy to determine the number of days in a year, calculate the size of Earth, propose that planets were spheres, and suggest that Earth spins on an axis. • Gupta builders used mathematics to design complex structures.	Possible response: Many advances were made in mathematics, which shows that the empire placed a high value on knowledge.
18.9	Roads Symbols will vary.	• Roads were built with care and precision. Roads of hard-packed dirt were smooth and level. • Roads built a few feet off the ground had ditches alongside to prevent flooding. • Roads promoted trade within the empire and with bordering countries like China.	Possible response: This time of peace and prosperity allowed the Guptas to use resources to build roads not for wars of conquest but for connecting cities and promoting trade.

Ancient India

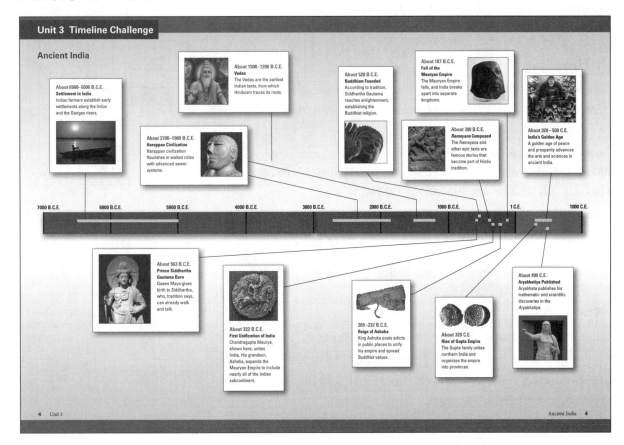

About 6500–5000 B.C.E.
Settlement in India
Indian farmers establish early settlements along the Indus and the Ganges rivers.

About 1500–1200 B.C.E.
Vedas
The Vedas are the earliest Indian texts, from which Hinduism traces its roots.

About 528 B.C.E.
Buddhism Founded
According to tradition, Siddhartha Gautama reaches enlightenment, establishing the Buddhist religion.

About 187 B.C.E.
Fall of the Mauryan Empire
The Mauryan Empire falls, and India breaks apart into separate kingdoms.

About 2700–1900 B.C.E.
Harappan Civilization
Harappan civilization flourishes in walled cities with advanced sewer systems.

About 300 B.C.E.
Ramayana **Composed**
The Ramayana and other epic texts are famous stories that become part of Hindu tradition.

About 320–550 C.E.
India's Golden Age
A golden age of peace and prosperity advances the arts and sciences in ancient India.

7000 B.C.E.   6000 B.C.E.   5000 B.C.E.   4000 B.C.E.   3000 B.C.E.   2000 B.C.E.   1000 B.C.E.   1 C.E.   1000 C.E.

About 563 B.C.E.
Prince Siddhartha Gautama Born
Queen Maya gives birth to Siddhartha, who, tradition says, can already walk and talk.

About 322 B.C.E.
First Unification of India
Chandragupta Maurya, shown here, unites India. His grandson, Ashoka, expands the Mauryan Empire to include nearly all of the Indian subcontinent.

269–232 B.C.E.
Reign of Ashoka
King Ashoka posts edicts in public places to unify his empire and spread Buddhist values.

About 320 C.E.
Rise of Gupta Empire
The Gupta family unites northern India and organizes the empire into provinces.

About 499 C.E.
Aryabhatiya Published
Aryabhata publishes his mathematic and scientific discoveries in the *Aryabhatiya*.

Overview

This Timeline Challenge helps students review the main events and ideas of this unit while providing practice in reading and interpreting timelines. You can vary and expand the activity according to students' needs and the amount of time available.

Basic Procedure

1 **Introduce the timeline in the Student Edition.** Direct students to the Ancient India Timeline at the end of Unit 3 in the Student Edition. You may wish to have students read aloud and discuss the timeline entries.

2 **Introduce the Timeline Challenge in the Interactive Student Notebook.** Direct students to the Unit 3 Timeline Challenge in their notebooks. Point out the two types of questions, "Timeline Skills" and "Critical Thinking," and model how to answer each type.

3 **Have students complete the Timeline Challenge.** Monitor students as they work. Use the Guide to Unit 3 Timeline Challenge to check their answers. You may wish to project a transparency of the Timeline Challenge as you work through the questions with the class and conduct a discussion of the "Critical Thinking questions."

4 **Complete the KWL chart.** Return to the KWL chart created at the beginning of the unit, and ask students to list the key information they have learned.

Classroom Timeline

1 **Prepare the Timeline Challenge Cards.** Copy and cut the cards from *Student Handout TC3: Unit 3 Timeline Challenge Cards.* You may wish to laminate the cards for future use.

2 **Create a timeline on a classroom wall.** On an empty wall or a large bulletin board, make a timeline with masking tape or colored paper. Mark off the time intervals in advance, or ask students to do so in class.

3 **Have students place the Timeline Challenge Cards.** Distribute cards to individual students or pairs and have them tape the cards to the timeline in the correct locations. Call on students to provide more information on the timeline topics, to review main events and issues.

Student Handout TC3

Internet Research

1 **Review students' suggestions for additional timeline entries.** Have students share their answers to the last question of the Timeline Challenge.

2 **Have students conduct Internet research.** Ask students to choose and research one of their suggested events.

3 **Have students create additional Timeline Challenge Cards.** Direct students to research an appropriate image for their cards and then use the computer to create an illustrated card, complete with timeline entry.

Timeline Skills

Score 1 point for each correct answer.

1. People first settled India from about 6500 to 5000 B.C.E. They settled along the Indus and the Ganges rivers.

2. India was first united nearly 1,600 years after the decline of Harappan civilization.

3. Harappan civilization had walled cities with advanced sewer systems.

4. Hinduism traces its early roots to the Vedas.

5. According to Buddhist tradition, Siddhartha was about 35 years old when he became the Buddha and established Buddhism.

6. The Mauryan Empire was the first to unite India.

7. India's golden age began about 320 C.E., during the Gupta Empire.

8. There were about 500 years between the fall of the Mauryan Empire and the rise of the Gupta Empire. During this time, separate kingdoms in India fought each other for land and power.

9. It would have been impossible for Ashoka to spread Buddhist values before about 528 B.C.E. because Buddhism didn't exist. About 528 B.C.E., the Buddha reached enlightenment and began teaching, but Ashoka's reign did not begin until about 269 B.C.E.

10. The timeline explains that the *Aryabhatiya* was published about 499 C.E. in India's golden age. During this period, many advances in learning were made, like the mathematical ones in Aryabhata's book.

Critical Thinking

Score 1 to 3 points for each answer, depending on the thoroughness of the response.

11. It took about 35 years for Siddhartha to become the Buddha because his search for a path to enlightenment took that long. As a child, and even as a young man, Siddhartha was kept sheltered from the world, for the king did not want his son to see suffering. The king had been told that his son would become a Buddha if Siddhartha saw suffering. After Siddhartha saw suffering at age 29, he became an ascetic. He tried different ways to reach enlightenment until he found a middle way.

12. One action that King Ashoka took was to fight wars of conquest to expand the empire. The Mauryan Empire occupied more land than before. After Ashoka rejected violence, he tried to spread Buddhist values. He posted edicts in public places throughout the empire so many people could see them and follow them. Through these edicts, King Ashoka helped unify the people of India and spread Buddhism.

13. a. The Guptas ruled by dividing their empire into provinces. This allowed local leaders to have some control and independence. The peace and stability of the Gupta Empire encouraged advances in the arts and sciences.
b. Answers will vary. Possible answer: One significant Gupta achievement was to promote learning. The Guptas built colleges and universities throughout the empire to instruct students in philosophy, mathematics, science, writing, medicine, and the arts.

14. Answers will vary. Students must explain why the events they chose merit inclusion.

Using Scores to Inform Instruction

Timeline Skills A score of 7 out of 10 indicates that students understand most of the key events of this unit.

Critical Thinking A score of 8 out of 12 indicates that students are able to think critically about most of the key issues of this unit.

If students score below these levels, consider reviewing timeline and critical thinking skills.

UNIT **4**

Ancient China

Geography Challenge

Chapter 19: Geography and the Early Settlement of China
How did geography affect life in ancient China?
Problem Solving Groupwork

Chapter 20: The Shang Dynasty
What do Shang artifacts reveal about this civilization?
Social Studies Skill Builder

Chapter 21: Three Chinese Philosophies
How did Confucianism, Daoism, and Legalism influence political rule in ancient China?
Experiential Exercise

Chapter 22: The First Emperor of China
Was the Emperor of Qin an effective leader?
Visual Discovery

Chapter 23: The Han Dynasty
In what ways did the Han dynasty improve government and daily life in China?
Social Studies Skill Builder

Chapter 24: The Silk Road
How did the Silk Road promote an exhange of goods and ideas?
Experiential Exercise

Timeline Challenge

Ancient China

Overview

This activity introduces the geographic information essential to Unit 4. Students read and interpret maps to learn about the ways in which geography affected the development of ancient China. Students annotate an outline map, answer questions in their Interactive Student Notebooks, and then discuss critical thinking questions. Students' comprehension of content and proficiency in map-reading and higher-order thinking skills will help you gauge their readiness for the unit. The pages that follow include a completed map, answers to questions, a scoring guide to inform your teaching, and suggestions for modifications to meet specific student needs.

Essential Geographic Understandings

1. Location of ancient China

2. Key physical features: Huang He (Yellow River), Chang Jiang (Yangtze River), Himalayas, Kunlun Mountains, Taklimakan Desert, Gobi Desert, Plateau of Tibet

3. Location of the Shang, Zhou, Qin, and Han dynasties

4. Impact of physical geography on the settlement of ancient China

Procedures

1 **Introduce the unit.** Tell students they will learn about civilizations of ancient China, including the rise of dynasties, and the developments of trade with western cultures.

2 **Create a KWL chart.** Ask students to identify what they already know about ancient China and what they want to learn. Use their responses to gauge how much additional background information they will need as you progress through the unit. Students will return to the KWL chart at the end of the unit and add the key information they have learned.

3 **Have students read Unit 4 "Setting the Stage" in the Student Edition.**

4 **Have students complete the Geography Challenge.** Monitor students as they work. Use the guide on the next two pages to check their answers. You may wish to project the map from the Interactive Student Notebook and have students annotate it as the class works through the map-reading questions. Make sure students have grasped Essential Geographic Understandings 1 to 3.

5 **Discuss the "Critical Thinking" questions.** Help students understand the geographic relationships described in Essential Geographic Understanding 4.

Ancient China

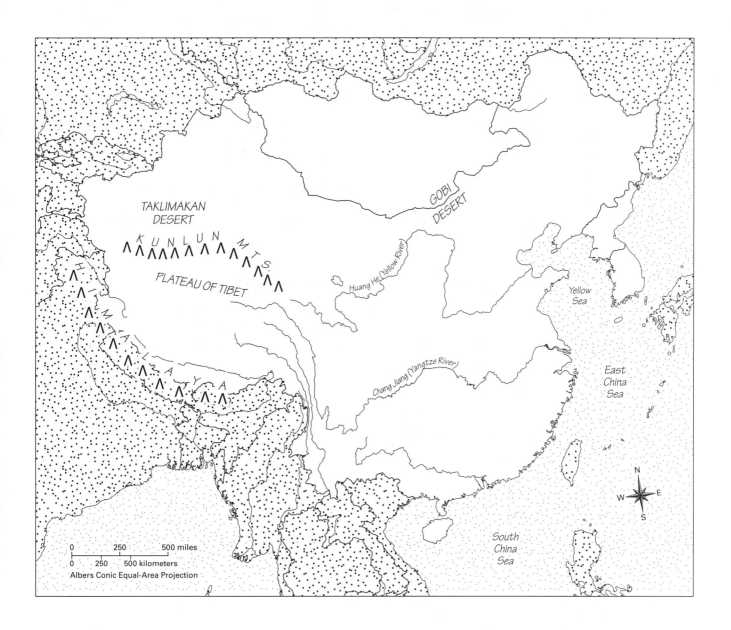

Geography Skills

Score 1 point for each correct answer. Use the map on the previous page to check labeling.

1. Students should label the Huang He (Yellow River) and the Chang Jiang (Yangtze River).

2. The Plateau of Tibet is located between the Himalayas and the Kunlun Mountains. Students should label these mountain ranges and the Plateau of Tibet.

3. Students should label the Taklimakan and the Gobi deserts.

4. Students should label the Yellow Sea, the East China Sea, and the South China Sea.

5. These seas may have isolated ancient China by forming a natural barrier that prevented contact with outsiders. As Chinese technology and society became more advanced, the seas would have provided a highway to trade with other countries.

6. The Han empire controlled the largest area.

7. The Han empire controlled territories that are not part of present-day China. Students may recognize that Vietnam and parts of North Korea and South Korea are present-day countries that were part of the Han empire in ancient times.

8. Geographical features shared by all four ancient empires include a coastline, rivers, and low elevation.

Critical Thinking

Questions may have more than one correct answer. Score 1 to 3 points for each reasonable answer, depending on the strength of students' geographic reasoning.

9. The majority ethnic group in China today may believe that they are descendants of the people who controlled the largest area of ancient China.

10. Students should choose a location that has flat land, which is easier to build on; access to fresh water for drinking and producing food; and a port to facilitate trade with other nations.

11. The territory controlled by each new empire may have grown larger because of an increase in population, causing people to move into areas that were less settled. Also, various rulers may have used force or military might to add new territory.

Using Scores to Inform Instruction

Geography Skills A score of 6 out of 8 or better indicates that students have acquired sufficient geographic information to proceed with the unit.

Critical Thinking A score of 6 out of 9 or better indicates that students are beginning to understand the relationships between physical geography and the different ways in which people live.

Modifying Instruction

ELL or Learners with Special Education Needs Consider focusing on map-reading questions or limiting the number of "Critical Thinking" questions.

Students with Weak Map or Critical Thinking Skills Assign appropriate pages from the Social Studies Skills Toolkit in the back of the Lesson Masters.

Geography and the Early Settlement of China

How did geography affect life in ancient China?

Overview

In a Problem Solving Groupwork activity, students create a relief map and a geographic poster of China's five regions and support hypotheses about the influence of geography on settlement and ways of life in ancient China. (**Note:** Pinyin spellings are used throughout this unit in accordance with the decision by the Library of Congress to join pinyin syllables.)

Objectives

In the course of reading this chapter and participating in the classroom activity, students will

Social Studies

- describe the geography of China's regions and analyze how each region's physical features, climate, and vegetation affect daily life.
- create a relief map.
- record, analyze, and present geographic data.
- locate the Huang He Valley and explain why Chinese civilization originated there.
- explain how China's geographic features isolated it from the rest of the world.

Language Arts

- analyze text with a compare-and-contrast organizational pattern.
- offer persuasive evidence to support a hypothesis.

Social Studies Vocabulary

Key Content Terms region, climate, oasis, North China Plain, tributary

Academic Vocabulary contrast, communicate, evaporate, enrich, isolate

Materials

*History Alive!
The Ancient World*

Interactive Student Notebooks

Visual 19

Lesson Masters

- Student Handouts 19A–19C (1 each per group of 4)
- Vocabulary Development handout (1 per student, on colored paper)

scissors

tape

glue

colored pencils or markers

poster board (optional; 1 sheet per group)

Activity	Suggested Time	Materials
Preview	15 minutes	• Interactive Student Notebooks
Vocabulary Development	30–40 minutes	• *History Alive! The Ancient World* • Interactive Student Notebooks • Vocabulary Development handout

Problem Solving Groupwork	120–150 minutes
	(3 regular periods)
	(2 block periods)
		• *History Alive! The Ancient World*
		• Interactive Student Notebooks
		• Student Handouts 19A–19C
		  (1 each per group of 4)
		• scissors
		• tape
		• glue
		• colored pencils or markers
		• poster board
		  (optional; 1 sheet per group)

Processing	20 minutes	• Interactive Student Notebooks • Visual 19
Assessment	40 minutes	• Chapter 19 Assessment

Preview

1 **Discuss the influence of geography on human settlement.** Tell students that physical features, climate, and vegetation influence human communities. For example, if a community is near the ocean (a physical feature), a major industry in the community might be fishing. If a community has hot summers (climate), houses often have air-conditioning. If a community has forests (vegetation), it may have a lumber industry. You may want to list each geographic aspect and its example on the board. See if students have any questions. Then have them complete the Preview activity.

2 **Have students share their answers in pairs or as a class.**

3 **Explain the connection between the Preview activity and Chapter 19.** Tell students that just as geography influences their lives, the geography of ancient China influenced the history of that country. In this chapter, students will learn about five important regions of China—the Tibet-Qinghai Plateau, the Northwestern Deserts, the Northeastern Plain, the North China Plain, and the Chang Jiang Basins—and how the geography of these regions affected the early settlement of China.

Vocabulary Development

1 **Introduce the Key Content Terms.** Have students locate the Key Content Terms for the chapter in their Interactive Student Notebooks. These are important terms that will help them understand the main ideas of the chapter. Ask volunteers to identify any familiar terms and how they might be used in a sentence.

2 **Have students complete a Vocabulary Development handout.** Give each student a copy of the Vocabulary Development handout of your choice from the Reading Toolkit at the back of the Lesson Masters. These handouts provide extra Key Content Term practice and support, depending on your students' needs. Review the completed handout by asking volunteers to share one answer for each term.

Reading

1 **Introduce the Essential Question and have students read Section 19.1.** Have students identify the Essential Question on the first page of the chapter: *How did geography affect life in ancient China?* Then have students read Section 19.1. Afterward, have students use information from Section 19.1 and from the chapter opener image to propose some possible answers to the Essential Question.

2 **Have students complete the Reading Notes for Chapter 19.** Assign Sections 19.2 to 19.10 during the activity, as indicated in the procedures for the Problem Solving Groupwork activity. Remind students to use the Key Content Terms where appropriate as they complete their Reading Notes.

Vocabulary Development: Shades of Meaning

Help students with Academic Vocabulary by exploring shades of meaning. For example, for *isolated*, present related meanings such as *lonely, apart, alone, remote,* and *separated*. Talk about how the word *isolated* is often applied to places; discuss how *remote* carries the same connotations as *isolated* does but also suggests somewhere far away. Also, discuss how things that are apart or separated are not necessarily isolated.

Problem Solving Groupwork

1 **Introduce the activity.** Tell students that China is a land of many geographic regions. There are towering mountains, scorching deserts, flat plains, flooding rivers, and narrow valleys. Each region has significantly affected China's history. In this activity, groups will create a relief map and a geographic poster of China's five regions. In their groups, students will share information about China's geography, and then analyze how geography affected settlement and ways of life in ancient China.

2 **Have students read Section 19.2 and complete the corresponding Reading Notes in their Interactive Student Notebooks.** Tell students that this section will present an overview of Chinese geography. Use Guide to Reading Notes 19 to review the answers as a class.

3 **Arrange students in groups of four and distribute materials.** You might prepare a transparency that shows group assignments and seating arrangements. Give each group the following materials:

   • one copy of *Student Handout 19A: Relief Map of China*

   • one copy of *Student Handout 19B: Geographic Data Sheets*

   • one copy of *Student Handout 19C: Steps for Creating a Geographic Poster of China*

   • scissors, colored pencils or markers, glue, tape

   • a sheet of poster board (optional)

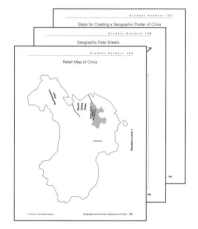

Student Handouts 19A–19C

4 **Review the steps for creating a geographic poster of China.** Review the roles in Step 1 of Student Handout 19C: Cartographer, Data Specialist, Production Supervisor, and Educational Coordinator. Note that a cartographer is someone who makes maps. Explain that each student will be responsible for reading one or two sections of Chapter 19 in *History Alive! The Ancient World* and completing a geographic data sheet for his or her region(s). Then review Steps 2 to 5, noting which student is to lead the group through each step.

5 **Monitor groups as they create their posters and share information about China's geography.** Allow students adequate time—at least one class period—to complete their posters. Check their work and initial Student Handout 19C as they complete each of the five steps. During Step 5, make sure students complete their Reading Notes for Sections 19.3 to 19.7 as group members share geographic data and describe each region.

6 **Explain the procedures for Reading Notes 19.8 to 19.10.** Have students turn to Sections 19.8 to 19.10 in their Interactive Student Notebooks. Explain that they will use their completed geographic posters to analyze the effect of geography on China. Remind students that a hypothesis is a statement about something that has not yet been proved either true or false. Explain that for each section, students should do the following:

- Complete Part 1 as a group, using only their poster for reference. Emphasize that for this portion of the Reading Notes, they are practicing their interpretation skills and will not be penalized for any incorrect responses. (**Note**: You may want to have students close their books during this part.)

- After students have come up with evidence to support the hypothesis, groups may complete Part 2. They will read the indicated section, add any additional information, correct errors in Part 1, and then complete the map at the bottom of the page. (**Note:** For Section 19.8, students will answer an additional question using information from the reading.)

7 **Have students complete their Reading Notes for Section 19.8, and then hold a class discussion.** Ask,

- Using only your poster, what reasons did you give to support this hypothesis: *Most early people settled on the North China Plain because of its geography*?

- In the reading, what information did you find to answer the question: *How were the first people to live in China affected by geography?*

- Ruins of early farming communities have also been found in the Chang Jiang Basins. Why do you think fewer people would have settled there?

8 **Have students complete their Reading Notes for Section 19.9, and then hold a class discussion.** Ask,

- Using only your poster, give reasons why you supported this hypothesis: *China was isolated from other civilizations because of its geography.*

- What additional reasons did you find in the reading?

- Do you think China's isolation helped or hurt the country? Why?

9 **Have students complete their Reading Notes for Section 19.10, and then hold a class discussion.** Ask,

- Using only your poster, what reasons did you give to support this hypothesis: *Because of geography, several ways of life developed in China*?

- What additional reasons did you find in the reading?

- Would the differences in ways of life make China stronger or weaker? Why?

Processing

1 **Introduce the Processing activity.** Project *Visual 19: Chinese Scroll.* Explain that the Chinese often drew or painted scenes on scrolls that illustrated the landscape of a place and the way of life for people living there. This is part of a scroll that shows peasants in the North China Plain trying to control the Huang He.

Visual 19

2 **Have students complete the Processing activity.** Explain to students that they will choose two geographic regions and create a scroll illustrating the geography and way of life in each region they chose. They will then write a paragraph to compare and contrast their two regions. Afterward, have students share their answers in pairs or as a class.

Quicker Coverage

Eliminate the Geographic Poster Rather than have students fill out geographic data and create a poster of China's regions in the Problem Solving Groupwork activity, do the following:

- Divide students into groups of five and assign each student to read one of the five sections from 19.3 to 19.7.

- Have each student complete the Reading Notes for his or her assigned section.

- When all group members are done, have them take turns describing the climate, natural vegetation, and important physical features of their assigned region, using their Reading Notes and the image in their books.

- Then have students complete their Reading Notes for Sections 19.8 to 19.10, using the procedures in Steps 6 to 9 of the Problem Solving Groupwork activity.

Deeper Coverage

Create a 3-D Relief Map Provide or have students bring in corrugated cardboard boxes. As groups work on Step 2 of Student Handout 19C, suggest that they cut small pieces of cardboard and glue them between each Elevation Level cutout. This will create a more realistic relief map and allow students to better visualize the terrain of China's regions.

Compare Local Geography with China's Geography Challenge students to decide which one of China's five regions is the most similar to the geography of their local area, and which one is the most different. Have students first discuss in pairs and then present evidence to the class to support their decisions. If time permits, have students visually illustrate how Chinese geography is similar to and different from their local area's geography.

Assessment

Mastering the Content

1. B	5. C	9. D	13. B
2. B	6. C	10. B	14. D
3. A	7. D	11. C	15. C
4. A	8. D	12. D	16. A

Applying Social Studies Skills

17. Tibet-Qinghai Plateau

18. Possible answers: Himalayas; Tibet-Qinghai Plateau; Taklimakan Desert; Turfan Depression; Gobi Desert, Yellow Sea, East China Sea, South China Sea (any three)

19. Answers will vary. Possible answer: The Huang He and the Chang Jiang ran west to east, allowing people and goods to travel by boat.

Exploring the Essential Question

20. Answers should include all of the elements requested in the prompt.

Scoring Rubric

Score	Description
3	Student completes all three parts of the task. Descriptions and final-arguments are clearly stated, supported by details, and demonstrate command of standard English conventions.
2	Student responds to most or all parts of the task, but descriptions and arguments may lack details or not be clearly stated.
1	Student responds to at least one part of the task. Descriptions and arguments may contain factual and/or grammatical errors and may lack details.
0	Response does not match the task or is incorrect.

English Language Learners

Add Visuals to the Preview Activity Find, or have students bring in, pictures of the geography of your local community. Display these images to help students identify and analyze the physical features, climate, and vegetation of your community.

Have Pairs Share a Role Pair up selected students for the Problem Solving Groupwork activity. They can work together to complete the following aspects of this activity:

- completing the geographic data sheets (Student Handout 19B)
- sharing information about their assigned region
- completing Reading Notes 19.8 to 19.10

Also, before class begins, consider reviewing the roles on Student Handout 19C with students, allowing them to choose the role that they think best matches their learning abilities and strengths.

Learners Reading and Writing Below Grade Level

Break Up Section 19.10 This section discusses ways of life for all five regions of China. Have students read only the introductory paragraph of Section 19.10. Tell students that this section will explain how geography affected life in each Chinese region, starting with the Tibet-Qinghai Plateau. To review with students what Tibet looks like, have them turn to the image in Section 19.3. Then have students read the two paragraphs about life in Tibet in Section 19.10 and complete the box in their Reading Notes that corresponds to this region. Repeat this process for the remaining regions.

Support the Processing Activity To help structure the paragraph portion of the Processing activity, give students the following partial sentences: *"The Chinese regions of _____ and _____ are similar to and different from each other. Two ways they are similar are . . . Two ways they are different are . . ."* Alternatively, rather than assign a compare-and-contrast paragraph, allow students to make a T-chart and list the similarities and differences of their two regions in bulleted form.

Learners with Special Education Needs

Support the Reading Notes Do the following:

- Read Section 19.2 aloud and complete the Reading Notes together.
- For Sections 19.3 to 19.7, use Guide to Reading Notes 19 to give students a Word Bank of adjectives and phrases describing the regions of China.
- For Part 1 of Sections 19.8 to 19.10, provide partial answers from Guide to Reading Notes 19. You might offer sentence starters or omit key words for students to fill in.

Support the Activity Use modifications below as groups use Student Handout 19C:

- During Steps 2 and 3, assign Elevation Level 4 and the Chang Jiang Basins (Section 19.7) to students who may need more time for the activity.
- During Step 5, debrief the geography of each region as a class. Have all students assigned to the Tibet-Qinghai Plateau display their geographic posters. Tell the class to turn to the related section in their books. Help presenters share information about the physical features, climate, and vegetation. Then allow students one minute to complete their Reading Notes. Repeat for the remaining regions.

Advanced Learners

Write a Travel Journal In lieu of the current Processing activity, assess students' understanding of Chinese geography by having them write and illustrate journal entries that describe a "trip" through China. Students should "travel" through at least three different regions of China. For each region, students should describe the physical features, climate, and vegetation they "see," and then explain how geography affects the way of life in that region.

Compare U.S. and Chinese Geography Challenge students to compare and contrast the overall geography of China to that of the United States. Ask, *What physical features, climates, and vegetation do these two nations have in common? How does the geography of China and the United States differ? How did the geography of both nations affect early settlement? How does the geography of both nations affect the way people live?*

Enrichment Resources

Find out more about the geography and early settlement of China by exploring the following Enrichment Resources for *History Alive! The Ancient World* at www.teachtci.com.

Enrichment Readings These in-depth readings encourage students to explore selected topics related to the chapter. You may also find readings that relate the chapter's content directly to your state's curriculum.

Internet Connections The recommended Web sites provide useful and engaging content that reinforces skills development and mastery of subjects within the chapter.

Literature Recommendations

The following books offer opportunities to extend the content in this chapter:

Ancient China by Arthur Cotterell (New York: Dorling Kindersley Publishing, 2005)

China by Hugh Sebag-Montefiore (New York: Dorling Kindersley Children, 2007)

China: People Place Culture History by Alison Bailey, et al (New York: Dorling Kindersley Publishing, 2007)

Section 19.2

Inner China was more attractive to early settlers because its two major regions, the North China Plain and the Chang Jiang Basins, contained rivers and flatter lands more suitable for farming. Outer China had harsh climates and extreme landforms, such as the Himalayas and the Northwestern Deserts.

Sections 19.3–19.7

Answers will vary but may include the following adjectives or phrases:

19.3 The Tibet-Qinghai Plateau: high, cold, large area, rocky, dry, sparse vegetation

19.4 The Northwestern Deserts: extreme temperatures, dangerous, sandy, dry, empty, large area, stony, sparse vegetation

19.5 The Northeastern Plain: grassland, low hills and plains, shallow and deep rivers, varied climates, cold and dry

19.6 The North China Plain: flat, grassland, range of temperatures, yellow silt, muddy river, floods, fertile

19.7 The Chang Jiang Basins: low coastal plains, long river, fertile, warm and wet

Section 19.8

Part 1:

Most early people settled on the North China Plain because of its geography.

Reasons that support this hypothesis will vary but may include these:

1. The Tibet-Qinghai Plateau and Northeastern Plain were too cold and dry for agriculture.

2. The Northwestern Deserts were too dry for agriculture, but the Chang Jiang Basins may have been too wet for farming and covered with rainforests.

3. The North China Plain was ideal because it had water, fertile soil, and a moderate climate.

Part 2:

1. Information about how geography affected the first people to live in China may include: Archaeologists believe that the first inhabitants of China lived in caves in northeastern China 500,000 years ago. Peking or Beijing man used local resources to live; for food these people hunted local animals, gathered plants, and fished. They also may have made tools from natural materials they found.

2. Students should draw in and label the Huang He and color the North China Plain yellow.

Section 19.9

Part 1:

China was isolated from other civilizations because of its geography.

Reasons that support this hypothesis will vary but may include these:

1. The high Tibet-Qinghai Plateau made it difficult to communicate with civilizations to the southwest of China.

2. The dry Gobi and Taklimakan Deserts made it difficult to communicate with civilizations to the northwest of China.

3. Most of the rest of China is bordered by water (but remind students that this will eventually lead to increased contact with other civilizations).

Part 2:

1. Students might add the following information not covered in Part 1: there is only a narrow coastal plain linking the Northeastern Plain to Inner China; the mountains and deserts formed natural barriers that restricted contact.

2. Students should color the Tibet-Qinghai Plateau, the Taklimakan Desert, and the Gobi Desert.

Section 19.10

Part 1:

Because of geography, several ways of life developed in China.

Reasons that support this hypothesis will vary but may include these:

1. In cold and dry areas like the Tibet-Qinghai Plateau and the Northeastern Plain, people needed to wear warm clothing and to raise animals for food.

2. In areas like the North China Plain, with good soil and water for irrigation, people grew crops, raised animals, and settled into permanent towns.

3. In areas like the Chang Jiang Basins, with lots of rain, people could grow rice.

Part 2

1. Students might add the following information not covered in Part 1: the people on the Tibet-Qinghai Plateau moved frequently to find grazing land for their livestock, especially yaks, which not only provided food but also wool and hair to make clothing and shelter; in the Northwestern Deserts, people lived near the oases and built houses of mud; in the Northeastern Plain, nomads raised animals and lived mostly in tents; on the North China Plain, people grew grains, raised animals, and built permanent homes of mud; in the Chang Jiang Basins, people raised pigs and poultry and built permanent shelters.

2. Drawings will vary but should include one type of food, shelter, or economic activity appropriate for each region.

The Shang Dynasty

What do Shang artifacts reveal about this civilization?

Overview

In a Social Studies Skill Builder, students "excavate" a tomb to learn about the government, social structure, religion, writing, art, and technology of the Shang dynasty. (**Note:** Pinyin spellings are used throughout this unit in accordance with the decision by the Library of Congress to join pinyin syllables.)

Objectives

In the course of reading this chapter and participating in the classroom activity, students will

Social Studies

- describe the government, social structure, religion, writing, art, and technology of the Shang dynasty.
- analyze artifacts to draw conclusions about the Shang dynasty.

Language Arts

- justify an argument with relevant evidence.

Social Studies Vocabulary

Key Content Terms Anyang, Shang dynasty, clan, bronze, ancestor worship, oracle bone

Academic Vocabulary chapter, expand, military, design

Materials

*History Alive!
The Ancient World*

Interactive Student Notebooks

Visual 20

Placards 20A–20H

Lesson Masters

- Student Handouts 20A and 20B (2 copies of each, on card stock)
- Student Handout 20C (1 copy per student and 1 transparency)
- Vocabulary Development handout (1 per student, on colored paper)

razor blade or utility knife

scissors

Activity	Suggested Time	Materials
Preview	15 minutes	• Interactive Student Notebooks
Vocabulary Development	30–40 minutes	• *History Alive! The Ancient World* • Interactive Student Notebooks • Vocabulary Development handout
Social Studies Skill Builder	100 minutes (2 regular periods) (1 block period)	• *History Alive! The Ancient World* • Interactive Student Notebooks • Visual 20 • Placards 20A–20H • Student Handouts 20A and 20B (2 copies of each, on card stock) • Student Handout 20C (1 copy per student, and 1 transparency) • razor blade or utility knife • scissors
Processing	15 minutes	• Interactive Student Notebooks
Assessment	40 minutes	• Chapter 20 Assessment

Preview

1   **Have students complete the Preview activity for in their Interactive Student Notebooks.** Students take on the role of future archaeologists and attempt to interpret contemporary objects.

2   **Have students share their answers in pairs or as a class.**

3   **Explain the connection between the Preview activity and Chapter 20.** Tell students that future archaeologists will interpret the objects we leave behind, just as modern archaeologists draw conclusions from artifacts left by ancient civilizations. In this chapter, students will learn about China's first complex civilization, the Shang (shung) dynasty, by studying artifacts unearthed by archaeologists.

Vocabulary Development

1   **Introduce the Key Content Terms.** Have students locate the Key Content Terms for the chapter in their Interactive Student Notebooks. These are important terms that will help them understand the main ideas of the chapter. Ask volunteers to identify any familiar terms and how they might be used in a sentence.

2   **Have students complete a Vocabulary Development handout.** Give each student a copy of the Vocabulary Development handout of your choice from the Reading Toolkit at the back of the Lesson Masters. These handouts provide extra Key Content Term practice and support, depending on your students' needs. Review the completed handout by asking volunteers to share one answer for each term.

Reading

1   **Introduce the Essential Question and have students read Section 20.1.** Have students identify the Essential Question on the first page of the chapter: *What do Shang artifacts reveal about this civilization?* Then have students read Section 20.1. Afterward, have students use information from Section 20.1 and from the chapter opener image to propose some possible answers to the Essential Question.

2   **Have students complete the Reading Notes for Chapter 20.** Assign Sections 20.2 to 20.9 during the activity, as indicated in the procedures for the Social Studies Skill Builder. Remind students to use the Key Content Terms where appropriate as they complete their Reading Notes.

Social Studies Skill Builder

1 Prepare materials for the activity. Before class, assemble the decoders by following the steps below. (**Note:** Use card stock or laminate the decoders for future use.)

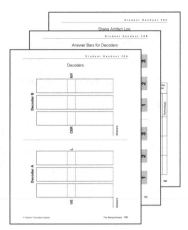

Student Handouts 20A–20C

- Make two copies of each of the four pages of *Student Handout 20A: Decoders* and *Student Handout 20B: Answer Bars for Decoders*.

- Cut all copies in half along the dashed lines to create 16 decoders and 16 sets of answers. Pair each set of answers with the proper decoder.

- Using a razor blade or utility knife, cut the nine dashed lines on the three decoder bars on Decoder A. Then cut out the three strips on the "Answers for Decoder A" sheet and insert them through the slits on the Decoder A bars, as shown in the diagram of Decoder A below. Make sure the strips slide up and down with ease.

- Prepare Decoders B–H in the same way.

Make a copy of *Student Handout 20C: Shang Artifact Log* for each student. Also, create one transparency of Student Handout 20C to project during the final discussion.

2 Prepare the classroom. Create a "Shang tomb" by placing eight desks near the front of the room, as shown in the classroom diagram below. Place *Placards 20A–20H: Shang Tomb Artifacts* underneath the desks. (**Note:** Consider writing "Shang Tomb" on a sign or on the board near the desks. Also, to avoid having pairs share placards, you might create additional sets as needed.) Place the decoders on a desk in the center of the room. Place the remaining desks along the other walls. Pairs will use these desks as "archaeologist workstations" during the activity.

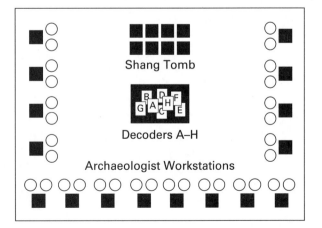

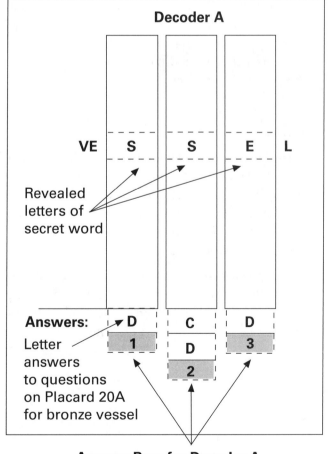

Answer Bars for Decoder A

3   **Place students in pairs and introduce the activity.** Project *Visual 20: A Shang Tomb*. Ask, *What do you see? Whose burial do you think this is? What items are people bringing to the tomb? Why might these objects be placed there?* Explain that students will become "archaeologists" who have just discovered a Shang tomb. The "archaeologists" will "excavate" the tomb to learn about this civilization. Remind students about the roles that chance, oversight, and error may play in interpreting ancient history. Have students brainstorm ways they can avoid misinterpretation as they analyze artifacts from a Shang tomb.

Placards 20A–20H

4   **Review the guidelines for excavating the tomb.** Distribute Student Handout 20C and review the instructions with the class. Emphasize these points:

- One student from each pair will "excavate" an artifact by retrieving a placard from the tomb and then finding the matching decoder. Tell students to rotate the job of excavating.

- Model how to use a decoder. Show students where the section number is revealed (by reading the numerals that appear after the letters in the decoder slots). Explain that students will read the section assigned by the decoder and complete the corresponding Reading Notes in their Interactive Student Notebook.

Visual 20

- For Step 5, remind students that artifacts can tell us about more than one characteristic of a civilization. For example, if an archaeologist finds a gold crown, it might indicate that a king ruled the country (government). It also reveals that the culture likely had artisans who worked with gold (social structure and art). Students should be able to justify any characteristics they check.

- When a pair has completed all the required information for an artifact, they return the placard and the decoder, and then excavate a new artifact.

5   **Have students excavate artifacts.** Circulate with the Guide to Reading Notes 20, assisting students as necessary. Give pairs time to analyze most of the artifacts and complete their Reading Notes. Then have all students return to their desks.

6   **Wrap up the activity.** Project a transparency of the first page of Student Handout 20C. For Artifact A, the bronze vessel, review answers to the placard questions as a class. Then ask which characteristics of the Shang dynasty are revealed by Artifact A (*government, social structure, religion, writing, art, technology*). As students explain why they may have checked each box, place a check in that cell. Do the same for Artifacts B–H. (**Note:** The secret words are: A-VESSEL; B-CEREMONY; C-HELMET; D-SHELLS; E-CHARIOT; F-TOOLS; G-BONE; H-VICTIM.)

Processing

Have students complete the Processing activity on a separate sheet of paper. Students will design a museum exhibit about one of the characteristics of Shang civilization. To help students visualize the activity, consider showing them an image of a museum exhibit displaying ancient Chinese artifacts.

Quicker Coverage

Eliminate the Classroom Setup In lieu of the tomb and workstations, place each placard in an envelope with its decoder. Assign each pair an envelope. When pairs have completed their analysis and the related Reading Notes, have them trade envelopes with another pair. Or, signal pairs to trade after a timed period.

Eliminate the Decoders Students love the kinesthetic aspect of the decoders. However, if you do not have time to assemble the decoders, follow these steps:

- Before copying Student Handout 20C, fill in the reading section numbers in the third column as follows:

Artifact	Section Number	Artifact	Section Number
A	20.7	E	20.3
B	20.2	F	20.4
C	20.8	G	20.6
D	20.9	H	20.5

- Have students "excavate" an artifact, complete the Reading Notes for the section indicated, and then guess the answers to the placard questions.

- Tell pairs to raise their hands when finished. Check their work and then have them excavate a new artifact.

Divide and Conquer Divide the class into eight groups. Assign each group a placard and a matching decoder. Have groups complete the steps on Student Handout 20C for their artifact. Then have groups present their placard questions and answers, their Reading Notes answers, and the characteristics of civilization they checked. Tell the class to take notes as each group presents. Ask the class to come up with other characteristics of civilization that the artifact reveals.

Deeper Coverage

Create Museum Exhibitions For the Processing activity, rather than have students design one part of a museum exhibit, have them create a comprehensive exhibition. Have students work in small groups. Tell them to create three or four exhibits, each one focusing on a different characteristic of Shang civilization and displaying artifacts that relate to the characteristic. Suggest that students create 3-D exhibits by making simple artifacts from construction paper or other materials. Conduct a gallery walk so that students can view each other's exhibitions.

Assessment

Mastering the Content

1. C	5. A	9. A	13. D
2. B	6. D	10. B	14. B
3. B	7. C	11. D	15. A
4. A	8. D	12. C	

Applying Social Studies Skills

16. bronze; Answers will vary. Possible answer: Bronze was important in Shang civilization. The Shang did not yet have iron, and other metals like copper, used alone, would not be strong enough.

17. Answers will vary. Possible answers: Handles: This would make the container much easier to carry, especially if it were hot. Legs: For cooking, one could simply build a fire directly under the vessel, without the need for a device to hold it above the fire.

18. Answers will vary; accept any that make sense and show student thinking. Possible answer: It might be an image of the owner's ancestor, turned into a god or supernatural being.

19. Answers will vary. Possible answer: The cooking vessel is very intricate and beautiful. It would have taken the artist a long time to make, so it was probably quite expensive.

Exploring the Essential Question

20. Answers should include all of the elements requested in the prompt.

Scoring Rubric

Score	Description
3	Student creates four characters and writes appropriate captions. Captions are clearly stated, supported by details, and demonstrate command of standard English conventions.
2	Student responds to most or all parts of the task, but captions may lack details or not be clearly stated.
1	Student responds to at least one part of the task. Captions may contain factual and/or grammatical errors and may lack details.
0	Response does not match the task or is incorrect.

English Language Learners

Review the Characteristics of Civilization On each of six pieces of poster paper, write one of the characteristics of civilization listed in the fourth column of Student Handout 20C. On each piece of poster paper, write a definition of the characteristic on that paper. Post the characteristics around the room so that students can refer to them during the activity.

Preteach Vocabulary Make sure students are familiar with all the "secret words" that will be revealed by the decoders. Determine if you should preteach the following terms: *vessel, ceremony, chariot,* and *victim.*

Learners Reading and Writing Below Grade Level

Model the Reading Notes Before the activity, have students turn to Sections 20.3 and 20.5 in their Interactive Student Notebooks. Use Guide to Reading Notes 20 to provide students with an example sensory figure statement. Tell students to locate the information in the text that was used to create the sample sensory statement. Have students write a different sensory statement about the same content. Invite volunteers to read their statements aloud, and answer any questions students may have.

Replace the Processing Activity Substitute a simpler activity for the Processing activity. Give the following instructions: *On a separate piece of paper, draw two artifacts from the Shang tomb. Next to each artifact, explain two or more characteristics of the Shang dynasty that the artifact reveals.*

Learners with Special Education Needs

Complete the Preview Activity as a Class Work together to identify each artifact, discuss possible interpretations of the artifact, and decide what each artifact reveals.

Model the Social Studies Skill Builder Follow these steps to explicitly model the activity:

- Hold up Placard 20C, the bronze helmet. Then hold up Decoder C and explain that students will use this matching decoder to check their answer choices to the placard questions.

- On the board, write *H E _ _ _ T.* Tell students that if their answer choices are correct, the decoder will reveal a word. One at a time, ask the placard questions, use students' answers to move the bars on the decoder, and record the letters that are revealed. If students have chosen the correct answers, the word *helmet* should be revealed. If not, have the class guess new answers.

- When students have found the secret word, tell them to use the correct answers from the placard to fill in the second column of Student Handout 20C.

- Then show students that the decoder has also revealed the numbers "20.8." Have students read Section 20.8 and complete the corresponding Reading Notes in their Interactive Student Notebooks.

Advanced Learners

Compare Shang Society to U.S. Society Revisit the Preview activity and have students compare Shang artifacts to American artifacts. Ask, *In what ways are the artifacts similar? In what ways are they different? How are the characteristics of Shang society similar to those of the United States? How are they different? How might future archaeologists misinterpret the U.S. artifacts? What other possible interpretations might be made from the Shang artifacts you examined in the activity?*

Enrichment Resources

Find out more about the Shang dynasty by exploring the following Enrichment Resources for *History Alive! The Ancient World* at www.teachtci.com.

Enrichment Readings These in-depth readings encourage students to explore selected topics related to the chapter. You may also find readings that relate the chapter's content directly to your state's curriculum.

Internet Connections The recommended Web sites provide useful and engaging content that reinforces skills development and mastery of subjects within the chapter.

Literature Recommendations

The following books offer opportunities to extend the content in this chapter.

The Ancient Chinese by Virginia Schlomp (New York: Franklin Watts, 2004)

The Jade Stone adapted by Caryn Yacowitz (Gretna, LA: Pelican Publishing Company, 2006)

Ten Suns: A Chinese Legend by Eric Kimmel (New York: Holiday House, 1998)

Section 20.2

1. Ruins of a Shang city were discovered at Anyang.

2. Shang cities included the king's palace on a platform, royal tombs, a temple, houses, and workshops.

Section 20.3

Sensory figure responses will vary. Possible statements:

With my ears, I hear . . . the rumble of the <u>chariot</u> that I am riding in.

With my eyes, I see . . . my <u>king</u> talking to his brothers and nephews.

With my heart, I feel . . . loyalty to my <u>clan</u> and the desire to defeat the other <u>clans</u>.

With my hands, I touch . . . weapons and armor made of <u>bronze</u>.

Section 20.4

Social classes should be listed from top to bottom: King, Nobles, Artisans and Traders (same level), Farmers, Slaves. Drawings of artifacts will vary but should be appropriate for each social class.

Section 20.5

Sensory figure responses will vary. Possible statements:

With my ears, I hear . . . the <u>oracle bone</u> crack and the holy man give advice.

With my eyes, I see . . . the holy man pressing a hot needle to an oracle bone as I do my <u>duty</u> by seeking advice from my ancestors.

With my heart, I feel . . . that it is important to honor my <u>ancestors</u>.

With my hands, I touch . . . the <u>offerings</u> of food we give our ancestors.

Section 20.6

1. Chinese writing was first found on oracle bones.

2. Logographs are characters that stand for words rather than sounds or objects.

3. Written language helped unify the Chinese people.

Section 20.7

1. A Shang artist might use bronze to make a vessel and use jade to make a pendant (jewelry).

2. Shang artisans decorated vessels and other objects with geometric designs and with pictures of mythical creatures, including an animal mask later called a taotie.

Section 20.8

1. Spoke diagrams should include the following weapons: arrowheads, spearheads, ax heads, helmets. Statements about the most important weapon will vary.

2. The Shang used their knowledge of bronze making to make many tools of war which helped their dynasty stay in power for more than 500 years.

Section 20.9

In the flowchart, students should include the following reasons for the fall of the Shang dynasty: a military weakened by too many wars, an economy weakened by excessive spending, and a society weakened by the corrupt practices of the last Shang king. Students may also note the short-term cause—that the Zhou armies caught the Shang armies unaware.

Three Chinese Philosophies

How did Confucianism, Daoism, and Legalism influence political rule in ancient China?

Overview

In an Experiential Exercise, students learn about Confucianism, Daoism, and Legalism under classroom conditions that reflect the main beliefs of each philosophy. (**Note:** Pinyin spellings are used throughout this unit in accordance with the decision by the Library of Congress to join pinyin syllables.)

Objectives

In the course of reading this chapter and participating in the classroom activity, students will

Social Studies

- identify political and cultural issues at the end of the Zhou dynasty.
- describe the lives and fundamental teachings of Confucius, Laozi, and Hanfeizi.
- explain how various schools of thought affected political rule in China.
- apply Confucian, Daoist, and Legalist principles to contemporary situations.

Language Arts

- clarify main ideas and connect them to a related issue.

Social Studies Vocabulary

Key Content Terms Zhou dynasty, Mandate of Heaven, feudalism, Confucianism, civil servant, Daoism, yin and yang, Legalism

Academic Vocabulary portion, emerge, sibling, laborer, pursue

Materials

History Alive! The Ancient World

Interactive Student Notebooks

Visual 21

Lesson Masters

- Information Masters 21A–21C (1 transparency of each)
- Vocabulary Development handout (1 per student, on colored paper)

Activity	Suggested Time	Materials
Preview	10 minutes	• Interactive Student Notebooks
Vocabulary Development	30–40 minutes	• *History Alive! The Ancient World* • Interactive Student Notebooks • Vocabulary Development handout
Experiential Exercise	120–140 minutes (3 regular periods) (2 block periods)	• *History Alive! The Ancient World* • Interactive Student Notebooks • Visual 21 • Information Masters 21A–21C (1 transparency of each)
Processing	10 minutes	• Interactive Student Notebooks
Assessment	40 minutes	• Chapter 21 Assessment

Preview

1 **Have students complete the Preview activity in their Interactive Student Notebooks.** Students evaluate the effectiveness of three different approaches to dealing with school violence.

2 **Have students share their answers in pairs or as a class.**

3 **Explain the connection between the Preview activity and Chapter 21.** Tell students that each approach to dealing with school violence represents a different way in which Chinese philosophers tried to bring order to their society. (*Approach 1 represents Confucianism, Approach 2 represents Daoism, and Approach 3 represents Legalism.*) In this chapter, students will learn about political developments during the Zhou (joh) dynasty, the problems of the Warring States period, and the approaches that three Chinese thinkers introduced to bring peace to this time of disorder.

Vocabulary Development

1 **Introduce the Key Content Terms.** Have students locate the Key Content Terms for the chapter in their Interactive Student Notebooks. These are important terms that will help them understand the main ideas of the chapter. Ask volunteers to identify any familiar terms and how they might be used in a sentence.

2 **Have students complete a Vocabulary Development handout.** Give each student a copy of the Vocabulary Development handout of your choice from the Reading Toolkit at the back of the Lesson Masters. These handouts provide extra Key Content Term practice and support, depending on your students' needs. Review the completed handout by asking volunteers to share one answer for each term.

Reading

1 **Introduce the Essential Question and have students read Section 21.1.** Have students identify the Essential Question on the first page of the chapter: *How did Confucianism, Daoism, and Legalism influence political rule in ancient China?* Then have students read Section 21.1. Afterward, have students use information from Section 21.1 and from the chapter opener image to propose some possible answers to the Essential Question.

2 **Have students complete the Reading Notes for Chapter 21.** Assign Sections 21.2 to 21.5 during the activity, as indicated in the procedures for the Experiential Exercise. Remind students to use the Key Content Terms where appropriate as they complete their Reading Notes.

Experiential Exercise

1 **Understand the intent of the activity—to learn about Confucianism, Daoism, and Legalism.** Students will participate in a three-phase activity, one for each philosophy. At the beginning of each phase, you will introduce the philosophy. Then, as students read and take notes, you will create classroom conditions appropriate for this school of thought. At the end of each phase, you will debrief the experience to help students make connections to the Chinese philosophy.

2 **Introduce the Zhou dynasty.** Project *Visual 21: Zhou Soldiers Destroying Peasants' Crops.* Ask, *What do you see? Who is the man in the helmet? Who do you think are the people holding sticks? What are they doing? Why do you think a military leader would order his men to destroy crops? How do you think the peasants to the left feel about what is happening? What does this image suggest about life during this time in Chinese history?* Tell students that scenes such as this were common at the end of the Zhou dynasty, which ruled China after the Shang dynasty.

3 **Have students complete the Reading Notes for Section 21.2.** Tell students that this section provides background information about the political and cultural conditions at the end of the Zhou dynasty. Have them read Section 21.2 and complete the corresponding Reading Notes in their Interactive Student Notebooks. Afterward, use Guide to Reading Notes 21 to review their responses.

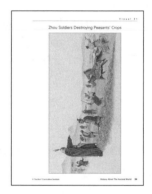

Visual 21

Phase 1: Learning About Confucianism

1 **Introduce Confucianism.** Tell students that they will now learn about Confucianism, a philosophy that was started by a man named Kongfuzi, or Confucius. He believed that society must have order and that order is achieved when people understand their relationships to others and behave in a virtuous way.

2 **Introduce the activity for Confucianism.** Tell students that they will learn more about Confucianism under classroom conditions that Confucius might have suggested. Confucius honored age and scholarly achievement. Therefore, four students will act as "elders" who will lead the activity. Select four students to act as elders. Have them stand in front of the overhead projector. (**Note:** Select students who can confidently guide others. You might select students in advance and suggest that they read Section 21.3 the night before.)

3 **Project a transparency of *Information Master 21A: Experiencing Confucianism,* revealing one step at a time.** First, show only the title. Explain that as you reveal each step, students must read the directions and respond appropriately. Follow these guidelines:

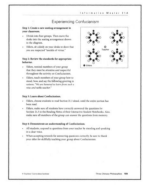

Information Master 21A

- *For Step 1*: Explain that the elders you have chosen will sit on their desks to represent a position of respect. They will show the class how to behave in a dignified way. (**Note:** If you have chosen the four elders in advance as suggested in the Note for number 2 of this phase, you may wish to prepare a seating chart based on the diagram on Information Master 21A.)

- *For Step 2*: Emphasize that students are to treat elders with respect throughout the activity. Model the formal greeting with the elders.

- *For Step 3*: Have elders tell students to read along silently as various group members read aloud parts of the section. Emphasize that elders should be certain all students have correctly answered the questions for Section 21.3 in their Reading Notes and can repeat the answers from memory.

- *For Step 4*: Be sure students have closed their Interactive Student Notebooks. Randomly select a student from one group to answer the first question from Section 21.3 of the Reading Notes. If the answer is correct, you might award that group some points or prizes. Compliment the group's elder for instructing the student properly. Continue until a student from every group has had an opportunity to answer a question, and all questions from the Reading Notes have been answered.

4 **Debrief the activity on Confucianism.** Hold a class discussion. Ask,

- How did it feel to learn about Confucianism in this way?

- "Elder" students sat on desks and led the discussion. How does this reflect the teachings of Confucius? (*Confucius encouraged respect for age.*)

- What are some of the advantages of learning from elders? What are some of the disadvantages?

- Students addressed elders with formal greetings. How is this like the teachings of Confucius? (*Confucius believed that proper conduct would encourage a peaceful state.*)

- Should you respect and obey a ruler? Your parents? Your older siblings (brother or sister)?

- Students learned about Confucianism and were rewarded when they could answer questions from memory. How is this similar to the way Confucian teachings influenced government in China? (*Civil service jobs were given to those who did well on exams based on Confucian teachings.*)

- Do you think government jobs should be given to people on the basis of test results? Why or why not?

- Why do you think Confucianism could have helped end the wars between competing states during the rule of the Zhou?

Writing: Response to Literature

To extend this chapter, present a selection of Confucian analects and/ or Daoist quotations or sayings. Have students read them carefully and then interpret them as they relate to the philosophy they represent. Remind students to develop and justify their interpretation by referring to the specific words of the quotation as well as to what students have learned about each philosophy.

Three Chinese Philosophies **263**

Phase 2: Learning About Daoism

1 **Introduce Daoism.** Tell students that they will now learn about Daoism, another Chinese philosophy that developed during the Zhou dynasty. Daoists believed that every individual should behave naturally, without restrictions from the government.

2 **Introduce the activity for Daoism.** Tell students that they will study about Daoism under conditions that Daoists might have suggested. Students will be allowed to study Section 21.4 in any manner that suits their learning style.

3 **Project *Information Master 21B: Experiencing Daoism,* revealing one step at a time.** First, show only the title. Tell students that as you reveal each step, they should read the directions and respond appropriately. Follow these guidelines:

Information Master 21B

   • *For Step 1:* To reduce confusion, tell students that they will have two minutes to find their new seats. To make the experience more realistic, you might take students outside. Or, you could place pillows around the room.

   • *For Step 2:* Explain that these standards create a natural, thoughtful atmosphere and avoid centering attention on themselves, two Daoist values.

   • *For Step 3:* Allow students to work together if they can do so quietly. Emphasize that they can use any means they want—such as writing the answers, drawing pictures to answer the questions, or using their bodies to pantomime the answers—to indicate that they understand the questions regarding Daoism.

   • *For Step 4:* Have students share their answers. Be sure those students who chose alternative methods to answer the questions (rather than the written form) have the opportunity to present their understanding of Daoism.

4 **Debrief the activity on Daoism.** Ask,

   • How did it feel to learn about Daoism in this way?

   • How was this activity different from the activity on Confucianism?

   • Which activity did you like better? Why?

   • In which activity do you feel you learned the most? Explain.

   • The teacher did not tell you where you had to sit. How is this like Daoism? (*Daoists opposed strong rules set by the government.*)

   • Students worked quietly and tried not to call attention to themselves. How is this like Daoism? (*Daoists encouraged people to avoid fame.*)

   • Students could answer the questions in the Reading Notes in any way they chose. How is this like Daoism? (*Daoists encouraged people to find their own way to live in harmony with the forces of nature.*)

   • Why do you think most Chinese rulers refused to accept Daoism?

Phase 3: Learning About Legalism

1 **Introduce Legalism.** Tell students that they will now learn about Legalism, a third Chinese philosophy that developed during the Zhou dynasty. Legalists believed that laws and punishments were necessary for a secure society.

2 **Introduce the activity for Legalism.** Tell students that they will study more about Legalism under classroom conditions that Legalists might have suggested. There will be strict rules and punishments, and you will be leading the discussion of the Reading Notes for Section 21.5.

3 **Project *Information Master 21C: Experiencing Legalism*, revealing one step at a time.** First, show only the title. Tell students that as you reveal each step, they must read the directions and respond appropriately. Follow these guidelines:

- *For Step 1*: This step is designed to make the classroom feel more regimented and less cooperative, and to emphasize the Legalist view that humans negatively influence one another.

- *For Step 2*: Tell students that if they do not follow the standards of behavior, you will remove them from the activity. (**Note**: To emphasize the strictness of the standards, you may want to tell them that if they are removed from the activity, they will lose points, but they will still have to complete their Reading Notes.)

- *For Step 3*: Do not allow students to work together. Circulate through the room to make sure they are reading Section 21.5 and obeying the standards for behavior. If necessary, have "disobedient" students move to the back of the room and stand silently. To make the experience more realistic, you may want to use a whistle to begin and end the reading, or march around the room with a serious expression on your face.

- *For Step 4*: Emphasize that students must never look directly in your eyes, as this, in Legalist tradition, is considered a sign of disrespect and a challenge to your authority. Explain that those students who answer correctly will be rewarded, whereas those who answer incorrectly will be punished. Have students close their Interactive Student Notebooks and sit up straight, with hands folded on their desks. Sternly read aloud one of the questions, and then choose a student to stand and answer it. If the student answers the question satisfactorily, reward him or her in some manner. If the student answers incorrectly, have him or her stand silently at the back of the classroom. Continue until all questions for Section 21.5 have been answered.

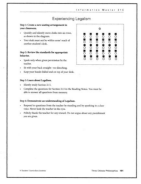

Information Master 21C

4 **Debrief the activity on Legalism.** Ask,

- How did it feel to learn about Legalism in this way?

- How was this activity different from the activities on Confucianism and Daoism? Which activity did you like the best? Why?

- In which activity do you feel you learned the most? Why?

- The teacher made students fold their hands and maintain a rigid posture to avoid punishment. How was this like Legalism? (*Legalists believed governments should have strong laws.*)

- The teacher led the discussion and did not allow students to talk to each other. How was this like Legalism? (*Legalists felt that people were naturally selfish and evil. They could not be trusted to help each other.*)

- Students with correct answers were rewarded; those with wrong answers were punished. How was this like Legalism? (*Legalists felt that there should be rewards and harsh punishments to promote a strong state.*)

- What do you think life in a Legalist country would be like?

- Why do you think Legalist rulers were unpopular in ancient China?

Processing

For homework, have students complete the Processing activity in their Interactive Student Notebooks. Students will analyze whether their family's homework policy is most like the practices of Confucianism, Daoism, or Legalism. Ask students to have a parent or a guardian sign their Processing activity page to verify that Questions 3 and 5 were completed. Check that the page is signed.

Quicker Coverage

Shorten Debriefing Eliminate some debrief questions for each phase of the activity. For Phases 1 and 2, ask the first four and the final question. For Phase 3, ask the first three and the final question. The discussion will focus students on each philosophy, comparing and contrasting the three philosophies, and applying what they have learned in the Experiential Exercise to the history of ancient China.

Deeper Coverage

Apply the Philosophies' Teachings To challenge students to apply their knowledge of the three schools of thought, have them respond to one or both of the contemporary situations below.

Situation 1: Alicia, a 13-year-old girl, and some friends want to go to the movies. Her parents are supportive but insist that they be chaperoned, either by them or by the parents of one of the other girls. Alicia feels that the presence of adults would prevent her and her friends from having fun. What advice do you think Confucius, Laozi, and Hanfeizi would give Alicia?

Situation 2: State officials are creating a bill that would require students in grades K–8 to wear uniforms. Many principals, teachers, and parents feel that uniforms would help establish a more serious academic environment and eliminate many discipline problems. Students, however, feel that wearing uniforms takes away a basic freedom that allows them to express their individuality. What advice do you think Confucius, Laozi, and Hanfeizi would give to the state officials?

Create a Triple Venn Diagram Have students create a triple Venn diagram to compare the ideas of Confucianism, Daoism, and Legalism. Encourage students to fill in at least *three* items that are unique to each philosophy (A, B, and C), at least *one* item that each philosophy has in common with only one other philosophy (D, E, and F), and at least *three* items that all three philosophies have in common with each other (G).

Create Character Collages Have students create character collages to represent Confucius, Laozi, and Hanfeizi. Each collage should consist of the following elements:

- an outline of the philosopher (students can create rough sketches, using the philosopher images in their book)
- at least three symbols and illustrations that represent the philosopher's beliefs
- a speech bubble containing a statement that the philosopher might make

Assessment

Mastering the Content

1. B	5. C	9. B	13. D
2. D	6. B	10. C	14. A
3. A	7. C	11. C	15. D
4. A	8. D	12. A	16. A

Applying Social Studies Skills

17. Answers will vary. Possible answers: its officials would likely be dignified, virtuous, generous, kind, and sincere

18. Answers will vary. Possible answer: its officials would be likely to do as little as possible to allow people the freedom to find their own happiness

19. Answers will vary. Possible answer: its officials would be likely to pay serious attention to making sure that everyone obeys the law

20. Answers should include all of the elements requested in the prompt.

Scoring Rubric

Score	Description
3	Student writes appropriate comments in all three boxes, relevant to the philosophy circled. Comments are clearly stated, supported by details, and demonstrate command of standard English conventions.
2	Student responds to most or all parts of the task, but comments may lack details or not be clearly stated.
1	Student responds to at least one part of the task. Comment(s) may contain factual and/or grammatical errors and may lack details.
0	Response does not match the task or is incorrect.

English Language Learners

Prepare Students for the Simulation In the Preview activity, explicitly connect each approach to dealing with school violence to one of the three philosophies in Chapter 21. Have students write next to each scenario the name of the corresponding philosophy and a description of its basic principles. Then explain that you are going to create a classroom environment that will let students feel what it would be like to live in a society that follows the teachings of each philosophy. For example, say, *Because Legalism has strict rules, we will use similar rules to imitate Legalism in our classroom.* Allow students to ask questions, and make sure they are comfortable before starting the activity.

Learners Reading and Writing Below Grade Level

Model the Reading Notes For Section 21.2, give students the following sentence to help them organize their speech bubbles: "Under feudalism, I have to give up _____, but I benefit because. . ." To assist students with the Warring States question, tell them to use the term *rival* in the left-hand banner and the term *Hundred Schools of Thought* in the right-hand banner. For each of Sections 21.3 through 21.5, designate three questions you would like students to answer during the simulation.

Use T-Charts to Debrief After each phase, have students create a T-chart and explicitly connect the ideas of each philosophy to the simulation they experienced. The example below might be part of a T-chart for Confucianism.

In-class Experience	Characteristics of Confucianism
• "Elder" students sat on desks and led small groups in discussions.	• Confucius encouraged respect for age and tradition.
• Students addressed elders with formal greetings.	• Confucius believed that proper conduct would encourage a peaceful state.

Learners with Special Education Needs

Support the Simulation Follow these steps to help the Experiential Exercise proceed more smoothly:

- Before starting, use Guide to Reading Notes 21 to provide complete answers for one or two questions in each section. For the remaining questions, offer sentence starters.

- Provide individual copies of Information Masters 21A–21C. Highlight the important direction words in Steps 2, 3, and 4 so that students are better able to participate in each phase of the activity.

Scaffold the Processing Activity Place students in pairs. Give them time to complete the first two steps of the Processing activity. Then prepare them for Step 3 by having them review their Reading Notes and highlight the main idea of each philosophy, to later teach to a parent or guardian. Allow pairs to practice "teaching" their parents or guardians before completing the activity for homework.

Advanced Learners

Attribute Quotations to Philosophers For each quotation below, challenge students to first summarize it in their own words, and then explain whether they think Confucius, Laozi, or Hanfeizi is the author:

- "The more laws and edicts are imposed, the more thieves and bandits there will be." (*Laozi*)

- "Be respectful at home, serious at work, faithful in human relations. Even if you go to uncivilized areas, these virtues are not to be abandoned." (*Confucius*)

- "In governing, one must use what works in most cases . . . Therefore, the sage does not work on his virtue, he works on his laws." (*Hanfeizi*)

Research "Daoism" Versus "Taoism" Challenge students to research why Daoism is often spelled "Taoism." (*The Chinese word way is romanized "dào" in the Pinyin system and "tao" in the Wade-Giles system.*) Ask students to research and explain the challenges of representing Chinese characters in English. Then, as a class, brainstorm other situations in which the translation or pronunciation of words may vary, e.g. "tuh-MAY-toh" vs. "tuh-MAH-toh" for *tomato*.

Enrichment Resources

Find out more about Confucianism, Daoism, and Legalism by exploring the following Enrichment Resources for *History Alive! The Ancient World* at www.teachtci.com.

Enrichment Readings This in-depth reading encourages students to explore selected topics related to the chapter. You may also find readings that relate the chapter's content directly to your state's curriculum.

Internet Connections The recommended Web sites provide useful and engaging content that reinforces skills development and mastery of subjects within the chapter.

Literature Recommendations

The following books offer opportunities to extend the content in this chapter.

Confucianism by Thomas Hoobler and Dorothy Hoobler (New York: Facts on File, 2004)

Confucius: The Golden Door by Russell Freedman (New York: Arthur A. Levine Books, 2002)

Taoism by Paula Nartz (New York: Facts on File, 2004)

Section 21.2

1. The Mandate of Heaven would support the belief that the drought occurred because Heaven was displeased with the king. Other leaders now have the right to overthrow him.

2. Speech bubbles will vary. Possible answers:

   King: "Under feudalism, I own all the land but give large pieces of it to my loyal lords. In return, they send soldiers to fight for me."

   Lord: "My role in the feudal system is to support the king, who granted me land, and to rule over my state and my peasants."

   Peasant: "I give part of my crops to my lord, in exchange for his protection."

3. *Causes*: The Warring States period was caused by the breakdown of the feudal system. As lords got more ambitious, their power rivaled that of the king. They grouped together and fought with each other. This led to instability.

   Results: The Warring States period resulted in the "Hundred Schools of Thought." Chinese scholars tried to answer serious questions about human nature and the best ways to govern. Confucianism, Daoism, and Legalism had a major influence on Chinese culture.

Section 21.3

1. Confucius was a philosopher whose teachings influenced Chinese government and culture.

2. China was in chaos during his lifetime.

3. The five basic relationships are ruler and subject, husband and wife, father and son, older sibling and younger sibling, and friend and friend.

4. People must respect and obey those above them in status. In return, those with authority must set a good example.

5. Civil servants had to take a test on Confucian teachings before they were awarded their positions. Government jobs were no longer given only to the sons of nobles.

6. Captions will vary but should include mention of the importance of respect and relationships.

Section 21.4

1. Students may answer through any means. However, their answer should indicate that Laozi was a great wise man and an adviser to the Zhou court.

2. Students may answer through any means. However, their answer should indicate that people discover how to behave by learning to live in harmony with the forces of nature.

3. Students may answer through any means. However, their answer should indicate that yin and yang are the opposite forces of nature.

4. Students may answer through any means. However, their answer should indicate that rulers should rule as little as possible.

5. Captions will vary but should mention the importance of nature and self-reflection.

Section 21.5

1. Hanfeizi was a prince of the royal family of Han.

2. According to Hanfeizi, the only way to create a strong society was for rulers to establish strict laws and enforce them, either with rewards for good behavior or with punishments for poor behavior.

3. Hanfeizi believed that a ruler should have absolute power backed by military might.

4. The Qin dynasty applied Hanfeizi's teachings by passing strict laws and harshly punishing people who disobeyed them.

5. Captions will vary but should mention the importance of punishing rule breakers.

The First Emperor of China

Was the Emperor of Qin an effective leader?

Overview

In a Visual Discovery activity, students analyze and bring to life images about Qin Shihuangdi's political and cultural unification of China, his efforts to protect China's northern boundaries, and his dispute with Confucian scholars. (**Note:** Pinyin spellings are used throughout this unit in accordance with the decision by the Library of Congress to join pinyin syllables.)

Objectives

In the course of reading this chapter and participating in the classroom activity, students will

Social Studies

- explain how the emperor Shihuangdi unified northern China under the Qin dynasty.
- analyze the policies and achievements of the Emperor of Qin.
- evaluate the extent to which Qin Shihuangdi was an effective leader.

Language Arts

- connect and clarify main ideas in text by relating them to images.
- select point of view; match purpose, message, and vocal modulation to an audience.

Social Studies Vocabulary

Key Content Terms Qin Shihuangdi, standardize, Great Wall, censor, immortal

Academic Vocabulary project, frontier, construct, conflict, revolt

Materials

History Alive!
The Ancient World

Interactive Student Notebooks

Visuals 22A–22D

Lesson Masters

- Student Handouts 22A and 22B (1 each per group of 3)
- Vocabulary Development handout (1 per student, on colored paper)

sticky notes

Activity	Suggested Time	Materials
Preview	10 minutes	• Interactive Student Notebooks
Vocabulary Development	30–40 minutes	• *History Alive! The Ancient World* • Interactive Student Notebooks • Vocabulary Development handout
Visual Discovery	120–140 minutes (3 regular periods) (1.5 block periods)	• *History Alive! The Ancient World* • Interactive Student Notebooks • Visuals 22A–22D • Student Handouts 22A–22B (1 each per group of 3) • sticky notes
Processing	20 minutes	• Interactive Student Notebooks
Assessment	40 minutes	• Chapter 22 Assessment

Preview

1   **Have students complete the Preview activity in their Interactive Student Notebooks.** Students will consider the extent to which certain actions make a leader effective or ineffective. Discuss the term *effective* before students complete the Preview activity.

2   **Have students share their answers in pairs or as a class.** Consider asking a couple of students to justify the action they chose as the most effective, and then the action they chose to be the least effective.

3   **Explain the connection between the Preview activity and Chapter 22.** Tell students that all the statements in the Preview activity have been used to describe the rule of the first emperor of China, Qin Shihuangdi (chin SHEE-hwahng-dee). Explain that accounts of his life have often been biased. Some people wrote about his greatness, and some people claimed he was a tyrant. In this chapter, students will learn about the policies and achievements of the first emperor of China and evaluate whether he was an effective ruler.

Vocabulary Development

1   **Introduce the Key Content Terms.** Have students locate the Key Content Terms for the chapter in their Interactive Student Notebooks. These are important terms that will help them understand the main ideas of the chapter. Ask volunteers to identify any familiar terms and how they might be used in a sentence.

2   **Have students complete a Vocabulary Development handout.** Give each student a copy of the Vocabulary Development handout of your choice from the Reading Toolkit at the back of the Lesson Masters. These handouts provide extra Key Content Term practice and support, depending on your students' needs. Review the completed handout by asking volunteers to share one answer for each term.

Reading

1   **Introduce the Essential Question and have students read Section 22.1.** Have students identify the Essential Question on the first page of the chapter: *Was the Emperor of Qin an effective leader?* Then have students read Section 22.1. Afterward, have students use information from Section 22.1 and from the chapter opener image to propose some possible answers to the Essential Question.

2   **Have students complete the Reading Notes for Chapter 22.** Assign Sections 22.2 to 22.6 during the activity, as indicated in the procedures for the Visual Discovery. Remind students to use the Key Content Terms where appropriate as they complete their Reading Notes.

Visual Discovery

1 **Place students in groups of three.** Make sure that all students can see the projections. You might want to prepare a transparency that shows group assignments and seating arrangements.

2 **Introduce the activity.** Explain that students will analyze four images and read sections of the chapter to learn about and evaluate the rule of the Emperor of Qin. For two of the images, groups will prepare an actor to "step into" the image and bring it to life.

3 **Project *Visual 22A: Creating an Empire* and have students analyze the image.** Tell students that this image shows one of the acts of Qin Shihuangdi: his unification of China. Point out the focus question that appears beneath the image. Explain that the image will help them answer this question. (**Note:** The image shows Qin Shihuangdi's army battling a rival kingdom.) Have students turn to Reading Notes Section 22.2 in their Interactive Student Notebooks and complete Step 1. Students may also refer to the same image shown in color in their books.

Visual 22A

4 **Have students share their responses.** Ask several students to come forward and point out details they labeled in their Reading Notes. For each detail, ask, *What might this detail reveal about the Emperor of Qin?* Allow the class to offer other interpretations.

5 **Have students complete Step 2 of Section 22.2 in their Reading Notes.** Tell students that they will now read their book to discover if their interpretations are correct. When students have finished reading, use Guide to Reading Notes 22 to review students' answers as a class.

6 **Have students complete Step 3 of Section 22.2 in their Reading Notes.** Follow these steps:

   • Tell groups to discuss how they would rate the actions of China's first emperor—very effective, very ineffective, or somewhere in between. Tell students to consider both the costs and benefits of the emperor's decisions.

   • As a reflection of their discussion, have students place an *X* on the spectrum in their Reading Notes. The more effective they think the emperor was, the farther to the right they should place their *X*. The more ineffective they think he was, the farther to the left they should place their *X*.

   • Assign each group a number to write on a sticky note. Then have one student from each group come forward and place their sticky note on the projected spectrum. Call on selected groups to justify their placements.

Visual 22B

7 **Repeat Steps 3–6 with *Visual 22B: Standardizing the Culture* and have students analyze the image.** Help guide students in analyzing the image in Section 22.3 of their Reading Notes. Tell students that these artifacts illustrate the Emperor of Qin's orders to standardize money, weights, measures, and written language.

8 **Repeat Steps 3–6 with *Visual 22C: Protecting the Northern Border* and have students analyze the image.** Help guide students in analyzing the image in Section 22.4 of their Reading Notes. Tell students that this image shows a modern artist's rendition of the building of the Great Wall of China. Peasants are shown carrying heavy stone blocks, while a foreman with a whip supervises the work.

9 **Have students prepare to bring Visual 22C to life by conducting an act-it-out.** Give each group a copy of *Student Handout 22A: Protecting the Northern Border Act-It-Out.* Assign each group a character in the image. (**Note:** More than one group can be assigned to act out the parts of the workers carrying baskets, standing on the wall, or digging up stones. Have each group represent a different specific individual in the image.) Emphasize that students should use their character's perspective to complete the steps on the handout. Give groups several minutes to prepare.

10 **Conduct the act-it-out.** Call up one actor from each group to stand in front of the appropriate character on the screen, taking on the posture and facial expression of that character. Assume the role of a reporter and interview the characters, asking questions like those they discussed in their groups.

11 **Repeat Steps 3–6 with *Visual 22D: Ending Opposition* and have students analyze the image.** Help guide students in analyzing the image in Section 22.5 of their Reading Notes. Direct students' attention to the top of the image, where the emperor is giving orders to execute Confucian scholars. At the bottom, soldiers are executing the scholars. The scholars to the right are being thrown into a pit. To the left are the texts burning in a pile.

12 **Repeat Steps 9 and 10 to have students prepare and perform an act-it-out for Visual 22D.** Give each group a copy of *Student Handout 22B: Ending Opposition Act-It-Out* to use in their preparation for the act-it-out.

13 **Have students read Section 22.6 and complete the corresponding Reading Notes.** Tell students that they will learn about Qin Shihuangdi's death and burial, and find out what happened to the Qin dynasty after his death. Use Guide to Reading Notes 22 to review the answers as a class.

14 **Wrap up the activity with a class discussion.** Ask,

- What interesting things did you learn about the Emperor of Qin?
- In what ways did Qin Shihuangdi's leadership have a positive impact on China? A negative impact?
- Was the Emperor of Qin an effective leader?

Processing

Have students complete the Processing activity on a separate sheet of paper. Students evaluate the rule of the Emperor of Qin by designing a commemorative plaque or a wanted poster.

Visual 22C

Student Handout 22A

Visual 22D

Student Handout 22B

Quicker Coverage

Provide Key Details During Step 1 of the Reading Notes, point out key details in the image, as suggested below. Students need then write only their hypothesis sentence telling what they think these details reveal about the Emperor of Qin.

For Visual 22A, Section 22.2: chariot, soldiers, and fire
For Visual 22B, Section 22.3: coin, measuring cup, and writing
For Visual 22C, Section 22.4: wall, whip, and workers
For Visual 22D, Section 22.5: emperor, guards, and books

Modify the Act-It-Outs Choose either Student Handout 22A or 22B and conduct only one act-it-out. Or, use "talking statues" by doing the following:

- Assign each group a character in one image. Tell groups to use information from the image and their Reading Notes to complete this sentence from the perspective of their assigned character: *"I think the Emperor of Qin was an effective/ineffective leader because . . ."*

- Have one student from each group come up to the image and freeze in the position of the group's character. As you tap them on the shoulder, have them "come to life," read their statement, and then freeze back into position.

- Quickly move through the statues, bringing them to life to hear their statements. After the act-it-out, lead the audience in a round of applause.

Speed Up the Processing Activity Rather than have students design their own plaques or wanted posters, provide templates. Use the contrasting images of Emperor Qin from Step 3 of the Reading Notes to create the templates. On the board, provide model statements that students can refer to. For example, "We remember the honorable Emperor of Qin because . . ." and "The Emperor of Qin must be found and punished because . . ."

Deeper Coverage

Return to the Preview Activity Have students review the Preview activity statements about leadership. For each statement, tell students to provide two specific pieces of evidence from their Reading Notes to show that the statement applies to Qin Shihuangdi. Then, in a well-written paragraph, have students answer the Essential Question: *Was the Emperor of Qin an effective leader?*

Expand the Processing Activity Give students these directions:

1. Because Qin Shihuangdi was both effective and ineffective as a ruler, create a commemorative plaque *and* a wanted poster for him.

2. Draw a picture of the emperor in the middle of a sheet of paper.

3. Above his picture, create a commemorative plaque and list actions that justify why this plaque salutes him.

4. Below his picture, create a wanted poster and list actions that justify why this poster dishonors him.

5. For each action you listed, include a reason why it made the emperor either effective or ineffective as a ruler.

Research Qin Shihuangdi's Tomb Challenge students to learn more about the Emperor of Qin's tomb. Consider having each student find one image of the tomb and one written detail about the tomb. Allow students to share their findings. Then ask, *Was the building of the tomb an effective use of manpower and resources?* You might also have students compare Qin Shihuangdi's tomb with those of the Egyptian pharaohs in the Old Kingdom period. Ask, *What were similarities and differences between the structure of the tombs and their contents? What do the tombs tell us about these leaders?*

Assessment

Mastering the Content

1. B	5. D	9. C	13. D
2. C	6. D	10. A	14. B
3. A	7. C	11. D	15. C
4. B	8. A	12. A	

Applying Social Studies Skills

16. the Great Wall

17. Huang He

18. to the east

19. Answers will vary. Possible answer: There were mountains, plateaus, and deserts to the west, and not many people lived there.

Exploring the Essential Question

20. Answers should include all of the elements requested in the prompt.

Scoring Rubric

Score	Description
3	Student completes accurate and relevant information in all six boxes and answers the question at the bottom of the page. Answers are clearly stated, supported by details, and demonstrate command of standard English conventions.
2	Student responds to most or all parts of the task; answers may lack details or not be clearly stated.
1	Student responds to at least one part of the task. Answers may contain factual and/or grammatical errors and may lack details.
0	Response does not match the task or is incorrect.

China's Great Walls

1   **Access students' prior knowledge about the Great Wall of China.** Have students brainstorm information they have read or heard about the Great Wall. List students' responses on the board.

2   **Read aloud the introduction to the Chapter 22 Reading Further in the Student Edition.** Discuss the reasons why there is so much contradictory information about the Great Wall of China.

3   **Have students read the first two pages of the Chapter 22 Reading Further.** Tell students that the Great Wall of China has been named a World Heritage Site by the United Nations. Ask them whether they think the Great Wall deserves such a designation, and to explain why or why not. Invite students to name other natural or human-made monuments they have visited or read about that could deserve such a designation.

4   **Have students read the rest of the Reading Further.** Have students consider reasons why some Chinese might be indifferent to the Great Wall or not think it worthy of preservation or study.

5   **Have students complete the first page of the Reading Further activity in their Interactive Student Notebooks.** Ask several volunteers to share the names of state and community monuments they have written about. Discuss the similarities and differences between these local monuments and the Great Wall in China.

6   **Have students complete the diary entries on the second page of the Reading Further activity in their Interactive Student Notebooks.** Invite students to share their diary entries about a visit to the Great Wall. Have students cite facts, either from the article or from the accompanying photographs, that they used in writing their entries.

English Language Learners

Rephrase the Preview Activity Statements Substitute the simplified statements below for those in the Preview activity:

A leader who has total control over his people.

A leader who keeps his country together.

A leader who makes rules for everyone to follow.

A leader who protects his people from attack.

A leader who has his enemies killed.

A leader who will be remembered for a long time after he dies.

Encourage Cue Cards Allow students to make a cue card for use during the act-it-out. On an index card, they should write brief answers to the questions on Student Handouts 22A and 22B. If chosen to be the "actor" for their group, students will be prepared to answer the reporter's questions.

Provide Models for the Processing Activity As you introduce the Processing activity, show real-life examples of commemorative plaques and wanted posters. Have students compare the similarities and differences between the Processing activity instructions and the real-life examples.

Learners Reading and Writing Below Grade Level

Connect Images to Text Before groups complete Step 2 of their Reading Notes (the questions about the section content), have them read the section to find as many sentences as possible that can be "seen" in the image they analyzed in Step 1. Have volunteers come to the front of the classroom, read the sentence, and point to the exact spot in the image that connects to the reading. Explicitly relating the text to the image will increase student comfort level with the content.

Highlight the Reading Provide a copy of the book pages for Sections 22.2 through 22.6. As students read, encourage them to highlight in one color all the things that made the Emperor of Qin an effective leader, and highlight in a second color those things that made the Emperor of Qin an ineffective leader. This exercise will help students mark their spectrums and complete the Processing activity.

Learners with Special Education Needs

Teach the Concept of a Spectrum To help students understand spectrums (used in Step 3 of the Reading Notes), draw a spectrum on the board, as shown below.

◀———————————————————————▶

Very Boring   Very Enjoyable

Explain that the more enjoyable an event is, the closer it should be placed to the right-hand side of the spectrum. The more boring an event is, the closer it should be placed to the left. Have students discuss where they would place these events on the spectrum:

birthday party   test at school

shopping   watching TV

When students are comfortable with how a spectrum works, change the labels to match Step 3 of the Reading Notes:

◀———————————————————————▶

Very Ineffective   Very Effective

Discuss what the term *effective* means. Then have students decide the effectiveness of each of the following studying methods and its appropriate place on the spectrum:

studying with the TV on   studying in a quiet room

studying with a friend   studying with a parent

Advanced Learners

Create a Report Card In place of, or in conjunction with, the current Processing activity, have students create a report card to evaluate the reign of China's first emperor. Have students give Qin Shihuangdi a letter grade—A, B, C, D, or F—and a written explanation for each of these "subject areas": Unifying China, Encouraging the Exchange of Ideas and Opinions, and Protecting the Chinese People. Tell students to use their report cards to write a well-written paragraph answering the Essential Question: *Was the Emperor of Qin an effective leader?*

Enrichment Resources

Find out more about the Qin dynasty by exploring the following Enrichment Resources for *History Alive! The Ancient World* at www.teachtci.com.

Enrichment Readings These in-depth readings encourage students to explore selected topics related to the chapter. You may also find readings that relate the chapter's content directly to your state's curriculum.

Internet Connections The recommended Web sites provide useful and engaging content that reinforces skills development and mastery of subjects within the chapter.

Literature Recommendations

The following books offer opportunities to extend the content in this chapter.

Emperor Qin's Terra Cotta Army by Michael Capek (Minneapolis, MN: Twenty-First Century Books, 2008)

The Great Wall of China by Lesley A. DuTemple (Minneapolis, MN: Lerner Publications Company, 2003)

Treasures from China by David Armentrout and Patricia Armentrout (Vero Beach, FL: Rourke Book, 2001)

Section 22.2

Step 1: Answers will vary. Students may circle, label, and discuss various soldiers, weapons, the horse and chariot, the walled city on fire, and the army marching across a bridge.

Step 2:

1. Qin Shihuangdi's strategy of conquest helped China because it increased the size of China. However, it also hurt China because it cost many lives, and he used harsh measures to maintain his power.

2. Qin Shihuangdi replaced feudalism with a government he controlled. He did this so that powerful lords would not be a threat to him.

Step 3: Answers will vary.

Section 22.3

Step 1: Answers will vary. Students may circle, label, and discuss the coin with a hole and written characters, the measuring cup, the bell-shaped weight, and the Chinese characters on narrow strips.

Step 2:

1. The emperor created a unified set of laws as part of his standardization of China's culture. Because of his Legalist beliefs, the laws were detailed and harsh, and they applied to all people.

2. Qin Shihuangdi improved trade by standardizing money, weights, and measures. He improved the writing system by reducing the number of Chinese characters.

Step 3: Answers will vary.

Section 22.4

Step 1: Answers will vary. Students may circle, label, and discuss the wall and its scaffolding, the overseer with a whip, the clothing of the characters, and the workers carrying heavy items.

Step 2:

1. The emperor protected China's northern border by building the Great Wall.

2. Soldiers, peasants, musicians, teachers, writers, and artists all helped build the Great Wall. Many died because they built the wall across dangerous physical features (high mountains, a desert, swamps, quicksand) and in extreme climate conditions.

Step 3: Answers will vary.

Section 22.5

Step 1: Answers will vary. Students may circle, label, and discuss the imperial palace and gates, the emperor in the palace, the heavily armed guards, the books burning, and the soldiers executing scholars and dropping them into a pit.

Step 2:

1. There was conflict between Confucian scholars and the emperor because the scholars believed in the ancient teachings of proper behavior and good examples, not in enforcing harsh laws, and they were critical of the government.

2. To prevent his subjects from learning about Confucianism, the emperor ordered all Confucian books burned. Anyone who discussed Confucian teachings would be guilty of criticizing the government and would be put to death.

Step 3: Answers will vary.

Section 22.6

1. *Goal 1*: The emperor failed to become immortal, even though he searched for a potion.

   Goal 2: The emperor succeeded in being remembered for a long time because of extraordinary achievements like the Great Wall and a tomb filled with treasures and an entire terra-cotta army.

2. Answers will vary. Objects buried in the emperor's tomb included a huge terra-cotta army, tools, precious jewels, and rare objects.

The Han Dynasty

In what ways did the Han dynasty improve government and daily life in China?

Overview

In a Social Studies Skill Builder, students visit seven stations to learn about Han achievements in the fields of warfare, government, agriculture, industry, art, medicine, and science. (**Note:** Pinyin spellings are used throughout this unit in accordance with the decision by the Library of Congress to join pinyin syllables.)

Objectives

In the course of reading this chapter and participating in the classroom activity, students will

Social Studies

- explain how the Han dynasty expanded their empire.
- describe the political contributions of the Han dynasty to the development of the imperial bureaucratic state.
- evaluate the impact of inventions and discoveries in the fields of warfare, government, agriculture, industry, art, medicine, and science during the Han empire.

Language Arts

- organize paragraphs that state clear positions and support them.

Social Studies Vocabulary

Key Content Terms Han dynasty, bureaucracy, industry

Academic Vocabulary estimate, release, series, suspend, benefit

Materials

History Alive! The Ancient World

Interactive Student Notebooks

Visuals 23A–23G

Placards 23A–23G

Lesson Masters

- Station Directions 23A–23G (2 copies of each)
- Station Materials 23A (2 copies)
- Station Materials 23B (5 copies, cut apart)
- Station Materials 23C (2 copies, cut apart)
- Vocabulary Development handout (1 per student, on colored paper)

file folders (2)

glasses (4)

straws (2)

sets of watercolors, with 2 brushes each (2)

containers of water (2)

6" squares of white drawing paper (1 per student)

masking tape

Activity	Suggested Time	Materials
Preview	15 minutes	• Interactive Student Notebooks • Visuals 23A–23G
Vocabulary Development	30–40 minutes	• *History Alive! The Ancient World* • Interactive Student Notebooks • Vocabulary Development handout
Social Studies Skill Builder	100–130 minutes (2–3 regular periods) (1.5 block periods)	• *History Alive! The Ancient World* • Interactive Student Notebooks • Placards 23A–23G • Station Directions 23A–23G (2 copies of each) • Station Materials 23A (2 copies) • Station Materials 23B (5 copies, cut apart) • Station Materials 23C (2 copies, cut apart) • file folders (2) • glasses (4) • straws (2) • sets of watercolors, with 2 brushes each (2) • containers of water (2) • 6" squares of white drawing paper (1 per student) • masking tape
Processing	15 minutes	• Interactive Student Notebooks
Assessment	40 minutes	• Chapter 23 Assessment

Preview

1   **Have students turn to the Preview activity in their Interactive Student Notebooks.** Students examine images and predict how the Chinese might have benefited from practices, discoveries, and inventions during the Han period.

2   **Project *Visual 23A: Warfare*.** Have students quickly scan the image and guess the answer to the first Preview activity question. Tell students that they will learn the correct answer to this question as they read Chapter 23.

3   **Repeat Step 2 for the remaining Preview activity questions by briefly projecting Visuals 23B to 23G, one at a time.**

4   **Explain the connection between the Preview activity and Chapter 23.** Tell students that the inventions and practices shown in the Preview activity had an important effect on the Chinese government and on people's daily lives during the Han dynasty. In this chapter, students will learn about Han achievements in the fields of warfare, government, agriculture, industry, art, medicine, and science.

Visual 23A

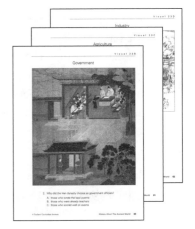

Visuals 23B–23G

Vocabulary Development

1   **Introduce the Key Content Terms.** Have students locate the Key Content Terms for the chapter in their Interactive Student Notebooks. These are important terms that will help them understand the main ideas of the chapter. Ask volunteers to identify any familiar terms and how they might be used in a sentence.

2   **Have students complete a Vocabulary Development handout.** Give each student a copy of the Vocabulary Development handout of your choice from the Reading Toolkit at the back of the Lesson Masters. These handouts provide extra Key Content Term practice and support, depending on your students' needs. Review the completed handout by asking volunteers to share one answer for each term.

Reading

1   **Introduce the Essential Question and have students read Section 23.1.** Have students identify the Essential Question on the first page of the chapter: *In what ways did the Han dynasty improve government and daily life in China?* Then have students read Section 23.1. Afterward, have students use information from Section 23.1 and from the chapter opener image to propose some possible answers to the Essential Question.

2   **Have students complete the Reading Notes for Chapter 23.** Assign Sections 23.2 to 23.8 during the activity, as indicated in the procedures for the Social Studies Skill Builder that follows. Remind students to use the Key Content Terms where appropriate as they complete their Reading Notes.

Social Studies Skill Builder

1 Prepare materials for the activity. Before class, allow sufficient time both to gather the required items from the materials list and to make the required number of copies of the Station Directions and Station Materials. The quantities listed will allow you to create two of each station (14 stations). For a class of more than twenty-eight students, consider placing some students in groups of three or creating triplicate stations.

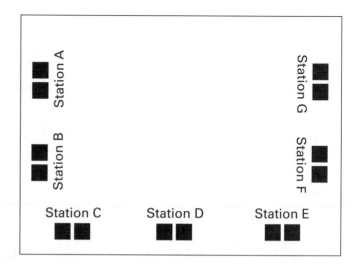

2 Prepare the classroom. Set up the station clusters as shown in the diagram. Follow the instructions on the back of Placards 23A–23G to set up materials at each station. Then post the appropriate placard on the wall between the two stations to which it corresponds. (**Note:** Alternatively, have students set up the stations at the beginning of class. Place the materials for each station in a large plastic bag and assign teams of students to set up each station.)

3 Introduce the activity. Have students sit on the floor and turn to the Chapter 23 Reading Notes in their Interactive Student Notebooks. Tell them that they will visit seven stations, each one representing a part of Chinese life that was improved by a new practice, discovery, or invention during the Han dynasty. At each station, they will be directed to do the following:

- Read a section of Chapter 23 in their books and take notes.

- Decide which Han achievement in the reading was the most important, and then illustrate a tomb brick by sketching an image of that achievement. (**Note:** You may want to explain that, during the reign of the Han, artists often engraved or painted scenes on the bricks used to construct tombs.)

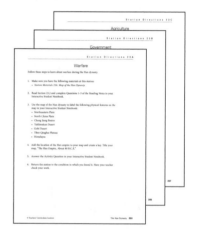

Station Directions 23A–23G

- Complete an activity and then answer a question related to the activity.

4 Divide students into pairs and have them begin working. Have pairs go to different stations. Consider having students raise their hands to indicate they are ready for you to check their work. Use Guide to Reading Notes 23 to check their answers. If their answers are satisfactory, award them points (optional), and have them move to a new station.

5 Have students correct their Preview activity answers. When most pairs have been to most of the stations, have them sit with their partners on the floor and review their answers to the Preview activity. While students are making corrections, grade the completed exams at Station B and announce which students are eligible for civil service appointment.

Station Materials 23A–C

6 Debrief the activity. Ask students,

- What practice, invention, or discovery did you find the most interesting?
- What practice, invention, or discovery do you think had the greatest effect on the government in China during the Han period?
- What practice, invention, or discovery do you think had the greatest effect on the daily lives of people in China during the Han period?

Processing

Have students complete the Processing activity on a separate sheet of paper. Students will evaluate the effect of Han achievements on daily life and on the expansion of the Han government and empire. Have students picture themselves living during the Han period and choose a practice, invention, or discovery that most influenced the Chinese people and government during that time.

Placards 23A–23G

Quicker Coverage

Omit Stations Use your state standards to determine which stations are the most important and which might be eliminated. Gather additional materials to create more of the stations you have decided to use. Alternatively, conduct Stations A, F, and G as a class, to speed up the activity. Create a transparency of the Station Directions and Station Materials for those stations. Then have students rotate through the remaining stations in groups.

Deeper Coverage

Expand the Stations Enrich the station materials. You might run a video clip on topics such as: Station E—calligraphy; Station F—acupuncture; Station G—seismograph. Find such clips on YouTube and other free video search sites. Other ideas: Station A—images of Han weapons; Station C—images of Han agricultural inventions; Station E—more Chinese characters for practice in writing.

Create a "Top Ten" Countdown Have students do the following:

- Ask students, working individually or with a partner, to choose from Chapter 23 ten practices, inventions, or discoveries of the Han dynasty.
- Tell students to rank these ten achievements according to their effect on people's daily lives, from least effect (10) to greatest effect (1).
- Have students use presentation software, overhead transparencies, or poster paper to create a mini-presentation, similar to a "Top Ten" countdown on television or the radio. Have students begin with the least important achievement (number 10) and build to the most important (number 1).
- Encourage students to be creative in their presentations by adding background music, props, and some dramatic flair as they reveal each successive achievement.

Assessment

Mastering the Content

1. B	5. D	9. B	13. D
2. C	6. A	10. C	14. A
3. B	7. D	11. B	15. D
4. A	8. C	12. A	

Applying Social Studies Skills

16. imperial university established, 124 B.C.E.; Buddhism enters China, ca. 50 C.E.; seismograph invented, 132 C.E.

17. Chang'an; Wudi

18. a period of unrest

19. Answers will vary. Possible answer: Wudi was emperor of China from about 141 B.C.E. to about 86 B.C.E., a reign of more than 50 years. He established a university. During his reign, the Han conquered Vietnam, Korea, and parts of Central Asia.

Exploring the Essential Question

20. Answers should include all of the elements requested in the prompt.

Scoring Rubric

Score	Description
3	Student writes an ad that addresses all four bulleted points. Ad is clearly stated, supported by details, and demonstrates command of standard English conventions.
2	Student responds to most or all parts of the task, but ad may lack details or not be clearly stated.
1	Student responds to at least one part of the task. Ad may contain factual and/or grammatical errors and may lack details.
0	Response does not match the task or is incorrect.

English Language Learners

Model the Station Activities Before sending pairs to work on their own, quickly review the procedures for all of the stations so that students have a general idea of how to complete each station activity. Pair students with a peer who can help them appropriately follow the directions at each station.

Conduct Station F Together The acupressure station can be difficult for students to grasp. Work through this station as a class. Have students complete their Reading Notes for Section 23.7. Then read aloud the description of acupressure from Station Directions 23F. Encourage students to ask questions. Draw a simple illustration that shows how qi might travel through a human body and become blocked, which, according to traditional Chinese medicine, causes pain or sickness. Then allow volunteers to follow the directions in Step 3.

Learners Reading and Writing Below Grade Level

Modify Station B Provide the following paraphrase to help students understand the quotation from Confucius: "In society, the highest group is made up of people who are born wise. The second-highest group is made up of people who become wise by studying. The third-highest group is made up of people who have to work very hard to learn. The lowest class is made up of people who work very hard but are never able to learn."

Support the Processing Activity Provide students with the following sentence starts for their Processing activity paragraphs:

1. "The Han achievement that most improved Chinese government or expanded the Han empire was _____. One reason why this was the most important achievement is . . . A second reason why this was the most important achievement is . . ."

2. "The Han achievement that most improved the daily lives of people in China was _____. One reason why this helped people the most is . . . A second reason why this helped people the most is . . ."

Learners with Special Education Needs

Limit the Number of Stations Consider requiring students to visit only four of the seven stations. For the stations that students don't visit, use Guide to Reading Notes 23 to provide answers to the questions. Review each station as a class and allow students to ask clarifying questions about the section content and station activities.

Support the Reading Notes Provide partial answers for the Reading Notes questions at each station by copying Guide to Reading Notes 23. You might omit key words, provide partial sentences, or give a "hint" word or phrase.

Provide a Template Give students a handout with the Processing activity instructions at the top of the page, and with the two bricks from the Interactive Student Notebook instructions already drawn and labeled. Make the bricks large enough so that students will have room to illustrate. Leave enough space underneath the bricks for students to explain the importance of the two Han practices, inventions, or discoveries. Scaffold the Processing activity by brainstorming a list of possible answers on the board. Conduct a "think aloud," in which you model how to fill out one of the bricks by using the brainstormed list and students' Reading Notes. Then allow students to complete the other brick on their own.

Advanced Learners

Link Han Achievements to Today For selected Han achievements, have students compare the Han practice, invention, or discovery with contemporary versions of these achievements. Consider assigning students to research and report to the class about one or more of the following:

- Compare Han military uses of the kite with creative military techniques used today.
- Compare Han government bureaucracy with the U.S. government bureaucracy.
- Compare Han agricultural techniques and tools with today's techniques and tools.
- Compare Han scientific instruments (seismograph and compass) with current versions.

Enrichment Resources

Find out more about the Han dynasty by exploring the following Enrichment Resources for *History Alive! The Ancient World* at www.teachtci.com.

Enrichment Readings These in-depth readings encourage students to explore selected topics related to the chapter. You may also find readings that relate the chapter's content directly to your state's curriculum.

Internet Connections The recommended Web sites provide useful and engaging content that reinforces skills development and mastery of subjects within the chapter.

Literature Recommendations

The following books offer opportunities to extend the content in this chapter.

Ancient Chinese by Tristan Boyar Binns (Minneapolis, MN: Compass Point Books, 2007)

Made in China: Ideas and Inventions from Ancient China by Suzanne Williams (Berkeley, CA: Pacific View Press, 1997)

Oracle Bones, Stars, and Wheelbarrows: Ancient Chinese Science and Technology by Frank R. Ross Jr. (Boston: Houghton Mifflin, 1989)

Section 23.2

1. The Han were able to expand their empire because of their military methods and new weapons. Their empire reached west into Central Asia, east to present-day Korea, and south to present-day Vietnam.

2. Improved iron armor was stronger and more flexible. Longer iron swords allowed Han soldiers to swing at enemies from a safer distance. The crossbow was a more advanced way to shoot arrows at enemies. The Han army used the kite to send messages for military purposes and to frighten enemies at night.

3. Answers will vary. Students will evaluate the weapon that they think most strengthened the Han army.

   Students who participate in the activity will annotate the map as shown below. They will explain how geography affected the expansion of the Han empire. Answers will vary.

Section 23.3

1. Han dynasty rulers softened the harsh ruling style of the Emperor of Qin and brought Confucian ideas back into government.

2. The Han government was a bureaucracy, which is a large, complex organization that functions under a fixed set of rules and conditions. People at each level of the bureaucracy direct those at the level below them. Han emperors used a civil service exam to decide who would get government jobs. Every three years, civil servants were evaluated to determine who would be promoted or demoted.

3. Answers will vary. Students will evaluate the way they think the Han most improved Chinese government.

   Students who participate in the activity will analyze the civil service test they took. Answers will vary.

The Han Empire, About 80 B.C.E

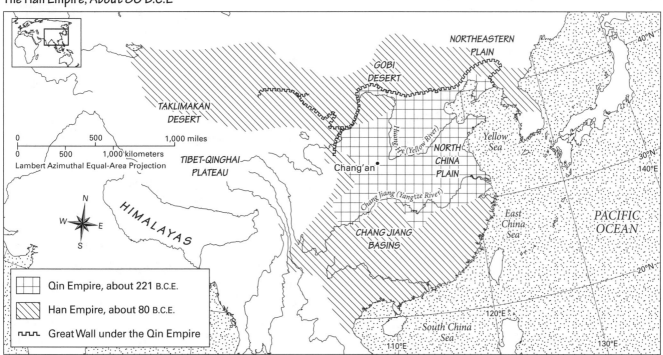

Section 23.4

1. Farmers had to grow food, make their clothing, build their homes, and give one month of unpaid labor to the government. Floods and drought often destroyed their crops.

2. The chain pump made it easier to move water from irrigation ditches and canals to fields. The iron plow made it easier to prepare fields for planting. The wheelbarrow allowed farmers to move heavy loads with less effort.

3. Answers will vary. Students will evaluate the tool that they think most improved agriculture during the Han dynasty. Accept any reasonable description of the benefits to farmers of one of the following: the chain pump, the iron plow, or the wheelbarrow.

   Students who participate in the activity will describe the effect of the agricultural inventions on Han farmers. Answers will vary but should include information on the effects of farming advancements such as the chain pump, the iron plow, or the wheelbarrow on farmers' lives.

Section 23.5

1. A foot-powered machine that could wind fibers onto large reels made silk production easier.

2. Salt was an important trade item in ancient times because it was used to help preserve meat and vegetables.

3. Answers will vary. Students will evaluate the invention that they think most improved industry during the Han period– the foot-powered machined to wind silk fibers or the iron-tipped bamboo drill.

   Students who participate in the activity will compare the Chinese drilling process with the model they used. Answers will vary. Possible answer: The glass of water represents the salt water or brine beneath Earth; the straw represents the hollow bamboo pole on the drill; and the empty glass represents the large iron pots into which the brine is placed.

Section 23.6

1. Chinese calligraphy writing was much like painting. It was a style of writing inspired by the flow of nature. Calligraphers created characters by making quick strokes in a particular order.

2. Before the invention of paper, the Chinese used a brush and ink to write on silk and bamboo. Paper was an improvement on silk and bamboo because it was inexpensive, easier to bind together, and better able to absorb ink.

3 Answers will vary. Students will determine what they think is the most important use of paper during the Han period.

   Students who participate in the activity will explain the advantages of writing on paper rather than on silk or bamboo. Answers will vary.

Section 23.7

1. The Han believed that illnesses were caused when the forces of yin and yang were out of balance in the body.

2. Acupuncture: *What is it?* It is the process of inserting thin needles into specific parts of the body. *Why is it used?* It is used to cure illnesses that strike quickly, like headaches.

   Moxibustion: *What is it?* It is the process of placing and burning a small cone of powdered leaves or sticks on or near the skin. *Why is it used?* It is used to treat long-term diseases, such as arthritis.

3. Chinese doctors discovered things about how the human body works. They learned that a pulse indicates a person's heartbeat and that blood circulates through the body.

4. Answers will vary. Students will evaluate what they think is the most important medical achievement during the Han period. They may choose a medical technique—acupuncture or moxibustion, or a discovery about how the human body works, such as using the heartbeat or pulse to judge health, or the knowledge of how blood circulates in the body.

   Students who participate in the activity will explain that acupressure is a way to clear blocked energy that can cause stress. Answers will vary.

Section 23.8

1. Chinese astronomers discovered why the moon shines and why solar eclipses happen.

2. The Han used the seismograph to detect earthquakes occurring far away and to determine in what direction they were occurring.

   The first compasses were used to determine the correct positioning for temples, graves, and homes to bring good fortune.

3. Answers will vary. Students will evaluate the scientific discovery that they think was the most important advancement during the Han period. They may choose the observations made by astronomers, the invention of the seismograph, or the invention of the magnetic compass.

   Students who participate in the activity will complete a bar graph and explain why the Chinese would want to invent a seismograph. Answers will vary but should mention that knowing where earthquakes occur could protect people.

Deadliest Earthquakes in China

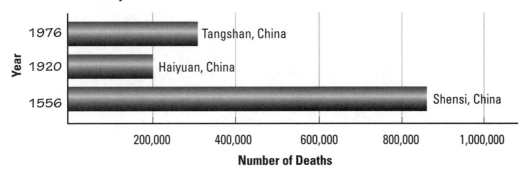

The Silk Road

How did the Silk Road promote an exchange of goods and ideas?

Overview

In an Experiential Exercise, students travel along a simulated Silk Road to learn about facing obstacles, trading products, and absorbing cultural exchanges that occurred along the Silk Road during the Han dynasty. (**Note:** Pinyin spellings are used throughout this unit in accordance with the decision by the Library of Congress to join pinyin syllables.)

Objectives

In the course of reading this chapter and participating in the classroom activity, students will

Social Studies

- locate trans-Eurasian trade routes in the period of the Han dynasty and the Roman Empire.
- identify travel difficulties along the Silk Road.
- explain how the Silk Road led to an exchange of goods, ideas, and beliefs.
- describe the diffusion of Buddhism northward from India to China.

Language Arts

- clarify main ideas in text and connect them to a classroom simulation.

Social Studies Vocabulary

Key Content Terms Silk Road, trade route, caravan, cultural diffusion

Academic Vocabulary dominate, link, acquire, oxygen, occur

Materials

History Alive! The Ancient World

Interactive Student Notebooks

Visual 24

Lesson Masters

- Student Handout 24 (6 copies of each of the 5 pages, on a different-colored paper for each page, cut apart)
- Information Masters 24A–24C (1 of each, cut apart)
- Information Master 24D (1 transparency)
- Vocabulary Development handout (1 per student, on colored paper)

resealable plastic bags (30)

masking tape

Activity	Suggested Time	Materials
Preview	10 minutes	• Interactive Student Notebooks
Vocabulary Development	30–40 minutes	• *History Alive! The Ancient World* • Interactive Student Notebooks • Vocabulary Development handout
Experiential Exercise	60 minutes (1–2 regular periods) (1 block period)	• *History Alive! The Ancient World* • Interactive Student Notebooks • Visual 24 • Student Handout 24 (6 copies of each of the 5 handout pages, on a different-colored paper for each page, cut apart) • Information Masters 24A–24C (1 of each, cut apart) • Information Master 24D (1 transparency) • resealable plastic bags (30) • masking tape
Processing	15 minutes	• Interactive Student Notebooks
Assessment	40 minutes	• Chapter 24 Assessment

Preview

1   **Have students complete the Preview activity in their Interactive Student Notebooks.** Students speculate about the origin of everyday items found and used in the United States today.

2   **Have students share their answers in pairs, and then reveal the answers as a class.** Tell students that the only item on the list that originated in the United States was the zipper. All the other items originated in cultures outside the United States.

3   **Challenge students to brainstorm how these items became a part of our culture.** Ask,

- How many of the items in the Preview activity did you think originated in the United States? Why?

- How do you think that these items became part of our culture? (*through trade, war, migration, media*)

4   **Explain the connection between the Preview activity and Chapter 24.** Tell students that the spreading of goods and ideas between cultures is known as *cultural diffusion*. For example, the ancient Maya chewed chicle, the sap from the sapodilla tree. When a Mexican general was exiled to New York, he happened to introduce chicle to Thomas Adams, who then used it to invent modern chewing gum. In this chapter, students will learn how the Silk Road, a network of trade routes across Europe and Asia, led to an important exchange of goods and ideas.

Vocabulary Development

1   **Introduce the Key Content Terms.** Have students locate the Key Content Terms for the chapter in their Interactive Student Notebooks. These are important terms that will help them understand the main ideas of the chapter. Ask volunteers to identify any familiar terms and how they might be used in a sentence.

2   **Have students complete a Vocabulary Development handout.** Give each student a copy of the Vocabulary Development handout of your choice from the Reading Toolkit at the back of the Lesson Masters. These handouts provide extra Key Content Term practice and support, depending on your students' needs. Review the completed handout by asking volunteers to share one answer for each term.

Reading

1 **Introduce the Essential Question and have students read Section 24.1.**
Have students identify the Essential Question on the first page of the chapter:
How did the Silk Road promote an exchange of goods and ideas? Then have
students read Section 24.1. Afterward, have students use information from
Section 24.1 and from the chapter opener image to propose some possible
answers to the Essential Question.

2 **Have students complete the Reading Notes for Chapter 24.** Assign Sections
24.2 to 24.5 during the activity, as indicated in the procedures for the
Experiential Exercise. Remind students to use the Key Content Terms where
appropriate as they complete their reading notes.

Experiential Exercise

1 **Understand the intent of the activity to simulate trading on the Silk Road.**
In this activity, students take on the role of traders along the Silk Road.
Students are assigned to one of five trading centers, given a set of products
to trade, and taught a simple greeting in a foreign language. In a fast-paced
game, students attempt to acquire five different products by traveling along
the Silk Road, greeting each other in their assigned languages, and exchanging products at the trading centers. As students move along the Silk Road,
they perform actions that represent the dangers of travel. (**Note:** For more
detailed historical connections between the activity and the Silk Road, review
the bulleted lists in Guide to Reading Notes 24.)

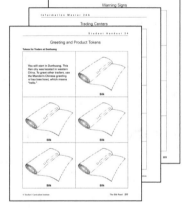

Student Handout 24

2 **Prepare the greeting and trading tokens.** Before class, prepare 30 bags of tokens, six bags for each of the five trading centers along the Silk Road. Consider
using card stock or laminating the tokens for future use. Follow these steps:

- Select a different-colored paper for each of the five trading centers. In the
  appropriate color for each trading center, make six copies of the related
  page of *Student Handout 24: Greeting and Product Tokens.*

- Prepare each bag. Cut one page of the handout along the dashed lines. Place
  the greeting token and the five product tokens into a plastic bag and seal it.
  Repeat for the remaining handout pages. Each center should have six
  bags of tokens.(**Note:**
  Alternatively, give each
  student a copy of one
  page from Student
  Handout 24 and have
  him or her cut out the
  tokens to be used.)

3 **Arrange the classroom.**
Simulate the Silk Road
by following the diagram
and these steps:

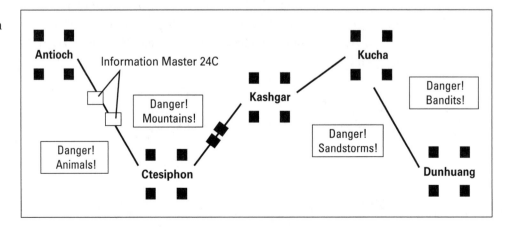

- Make five squares to represent trading centers along the Silk Road. Use four desks to mark the corners of each square. Squares should be (a) large enough to accommodate six students, (b) arranged so that students move in a fairly straight line from one end of the road to the other, and (c) far enough apart so students must "journey" from one square to another.

- In the middle of each square, tape the appropriate location label from *Information Master 24A: Trading Centers*.

- Connect the squares with masking tape to indicate the road from one trading center to the next.

4 **Simulate travel conditions along the Silk Road.** Do the following:

- Between Dunhuang and Kucha, tape the "Danger! Bandits!" warning sign from *Information Master 24B: Warning Signs* next to the masking tape. Students will crawl between these two trading stations to represent the evasive measures traders had to take to avoid bandits who attacked caravans.

- Between Kucha and Kashgar, tape the "Danger! Sandstorm!" warning sign next to the masking tape. Students will cover their eyes and look down to represent the measures traders had to take to protect themselves during sandstorms in the Taklimakan Desert.

- Between Kashgar and Ctesiphon, place two desks. Tape the "Danger! Mountains!" warning sign to one of the desks. Students will climb over the desks to represent the difficulties of traveling over the steep mountain trails of the Pamir Mountains, which were often covered in snow.

- Between Ctesiphon and Antioch, tape the illustrations of the lion and the scorpion from *Information Master 24C: Animals* over the masking tape. Tape the "Danger! Animals!" warning sign next to the masking tape. Students will hop over the animal pictures to represent the dangers encountered in crossing the Syrian Desert on the way to Antioch.

5 **Introduce the Silk Road.** Have students sit anywhere in the classroom where they can see the screen. Project *Visual 24: The Silk Road* and ask, *What do you see? What do the red lines represent? What do you think happened along the Silk Road? Why do you think it was called the Silk Road? What cities were at the ends of the Silk Road? Which parts of the Silk Road do you think would be most dangerous to travel?*

6 **Introduce the activity, traveling and trading along the Silk Road.** Explain that in this activity, students will take on the role of traders along the ancient Silk Road. They will experience the challenges of traveling and the rewards of trading along this important network of trade routes.

7 **Have students read and complete items 1–4 in the corresponding Reading Notes for Section 24.2.** Tell students that this section will give them background information that will help them participate in the upcoming activity about the Silk Road. Tell them to leave the T-chart incomplete at this time. Use Guide to Reading Notes 24 to review students' answers to the questions.

Information Master 24A

Information Masters
24B and 24C

Visual 24

The Silk Road **301**

8 Assign students to starting locations and distribute materials.

- Divide students into five equal-size groups. (**Note:** If your class is not evenly divisible by five, assign some students to work in pairs or to act as "checkers" along the route, making sure "traders" are following the rules.)

- Have each group sit in one of the trading centers.

- Give every student a bag of tokens corresponding to his or her trading center. Have students verify that they have each received one greeting token and five product tokens.

9 Go over the rules of trading. Project *Information Master 24D: Rules for Trading Along the Silk Road* and review the rules as a class. Emphasize the following:

Information Master 24D

- As students travel, they may move in either direction, but they must stop at the next nearest center they come to. When students climb over desks or walk with their eyes covered, they must do so very carefully.

- Only students who are new arrivals to a trading center may initiate a trade, and they may take part in only one exchange each time they stop. This ensures that students will have to move along the Silk Road, rather than staying at their starting location.

- Before every trade, students must greet each other in the language assigned to their trading center. Have each group practice aloud the pronunciation of their greeting. These greetings represent the diffusion of culture and beliefs that occurred along the Silk Road. The languages are not meant to represent the exact languages spoken at each location during this specific time period. They have been chosen to represent different cultures that were involved in trade along the Silk Road.

10 Conduct the simulation. Have students in each group number off, starting with 1. Remind students that they may not trade until you call their numbers. Then call the numbers in any order, but be certain that everyone has had a turn before repeating numbers. This will ensure students' attention and add to the excitement. Give each group approximately 45 seconds to move and trade; allow sufficient time for trading but keep the game moving at a brisk pace.

11 Debrief the experience. Project Visual 24 again and ask,

- What did you like about the activity? What did you dislike?

- What aspects of the activity were the most challenging? Why?

- Would you have wanted to be a trader along the Silk Road? Why or why not?

12 Connect the experience to history. Have students turn to the "Trading Along the Silk Road" T-chart in their Reading Notes for Section 24.2. Examine the answers filled in for the first bullet in each column on the chart as a model for the remaining bullets to be completed. Be sure that students understand the relationship between their actions in the classroom (moving only to the next nearest trading center) and those of traders on the Silk Road (traveling long distances and then resting). Next, ask the first bulleted set of questions below, guiding students to identify how the travel challenges they experienced connect to actual obstacles traders may have faced. During the discussion, students should fill in the second bullet on both sides of the T-chart. (**Note:** Use the two bulleted lists in Guide to Reading Notes 24 as a reference.) Repeat this procedure for the remaining bullets, giving students time to fill in the T-chart between each set of questions.

- What were some of the difficulties of traveling the Silk Road? What did crawling represent? What did covering your eyes and looking down represent? What did the desks represent? What did the animal pictures represent?

- What happened if you did not complete a task properly? What might have happened to traders who failed to take precautions while traveling?

- What did traders from Dunhuang, the trading center for Chinese products, have to trade? What did traders from Antioch, the trading center for Roman products, have to trade? What were some of the other products traded along the Silk Road?

- Which students finished first? Which had to travel the farthest to get the products they wanted? What do you think this illustrates?

- How many of you traveled from one end of the Silk Road to the other? Why do you think most traders did not travel the entire route?

- In how many different languages were you greeted during your travels? What other cultural ideas or beliefs do you think traders experienced on the Silk Road?

13 Have students read and complete the corresponding Reading Notes for Sections 24.3 to 24.5. You may wish to invite students to add historical details to their T-charts as they read these sections. Use the bulleted lists in Guide to Reading Notes 24 to review the answers with them.

14 Wrap up the activity with a class discussion. Ask,

- What aspects of the activity were similar to what traders may have actually experienced along the historical Silk Road? What aspects were different?

- What were the benefits of trading along the Silk Road? What were the costs or risks?

- How did trade along the Silk Road result in cultural diffusion?

Listening and Speaking: Narrative

An alternative assignment is an oral narrative that relates a trader's experiences along the Silk Road. Require a story map as a planning or prewriting step; it must include the setting or settings, main characters, point of view, and events. Remind students to develop their narrative through the use of concrete details and dialogue. Encourage them to build suspense as they incorporate one or more of the dangers of the Silk Road. Then ask students to practice delivering their narratives before they present them to the class.

Processing

Have students complete the Processing activity. Students should use a separate sheet of paper to write and illustrate a journal entry about the challenges and rewards of travel along the Silk Road.

Quicker Coverage

Complete Section 24.2 Together As part of the introduction to the activity, summarize the key points from Section 24.2 for the class. As you review the images and summarize the main ideas in that section, have students fill out their Reading Notes. Emphasize the following points:

- Zhang Qian's travels introduced China to new places and established trade relations across Asia.
- The Silk Road was a network of many smaller trade routes across Europe and Asia.
- China's most valuable trade good was silk. The Romans traded gold and glassware for silk.

Then conduct the Experiential Exercise.

Conduct a Class Demonstration Rather than have all students participate in the trading game, have a limited number of students demonstrate the activity. Choose ten volunteers and assign two to each of the five trading stations. Follow all other procedures for the activity. As part of the debrief questions, ask the class, *What did you notice during the demonstration?* (**Note:** You may want to simplify the classroom setup by using one desk to represent each trade center. Have the two students sit on the desk that represents their center.)

Deeper Coverage

Research the Origin of Preview Activity Items Have students research the origin of the items listed in the Preview activity. Tell students to first look in a dictionary to find the origin of each word or phrase. Then students can research more information online and in their school library. (**Note:** All the Preview Activity items are discussed in Charles Panati's *Extraordinary Origins of Everyday Things*.) Have students present their findings to the class. If students present conflicting stories of origin, have the class analyze why there might be varying accounts of the origin of an item.

Add Perspectives to the Processing Activity Have students write the Processing activity from the viewpoint of a Buddhist monk, a caravan leader, or a merchant. Students' journal entries should be written from their character's perspective, reflecting the different goals and experiences of travelers on the Silk Road. Ask volunteers to read their journal entries aloud.

Explore the Silkworm Bring samples of silk and live silkworms to class, or show images of each. Challenge students to guess how worms could possibly be the source of such a beautiful fabric. Consider reading aloud *The Empress and the Silkworm* by Lily Toy Hong, a storybook about the discovery of silk in China. An endnote explains what is known about the history of Chinese silk, and describes how silk is made. Students may want to research more about the cycle of the silkworm, the process of making silk, or the various types of silk.

Assessment

Mastering the Content

1. A	5. D	9. B	13. D
2. B	6. A	10. D	14. A
3. C	7. C	11. C	15. A
4. D	8. B	12. A	16. C

Applying Social Studies Skills

17. Taklimakan Desert; Tian Shan Mountains (must be in this order)

18. Chang'an; Dunhuang (either order)

19. Answers will vary. Possible answers: it was about halfway along the Silk Road; several different routes came together there; it was accessible to Persia, India, and China

Exploring the Essential Question

20. Answers should include all of the elements requested in the prompt.

Scoring Rubric

Score	Description
3	Student completes a billboard that meets the requirements of all five bulleted points. Billboard is clearly stated, supported by details, and demonstrates command of standard English conventions.
2	Student responds to most or all parts of the task, but billboard may lack details or not be clearly stated.
1	Student responds to at least one part of the task. Billboard may contain factual and/or grammatical errors and may lack details.
0	Response does not match the task or is incorrect.

English Language Learners

Model the Rules for Trading Before having students conduct the Experiential Exercise, explicitly model the rules on Information Master 24D. Have a couple of students with appropriate bags of tokens stand at different trading centers. As you explain each rule, have these students model what to do, such as moving only when their number is called, carefully dealing with each obstacle, greeting one another in their assigned language (on their greeting token), conducting a trade, and so on.

Introduce the Concept of Diffusion Before students complete their Reading Notes for Section 24.5, introduce the term *cultural diffusion*. Have students think about the spread of cultural fads. Ask students, *What do you do when you find a new phone, shirt, song, or video game that you like?* (Students tell their friends about it, or they buy it and their friends see it.) *What do your friends do then?* (They want it or buy it or share the information with other friends.) Explain that, just as students share today's fads, ancient people traded and spread ideas they liked.

Learners Reading and Writing Below Grade Level

Provide a Word Bank Use Guide to Reading Notes 24 to create a "master" list, in random order, of the key dangers, products, and plants involved in trade along the Silk Road. Students can match the items on the master list to the appropriate question in their Reading Notes to help them complete the tasks on the map.

Support the Debrief Give students the answers to either the classroom experiences (left column) or the historical connections (right column) on the T-chart. These are provided in Guide to Reading Notes 24 in two bulleted lists titled "Classroom Experience" and "Historical Connection." Providing these answers will reduce the amount of writing necessary while debriefing the activity and connecting students' experience to history. Consider making a transparency of the T-chart from the Interactive Student Notebook and completing it with students.

Learners with Special Education Needs

Provide T-Chart Answers Copy and cut apart the statements in the two bulleted lists in Section 24.2 in Guide to Reading Notes 24. After the Experiential Exercise, read each statement aloud randomly. Have students categorize it as either something that happened in the classroom or something that happened in history. Write both headings on the board and then write each statement under the heading that students have agreed on. Starting with the first statement for the classroom experience, ask students to find the matching historical connection. Draw a line connecting the two matching statements on the board and examine the connection as a class. Repeat this process for the remaining connections.

Model the Reading Notes Make a transparency of the Reading Notes for Section 24.3. After students have read the section, model the required map tasks. To model Question 1, explain that one of the dangers along the Eastern Silk Road was bandits. Then, on the overhead map, between Dunhuang and Kucha, sketch a simple warning sign that says "Careful—You Might Get Robbed!" To model Questions 2 to 4, remind students that silk was China's most valuable trading good. On the overhead map, near Dunhuang, sketch a simple drawing of a piece of silk and label it. Note that the label is more important than the quality of the art.

Advanced Learners

Discuss Trade and Prices In the debrief, ask, *What do you think happened to the price of a product the farther it was sold from its original location? Why?* Have students consider how the "middle man" affects prices in a market economy. Ask, *Where does your family buy food? Would it be cheaper to buy food from a grocery store or directly from a farmer? What is the advantage of buying from the store rather than the farmer? What else do we buy from "middle men"?*

Research Cultural Diffusion Ask student pairs to find a historical or current example of cultural diffusion, e.g., the Columbian exchange or the spread of modern cultural fads. Have students map the movement of their chosen good or idea and explain how it has been adapted by and into the new culture(s).

Enrichment Resources

Find out more about the Silk Road by exploring the following Enrichment Resources for *History Alive! The Ancient World* at www.teachtci.com.

Enrichment Readings These in-depth readings encourage students to explore selected topics related to the chapter. You may also find readings that relate the chapter's content directly to your state's curriculum.

Internet Connections The recommended Web sites provide useful and engaging content that reinforces skills development and mastery of subjects within the chapter.

Literature Recommendations

The following books offer opportunities to extend the content in this chapter.

Legacies from Ancient China by Anita Ganeri (Mankato, MN: Thameside Press, 2000)

The Silk Route: 7,000 Miles of History by John S. Major (New York: HarperCollins, 1996)

Stranger on the Silk Road: A Story of Ancient China by Jessica Gunderson (Minneapolis, MN: Picture Window Books, 2009)

Section 24.2

1. The Han empire opened the Silk Road by defeating the nomadic people in northwestern China.

2. Three things Zhang Qian brought back to China were more powerful horses, grapes, and cultural knowledge of such places as Persia, Syria, India, and Rome.

3. Silk was China's most valuable trade good because, at first, the Chinese were the only people who knew how to make it. A Roman trading product that was new to the Chinese was glassware.

Trading Along the Silk Road

Classroom Experience

- Students were allowed to move to only one trading center at a time.

- Students had to crawl, cover their eyes, climb over desks, and hop over pictures.

- Students lost a turn if they did not complete a task properly.

- Students started with one type of product token and traded for others.

- Students in middle trading centers finished sooner than students at trading centers at the ends.

- Most students did not travel to all the stations.

- Students learned greetings in five different languages.

Historical Connection

- Traders had to travel long distances and then rest for days or weeks.

- Traders faced many dangers such as bandits, desert sandstorms, mountains, and threats from animals.

- If traders were not carefully prepared, they could lose their camels and goods, and possibly die.

- Products from different cultures were traded all along the Silk Road.

- It took a long time for goods from China and Rome to reach the opposite location.

- Traders used local trade routes rather than using the entire Silk Road.

- Ideas, culture, and religion spread along the Silk Road.

Section 24.3

Map Tasks:

1. "Warning signs" should reference two of the following dangers of the Eastern Silk Road: bandits, sandstorms, and mirages.

2. Near Dunhuang, students should draw and label symbols for two of the following Chinese trade products: silk, dishware, jewelry, cast-iron products, and decorative boxes.

3. Near Kucha, students should draw and label symbols for two of the following Central Asian trade products: horses, jade, furs, and gold.

4. Near Kashgar, students should draw and label symbols for two of the following Indian trade products: cotton, spices, pearls, and ivory.

Questions:

1. Traders survived desert travel by stopping at oases, avoiding mirages, and forming caravans of Bactrian camels.

2. Silk was the perfect trading good because it was light and valuable.

Section 24.4

Map Tasks:

1. "Warning signs" should reference two of the following dangers of the Western Silk Road: difficult passes and a lack of oxygen high in the mountains, and the threat of animals and insects in the desert.

2. Near Ctesiphon, students should draw and label symbols for two of the following Egyptian, Arabian, and Persian trade products: perfumes, cosmetics, and carpets.

3. Near Antioch, students should draw and label symbols for two of the following Roman trade products: glassware, gold, and asbestos.

Questions:

1. After they reached Antioch, many goods were transported by ship throughout the Mediterranean world, including Rome.

2. The Roman emperor forbid men from wearing silk because he wanted to reduce the amount of gold lost to his empire.

Section 24.5

Map Tasks:

1. Near China, students should draw and label symbols for two of the following plants China learned about from trade along the Silk Road: grapes, cucumbers, figs, pomegranates, walnuts, chives, sesame, and coriander.

2. Near Rome, students should draw and label symbols for two of the following plants the West learned about from trade along the Silk Road: roses, azaleas, chrysanthemums, peonies, camellias, oranges, pears, and peaches.

3. Near India, students should draw a symbol for Buddhism. To show the spread of Buddhism, they should draw an arrow up to Kashgar and then eastward along the Silk Road into China.

Question: Answers will vary but should concisely respond to the Essential Question for the chapter.

Ancient China

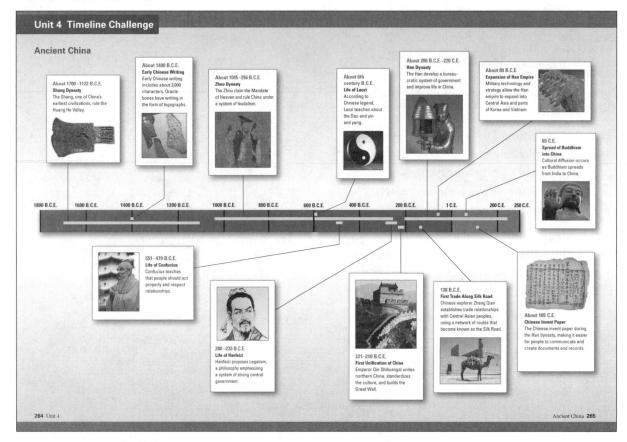

Overview

This Timeline Challenge helps students review the main events and ideas of this unit while providing practice in reading and interpreting timelines. You can vary and expand the activity according to students' needs and the amount of time available.

Basic Procedure

1 **Introduce the timeline in the Student Edition.** Direct students to the Ancient China Timeline at the end of Unit 4 in the Student Edition. You may wish to have students read aloud and discuss the timeline entries.

2 **Introduce the Timeline Challenge in the Interactive Student Notebook.** Direct students to the Unit 4 Timeline Challenge in their notebooks. Point out the two types of questions, "Timeline Skills" and "Critical Thinking," and model how to answer each type.

3 **Have students complete the Timeline Challenge.** Monitor students as they work. Use the Guide to Unit 4 Timeline Challenge to check their answers. You may wish to project a transparency of the Timeline Challenge as you work through the questions with the class and conduct a discussion of the "Critical Thinking" questions.

4 Complete the KWL chart. Return to the KWL chart created at the beginning of the unit, and ask students to list the key information they have learned.

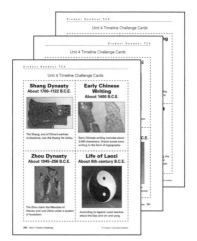

Student Handout TC4

Classroom Timeline

1 Prepare the Timeline Challenge Cards. Copy and cut the cards from *Student Handout TC4: Unit 4 Timeline Challenge Cards.* You may wish to laminate the cards for future use.

2 Create a timeline on a classroom wall. On an empty wall or a large bulletin board, make a timeline with masking tape or colored paper. Mark off the time intervals in advance, or ask students to do so in class.

3 Have students place the Timeline Challenge Cards. Distribute cards to individual students or pairs and have them tape the cards to the timeline in the correct locations. Call on students to provide more information on the timeline topics, to review main events and issues.

Internet Research

1 Review students' suggestions for additional timeline entries. Have students share their answers to the last question of the Timeline Challenge.

2 Have students conduct Internet research. Ask students to choose and research one of their suggested events.

3 Have students create additional Timeline Challenge Cards. Direct students to research an appropriate image for their cards and then use the computer to create an illustrated card, complete with timeline entry.

Timeline Skills

Score 1 point for each correct answer.

1. The Shang dynasty was the first to rule China, from about 1700 to 1122 B.C.E. They controlled the Huang He Valley.

2. Early Chinese writing, called logographs, was placed on oracle bones during the Shang dynasty.

3. The Zhou justified their rule by claiming the Mandate of Heaven.

4. The Zhou dynasty ended in about 256 B.C.E.

5. Confucius lived from 551 to 479 B.C.E., which was before the first unification of China in 221 B.C.E.

6. Emperor Qin Shihuangdi united northern China, standardized the culture, and built the Great Wall.

7. The Han dynasty ruled China for about 426 years.

8. Expansion of the Han dynasty began in 80 B.C.E., which was in the earlier half of the dynasty's rule. They expanded into Central Asia and parts of Korea and Vietnam.

9. Trading began along the Silk Road in 138 B.C.E., which opened up China to foreign trade. In 65 C.E., Buddhism spread to China from India, in the cultural diffusion that occurred with trade.

10. The Chinese invented paper about 105 C.E. It was important because it made it easier for people to communicate and create records and documents.

Critical Thinking

Score 1 to 3 points for each answer, depending on the thoroughness of the response.

11. Confucianism taught that people should act properly and respect relationships. Daosim taught that people gained happiness and peace by living in harmony with the way of nature. Legalism taught that people needed strict laws, enforced with either rewards for good behavior or harsh punishments for bad behavior. These philosophies developed during the later years of the Zhou dynasty, when several states were fighting for power. So much instability led Chinese thinkers to ask questions about the way people should be governed.

12. Answers will vary. Students must clearly state their opinion and use supporting examples to explain their ideas. Examples of effective actions *may* include unifying China, standardizing weights and measures, simplifying the writing system, and protecting the northern border. Examples of ineffective actions *may* include using physical punishment, exiling people, burning Confucian books, and executing Confucian scholars.

13. a. By adopting Confucian ideas, the Han changed the way China was ruled. They created a bureaucracy to help run the vast empire. Civil servants were chosen by merit, not by social class.
    b. Answers will vary. Possible answer: Another important Han contribution that helped people was improvements in agriculture. The inventions of the chain pump, the iron plow, and the wheelbarrow all made farming easier, which helped create a stable food supply. (Accept answers about advances in industry, art, medicine, or science.)

14. Answers will vary. Students must explain why the events they chose merit inclusion.

Using Scores to Inform Instruction

Timeline Skills A score of 7 out of 10 indicates that students understand most of the key events of this unit.

Critical Thinking A score of 8 out of 12 indicates that students are able to think critically about most of the key issues of this unit.

If students score below these levels, consider reviewing timeline and critical thinking skills.

Ancient Greece

Ancient Greece

Overview

This activity introduces the geographic information essential to Unit 5. Students read and interpret maps to learn about key physical features of ancient Greece and the unique ways in which those features affected not only the interaction between ancient Greek communities, but also the interaction between the ancient Greeks and people from other cultures. Students annotate an outline map of ancient Greece, answer questions in their Interactive Student Notebooks, and then discuss critical thinking questions. Students' comprehension of content and proficiency in map-reading and higher-order thinking skills will help you gauge their readiness for the unit. The pages that follow include a completed map, answers to questions, a scoring guide to inform your teaching, and suggestions for modifications to meet specific student needs.

Essential Geographic Understandings

1. Location of ancient Greece

2. Key physical features: Mediterranean Sea, Adriatic Sea, Ionian Sea, Aegean Sea, Black Sea, Asia Minor

3. Location of Greek colonies

4. Location of key Greek cities

Procedures

1 **Introduce the unit.** Tell students they will learn about ancient Greek civilization and its enduring influence on the world today.

2 **Create a KWL chart.** Ask students to identify what they already know about ancient Greece and what they want to learn. Use their responses to gauge how much additional background information they will need as you progress through the unit. Students will return to the KWL chart at the end of the unit and add the key information they have learned.

3 **Have students read Unit 5 "Setting the Stage" in the Student Edition.**

4 **Have students complete the Geography Challenge.** Monitor students as they work. Use the guide on the next two pages to check their answers. You may wish to project the map from the Interactive Student Notebook and have students annotate it as the class works through the map-reading questions. Make sure students have grasped Essential Geographic Understandings 1 to 3.

5 **Discuss the "Critical Thinking" questions.** Help students understand the geographic relationships described in Essential Geographic Understanding 4.

The World of the Ancient Greeks, About 550 B.C.E.

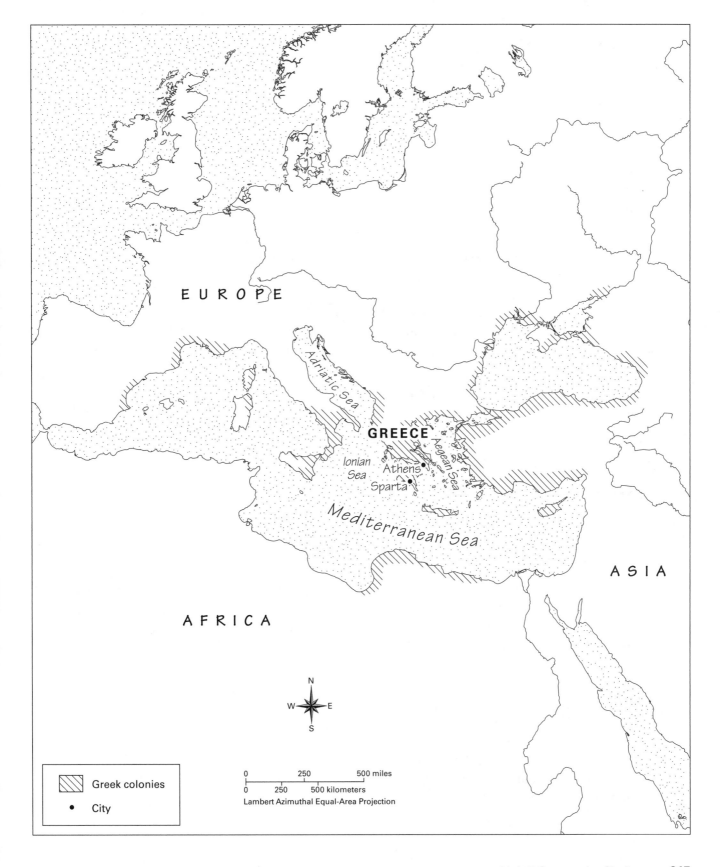

EUROPE

Adriatic Sea

GREECE

Ionian Sea

Athens

Sparta

Aegean Sea

Mediterranean Sea

ASIA

AFRICA

N
W E
S

0	250	500 miles
0	250	500 kilometers

Lambert Azimuthal Equal-Area Projection

Greek colonies

• City

Geography Skills

Score 1 point for each correct answer. Use the map on the previous page to check shading and labeling.

1. Students' labels should indicate that the Mediterranean Sea lies south of ancient Greece and that the Aegean Sea lies along the eastern coast of Greece.

2. Students should label the continent of Europe.

3. Use the annotated map to check students' locations of colonies and continent labels.

4. The Greek colonies on the Iberian Peninsula were the farthest from Greece. They were located about 1,100 miles from mainland Greece.

5. Use the annotated map to check students' labels for the Adriatic and the Ionian seas. The seas surrounding ancient Greece meant that the country had a good deal of coastline and natural harbors. The seas also provided highways to other countries, which made establishing colonies and trade with those countries much easier.

6. You would travel south to get from ancient Greece to Egypt.

7. Check students' labels for the cities of Athens and Sparta. Athens was farther north.

Critical Thinking

Questions may have more than one correct answer. Score 1 to 3 points for each reasonable answer, depending on the strength of students' geographic reasoning.

8. Greek farmers met the challenge of their steep and rocky land by cultivating crops such as olives and grapes that did not require a great deal of land. The Greeks also raised sheep and goats, rather than cattle. Unlike cattle, sheep and goats could graze on the steep hillsides.

9. Students should use the large map in the Unit 5 Setting the Stage feature to predict that the ancient Greeks set up colonies and trade routes to overcome the problem of not having enough farmland to produce food.

10. Answers will vary. Possible answer: Because so many islands dotted the Aegean Sea, travel to Asia Minor would have been easier. Ships would have been able to stop along the route at these islands, resting and restocking provisions if necessary.

11. Answers will vary. Possible answer: The contact between the ancient Greeks and the people of other cultures might have had several possible consequences. One could have been the growth of trade, which could have made Greece a thriving and wealthy nation. Another consequence might have been cultural diffusion between the Greeks and the people of other lands. Finally, this contact may have allowed the Greeks to absorb other nations into its realm of power. Accept any other reasonable hypotheses.

Using Scores to Inform Instruction

Geography Skills A score of 5 out of 7 or better indicates that students have acquired sufficient geographic information to proceed with the unit.

Critical Thinking A score of 8 out of 12 or better indicates that students are beginning to understand the relationships between physical geography and the different ways in which people live.

Modifying Instruction

ELL or Learners with Special Education Needs Consider focusing on map-reading questions or limiting the number of "Critical Thinking" questions.

Students with Weak Map or Critical Thinking Skills Assign appropriate pages from the Social Studies Skills Toolkit in the back of the Lesson Masters.

CHAPTER

Geography and the Settlement of Greece

25

How did geography influence settlement and way of life in ancient Greece?

Overview

In a Visual Discovery activity, students examine and analyze thematic maps to learn about the physical geography of ancient Greece and how it influenced the development of Greek civilization.

Objectives

In the course of reading this chapter and participating in the classroom activity, students will

Social Studies

- examine the physical geography of the Greek peninsula.
- analyze thematic maps of ancient Greece, including locations of colonies and trade routes.
- discuss connections between the geography of Greece and the development of ancient Greek city-states.

Language Arts

- connect and clarify main ideas by identifying their relationship to other sources.
- write sentences for a specific audience.

Social Studies Vocabulary

Key Content Terms peninsula, Aegean Sea, colony

Academic Vocabulary consult, participate, rely

Materials

History Alive!
The Ancient World

Interactive Student Notebooks

Visuals 25A–25C

Lesson Masters

- Vocabulary Development handout (1 per student, on colored paper)

masking tape

scrap paper

Activity	Suggested Time	Materials
Preview	30 minutes	• Interactive Student Notebooks • Visual 25A • masking tape • scrap paper
Vocabulary Development	30–40 minutes	• *History Alive! The Ancient World* • Interactive Student Notebooks • Vocabulary Development handout
Visual Discovery	45 minutes (1 regular period) (0.5 block period)	• *History Alive! The Ancient World* • Interactive Student Notebooks • Visuals 25B and 25C
Processing	20 minutes	• Interactive Student Notebooks
Assessment	40 minutes	• Chapter 25 Assessment

Preview

Visual 25A

1   **Re-create the area of mainland Greece.** Create an open space in the class-room. Project *Visual 25A: Physical Features of the Greek Peninsula*. With a piece of paper, cover the map to reveal only the title. Use masking tape to create a 6-by-8-foot rectangle on the floor, and tell students that it represents the area of mainland Greece. (**Note**: Alternatively, use string or a twin-size bedsheet to designate the area of Greece.)

2   **Introduce the physical geography of Greece.** Tell students that Greece does not have any major rivers, but is surrounded on three sides by seas. Then direct students' attention to the rectangle on the floor. Tell them that the bottom and the sides of the rectangle simulate the coastline of Greece, and point out the location of the Mediterranean, Aegean, and Ionian seas. Ask the class, *How did the physical geography affect where ancient Greeks settled?*

3   **Have volunteers "settle" Greece.** Invite 12 students to settle Greece by having them stand anywhere they would like inside the rectangle. Ask these students, *Why did you settle in this particular area? Do you have enough space?*

4   **Reveal the top third of Visual 25A.** Pull down the paper covering Visual 25A to reveal the top third of the map of Greece. Ask the class, *What physical feature covers most of the land? What effect will the mountains have on settlement?*

5   **Simulate the mountains and have settlers move.** Create mountains by placing two chairs in the center of the top third of the rectangle. Announce that these mountains make this area unsuitable for settlement. Settlers must move to a more suitable area. Ask settlers, *Why did you move to this particular location?*

6   **Repeat Steps 4 and 5 with the middle and bottom thirds of the map on Visual 25A.**

7   **Simulate the islands and have settlers move.** Have the class reexamine the map on Visual 25A. Ask students, *What other physical features do you see on the map? About how many islands do you think there are?* Create islands by placing four or five pieces of scrap paper on the floor, near the bottom and sides of the rectangle. Offer settlers the option of moving to these islands. Then ask settlers, *Why did you choose to move or to stay where you are?*

8   **Debrief the exercise.** Have settlers return to their seats. Ask students,

- What are the advantages of the physical geography of Greece? What are the disadvantages?

- In what ways does the physical geography create challenges for human settlement? How might people deal with these challenges?

9   **Have students complete the Preview activity in their Interactive Student Notebooks.** Students predict the ways in which the physical geography of Greece may have influenced settlement and way of life in ancient Greece.

10 Explain the connection between the Preview activity and Chapter 25. Tell students that Greece has a unique geography that influenced where people settled and how they lived. For example, the mountainous land and the lack of major rivers made farming difficult. In this chapter, students will learn about the physical geography of ancient Greece and how it influenced the development of communities in the region.

Vocabulary Development

1 Introduce the Key Content Terms. Have students locate the Key Content Terms for the chapter in their Interactive Student Notebooks. These are important terms that will help them understand the main ideas of the chapter. Ask volunteers to identify any familiar terms and how they might be used in a sentence.

2 Have students complete a Vocabulary Development handout. Give each student a copy of the Vocabulary Development handout of your choice from the Reading Toolkit at the back of the Lesson Masters. These handouts provide extra Key Content Term practice and support, depending on your students' needs. Review the completed handout by asking volunteers to share one answer for each term.

Reading

1 Introduce the Essential Question and have students read Section 25.1. Have students identify the Essential Question on the first page of the chapter: *How did geography influence settlement and way of life in ancient Greece?* Then have students read Section 25.1. Afterward, have students use information from Section 25.1 and from the chapter opener image to propose some possible answers to the Essential Question.

2 Have students complete the Reading Notes for Chapter 25. Assign Sections 25.2 to 25.5 during the activity, as indicated in the procedures for the Visual Discovery. Remind students to use the Key Content Terms where appropriate as they complete their Reading Notes.

Visual Discovery

1 Place students in pairs and introduce the activity. Tell students that they are going to analyze two thematic maps of ancient Greece. They will use the maps to make predictions about where ancient Greeks settled and how they lived. Students will then read to discover if their predictions were correct.

2 Have students analyze a physical map of Greece. Project *Visual 25B: Physical Geography of Greece.* This visual shows a physical map of Greece and also gives information about climate (temperature and precipitation) and vegetation. Point out to students the elevation key on the map. Ask these questions to help students analyze the map:

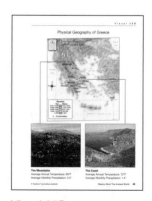

Visual 25B

- What type of information does this map show?

- What physical features do you see on the map? What is the elevation in most parts of Greece?

- How would you describe the climate and vegetation of the mountain regions? Of the coastal regions?

- Where are most people likely to settle? Why do you think so?

- What challenges would physical geography likely create for settlers? How might people deal with these challenges?

3 **Have pairs complete the Reading Notes for Sections 25.2 and 25.3.** Tell students that these sections reveal where people settled in ancient Greece and what challenges they faced. Have pairs read Sections 25.2 and 25.3 and complete the corresponding Reading Notes in their Interactive Student Notebooks.

4 **Have students reexamine Visual 25B.** Encourage students to use their Reading Notes to answer this question: *What challenges did geography create for settlement in ancient Greece, and how did people deal with those challenges?*

5 **Have students analyze settlements and trade routes of ancient Greece.** Project *Visual 25C: Ancient Greek Colonies and Trade Routes.* This map shows the locations of ancient Greek settlements and trade routes. Ask these questions to help students analyze the map:

Visual 25C

- What information does this map show?

- Where were most ancient Greek settlements located before 800 B.C.E.? After 800 B.C.E.?

- Why do you think ancient Greeks settled outside mainland Greece?

- What places traded with ancient Greece?

- Why might ancient Greece have needed to trade with these places?

- What relationship might exist between the trade routes and the colonies?

6 **Have pairs complete the Reading Notes for Sections 25.4 and 25.5.** Tell students that these sections discuss how and why the ancient Greeks established colonies and trade. Have pairs read Sections 25.4 and 25.5 and complete the corresponding Reading Notes in their Interactive Student Notebooks.

7 **Have students reexamine Visual 25C.** Encourage students to use their Reading Notes to answer this question: *Why did the ancient Greeks establish colonies and trade?*

8 **Debrief the activity. Hold a class discussion.** Ask,

- What adjectives would you use to describe the physical geography of Greece?

- How did geography influence settlement in ancient Greece?

- How did geography influence the way of life in ancient Greece?

Processing

Have students complete the Processing activity in their Interactive Student Notebooks. Students complete a storyboard draft of a children's book about the geography of ancient Greece and how it influenced the Greeks' way of life.

Quicker Coverage

Skip the Settlement Exercise in the Preview Activity Eliminate Steps 1 through 8 to skip the settlement exercise in the Preview activity. Instead, project Visual 25A and have students complete the Preview activity prompt in their Interactive Student Notebooks.

Deeper Coverage

Conduct a Mapping Lab Before the class examines the maps in the Visual Discovery activity, have pairs use each map to answer specific questions. Create workstations by making several copies of each visual and posting them on the walls around the room. Have pairs work at the stations to answer the questions. Sample questions are listed below.

Visual 25B:

- What is the name of the mountain range that covers most of Greece?
- What are the names of the seas that surround Greece?
- What is the name of Greece's largest island?
- What is the highest elevation in Greece? The lowest?
- What is the average annual temperature in the mountains? At the coast?
- What is the average monthly precipitation in the mountains? At the coast?

Visual 25C:

- Near what sea were most Greek colonies located?
- On what continent were most Greek colonies located?
- Where were the closest colonies located? The farthest colonies?
- Which seas did Greek traders travel through?
- Which continents did Greek traders travel to?
- How many colonies were connected to trade routes?

Add a Student Skit When pairs have completed the Reading Notes for Sections 25.4 and 25.5, conduct an act-it-out for Visual 25C. Divide students into groups of four. Assign one-third of the groups to be Farming Settlements, one-third to be Trading Settlements, and one-third to be Colonies. Have each group prepare a short skit illustrating what life was like for the people in each of these types of settlements. Invite the groups representing the Farming Settlements to perform their skits one at a time. Repeat for the groups representing the Trading Settlements and then the Colonies.

Assessment

Mastering the Content

1. B	5. C	9. D	13. B
2. A	6. B	10. D	14. D
3. D	7. C	11. C	15. A
4. B	8. A	12. A	

Applying Social Studies Skills

16. any three places named on the map

17. a. On the map, the X should be placed in the body of water to the right of Greece.
b. Answers will vary. Possible answer: east of Greece; between Greece and Asia Minor; between Greece and Sardis; the part of the Mediterranean Sea that is closest to the Black Sea

18. Answers will vary. Possible answers:
a. at the seacoast; on sailing routes; near the Mediterranean Sea and the Black Sea
b. Those locations were chosen for their natural harbors and good farmland. The colonies needed to trade by sea with mainland Greece.

19. a. Ships
b. Answers will vary. Possible answer: The mountains were hard to cross, and land travel was difficult, so most shipping of goods was done by water.

Exploring the Essential Question

20. Answers should include all of the elements requested in the prompt.

Scoring Rubric

Score	Description
3	Student completes all four parts of the task, selecting at least one influence for each geographical feature. Writing in ovals is clearly stated, supported by details, and demonstrates command of standard English conventions.
2	Student responds to most or all parts of the task, but writing may lack details or not be clearly stated.
1	Student responds to at least one part of the task. Writing may contain factual and/or grammatical errors and may lack details.
0	Response does not match the task or is incorrect.

English Language Learners

Discuss Examples Before students complete the Preview activity in their Interactive Student Notebooks, review the concept of how geography affects the way people live. Consider discussing examples from other civilizations, such as China. In China, for example, people grew rice in the warm, wet regions that were unsuitable for growing wheat. Or use U.S. regions as examples.

Provide Metric Conversions Some students may be more familiar with Celsius (temperature) and with metric measurements (precipitation) than with the information given on Visual 25B. Give students the following Celsius and metric conversions:

- The Mountains: 18° C, 89 mm
- The Coast: 22° C, 36 mm

Learners Reading and Writing Below Grade Level

Read One Section at a Time Break up the reading during the Visual Discovery activity so that students read only one section at a time.

To break up the reading for Visual 25B:

- Ask all but the last bulleted question in Step 2. Have students read Section 25.2 and complete the corresponding Reading Notes.
- Ask the last bulleted question in Step 2. Have students read Section 25.3 and complete the corresponding Reading Notes.

To break up the reading for Visual 25C:

- Ask all but the last two bulleted questions in Step 5. Have students read Section 25.4 and complete the corresponding Reading Notes.
- Ask the last two bulleted questions in Step 5. Have students read Section 25.5 and complete the corresponding Reading Notes.

Scaffold the Reading Notes Use Guide to Reading Notes 25 to scaffold the Reading Notes so that students take steps toward working more independently.

- For Section 25.2, omit key words that students can fill in.

- For Sections 25.3 and 25.4, provide prompts that students can complete.
- For Section 25.5, have students complete as written.

Learners with Special Education Needs

Divide the Preview Question Divide the Preview question in the Interactive Student Notebook into two separate questions: *How do you think the physical geography of Greece influenced where people settled?* and *How do you think the physical geography of Greece influenced how people lived?* Students should write a brief response to each question.

Offer a Choice for the Processing Activity Have students complete two of the four storyboard pages for the Processing activity. Allow students the choice of doing Pages 1 and 2 or Pages 3 and 4. Alternatively, consider pairing students to work together to complete all four pages of the storyboard.

Advanced Learners

Add Questions to the Debrief Add the following questions to Step 8 in the Visual Discovery activity:

- How is the physical geography of Greece similar to or different from that of other civilizations you have studied, such as Mesopotamia, Egypt, Kush, Canaan, India, and China?
- How was life in ancient Greece similar to and different from life in other ancient civilizations? What influence does physical geography have on these similarities and differences?
- Do you think the settlements of ancient Greece will develop into a unified empire? Why or why not?

Research a Traditional Greek Dish In addition to, or as an alternative to, the Processing activity, have students research the ingredients of a traditional Greek dish, for example, a Greek salad. Students should identify each ingredient, how it is produced, and how it relates to ancient Greece. For the Greek salad, students might explain that olive oil is made from olives, which are grown on trees on Greek hillsides. In small groups, students should share their findings and discuss how their research on the Greek dish ingredients relates to what they learned about in the chapter.

Enrichment Resources

Find out more about the geography and settlement of ancient Greece by exploring the following Enrichment Resources for *History Alive! The Ancient World* at www.teachtci.com.

Enrichment Readings These in-depth readings encourage students to explore selected topics related to the chapter. You may also find readings that relate the chapter's content directly to your state's curriculum.

Internet Connections The recommended Web sites provide useful and engaging content that reinforces skills development and mastery of subjects within the chapter.

Literature Recommendations

The following books offer opportunities to extend the content in this chapter.

Ancient Greece by Andrew Solway (New York: Oxford University Press, 2001)

The Ancient Greek World by Jennifer T. Roberts and Tracy Bennett (New York: Oxford University Press, 2004)

Seven Wonders of Ancient Greece by Michael and Mary B. Woods (Minneapolis, MN: Twenty-First Century Books, 2008)

Section 25.2

1. The ancient Greeks mostly settled on the coast near the seas.

2. Ancient Greek communities were isolated from each other by mountains, which made travel and communication difficult.

3. Answers will vary. Possible answers:
   - Travel by land was hard because roads were not paved.
   - People had to bring their own food and other supplies with them.
   - Sudden storms might send ships off course or sink them.

Section 25.3

1. Answers in chart will vary. Possible answers:

   Challenges to Greek Farmers:
   - The land in ancient Greece was mostly mountainous.
   - Even in the plains and valleys, the land was rocky, and water was scarce.
   - The rainy season was mostly during the winter months.
   - No major rivers flowed through Greece.

   How Farmers Met These Challenges:
   - Some farmers built wide earth steps into the hills to create more flat land for farming.
   - Most farmers grew crops like grapes and olives, which needed less land.
   - Farmers planted hillside orchards of fruit and nut trees.
   - Greek farmers raised sheep and goats, which can graze on the sides of mountains.

2. Some Greek settlements fought each other because of the shortage of good land.

Section 25.4

1. The ancient Greeks started colonies primarily because they needed more farmland to raise enough crops to feed their people.

2. The ancient Greeks consulted an oracle to see whether their efforts would be successful. Then they gathered food and supplies, took a flame from the town's sacred fire, and began their long sea voyages. Finally, after finding a safe place with good farmland and natural harbors, they established their colony.

3. The Greeks established colonies over a period of 300 years, from 1000 to 650 B.C.E. Colonies were located in Asia Minor (Turkey), Spain, France, Italy, Africa, and along the coast of the Black Sea.

Section 25.5

1. Some ancient Greek settlements traded to get the goods they needed.

2. Olive oil and pottery from the Greek mainland were traded (exported). In exchange, the Greeks got (imported) grain, timber, and metal.

3. Answers will vary. Possible answers:
   - Merchant ships were built not for speed but for carrying large amounts of goods. Journeys were long, and a one-way trip from the mainland could take two months.
   - The lack of compasses or charts made navigation difficult.

The Rise of Democracy

How did democracy develop in ancient Greece?

Overview

In an Experiential Exercise, students use the principles of monarchy, oligarchy, tyranny, and democracy to select and play music for the class, as a way to examine and experience the various forms of government in ancient Greece that led to the development of democracy.

Objectives

In the course of reading this chapter and participating in the classroom activity, students will

Social Studies

- examine forms of government in ancient Greece.
- identify the advantages and disadvantages of monarchy, oligarchy, tyranny, and democracy as ways of governing in ancient Greece.
- explain key differences between direct and representative democracy.

Language Arts

- state and support a clear position.
- connect and clarify main ideas.

Social Studies Vocabulary

Key Content Terms monarchy, aristocrat, oligarchy, tyranny, democracy, citizen, assembly

Academic Vocabulary insist, ignore, hostile, reverse

Materials

History Alive! The Ancient World

Interactive Student Notebooks

Lesson Masters

- Vocabulary Development handout (1 per student, on colored paper)

music CDs (brought to class by students)

headband made of yellow paper

headband made of green paper

play money, in large denominations

yardstick or meterstick

Activity	Suggested Time	Materials
Preview	15 minutes	• Interactive Student Notebooks
Vocabulary Development	30–40 minutes	• *History Alive! The Ancient World* • Interactive Student Notebooks • Vocabulary Development handout
Experiential Exercise	60–80 minutes (1–2 regular periods) (1 block period)	• *History Alive! The Ancient World* • Interactive Student Notebooks • music CDs (brought to class by students) • CD player • headband made of yellow paper • headband made of green paper • play money, in large denominations • yardstick or meterstick
Processing	20 minutes	• Interactive Student Notebooks
Assessment	40 minutes	• Chapter 26 Assessment

Preview

1   **Have students complete the Preview activity in their Interactive Student Notebooks.** Students act as members of a sports team to determine the best way to make a team decision.

2   **Have students share their responses in pairs or as a class.**

3   **Explain the connection between the Preview activity and Chapter 26.** Tell students that the four options for how best to make the team's decision relate to the four forms of government used in ancient Greece. Many Greek city-states tried more than one form of government. Athens is the city-state that became known for developing democracy. In a democracy, all citizens share the power to rule. In this chapter, students will learn about various forms of government in ancient Greece that led to the development of democracy.

Vocabulary Development

1   **Introduce the Key Content Terms.** Have students locate the Key Content Terms for the chapter in their Interactive Student Notebooks. These are important terms that will help them understand the main ideas of the chapter. Ask volunteers to identify any familiar terms and how they might be used in a sentence.

2   **Have students complete a Vocabulary Development handout.** Give each student a copy of the Vocabulary Development handout of your choice from the Reading Toolkit at the back of the Lesson Masters. These handouts provide extra Key Content Term practice and support, depending on your students' needs. Review the completed handout by asking volunteers to share one answer for each term.

Reading

1   **Introduce the Essential Question and have students read Section 26.1.** Have students identify the Essential Question on the first page of the chapter: *How did democracy develop in ancient Greece?* Then have students read Section 26.1. Afterward, have students respond to these questions:

   • What did the ancient Greeks from isolated communities have in common with each other?

   • Did the ancient Greeks think of themselves as belonging to one country? Why or why not?

   • In what ways were ancient Greek city-states different from each other?

2   **Have students complete the Reading Notes for Chapter 26.** Assign Sections 26.2 to 26.5 during the activity, as indicated in the procedures for the Experiential Exercise. Remind students to use the Key Content Terms where appropriate as they complete their Reading Notes.

> **Vocabulary Development: Multiple-Meaning Words**
>
> Help students think about multiple meanings for *assembly* by talking about how the term is used at school. Discuss other meanings, too, such as "the act of making something" or "the putting together of parts," as in automobile assembly. Mention the right to assembly given by the First Amendment. Point out that the meanings, including the one that applies to ancient Greece, all have at the core of their meaning some sense of a group or of a group working together.

Experiential Exercise

1 **Collect music CDs several days in advance.** Before you conduct the activity, give students several days to bring in their favorite songs on CDs. Tell students that the first ten CDs brought to class will be used for a musical listening activity. Have students label the CDs or CD cases with their names and the track numbers of their favorite songs. Preview the songs ahead of time to make sure the songs are appropriate in content and length. (**Note:** Alternatively, have students list their favorite songs, and download digital versions of the music. For the activity, make a CD, or use a digital music player and speakers.)

2 **Arrange the classroom.** Place the CD player and three chairs at the front of the room.

3 **Introduce the activity.** Tell students that they will listen to some of their favorite songs from the CDs they brought to school. Ask the class, *Which songs should we listen to? How loudly should the music be played?* Allow students to offer several suggestions, and thank them for their participation. But then explain to students that they will be using the principles of four forms of government from ancient Greece to select the songs and set the volume. After students have experienced each form of government, they will read to connect their experience with actual history. (**Note:** You may want to conduct all four phases of the Experiential Exercise before you have students read the chapter and complete their Reading Notes.)

Phase 1: Monarchy

1 **Introduce the concept of monarchy.** Write the word *monarchy* on the board. Explain that the earliest form of government in ancient Greece was monarchy, in which one person, most likely a king, had the power to make all government decisions.

2 **Have students sit on the floor.** Explain that in this activity, students who are sitting on the floor have no power. They cannot speak or move without permission.

3 **Choose music according to the principles of monarchy.**

   • Select two students to come to the front of the room. Place the yellow headband on one student and have him or her sit in a chair. Explain that this student is the king and has absolute power. Place the green headband on the other student and have him or her kneel next to the king. Tell the class that this student is the prince and is next in line to become king.

   • Tell the king to select a song to play. Announce that he or she will ignore any earlier suggestions from the class because a king has absolute power. Allow the king to play the song, at any volume he or she chooses. (**Note:** In the interest of time, you may want to have students play only a sample, perhaps 20 to 30 seconds, of the selected songs.)

- When the song ends, tell the king that he or she has just died. Remove the yellow headband and have the king lie on the floor. Tell the prince that he or she has now inherited the power from the king. Remove the prince's green headband, replace it with the yellow one, and have the prince sit in the chair.

- Have the prince (the new king) select and play a new song, following the same guidelines given to the former king.

4 **Debrief the experience.** Ask students,

- How did you feel during this part of the activity?

- Did you like how the king and prince chose and played the music? Was there anything you could have done if your ideas differed from your leader's?

- Who makes the decisions in a monarchy? How did an individual become a king?

- What are the advantages of a monarchy? What are the disadvantages?

5 **Have students complete the Reading Notes for Section 26.2.** Have students read Section 26.2 and complete the corresponding Reading Notes in their Interactive Student Notebooks. Then ask students to talk about connections between their classroom experience and the reading.

Phase 2: Oligarchy

1 **Introduce the concept of oligarchy.** Write the word *oligarchy* on the board. Explain that oligarchy developed in ancient Greece as an alternative to monarchy. In an oligarchy, a small group of people have the power to make political decisions.

2 **Choose music according to the principles of oligarchy.**

- Continue having students sit on the floor. Remind them that, in this position, they have no power.

- Select three students to come to the front of the room. Give them the play money and have them sit in the chairs. Explain that these students are oligarchs. Most oligarchs in ancient Greece were wealthy aristocrats. They lived very comfortably. (**Note:** Consider either placing a soft blanket over the chairs or allowing students to put their feet up on chairs.)

- Have the oligarchs select a song to play. Announce that they will ignore any earlier suggestions from the class because oligarchs typically look after their own interests. Allow the oligarchs to play the song, at any volume they choose.

3 **Debrief the experience.** Ask students,

- How did you feel during this part of the activity?

- Did you like how the oligarchs chose and played the music? Was there anything you could have done if your ideas differed from your leaders'?

- Who makes the decisions in an oligarchy? How did an individual become an oligarch?

- What are the advantages of an oligarchy? What are the disadvantages?
- Why do you think oligarchy developed as an alternative to monarchy?

4 **Have students complete the Reading Notes for Section 26.3.** Have students read Section 26.3 and complete the corresponding Reading Notes in their Interactive Student Notebooks. Then ask students to talk about connections between their classroom experience and the reading.

Phase 3: Tyranny

1 **Introduce the concept of tyranny.** Write the word *tyranny* on the board. Explain that discontent with the oligarchies in ancient Greece led to the rise of new leaders called tyrants. In a tyranny, one individual seizes power by force and rules single-handedly.

2 **Choose music according to the principles of tyranny.**

- Continue having students sit on the floor. Remind them that, in this position, they have no power.
- Ask for three or four volunteers, who would each like to choose the next song. Have the volunteers stand. Tell the remaining students to each stand next to the volunteer who, in their opinion, should be the one to choose the next song. Identify the student with the greatest number of supporters. Have everyone else again sit down on the floor.
- Ask the selected volunteer to come to the front of the class. Give the student a yardstick or meterstick to hold, and have him or her sit in a chair. Explain that this student is a tyrant. Most Greek tyrants were military leaders who promised improvements and who rose to power with the support of their soldiers and some of the people.
- Have the tyrant select a song to play. Announce that he or she will ask for the advice of those students who supported him or her, because tyrants need to please their supporters to stay in power. Allow the tyrant to play the suggested song, at a volume recommended by his or her supporters.

3 **Debrief the experience.** Ask students,

- How did you feel during this part of the activity?
- Did you like how the tyrant chose and played the music? Was there anything you could have done if your ideas differed from your leader's?
- Who makes the decisions in a tyranny? How did an individual become a tyrant?
- What are the advantages of a tyranny? What are the disadvantages?
- Why do you think tyrannies developed after oligarchies and monarchies?

4 **Have students complete the Reading Notes for Section 26.4.** Have students read Section 26.4 and complete the corresponding Reading Notes in their Interactive Student Notebooks. Then ask students to talk about connections between their classroom experience and the reading.

Phase 4: Democracy

1 **Introduce the concept of democracy.** Write the word *democracy* on the board. Explain that around 500 B.C.E., after the overthrow of a harsh tyrant, the citizens of Athens decided that they would rule themselves. In a democracy, people vote to make political decisions.

2 **Choose music according to the principles of democracy.**

   - Have all students sit in their seats. Tell students that everyone now has equal power to make the decisions about the choice of song and its volume.

   - Ask students to share suggestions for which songs to play. Have a volunteer record the titles on the board.

   - Have the class choose a song by voting on the titles on the board. Announce that you will play the song that receives the majority, or more than 50 percent, of the votes. If, after the first vote, there is no winner, the class will vote again, but this time, choosing between the top two songs. (**Note:** If time allows, repeat these steps to have students choose the volume.)

   - Play the song voted on by the majority of students.

3 **Debrief the experience.** Ask,

   - How did you feel during this part of the activity?

   - Who makes decisions in a democracy? How are these decisions made?

   - What are the advantages of a democracy? What are the disadvantages?

   - Why do you think democracy developed after the other three forms of government?

4 **Have students complete the Reading Notes for Section 26.5.** Have students read Section 26.5 and complete the corresponding Reading Notes in their Interactive Student Notebooks. Then ask students to talk about connections between their classroom experience and the reading. Afterward, ask, *In what ways is American government similar to and different from ancient Greek democracy?*

Processing

Have students complete the Processing activity in their Interactive Student Notebooks. Students will complete a report card to evaluate the four forms of government practiced in ancient Greece.

Quicker Coverage

Break Up the Reading Conduct all four phases of the Experiential Exercise before having students read and complete their Reading Notes for Chapter 26. To complete the Reading Notes, divide the class into four groups. Assign one section of Sections 26.2–26.5 to each of the four groups. Have students work in pairs to complete the Reading Notes for their assigned section. Then create new groups of four or five, with students from each of the assigned sections. Have group members share their Reading Notes in their groups, one section at a time, beginning with Section 26.2.

Conduct Two of Four Phases Conduct only the first and fourth phases of the Experiential Exercise. After following the procedures for the first phase on monarchy, introduce oligarchy as a form of government. Have students read and complete the Reading Notes for Section 26.3. Afterward, have students offer suggestions on how the principles of oligarchy might be used to choose a song to play in the classroom. Then introduce tyranny and follow the same procedures as those for oligarchy, using Section 26.4. Finally, conduct the fourth and final phase of the Experiential Exercise in which students experience and read about democracy.

Deeper Coverage

Create Pictowords Have students work individually or in pairs to create pictowords for each of the four forms of government practiced in ancient Greece. Explain that a pictoword is a drawing that uses the letters in a word to symbolize the word's meaning. A pictoword might change a letter into an object or change the form of the letters. For example, a pictoword for the term *vote* might have hands at the ends of the letters. Another pictoword for the term *vote* might replace the letter *o* with a ballot box.

Compare Direct Democracy and Representative Democracy Compare and contrast direct and representative democracy by examining the ancient city-state of Athens and the modern United States. Have students work in pairs or in small groups to complete a chart for each government. Consider having students do research to learn about the following:

- Who may become a citizen?
- Who may vote?
- Who makes laws?
- How long may lawmakers serve?

Afterward, have students discuss the strengths and weaknesses of each type of democracy. You might consider asking about the degree to which all people are represented, the amount of time it might take to pass laws, and the effectiveness or longevity of each system.

Assessment

Mastering the Content

1. B	5. C	9. C	13. D
2. C	6. B	10. B	14. D
3. A	7. D	11. A	15. A
4. A	8. D	12. D	16. B

Applying Social Studies Skills

17. Kypselos or Periander (accept either)

18. oligarchy

19. Answers will vary. Possible answer: A tyrant had taken power and would likely treat them harshly if they stayed.

Exploring the Essential Question

20. Answers should include all of the elements requested in the prompt.

Scoring Rubric

Score	Description
3	Student completes all five parts of the task. Notes are clearly stated, supported by details, and demonstrate command of standard English conventions.
2	Student responds to most or all parts of the task, but notes may lack details or not be clearly stated.
1	Student responds to at least one part of the task. Note(s) may contain factual and/or grammatical errors and may lack details.
0	Response does not match the task or is incorrect.

English Language Learners

Brainstorm Symbols After the debrief step in each phase of the Experiential Exercise, have students work in small groups to brainstorm simple symbols that represent each one of the forms of government. Students can use these examples to help them complete the first part of the Reading Notes for each section. Sample symbols include the following:

- a crown for monarchy
- three smaller crowns for oligarchy
- a sword or fist for tyranny
- a ballot or ballot box for democracy

Use a Word Bank Provide a Word Bank to support students in completing the Reading Notes. Using Guide to Reading Notes 26, make a list of all the answers. Students will choose their answers from the list to fill in the blank lines in each section. For the speech bubbles for each section, provide the following words:

- Section 26.2: *laws, lead, punish, aristocrats, power*
- Section 26.3: *laws, wealth, poor, ignore, unjust*
- Section 26.4: *force, promise, poor, harshly, people*
- Section 26.5: *assembly, free man, vote, citizens*

Learners Reading and Writing Below Grade Level

Conduct a Prereading Exercise For the steps of the Experiential Exercise that involve reading the text, have students work in pairs to read aloud to each other. As they read, have them work together to jot down four words or phrases that are associated with each government type. Examples for oligarchy might include *wealthy, army, unfairness, ruled as a group*. After everyone has completed the reading, ask pairs to share their words, writing them on the board or using an overhead transparency. Then have students complete their Reading Notes individually or with their partners.

Learners with Special Education Needs

Prepare for the Activity Before conducting the Experiential Exercise in class, discuss with students, in advance, what will happen in each phase of the activity. Determine with these students whether any accommodations are needed that will help them feel comfortable participating in the activity. You might consider assigning them to the role of on-scene reporter, whose job it is to observe the activity in each phase and summarize the events that happen, before the class begins the debrief step.

Model the Reading Notes Before class, make a transparency of the Reading Notes for Section 26.2. After conducting Phase 1 of the Experiential Exercise, have students take turns reading aloud Section 26.2 on monarchy. Project the transparency of the Reading Notes for Section 26.2 and work as a class to complete them. Consider using this procedure to complete the Reading Notes for the remaining sections, or consider pairing students to work together.

Modify the Processing Activity Provide additional structure for the Processing activity by breaking up each of the tasks. Together with students, review the concept of a report card. Then, for each of the four governments, work together as a class to complete the grades in the first column. Have students work in pairs to complete the grades for the second column, and then review as a class. Finally, have students, on their own, complete the grades for the last column.

Advanced Learners

Research Forms of Government Have students work in pairs or in small groups to research historical or modern examples of each form of government discussed in Chapter 26. Have students create a poster or a digital presentation to share their research. For each form of government, they should include the name of the country or empire; the name(s) of the leader(s); an explanation for why their example meets the criteria of that form of government; and a simple visual, such as a flag, map, or photograph.

Enrichment Resources

Find out more about democracy and other forms of government in ancient Greece by exploring the following Enrichment Resources for *History Alive! The Ancient World* at www.teachtci.com.

Enrichment Readings These in-depth readings encourage students to explore selected topics related to the chapter. You may also find readings that relate the chapter's content directly to your state's curriculum.

Internet Connections The recommended Web sites provide useful and engaging content that reinforces skills development and mastery of subjects within the chapter.

Literature Recommendations

The following books offer opportunities to extend the content in this chapter.

The Greeks: Life in Ancient Greece by Michelle Levine (Minneapolis, MN: Millbrook Press, 2009)

The Pocket Timeline of Ancient Greece by Emma McAllister (New York: Oxford University Press, 2006)

Tools of the Ancient Greeks: A Kid's Guide to the History and Science of Life in Ancient Greece by Kris Bordessa (White River Junction, VT: Nomad Press, 2006)

Section 26.2

1. Students should shade in the timeline from 2000 to 800 B.C.E. Symbols for monarchy will vary.

2. Under a monarchy, the power to make political decisions is in the hands of one person, usually called a monarch, or king.

3. Answers will vary. Possible answer:

   I ruled by making laws, acting as judge, conducting religious ceremonies, and leading the army. I punished people who disobeyed the law or didn't pay their taxes. I had a council of aristocrats to advise me.

4. Answers will vary. Possible answer:

   I lost power because I depended heavily on the aristocrats to help me during wartime. They grew stronger as a group, demanded more of my power, and finally overthrew me.

Section 26.3

1. Students should shade in the timeline from 800 to 650 B.C.E. Symbols for oligarchy will vary.

2. Under an oligarchy, the power to make political decisions is in the hands of a few people, called oligarchs.

3. Answers will vary. Possible answer:

   We ruled by passing laws that protected and increased our own wealth. We lived comfortable lives, while the poor worked all day in the fields.

4. Answers will vary. Possible answer:

   We lost power because we ignored the needs of the majority of the people. We passed unpopular laws and used the army to enforce them. The rich got richer and the poor got poorer. Eventually, the poor turned to leaders in the army. These new leaders overthrew us.

Section 26.4

1. Students should shade in the timeline from 650 to 500 B.C.E. Symbols for tyranny will vary.

2. Under a tyranny, the power to make political decisions is in the hands of one person who is not a lawful king, called a tyrant.

3. Answers will vary. Possible answer:

   I ruled by force, though I was not always unpopular. I promised people more rights and made changes to help the poor.

4. Answers will vary. Possible answer:

   I lost power because I sometimes ruled harshly and ignored the needs of the people. In Athens, the people forced me out of power.

Section 26.5

1. Students should shade in the timeline from 500 to 400 B.C.E. Symbols for democracy will vary.

2. Under a democracy, the power to make political decisions is in the hands of all people, called citizens.

3. Answers will vary. Possible answer:

   We ruled by having an assembly. Any free man could speak at an assembly and vote on a new law or a proposal to go to war. Free men also ran the city's day-to-day business.

4. Answers will vary. Possible answer:

   Not all Greeks thought democracy was a good idea because powerful speakers sometimes persuaded ordinary citizens to vote unwisely. Often, an assembly reversed important decisions after just a few weeks. Most city-states returned to earlier forms of government, such as tyrannies (dictatorships) and oligarchies.

Life in Two City-States: Athens and Sparta

What were the major differences between Athens and Sparta?

Overview

In a Social Studies Skill Builder, students examine the major differences between Athens and Sparta by working in pairs to create placards with illustrations and challenge questions about each city-state.

Objectives

In the course of reading this chapter and participating in the classroom activity, students will

Social Studies

- locate ancient Athens and Sparta and explain the connection between geography and the development of these city-states.
- describe Athenian and Spartan government, economy, education, and treatment of women and slaves.
- compare and contrast life in Athens and Sparta.

Language Arts

- analyze text that is organized by comparison and contrast.
- clarify an understanding of text using illustrations and summary notes.
- express complete thoughts using effective coordination and subordination of ideas.

Social Studies Vocabulary

Key Content Terms Athens, Sparta, Peloponnesus, Council of 500, agora, Council of Elders

Academic Vocabulary select, obtain, capable, abandon, eliminate

Materials

*History Alive!
The Ancient World*

Interactive Student Notebooks

Visuals 27A and 27B

Lesson Masters

- Information Masters 27A and 27B (1 transparency of each)
- Student Handout 27 (1 copy per pair of students)
- Vocabulary Development handout (1 per student, on colored paper)

colored pencils or markers

blank paper (1 piece per pair of students)

masking tape

Activity	Suggested Time	Materials
Preview	15 minutes	• Interactive Student Notebooks • Visual 27A
Vocabulary Development	30–40 minutes	• *History Alive! The Ancient World* • Interactive Student Notebooks • Vocabulary Development handout
Social Studies Skill Builder	90 minutes (2 regular periods) (1 block period)	• *History Alive! The Ancient World* • Interactive Student Notebooks • Visual 27B • Information Masters 27A and 27B (1 transparency of each) • Student Handout 27 (1 copy per pair of students) • colored pencils or markers • blank paper (1 piece per pair of students) • masking tape
Processing	20 minutes	• Interactive Student Notebooks
Assessment	40 minutes	• Chapter 27 Assessment

Preview

1 **Have students predict differences between Athens and Sparta.** Project *Visual 27A: Athens and Sparta* and have students complete the Preview activity in their Interactive Student Notebooks. Students use the illustrations of Athens and Sparta to make predictions about how life differed in each city-state.

2 **Have students share their responses in pairs or as a class.**

3 **Explain the connection between the Preview activity and Chapter 27.** Tell students that the illustration at the top of the projection is the city-state of Athens. Athens was located just miles from the sea, and its economy was based on trade. The illustration at the bottom is the city-state of Sparta. Sparta was located on a narrow plain, surrounded on three sides by mountain ranges. Its economy depended on farming. These were only a few of the differences between the two city-states. In this chapter, students will learn how life differed between Athens and Sparta.

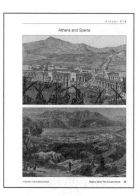

Visual 27A

Vocabulary Development

1 **Introduce the Key Content Terms.** Have students locate the Key Content Terms for the chapter in their Interactive Student Notebooks. These are important terms that will help them understand the main ideas of the chapter. Ask volunteers to identify any familiar terms and how they might be used in a sentence.

2 **Have students complete a Vocabulary Development handout.** Give each student a copy of the Vocabulary Development handout of your choice from the Reading Toolkit at the back of the Lesson Masters. These handouts provide extra Key Content Term practice and support, depending on your students' needs. Review the completed handout by asking volunteers to share one answer for each term.

> **Writing: Capitalization**
>
> Use the chapter Key Content Terms and other vocabulary to teach or review some rules of capitalization:
>
> 1. Capitalize the names of countries, states, cities, and other political divisions, such as city-states (Athens, Sparta);
>
> 2. Capitalize the names of geographical places (Peloponnesus);
>
> 3. Capitalize important words in the names of political bodies and associations (Council of 500, Council of Elders).

Reading

1 **Introduce the Essential Question and have students read Section 27.1.** Have students identify the Essential Question on the first page of the chapter: *What were the major differences between Athens and Sparta?* Then have students read Section 27.1. Afterward, have students use information from Section 27.1 to propose some possible answers to the Essential Question.

2 **Have students complete the Reading Notes for Chapter 27.** Assign Sections 27.2 to 27.10 during the activity, as indicated in the procedures for the Social Studies Skill Builder. Remind students to use the Key Content Terms where appropriate as they complete their Reading Notes.

Social Studies Skill Builder

1 **Place students in pairs.** You may want to prepare a transparency that shows pair assignments and seating arrangements.

2 **Have pairs complete the Reading Notes for Section 27.2.** Tell students that this section will introduce them to Athens and Sparta. Have pairs read Section 27.2 and complete the corresponding Reading Notes in their Interactive Student Notebooks. Afterward, use Guide to Reading Notes 27 to review their responses.

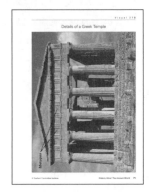

Visual 27B

3 **Introduce the activity in which students prepare placards about Athens and Sparta.** Tell students that they will become experts on one of four topics for either Athens or Sparta. The topics are government, economy, education, and treatment of women and slaves. Each pair of students will prepare a placard with illustrations, information, and a challenge question for an assigned topic. Afterward, pairs will post their placards. Their classmates will use the placards to learn about all four topics for both Athens and Sparta.

4 **Show an example of a Greek temple and its *metopes*.** Tell students that their placards will take the form of a Greek temple. Project *Visual 27B: Details of a Greek Temple*. Explain that the square sections in the rectangular strip that runs across the front of the temple above the columns are called *metopes* (MEH-tuh-pees). Ancient Greeks would use these sections to carve scenes from their legends or religion. Tell students that they will illustrate the metopes on their placards to show life in Athens or Sparta.

Student Handout 27

5 **Review the steps for creating placards.** Distribute a copy of *Student Handout 27: Placard Template* to each pair. Have students locate the metopes near the top of the handout. Then project *Information Master 27A: Creating Placards for Athens and Sparta* and review the steps with students. Explain that the challenge question should be a trivia-like question that will "challenge" those who examine the placard. The answer must be somewhere in the reading so that those students who carefully read the section will be able to find the correct information.

Information Master 27A

6   **Have pairs create their placards.** Assign each pair to one of Sections 27.3–27.10. Pairs should write both the section number and the title on their copy of Student Handout 27. (**Note:** In classes larger than 16, more than one pair will be assigned to a section.) Monitor pairs as they complete the Reading Notes for their section and create their placards. When students have finished, make sure they have clearly and accurately summarized the key information. Give each pair a blank piece of paper on which to create their challenge question answer key.

7   **Have pairs post their placards.** Designate one classroom wall for each of the four topics. For each topic, create a station for Athens and a station for Sparta by putting two or three desks together. Place two or three copies of *History Alive! The Ancient World* at each station. Have pairs post their placards on the wall at the appropriate station and place their challenge question answer keys directly below their placards.

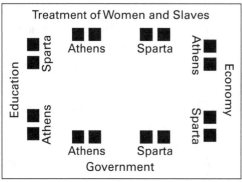

8   **Have pairs examine the placards.** Assign one or two pairs to each station. Have pairs use the visual and written information on each placard to complete the corresponding Reading Notes in their Interactive Student Notebooks. Then pairs should read the section to answer the challenge question and to add information to their Reading Notes, if necessary. Pairs can use the answer key below the placard to check the answer to the challenge question.

9   **Wrap up the activity.** Project *Information Master 27B: Comparing and Contrasting Athens and Sparta* and hold a class discussion. Follow these steps:

* Ask, *In what ways were Athens and Sparta the same?* Have volunteers write their responses in the middle of the Venn diagram.

* Ask, *How did the governments of Athens and Sparta differ?* Have volunteers write their responses on the appropriate side of the Venn diagram. Repeat for economy, education, and treatment of women and slaves.

* Ask, *In which city-state would you have liked to live and why?*

Information Master 27B

Processing

Have students complete the Processing activity in their Interactive Student Notebooks. Students compare and contrast Athens and Sparta by writing statements for an Athenian citizen and a Spartan soldier.

Quicker Coverage

Eliminate Topics for Placards For the Social Studies Skill Builder, eliminate one or two topics for which pairs create placards. Focus on the topics of government and economy for both Athens and Sparta. Since there will be multiple placards for each topic, require pairs to examine only one of the placards at each station. Consider having students complete the Reading Notes for the remaining topics as homework.

Reduce the Number of Wrap-Up Questions In Step 9 of the Social Studies Skill Builder, reduce the number of specific wrap-up questions. Rather than ask students to identify differences for each topic, ask a more general question: *In what ways were Athens and Sparta different?* Encourage students to consider all four topics when sharing their responses.

Deeper Coverage

Add a Topic for Placards For the Social Studies Skill Builder, add the topic of geography to the placard activity. When you begin the activity, skip Step 2, in which students are asked to read Section 27.2 about the geography of Athens and Sparta. Instead, assign at least one pair to create a placard on the geography of Athens, and another pair to do the same for Sparta. These pairs should use the information in Sections 27.1 and 27.2 to create their placards, which other pairs will then examine to complete their Reading Notes for Section 27.2.

Design Real-Estate Ads Have students create a poster that would encourage people to move to either Athens or Sparta. These posters should show not only the strengths of the city-state students select, but also the weaknesses of the opposing city-state. Have students include a catchy phrase to attract viewers, one or more visuals with captions, and several key details about life in the city-states.

Assessment

Mastering the Content

1. A	5. A	9. D	13. C
2. B	6. B	10. D	14. A
3. D	7. A	11. C	15. D
4. C	8. A	12. B	16. B

Applying Social Studies Skills

17. Answers will vary. Possible answer: They will fight and not surrender, even if their numbers are small.

18. Answers will vary. Possible answer: They must obey a law that forbids them to run away in battle.

19. Answers will vary. Possible answer: I think he admired the Spartans. He talks about how brave they were.

Exploring the Essential Question

20. Answers should include all of the elements requested in the prompt.

Scoring Rubric

Score	Description
3	Student completes all four parts of the task. Reasons are clearly stated, supported by details, and demonstrate command of standard English conventions.
2	Student responds to most or all parts of the task, but notes may lack details or not be clearly stated.
1	Student responds to at least one part of the task. Note(s) may contain factual and/or grammatical errors and may lack details.
0	Response does not match the task or is incorrect.

English Language Learners

Review Concepts for the Preview Activity Before students view the transparency images of Athens and Sparta in the Preview activity, review the characteristics of farming and trading communities in ancient Greece. Have students use their Reading Notes for Chapter 25 to list the characteristics of each type of community, and write these on the board. Then have students reference this list as they answer the questions for the Preview activity in their Interactive Student Notebooks.

Eliminate Challenge Questions Eliminate the challenge questions as a requirement for the placards. Consider requiring pairs to include an additional piece of information on their placards as a substitute for the challenge questions.

Learners Reading and Writing Below Grade Level

Conduct the Preview Activity Orally Rather than have students write their answers to the Preview activity, use the Preview questions to conduct a class discussion of the two images of Athens and Sparta.

Provide a Word Bank for Placards As pairs create their placards, give them a Word Bank to use for their assigned section, to make sure they highlight the important information. Pairs must incorporate terms from their Word Bank as they fill out their placard. Consider using the terms listed below.

- Section 27.3: *citizens, Council of 500, day-to-day business, Assembly, vote*
- Section 27.4: *trade, goods, agora, merchants, coins*
- Section 27.5: *citizen, boys, home, school, girls*
- Section 27.6: *women, home, slaves, skilled jobs, silver mines*
- Section 27.7: *oligarchy, Council of Elders, noble, power, Assembly*
- Section 27.8: *farming, slaves, noncitizens, trade, money*
- Section 27.9: *discipline, boys, girls, military, barracks*
- Section 27.10: *women, rights, slaves, harsh treatment, buy freedom*

Learners with Special Education Needs

Complete Two Topics Have pairs examine the placards for two of the four topics for Athens and Sparta. Have pairs examine the "Government" placards for both city-states. Then allow pairs to choose one of the three remaining topics and examine the placards for both city-states.

Provide Phrases for the Wrap-Up For Step 9 of the Social Studies Skill Builder, provide a list of phrases for students to use as they complete an individual copy of the Venn diagram. Or provide the phrases on slips of paper and have students post them on the projected image of the Venn diagram. Below are some suggested phrases:

- formed a democratic government
- ruled by an oligarchy
- gave women few rights
- let women own and control property
- traded with other city-states for goods
- used slaves to produce most goods
- bought and sold goods in the agora
- had an Assembly as part of the government

Advanced Learners

Explain Differences After students have completed the Venn diagram, in Step 9 of the Social Studies Skill Builder, ask them to reflect on why they think many differences existed between Athens and Sparta, aside from the influence of geography. Encourage students to consider how the topics they learned about are related (i.e., government and economy, economy and education).

Compare Other City-States Have students do research to learn about government, economy, education, and the treatment of women and slaves in other ancient Greek city-states. Some other city-states include Argos, Corinth, and Thebes. Afterward, have students first form a conclusion about whether their researched city-state is more like Athens or Sparta, and then hypothesize why these similarities exist.

Enrichment Resources

Find out more about Athens and Sparta by exploring the following Enrichment Resources for *History Alive! The Ancient World* at www.teachtci.com.

Enrichment Readings These in-depth readings encourage students to explore selected topics related to the chapter. You may also find readings that relate the chapter's content directly to your state's curriculum.

Internet Connections The recommended Web sites provide useful and engaging content that reinforces skills development and mastery of subjects within the chapter.

Literature Recommendations

The following books offer opportunities to extend the content in this chapter.

Inside Ancient Athens by Fiona McDonald (New York: Enchanted Lion Books, 2005)

Pericles: Great Leader of Ancient Athens by Don Nardo (Berkeley Heights, NJ: Enslow Publishers, 2006)

You Wouldn't Want to Be a Slave in Ancient Greece by Fiona McDonald, author, and Mike Berginn, illustrator (Danbury, CT: Children's Press, 2000)

Section 27.2

1. Students should circle Athens. Check the location against the map in Section 27.2 of *History Alive! The Ancient World*.

2. Athens was located in central Greece, only four miles from the Aegean Sea.

3. Students should circle Sparta. Check the location against the map in Section 27.2 of *History Alive! The Ancient World*.

4. Sparta was located on a narrow plain in the part of Greece known as the Peloponnesus; it was surrounded on three sides by mountain ranges, and was about 25 miles from the sea.

Sections 27.3–27.10

Government

Athens (Section 27.3)

Why was Athens called a democracy?
Answers will vary. Possible answers:

- Every citizen (free males over 18 and born in Athens) could take part in the city's government.

- A group of 500 citizens were chosen to be on the Council of 500 that ran the day-to-day business of the government.

- Every citizen belonged to the Assembly, which met every ten days to debate issues and vote on laws.

Sparta (Section 27.7)

Why was Sparta called an oligarchy?
Answers will vary. Possible answers:

- The ruling power of Sparta was in the hands of a few people who were called the Council of Elders.

- The Council of Elders consisted of men who were at least 60 years old, from noble families, and elected to lifetime terms.

- The Assembly in Sparta had very little power and did not debate issues.

Economy

Athens (Section 27.4)

How did Athenians get the goods they needed for everyday life? Answers will vary. Possible answers:

- Athenians traded with other city-states and with several foreign lands to get the goods and resources they needed.

- Athenians bought and sold goods at a huge marketplace called the agora.

- Athenians developed their own metal coins to make trade easier.

Sparta (Section 27.8)

How did Spartans get the goods they needed for everyday life? Answers will vary. Possible answers:

- Spartans relied on farming and on conquering other people to get what they needed.

- Slaves and noncitizens grew food and made goods, while Spartan men served as soldiers.

- Sparta did conduct some trade, but discouraged trade, in general. Its system of money (heavy iron bars) was difficult to use.

Education

Athens (Section 27.5)

How did Athenians educate their children?
Answers will vary. Possible answers:

- Boys were taught at home until about 6 or 7, and then went to school until age 14. They learned reading, writing, arithmetic, literature, sports, and music.
- Boys began military training at age 18. Afterward, some wealthy young men studied with private teachers.
- Girls did not learn to read or write. Instead they learned by helping their mothers with household tasks, such as cooking, cleaning, spinning, and weaving. Some girls also learned ancient secret songs and dances for festivals.

Sparta (Section 27.9)

How did Spartans educate their children?
Answers will vary. Possible answers:

- Boys and girls received military training from the age of 7. Boys lived and trained in barracks.
- Boys were taught to be brave soldiers by learning how to suffer physical pain without complaining.
- At the age of about 20, Spartan men were given a test of fitness, military ability, and leadership skills. If they passed, they became soldiers and citizens.

Treatment of Women and Slaves

Athens (Section 27.6)

How were women and slaves treated in Athens?
Answers will vary. Possible answers:

- Women and slaves were not citizens and had far fewer rights than free men did.
- A few women had jobs, but most women managed the household and raised children.
- Slaves performed a variety of jobs, some of them highly skilled. Some slaves worked under harsh conditions in the silver mines.

Sparta (Section 27.10)

How were women and slaves treated in Sparta?
Answers will vary. Possible answers:

- Women lived the same simple life as men but had many more rights than other Greek women had.
- There were more slaves (also called helots) in Sparta than there were citizens. Helots were treated very harshly because the Spartans were afraid the slaves would revolt.
- Helots had some rights, such as buying their freedom if they saved enough money.

Fighting the Persian Wars

What factors influenced the outcome of the Persian wars?

Overview

In a Response Group activity, students learn about the wars between the Greek city-states and the Persian Empire by dramatizing key events and debating which factors contributed to the eventual outcome of the wars.

Objectives

In the course of reading this chapter and participating in the classroom activity, students will

Social Studies

- locate the Persian Empire and describe its founding, expansion, and political organization.
- describe the roles of Athens and Sparta in the Persian wars.
- summarize the details of key battles of the Persian wars.
- evaluate the factors that contributed to a Greek victory in the Persian wars.

Language Arts

- use relevant evidence to support an opinion.
- write an explanatory paragraph with persuasive evidence.

Social Studies Vocabulary

Key Content Terms Persian Empire, Darius, Persian wars, cavalry, Xerxes, Hellespont

Academic Vocabulary initial, convince, navy, approach

Materials

History Alive! The Ancient World

Interactive Student Notebooks

Visuals 28A–28E

CD Tracks 16 and 17

Lesson Masters

- Information Master 28A (1 transparency)
- Information Master 28B (1 transparency)
- Student Handouts 28A– 28D (10 copies of each; copies may be reused)
- Vocabulary Development handout (1 per student, on colored paper)

Activity	Suggested Time	Materials
Preview	15 minutes	• Interactive Student Notebooks • CD Track 16
Vocabulary Development	30–40 minutes	• *History Alive! The Ancient World* • Interactive Student Notebooks • Vocabulary Development handout
Response Group	100 minutes (2–3 regular periods) (1–1.5 block period)	• *History Alive! The Ancient World* • Interactive Student Notebooks • Visuals 28A–28E • Information Master 28A (1 transparency) • Information Master 28B (1 transparency) • Student Handouts 28A–28D (10 copies of each; copies may be reused) • CD Track 17
Processing	20 minutes	• Interactive Student Notebooks
Assessment	40 minutes	• Chapter 28 Assessment

Preview

1 **Have students reflect on the strengths and weaknesses of a team.** Play CD Track 16, "The Lions Versus the Wildcats" while students read along in thier Interactive Student Notebooks. Then have students complete the Preview activity. Students reflect on the strengths and weaknesses of two seemingly mismatched fictional basketball teams.

2 **Have students share their responses in pairs or as a class.** Then ask, *Who do you think will win the game and why?*

3 **Explain the connection between the Preview activity and Chapter 28.** Tell students that the differences between the Lions and the Wildcats reflect the differences that existed between the Persian Empire and the Greek city-states in 499 B.C.E. Like the Lions, the Persian Empire was well-organized under a strong leader. Similar to the Wildcats, the Greek city-states fought among themselves. In this chapter, students will learn about the war between the Persian Empire and the Greek city-states, and what factors contributed to the eventual outcome of the Persian wars.

Vocabulary Development

1 **Introduce the Key Content Terms.** Have students locate the Key Content Terms for the chapter in their Interactive Student Notebooks. These are important terms that will help them understand the main ideas of the chapter. Ask volunteers to identify any familiar terms and how they might be used in a sentence.

2 **Have students complete a Vocabulary Development handout.** Give each student a copy of the Vocabulary Development handout of your choice from the Reading Toolkit at the back of the Lesson Masters. These handouts provide extra Key Content Term practice and support, depending on your students' needs. Review the completed handout by asking volunteers to share one answer for each term.

Reading

1 **Introduce the Essential Question and have students read Section 28.1.** Have students identify the Essential Question on the first page of the chapter: *What factors influenced the outcome of the Persian wars?* Then have students read Section 28.1. Afterward, have students use information from Section 28.1 and from the map to propose some possible answers to the Essential Question.

2 **Have students complete the Reading Notes for Chapter 28.** Assign Sections 28.2 to 28.6 during the activity, as indicated in the procedures for the Response Group. Remind students to use the Key Content Terms where appropriate as they complete their Reading Notes.

Response Group

1 **Place students in groups of three.** You may want to create a transparency that shows group assignments and seating arrangements.

2 **Have groups complete the Reading Notes for Section 28.2.** Tell students that this section outlines the founding of the Persian Empire and the beginning of the Persian wars. Have groups read Section 28.2 and complete the corresponding Reading Notes in their Interactive Student Notebooks. Use Guide to Reading Notes 28 to review their responses.

3 **Introduce the activity.** Tell students that the Persian wars became the subject of a famous Greek play, *The Persians*. Written in 472 B.C.E. by Greek playwright Aeschylus (ES-kuh-luhs), the play describes the events that took place during one of the war's important battles. Similarly, groups will use the elements of Greek drama to bring to life four key battles of the Persian wars. After reading about each battle, groups will discuss which factors most contributed to the eventual outcome of the Persian wars.

4 **Introduce Greek drama.** Project *Information Master 28A: A Greek Play* and tell students that this is an excerpt from the play, *The Persians*. Explain that Greek plays had a chorus and only a few actors. In this excerpt, the messenger is the only actor. The chorus, usually made up of about fifteen men, sang or spoke their lines in unison. By explaining and commenting on the story, the chorus helped the audience understand the play. Play CD Track 17, "A Greek Chorus," and have students listen as the chorus performs an excerpt from *The Persians*.

5 **Have students perform the first dramatization.** Tell students that they will use Greek drama to bring to life the events leading up to the Battle of Marathon. Project *Information Master 28B: Performing a Greek Play* and review the steps with students. Then conduct the dramatizations as follows:

- Ask for a volunteer from each group to be a performer.

- Give each performer a copy of *Student Handout 28A: Script for Battle of Marathon*.

- Assign each performer to play a character or to be in the chorus.

- Project *Visual 28A: Battle of Marathon*. Have each actor "step into" the image and assume his or her character's position. Have chorus members stand together outside the image.

- Have performers read their lines and perform their actions as directed by the script on Student Handout 28A.

- Afterward, have the audience give the performers a round of applause.

6 **Have groups complete the Reading Notes for Section 28.3.** Tell students that they will learn what happened at the Battle of Marathon. Have groups read Section 28.3 and complete the corresponding Reading Notes in their Interactive Student Notebooks. Use Guide to Reading Notes 28 to review their responses.

Information Master 28A

Information Master 28B

Student Handout 28A

Visual 28A

7   **Repeat Steps 5 and 6 for the remaining three dramatizations.** Rotate students who act as performers, and make these changes:

- Use Visual 28B and Student Handout 28B for the Battle of Thermopylae. Have groups read and complete the Reading Notes for Section 28.4.
- Use Visual 28C and Student Handout 28C for the Battle of Salamis. Have groups read and complete the Reading Notes for Section 28.5.
- Use Visual 28D and Student Handout 28D for the Battle of Plataea. Have groups read and complete the Reading Notes for Section 28.6.

8   **Have groups discuss the Critical Thinking Question.** Project *Visual 28E: Critical Thinking Question.* Tell students that groups will now discuss which of the factors they think most contributed to the outcome of the Persian wars. Review the factors that influenced the outcome of each battle with students. Give groups several minutes to discuss the Critical Thinking Question.

9   **Facilitate a class discussion.** Follow these steps:

- Designate each corner of the classroom for one of the four factors listed on Visual 28E.
- Have each group appoint a Spokesperson who will then stand in the "factor" corner that reflects their group's opinion.
- Addressing one factor at a time, have Spokespersons each give one reason for their group's choice.
- After Spokespersons have shared reasons, encourage the remaining students to challenge the Spokespersons and discuss any of the reasons in more depth. If any factor is not chosen, take on the role of a Spokesperson and present reasons why that factor might best explain why the Greeks won the Persian wars. (**Note:** Afterward, consider having Spokespersons briefly confer with their groups and then move to different corners if group members decide as such.)

Visuals 28B–28D

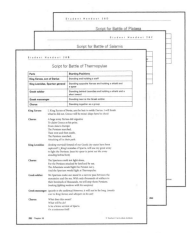

Student Handouts 28B–28D

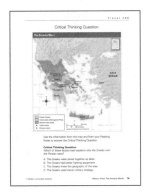

Visual 28E

Processing

Have students complete the Processing activity in their Interactive Student Notebooks. Students rank a list of factors that contributed to a Greek victory in the Persian wars, and then write a paragraph justifying their choice of the most important factor.

Quicker Coverage

Skip the Dramatizations Eliminate Steps 3 to 7 in the Response Group activity that guide students through the dramatizations for each battle. Instead, follow these procedures:

- Have groups read a section and complete the corresponding Reading Notes.
- Then project the corresponding visual. Have students share their headlines and point out details that relate to their summaries.
- Repeat these procedures until students have learned about all four battles.
- Follow Steps 8 and 9 for the discussion of the Critical Thinking Question.

Skip the Class Discussion Eliminate Steps 8 and 9 that outline procedures for the class discussion. Instead, wrap up the activity by projecting Visual 28E and asking students to write one piece of evidence to support each factor listed.

Deeper Coverage

Add Discussions After groups have completed their Reading Notes for each of Sections 28.3–28.6, conduct a class discussion about which factors they think most contributed to the outcome of the battle they just learned about. Either list the factors on the board, or make a transparency of the factors listed in the Reading Notes. Follow the procedures (Steps 8 and 9) for the class discussion of the Critical Thinking Question. Have groups appoint a different Spokesperson for each factor discussion. Also, after discussing each of the first three battles, consider having students predict whether the Persians or the Greeks will win the wars overall.

Write Dramas After students have dramatized and learned about the Battle of Marathon, have groups write their own lines for the dramas. Assign each group to one of Sections 28.4–28.6. Have groups read the section and complete the corresponding Reading Notes in their Interactive Student Notebooks. Give groups a copy of the Student Handout that corresponds to their assigned battle. Have groups add to the script on the Student Handout by writing a second scene describing events that might follow. Their dramas should include at least four characters and a chorus. (**Note:** Emphasize to students that Greek dramas never showed violence on stage. Rather, the Greeks used the chorus to narrate what happened.) Then, in chronological order, have groups perform their dramas.

Writing: Spelling

After students draft their paragraphs for the Processing activity, ask them to identify every use they made of these homophones: *their* and *there*; *its* and *it's*. Call for examples from students' work, write them on the board, and talk about why each use of these frequently misspelled words is either correct or needs to be revised.

Assessment

Mastering the Content

1. C	5. D	9. B	13. A
2. A	6. D	10. B	14. C
3. D	7. A	11. D	15. C
4. B	8. A	12. B	16. D

Applying Social Studies Skills

17. Battle of Marathon

18. 480 B.C.E.

19. Answers will vary. Possible answer: The Persian wars started more slowly and built up to a quick series of big battles. The period of most activity in the Persian wars was during the years 480 and 479 B.C.E.

Exploring the Essential Question

20. Answers should include all of the elements requested in the prompt.

Scoring Rubric

Score	Description
3	Student completes all three parts of the task. Three pieces of advice are clearly stated and then explained, and demonstrate command of standard English conventions.
2	Student responds to most or all parts of the task, but advice may not be clearly stated or may lack explanation.
1	Student responds to at least one part of the task. Advice may contain factual and/or grammatical errors and may lack explanation.
0	Response does not match the task or is incorrect.

English Language Learners

Explain the Factors Help students understand the factors listed in Question 3 of Sections 28.3–28.6 in the Reading Notes. Have groups follow the procedures to complete Questions 1 and 2. Then, write Question 3 on the board. Review the four factors as a class. Have students explain each factor's meaning and provide an example from ancient Greece or from students' knowledge. Some examples for each factor might be:

A. Athens and Sparta agreed to help each other out.

B. Sharper swords and stronger armor helped the Greeks defeat the Persians.

C. The Greeks knew places where their soldiers could hide.

D. A Greek general trapped the Persians in a narrow waterway to prevent their escape.

Assign Students as Actors When inviting volunteers to perform in each battle drama, assign students to be actors rather than chorus members. Choose characters whose straightforward lines can be easily read aloud.

Learners Reading and Writing Below Grade Level

Provide Steps for Reading Provide steps for student groups as they read the sections in Chapter 28 and complete the Reading Notes. Have group members take turns whisper-reading the section to each other. Next, have them discuss how to summarize the main events of the battle. Then they should individually write their responses and create their headlines. Have students complete Question 3, on their own, and then share their ideas with group members.

Give Summary Sentence Starters Help students write the summaries in the Reading Notes for Sections 28.3–28.6. Have students make an outline using these sentence starters and filling in the appropriate details.

- Before the battle, . . .
- At the beginning of the battle, . . .
- During the battle, . . .
- At the end of the battle, . . .

As an alternative, consider providing a simpler outline using these terms: *first, then,* and *finally*.

Learners with Special Education Needs

Eliminate a Factor Remove factor B about "better fighting equipment" in Question 3 of the Reading Notes for Sections 28.3–28.6 and on Visual 28E.

Support Discussion Provide note cards and a copy of Visual 28E while groups discuss the Critical Thinking Question. Have groups circle their choice and write three or more reasons. Each group member should write one reason on a note card. Pair each group with another group that has chosen a different factor, and have students share their reasons. Invite the paired groups to ask clarifying questions of each other. Then lead the class discussion as outlined in the procedures.

Advanced Learners

Add Factors For the Critical Thinking Question, have students consider factors that represent the Persians' weaknesses. Add these factors on Visual 28E:

- The vastness of the Persian Empire made it difficult to get supplies and reinforcements.
- The Persians were an invading army, and were not defending their homes.
- Persian leaders were arrogant and overconfident.

Then add students' suggestions for factors to the list of factors they rank for the Processing activity.

Compare and Contrast Wars Have students work in small groups to research other historical examples of an underdog defeating an advantaged force. Students should identify the strengths and weaknesses of each side, describe the major battles and subsequent outcome, and explain what factors contributed to victory. Have students share their research with the class. Then have the class discuss any similarities to and differences from the Persian wars. Offer these examples or allow students to find their own:

- Carthage v. Rome in the Punic Wars
- England v. Spain in 1588
- American colonies v. Great Britain in the American Revolution
- France v. Vietnam in the First Indochina War
- Afghanistan v. the U.S.S.R. in the Soviet-Afghan War

Enrichment Resources

Find out more about the Persian wars by exploring the following Enrichment Resources for *History Alive! The Ancient World* at www.teachtci.com.

Enrichment Readings These in-depth readings encourage students to explore selected topics related to the chapter. You may also find readings that relate the chapter's content directly to your state's curriculum.

Internet Connections The recommended Web sites provide useful and engaging content that reinforces skills development and mastery of subjects within the chapter.

Literature Recommendations

The following books offer opportunities to extend the content in this chapter.

The Ancient Greece of Odysseus by Peter Connolly (New York: Oxford Press, 1999)

Going to War in Ancient Greece by Adrian Gilbert, author, and Mark Bergin, illustrator (Danbury, CT: Franklin Watts, 2001)

The Story of the Persian War from Herodotus by Alfred P. Church (Chapel Hill, NC: Yesterday's Classics, 2009)

Section 28.2

1. Check that students' maps reflect the Persian Empire and Greece as shown on the map in Section 28.1 of *History Alive! The Ancient World.* Students should color in the Persian Empire to reflect that the empire extended from Egypt, in northern Africa, east to present-day Pakistan. Students should use a different color to indicate the mainland peninsula and the islands of Greece.

2. The Persians built their empire by conquering their neighbors in Mesopotamia, Asia Minor, Egypt, and parts of India and Europe.

3. King Darius ruled his large empire by dividing it into 20 provinces. He established a system of tax collection and appointed officials to rule local areas.

4. The Ionian Revolt began in 499 B.C.E. and led to the Persian wars. The revolt began because the Persians had conquered the wealthy Greek settlements in Ionia, and had taken their land. They forced the Ionians to pay tribute and serve in the Persian army. After some success rebelling against the Persians, the Ionians were defeated in 493 B.C.E. The revolt was important because it showed the Greeks that small city-states needed to work together to fight Persia, and because it led to the Persian wars.

Section 28.3

1. King Darius sent a large army of foot soldiers and cavalry by boat to Greece, and they assembled on the plain of Marathon. The king was furious because the Greeks had refused to pay tribute after the Ionian Revolt. The Athenians were outnumbered. After several days of waiting, the Athenian general Miltiades used clever military strategy to attack the Persians. Athenian soldiers attacked the Persians on three sides, and the Persians retreated to their ships.

2. Answers will vary. Possible answer: Athenians Outsmart Persians to Win Battle of Marathon

3. Answers will vary.

Section 28.4

1. After King Darius died, his son, Xerxes, organized another attack on Greece. His large army crossed the Hellespont and marched to Greece. Athens used its navy to fight the Persians at sea, and Sparta attempted to stop the Persian army. The Spartans made their stand at the narrow pass of Thermopylae, and drove the Persians back. But a Greek traitor showed the Persians a secret route that allowed the Persians to surround the Spartans. King Leonidas of Sparta kept about 300 men to defend the pass, while the rest of his army escaped. All the Spartan soldiers were killed.

2. Answers will vary. Possible answer: Brave Spartans Die Saving Army at Thermopylae

3. Answers will vary.

Section 28.5

1. After Thermopylae, fearful Athenians left the city, and the Persians destroyed Athens. The leader of the Athenian navy, Themistocles, thought that he could defeat the Persian navy by fighting in the narrow channels between the islands and the mainland. He set a trap to lure the Persian ships into a channel near Salamis, by sending a message that he was going to surrender and join the Persians. Persian King Xerxes ordered his ships into the channel, where the Greeks were hiding. The Greek ships surrounded them and sank 300 Persian ships.

2. Answers will vary. Possible answer: Greek Ships Trick Persians Navy and Claim Victory

3. Answers will vary.

Section 28.6

1. After Salamis, Xerxes and some of his soldiers fled back across the Hellespont. He left the rest of his army in Greece, with orders to attack again in the spring. The Spartans feared that the Athenians, with their city destroyed, would make peace with the Persians. But the Athenians agreed to fight alongside the Spartans. In 479 B.C.E., a force of 80,000 Greeks, led by the Spartans, destroyed the Persian army in a battle outside the town of Plataea. The Persian wars were over.

2. Answers will vary. Possible answer: Xerxes Makes a Run for It! Greeks Claim Victory at Battle of Plataea

3. Answers will vary.

4. The Greek victory in the Persian wars ended any future Persian threat against the Greeks.

The Golden Age of Athens

What were the major cultural achievements of Athens?

Overview

In a Writing for Understanding activity, students take a "walking tour" of Athens, visiting six sites to learn about various aspects of Greek culture. Students then write a speech describing Athens during its Golden Age.

Objectives

In the course of reading this chapter and participating in the classroom activity, students will:

Social Studies

- describe the role of Pericles in leading Athens into its Golden Age.
- discuss the significance of religion in the everyday life of the ancient Greeks.
- identify ways in which Greek literature permeates modern English language and literature.
- explain how Athenian achievements in architecture, sculpture, drama, philosophy, and sports contributed to its Golden Age.

Language Arts

- support a clearly stated position, using organized and relevant evidence.
- revise writing to improve the organization and clarity of ideas within paragraphs.
- deliver a persuasive presentation that is focused and coherent.

Social Studies Vocabulary

Key Content Terms Pericles, Parthenon, acropolis, myth, drama, Socrates, Panathenaic Games

Academic Vocabulary reform, dedicate, conduct, column, muscle

Materials

History Alive! The Ancient World

Interactive Student Notebooks

Placards 29A–29F

CD Track 18

Lesson Masters

- Station Directions 29A–29F (2 copies of each)
- Station Materials 29A and 29C (2 copies, each page cut apart and kept separate)
- Station Materials 29B (1 copy for every 2 students)
- Station Materials 29D (4 copies)
- Station Materials 29E and 29F (2 copies)
- Information Master 29 (1 transparency)
- Vocabulary Development handout (1 per student, on colored paper)

masking tape, colored pencils (12 sets), straws (4), yardsticks (2), stopwatches (2, optional)

Activity	Suggested Time	Materials
Preview	15 minutes	• Interactive Student Notebooks
Vocabulary Development	30–40 minutes	• *History Alive! The Ancient World* • Interactive Student Notebooks • Vocabulary Development handout
Writing for Understanding	Walking tour of Athens, Steps 1–6 90 minutes (2 regular periods) (1 block period) Completing the writing assignment, Steps 7–10 90 minutes (2 regular periods) (1 block period)	• *History Alive! The Ancient World* • Interactive Student Notebooks • Placards 29A–29F • CD Track 18 • Station Directions 29A–29F (2 copies of each) • Station Materials 29A and 29C (2 copies, each page cut apart and kept separate) • Station Materials 29B (1 copy for every 2 students) • Station Materials 29D (4 copies) • Station Materials 29E and 29F (2 copies) • Information Master 29 (1 transparency) • masking tape • colored pencils (12 sets) • straws (4) • yardsticks (2) • stopwatches (2, optional)
Processing (optional)	20 minutes	• Interactive Student Notebooks
Assessment	40 minutes	• Chapter 29 Assessment

Preview

1   **Have students complete the Preview activity in their Interactive Student Notebooks.** Students analyze an excerpt from Pericles' Funeral Oration to explore what made Athens a unique city during the fifth century B.C.E.

2   **Have students share their responses in pairs or as a class.**

3   **Explain the connection between the Preview activity and Chapter 29.** Tell students that Pericles had many reasons to think of Athens as a great city and as the "school of Greece." At the time he gave his speech, Athens had just ended a period of peace and prosperity known as the Golden Age. During that time, Athens had become the artistic and cultural center of Greece. In this chapter, students will learn about several aspects of Greek culture that thrived during the Golden Age of Athens.

Vocabulary Development

1   **Introduce the Key Content Terms.** Have students locate the Key Content Terms for the chapter in their Interactive Student Notebooks. These are important terms that will help them understand the main ideas of the chapter. Ask volunteers to identify any familiar terms and how they might be used in a sentence.

2   **Have students complete a Vocabulary Development handout.** Give each student a copy of the Vocabulary Development handout of your choice from the Reading Toolkit at the back of the Lesson Masters. These handouts provide extra Key Content Term practice and support, depending on your students' needs. Review the completed handout by asking volunteers to share one answer for each term.

Reading

1   **Introduce the Essential Question and have students read Section 29.1.** Have students identify the Essential Question on the first page of the chapter: *What were the major cultural achievements of Athens?* Then have students read Section 29.1. Afterward, have students use information from Section 29.1 and from the chapter opener image to propose some possible answers to the Essential Question.

2   **Have students complete the Reading Notes for Chapter 29.** Assign Sections 29.2 to 29.8 during the activity, as indicated in the procedures for the Writing for Understanding activity. Remind students to use the Key Content Terms where appropriate as they complete their Reading Notes.

Reading: Persuasion and Propaganda

Discuss with students Pericles' reasons for delivering such a stirring speech. Guide students to see that this oration in honor of the dead is only partly to honor the dead. Then ask whether Pericles might in any way have overstated the glories of Athens in order to achieve a persuasive purpose. Have students find concrete examples in the text of things that might have been true or somewhat true, yet overstated for the purpose of motivating his audience.

Writing for Understanding

1   **Prepare materials.** Before class, allow sufficient time to gather the required items from the materials list, as well as to make copies of Station Directions 29A–29F and Station Materials 29A–29F. The quantities listed will allow you to create 12 stations, two of each station. For a class of more than 24 students, consider placing students in groups of three or creating triplicate stations.

2   **Arrange the classroom.** Use desks to set up the stations as shown in the diagram. Follow the instructions on the back of Placards 29A–29F to place the materials at each station. Then post the appropriate placard on each station wall, in between the two desks. You may want to print additional placards. Set up CD Track 18 between the two desks at Station E. During the activity, play CD Track 18, "Socrates Speaks." (**Note:** Alternatively, have students set up the stations at the beginning of class. Place the materials for each station in a large plastic bag and assign teams of students to set up each station.)

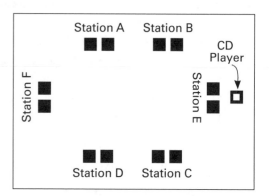

3   **Introduce the activity—a "walking tour" of Athens.** Tell students that they are going to take a "walking tour" of Athens during its Golden Age in the fifth century B.C.E. They will learn about different aspects of Greek culture by visiting six sites in or near the city. Afterward, students will use the notes from their tour to help them write a speech for Pericles, describing the greatness of Athens during its Golden Age.

4   **Have students complete the Reading Notes for Section 29.2.** Tell students that this section provides background information about Athens after the Persian wars. Have students read Section 29.2 and complete the corresponding Reading Notes in their Interactive Student Notebooks. Use Guide to Reading Notes 29 to review their responses.

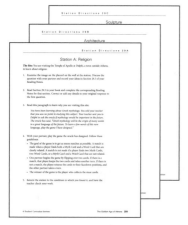

Station Directions 29A–29F

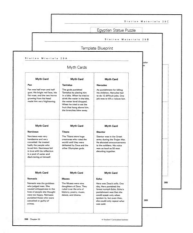

Station Materials 29A–29F

Placards 29A–29F

5 **Review the steps for the walking tour of Athens.** Tell students that there are six stations set up around the classroom. Each station represents a different site in or near ancient Athens. At each site, students will learn about an aspect of Greek culture. They will also be directed to do the following:

- Examine an image and respond to a question on a placard.
- Read and complete the Reading Notes for a section of Chapter 29.
- Complete a short activity, such as designing a temple or performing a play.

6 **Place students in pairs and conduct the walking tour.** Have pairs go to different stations. Remind students to follow the steps at each station. Monitor pairs as they work, and use Guide to Reading Notes 29 to provide feedback. (**Note:** Consider reviewing the stations as a class, after students have finished the tour. For example, you might review the correct card matches for Station A and who won the events at Station F.)

7 **Introduce the writing activity—a speech for Pericles.** Remind students of the speech they examined in the Preview activity for this chapter. In the speech, the Athenian leader Pericles described the greatness of Athens. He called the city the "school of Greece." Tell students that they will now write an additional speech for Pericles, using what they learned in their walking tour of Athens.

8 **Review the directions for writing speeches about Athens.** Project a transparency of *Information Master 29: Writing a Persuasive Speech About Athens.* Review the instructions for writing the speeches, and answer any questions students may have.

Information Master 29

9 **Have students write their speeches.** Give students adequate time to draft, edit, and revise their speeches. Allow time for students to practice quietly reading aloud their drafts to partners.

10 **Form groups and have students deliver their speeches.** Form groups of four by placing two pairs of students together. In groups, each student should read his or her speech aloud to group members. As group members listen, have them record the most persuasive statement they hear from each speech. Afterward, ask volunteers to share with the class their group's most persuasive quotations.

Processing (optional)

1 **Understand the intent of the Processing activity.** The persuasive speech serves as this chapter's Processing activity. Should you choose not to have students do the writing activity, you might use the optional Processing activity in the Interactive Student Notebook.

2 **Have students complete the Processing activity.**

3 **Have students share their paragraphs with their partners or with the class.**

Quicker Coverage

Have Students Choose Sites After students complete Step 4 in the Writing for Understanding procedures, introduce the writing activity and review the speech guidelines on Information Master 29. Tell students that they will choose to visit three of the six sites in their walking tour. They should choose the sites they would most like to write about in their speeches. Have students complete their three stations for the walking tour. Before they begin the writing activity, they should read and complete the Reading Notes for the remaining three sections.

Eliminate the Speech Writing After students complete their walking tour of Athens, wrap up the activity with a brief discussion. Ask students these questions: *What was the most interesting place you visited? Which site did you find most impressive and why? How did the city of Athens support the growth of Greek culture? What were the major cultural achievements of Athens?*

Deeper Coverage

Research Pericles Have students work in pairs or in small groups to research the life of Pericles. To share what they learn, students should write a funeral oration, or eulogy, for Pericles. In their eulogies, students should summarize three important details about the life of Pericles, highlight his beliefs about democracy, and present evidence for why he should be remembered. Consider having students also include a quotation from Pericles, such as one from his Funeral Oration speech that he gave at the beginning of the Peloponnesian War.

Replace the Speech with a Scrapbook In place of the speech-writing activity, have students create a scrapbook of their walking tour of Athens. Their scrapbook should include an appropriately decorated cover and three or more pages about their visit. Each page should focus on what students learned at one of the six sites, and include the following:

- an illustration of the student at the site
- a description of what the student learned at the site
- a memento from the site (e.g., a postcard from Delphi, a theater ticket, a note from Socrates)

Allow students to utilize technology to find or create their illustrations, write their descriptions, and make their mementos.

Writing: Research and Technology

Guide students in how to use efficient keyword searches to find information about Pericles' life. For example, students might search *Pericles biography, Pericles democracy,* and *Pericles quotation.* If students have access to a library database, this assignment may serve as a good opportunity for demonstrating its features and use to students.

Assessment

Mastering the Content

1. C	5. B	9. B	13. D
2. D	6. B	10. C	14. D
3. B	7. C	11. B	15. A
4. A	8. A	12. D	16. C

Applying Social Studies Skills

17. southwest

18. Marathon; Salamis

19. Answers will vary but should mention the Panathenaic Way and the agora, or the main marketplace.

Exploring the Essential Question

20. Answers should include all of the elements requested in the prompt.

Scoring Rubric

Score	Description
3	Student completes all four parts of the task. Drawings and captions highlight and explain points of interest, and captions demonstrate command of standard English conventions.
2	Student responds to most or all parts of the task, but may be missing one or more of the drawings and captions.
1	Student responds to at least one part of the task. Captions may contain factual and/or grammatical errors.
0	Response does not match the task or is incorrect.

English Language Learners

Simplify the Preview Activity Separate and simplify the main points of the quotation from Pericles, provided on the Preview page in the Interactive Student Notebook. Consider bulleting these main points:

- We provide entertainment so people can relax after working hard.
- We hold athletic games.
- We have beautiful homes.
- We are happy because we have nice things in our city.
- We enjoy products from many places.

Simplify the Station Directions and Activities Modify Station Directions 29A–29F to ensure that students understand what they need to do. Also consider modifying those activities that require a lot of reading. Below are several suggestions:

- Station A: draw pictures to show how the oracle's matching game should work; eliminate four Myth Cards and their corresponding Word Cards so that students make only five matches.
- Station B: annotate the temple blueprint with the specific tasks listed in Step 4 of Station Directions 29B.
- Station D: ahead of time, have two volunteers record a performance of the play so that students can listen to the recording while reading the script; define any difficult words in the script.
- Station E: allow students to choose one quotation to respond to, and to replay the track if necessary.
- Station F: find or draw simple visuals of each of the events in Step 4 of Station Directions 29F.

Design a Poster As an alternative to the writing activity, have students work individually or in pairs to design a poster advertising why Athens would be a great city to visit during its Golden Age. The poster should highlight the top three things to do while visiting Athens, and include a catchy title and three or more visuals with captions.

Learners Reading and Writing Below Grade Level

Conduct a Prewriting Activity After students have completed the walking tour, have them work with partners to complete a brief prewriting activity. For each of the sites they visited, have students write a sentence describing what they learned, and a sentence explaining its relation to Athens's Golden Age. You might provide sentence starters, such as these:

- At Delphi, I learned . . .
- This shows that Athens was in its Golden Age because . . .

Learners with Special Education Needs

Preview and Limit Stations Require that students visit three of the six stations and complete the Reading Notes for only those stations they visit. To help students choose their three stations, introduce the topics at each station, provide a brief overview of the topic, and summarize the activity students would complete at each station.

Adapt the Speech-Writing Activity Eliminate the requirement to appeal to those listeners who might say that Athens is not a great city. Alternatively, provide a list of counterarguments. Examples are below:

- Athens is not a great city because Socrates was killed.
- Athens is not a great city because its achievements are not anything special.
- Athens is not a great city because Sparta is better.
- Athens is not a great city because other civilizations had better achievements.

Advanced Learners

Discuss the End of the Golden Age Provide students with or have students research historians' different points of view about why the Golden Age of Athens ended. Examples might include a discussion of the trial of Socrates, the role of Pericles, and the start of the Peloponnesian War. Have students identify the main points of view and then discuss as a class the one they think is most valid.

Enrichment Resources

Find out more about the cultural achievements of ancient Athens during its Golden Age by exploring the following Enrichment Resources for *History Alive! The Ancient World* at www.teachtci.com.

Enrichment Readings These in-depth readings encourage students to explore selected topics related to the chapter. You may also find readings that relate the chapter's content directly to your state's curriculum.

Internet Connections The recommended Web sites provide useful and engaging content that reinforces skills development and mastery of subjects within the chapter.

Literature Recommendations

The following books offer opportunities to extend the content in this chapter.

Dramatizing Greek Mythology by Louise Thistle (Lyme, NH: Smith and Kraus, 2002)

Life in Ancient Athens (Picture the Past) by Jane Shuter (Mankato, MN: Heinemann-Raintree, 2005)

Socrates: The Public Conscience of Golden Age Athens by Jun Lim (New York: Rosen Central, 2006)

Section 29.2

1. Pericles led the rebuilding of Athens after the Persian wars. He encouraged the arts and made reforms to encourage the growth of democracy.

2. The people of Athens lived in small, uncomfortable houses, but the city's public spaces were large and beautiful.

Section 29.3

On the map, students should locate the Temple at Delphi.

1. A person would go to an oracle to ask a god questions. Each god or goddess had power over a certain area of life. People needing advice would go to the oracle who spoke for a particular god or goddess.

2. The ancient Greek gods and goddesses lived on Mount Olympus. They looked and acted like humans, but they did not age or die.

3. The ancient Greeks asked the gods for help before setting out on journeys. The Greeks dedicated festivals and sporting events to their gods. Temples were dedicated to the gods and decorated with their images.

Section 29.4

On the map, students should locate the acropolis and the Parthenon.

1. The ancient Greeks built their temples as beautiful dwelling places for the gods and goddesses. These temples were not places of worship because the Greeks conducted religious ceremonies outside.

2. The simple Doric column had no base and got slimmer toward the top. The Ionic column was thinner, sat on a base, and had scrolls carved into the top. The Corinthian column was the most complex, with carvings that looked like leaves at the top.

3. The Parthenon had 8 columns across the front and back, and 17 along each side. The top of the temple was decorated with a band of sculptures called a frieze. Inside the temple was a magnificent statue of Athena.

Section 29.5

On the map, students should locate the marble workshop.

1. The earliest Greek statues were influenced by ancient Egypt. Statues were larger-than-life figures that faced front, with arms held stiffly at their sides.

2. Later Greek statues were more realistic. They were sculpted in natural poses, with muscles, hair, and clothing in much greater detail.

3. Phidias was one of the most famous sculptors in Athens. He designed the figures at the top of the Parthenon and sculpted the statue of Athena that stood inside the temple.

Section 29.6

On the map, students should locate the Theater of Dionysus.

1. The Theater of Dionysus could hold thousands of people. Because it was shaped like a bowl, everyone could hear what was said on the stage.

2. Answers will vary. Possible answers: Greek drama differed from modern plays and movies because (1) it relied on a chorus to help explain the story, and (2) it had no women actors.

Section 29.7

On the map, students should locate the agora.

1. Greek philosophers talked and argued about the world around them. They talked about things they could see, such as nature and how it worked. They talked about things they could not see, such as the meaning of life, justice, truth, and beauty.

2. Socrates asked people questions that led them to think about their beliefs.

3. Socrates was arrested and brought to trial. His enemies accused him of not honoring the gods and of leading young people into error and disloyalty. He was found guilty and sentenced to death. He died by drinking the poison hemlock.

Section 29.8

On the map, students should locate the site of the Panathenaic Games.

1. The Panathenaic Games were a series of competitive athletic events that were held as part of a festival that honored the goddess Athena. These games showed how much the Greeks valued physical fitness and a healthy body.

2. The Panathenaic Games included events like horse races, chariot races, footraces, boxing, wrestling, and the pancratium.

3. Answers will vary.

Alexander the Great and His Empire

How did Alexander build his empire?

Overview

In a Response Group activity, students learn about the rise of Macedonia after the Peloponnesian War and debate the degree of success Alexander the Great had in uniting the diverse peoples of his empire.

Objectives

In the course of reading this chapter and participating in the classroom activity, students will

Social Studies

- summarize the roles of Athens and Sparta in the Peloponnesian War.
- describe the rise of Macedonia under the reigns of Philip and Alexander.
- rate the success of Alexander the Great in uniting his empire, including his efforts to spread Greek culture eastward.
- evaluate the achievements of Alexander the Great.

Language Arts

- support opinions, using detailed and relevant evidence.
- engage listeners by emphasizing main points and using effective speaking skills.

Social Studies Vocabulary

Key Content Terms Peloponnesian War, Macedonia, Aristotle, Alexander the Great, custom, Alexandria

Academic Vocabulary ally, appreciate, involve, require, reluctantly

Materials

*History Alive!
The Ancient World*

Interactive Student Notebooks

Visuals 30A–30D

Lesson Masters

- Student Handout 30 (1 per group of 3, plus a transparency)
- Vocabulary Development handout (1 per student, on colored paper)

tokens, such as buttons or pennies (1 per student)

masking tape

colored pencils or markers

Activity	Suggested Time	Materials
Preview	15 minutes	• Interactive Student Notebooks
Vocabulary Development	30–40 minutes	• *History Alive! The Ancient World* • Interactive Student Notebooks • Vocabulary Development handout
Response Group	90 minutes (2 regular periods) (1 block period)	• *History Alive! The Ancient World* • Interactive Student Notebooks • Visuals 30A–30C • Student Handout 30 (1 per group of 3, plus a transparency) • tokens (1 per student) • masking tape
Processing	20 minutes	• Interactive Student Notebooks • Visual 30D • colored pencils or markers
Assessment	40 minutes	• Chapter 30 Assessment

Preview

1 **Have students complete the Preview activity in their Interactive Student Notebooks.** Explain that students will predict reasons why a ruler from ancient times might be given the title "Great."

2 **Have students share their responses in pairs or as a class.**

3 **Explain the connection between the Preview activity and Chapter 30.** Tell students that there are different reasons why a ruler might earn the title "Great." In many cases, the ruler achieved great deeds. As an example, you might wish to discuss the characteristics and achievements of Ramses the Great, of Egypt. He ruled for more than 60 years. He was known for both his military leadership and his construction of numerous monuments. In this chapter, students will learn about Alexander the Great, a ruler who conquered many lands and built one of the largest empires of ancient times.

Vocabulary Development

1 **Introduce the Key Content Terms.** Have students locate the Key Content Terms for the chapter in their Interactive Student Notebooks. These are important terms that will help them understand the main ideas of the chapter. Ask volunteers to identify any familiar terms and how they might be used in a sentence.

2 **Have students complete a Vocabulary Development handout.** Give each student a copy of the Vocabulary Development handout of your choice from the Reading Toolkit at the back of the Lesson Masters. These handouts provide extra Key Content Term practice and support, depending on your students' needs. Review the completed handout by asking volunteers to share one answer for each term.

Reading

1 **Introduce the Essential Question and have students read Section 30.1.** Have students identify the Essential Question on the first page of the chapter: *How did Alexander build his empire?* Then have students read Section 30.1. Afterward, have them respond to the following questions:

   • Who was Alexander the Great?

   • Where was he from?

   • Where is Macedonia?

   • What did Alexander accomplish?

2 **Have students complete the Reading Notes for Chapter 30.** Assign Sections 30.2 to 30.8 during the activity, as indicated in the procedures for the Response Group activity. Remind students to use the Key Content Terms where appropriate as they complete their Reading Notes.

Response Group

1 **Place students in groups of three.** You may want to prepare a transparency before class that shows group assignments and seating arrangements. Students should arrange their desks so that group members can talk among themselves and clearly see the front of the classroom.

2 **Introduce the activity in which students examine and rate the success of three parts of Alexander's plan for uniting his empire.** Tell students that they are going to learn about Alexander the Great's rise to power and his plan to rule and unify his vast empire. After reading about the three parts of his plan, groups will discuss the degree to which they think each part was successful. Afterward, they will share and defend their ratings against those of other groups.

3 **Have groups complete the Reading Notes for Sections 30.2 to 30.4.** Have groups read Sections 30.2 to 30.4 and complete the corresponding Reading Notes in their Interactive Student Notebooks. Afterward, use Guide to Reading Notes 30 to review their responses.

4 **Have groups complete the Reading Notes for Section 30.5.** Tell students that they will read about Alexander's plan to spread Greek culture and ideas to unite his empire. Have groups read Section 30.5 and complete the corresponding Reading Notes in their Interactive Student Notebooks. Afterward, use Guide to Reading Notes 30 to review their responses.

5 **Have groups discuss Alexander's plan to spread Greek ideas.** Project *Visual 30A: Spreading Greek Ideas* and review the steps. Distribute a token to each student. To each group, distribute a copy of *Student Handout 30: Group Spectrum*. Give groups several minutes to complete the steps and discuss the critical thinking question. Afterward, have each group choose a Presenter for the class discussion. (**Note**: Consider laminating copies of Student Handout 30 to make permanent, reusable handouts.)

Visual 30A

6 **Facilitate a student-centered class discussion.** Project the transparency of Student Handout 30. Assign each group a number. Have Presenters write their group's number in the position on the spectrum that reflects the group's decision. Then follow these guidelines for the class discussion:

- Select one Presenter to stand and explain his or her group's rating for Critical Thinking Question A.

- Ask all other Presenters to raise their hands, and have the first Presenter call on one of the other Presenters by name. Encourage lively debate between Presenters whose group's ratings differ.

- Have the new Presenter, and subsequent Presenters, begin his or her response as follows: *[Name of previous speaker], our group agrees/disagrees with your group because . . .*

After most Presenters have spoken, consider allowing groups time to discuss their original ratings. Then have the groups decide whether to change their position on the spectrum.

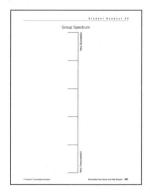

Student Handout 30

7 **Repeat Steps 4 through 6 to discuss the two other key parts of Alexander's plan.**

- For the part of Alexander's plan in which he used religion to unite his empire, have groups complete the Reading Notes for Section 30.6. Use *Visual 30B: Using Religion* and have each group choose a different Presenter for the class discussion.

- For the part of Alexander's plan in which he adopted other cultural practices to unite his empire, have groups complete the Reading Notes for Section 30.7. Use *Visual 30C: Adopting the Ways of Conquered Cultures* and have groups choose a different Presenter for the class discussion.

8 **Have groups complete the Reading Notes for Section 30.8.** Have groups read Section 30.8 and complete the corresponding Reading Notes in their Interactive Student Notebooks. Afterward, use Guide to Reading Notes 30 to review their responses.

9 **Debrief the activity.** Ask the class,

- Which part of Alexander's plan did you think was the most successful and why?

- Which part of Alexander's plan did you think was the least successful and why?

- How successful do you think Alexander the Great was in his efforts to build and unify his empire?

Visual 30B

Visual 30C

Processing

1 **Introduce the Processing activity.** Project *Visual 30D: Medallion.* Explain that in ancient times, artists often made medallions such as this one to commemorate important events. On this medallion, Alexander is on Bucephalus (byoo-SEF-uh-luhs), his warhorse. He is attacking the elephant of Porus (POH-ruhs), a famous Indian leader who fought Alexander during one of the king's last campaigns. Tell students that they will design their own medallions to evaluate the achievements of Alexander the Great.

2 **Have students complete the Processing activity on a separate piece of paper.** Consider having students share their medallions with a partner, or have volunteers share their work with the class.

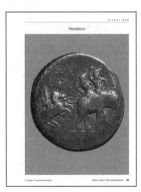

Visual 30D

Quicker Coverage

Conduct One Large Discussion Rather than have groups rate the success of each part of Alexander's plan, have them rate the overall success of Alexander's efforts to build and unify his empire.

- Have groups read and complete the Reading Notes for Sections 30.2–30.8.
- Give each group a copy of Student Handout 30.
- Have groups use the spectrum to rate the overall success of Alexander's plans to build and unify his empire.
- Use the guidelines in Step 6 of the Response Group activity to facilitate a student-centered class discussion.

Jigsaw Reading for Discussions Do not form groups of three in Step 1 of the Response Group activity. Have students complete the reading for Sections 30.2–30.4. Then divide the class into three large groups. Assign each group to one of Sections 30.5–30.7. Have students read and complete the Reading Notes for their assigned section. Then form small groups, each with members representing all three sections of reading. Have group members present and share their Reading Notes for their assigned section before you conduct the class discussion for that part of Alexander's plan.

Deeper Coverage

Add a Group Discussion Have groups read and complete the Reading Notes for Sections 30.2 and 30.3. Then tell students that they are going to rate the success of Alexander the Great's efforts to build his empire. Use the format on Visuals 30A–30C to conduct an additional group discussion. Substitute this information:

- Critical Thinking Question: *Alexander planned to use a strategy of terror and kindness to build an empire. How successful was this plan?*
- Questions for Step 1: *Why do you think Alexander planned to destroy some of the cities he conquered, and then sell the people into slavery? Was this a good or bad idea? Why? Why do you think Alexander planned to rebuild destroyed property in some of the cities he conquered, and then appoint local leaders to rule? Was this a good or bad idea? Why?*

Use the guidelines in Step 6 of the Response Group activity to guide a student-centered class discussion.

Assessment

Mastering the Content

1. B	5. A	9. A	13. C
2. D	6. A	10. A	14. D
3. C	7. D	11. B	15. C
4. D	8. B	12. D	16. B

Applying Social Studies Skills

17. the Indus River

18. the Mediterranean Sea, the Arabian Sea, the Caspian Sea (accept any two)

19. Answers will vary. Possible answers: To take a more direct route, he would have had to cross the desert. He may have wanted to go back to Persia. He wanted to travel along rivers and seacoasts.

Exploring the Essential Question

20. Answers should include all of the elements requested in the prompt.

Scoring Rubric

Score	Description
3	Student completes all four parts of the task. Details, descriptions, and feelings are clearly stated, relate to two parts of the plan, and demonstrate command of standard English conventions.
2	Student responds to most or all parts of the task, but may omit details, descriptions or feelings, only relate to one part of the plan, or not be clearly stated.
1	Student responds to at least one part of the task. Writing may contain factual and/or grammatical errors and may lack details.
0	Response does not match the task or is incorrect.

English Language Learners

Offer Examples of Rulers For the Preview activity, give students examples of other rulers with the title "Great" to help them access prior knowledge. These rulers appear in the following chapters of *History Alive! The Ancient World*:

- *Exploring Four Empires of Mesopotamia:* Sargon of Akkad, also known as Sargon the Great
- *The Ancient Egyptian Pharaohs:* Ramses II of Egypt, also known as Ramses the Great
- *The First Unification of India:* King Ashoka, also known as Ashoka the Great
- *Fighting the Persian Wars:* King Darius of Persia, also known as Darius the Great

Prepare Presenters Have Presenters write out their group's reasons for the rating on the spectrum. Presenters may read from or refer to the written statement when participating in the class discussion. Also consider having Presenters rehearse their comments with their groups before the class discussion.

Provide Sample Titles For the Processing activity, provide sample titles for students to reference on their medallions. Use titles and language that are familiar references for students. Titles might include *Alexander the Conqueror, Alexander the Builder, Alexander the Greek, Alexander the Religious, Alexander the God, Alexander the Borrower,* and *Alexander the Persian.*

Learners Reading and Writing Below Grade Level

Supply Cloze Notes For Sections 30.2 to 30.4, provide cloze notes for the Reading Notes. Copy these sections in Guide to Reading Notes 30. White-out selected details so that the remaining information is a cue for students as they read.

Allow an Oral Option For the Processing activity, allow students a choice to describe and explain their medallions orally. After drawing and titling their medallions, students can share their captions and explanations with a teacher, a partner, or the class.

Learners with Special Education Needs

Have Presenters Use Note Cards Give groups a note card for each critical thinking question. After groups have agreed on a rating on the spectrum, have group members write down their reasons on the note card. Encourage Presenters to use the note cards during the student-centered class discussion.

Simplify the Processing Activity Have students complete two of the three medallions for the Processing activity. Support students by giving them a blank outline of the medallions to use.

Advanced Learners

Use Historical Sources Give groups excerpts from historical sources written by ancient and/or modern historians, for students to use as resources for their discussions. Encourage groups to use the excerpts as supporting evidence when explaining their ratings. For ancient writers, consider the following:

- Arrian, *Anabasis Alexandri (Campaigns of Alexander)*
- Diodorus of *Sicily, Library of World History*
- Plutarch, *Life of Alexander*
- Quintus Curtius Rufus, *History of Alexander the Great*

Assign an Essay As an alternative to the Processing activity, have students write a short essay. Ask them to argue whether they think Alexander was successful in uniting his empire. Their essay should include these elements:

- a beginning statement that defines their opinion
- a summary of Alexander's plan to build and unite his empire
- at least three pieces of evidence (facts, quotations, or examples) to support their opinion

Enrichment Resources

Find out more about Alexander the Great by exploring the following Enrichment Resources for *History Alive! The Ancient World* at www.teachtci.com.

Enrichment Readings These in-depth readings encourage students to explore selected topics related to the chapter. You may also find readings that relate the chapter's content directly to your state's curriculum.

Internet Connections The recommended Web sites provide useful and engaging content that reinforces skills development and mastery of subjects within the chapter.

Literature Recommendations

The following books offer opportunities to extend the content in this chapter.

Alexander the Great by John Gunther (New York: Sterling, 2007)

Alexander the Great Rocks the World by Vicky Alrear Shecter (Plain City, OH: Darby Creek Publishing, 2006)

You Wouldn't Want to Be in Alexander the Great's Army!: Miles You'd Rather Not March by Jacqueline Morley, author, and David Antram, illustrator (New York: Franklin Watts, 2005)

Sections 30.2 to 30.3

Students' visuals for the timeline will vary.

404 B.C.E.: Peloponnesian War ends.

338 B.C.E.: King Philip of Macedonia conquers most of Greece.

336 B.C.E.: King Philip is murdered, and his son, Alexander, becomes king.

334 B.C.E.: Alexander invades Asia Minor.

1. Quarreling between Athens and Sparta led to the Peloponnesian War. Other city-states were also drawn in to the war as allies of either Athens or Sparta. Sparta won the war and became the most powerful city-state in Greece for a time.

2. When the Greeks were at war, they were not aware that Macedonia was getting stronger. King Philip had been unifying his country and creating a well-trained army. Philip was able to conquer the Greeks because the Peloponnesian War had left them weak and divided.

3. Alexander was well trained to be a leader because, as a youth, he had been tutored by the Greek philosopher Aristotle. Aristotle had taught Alexander public speaking, science, philosophy, and an appreciation of Greek culture.

4. Alexander planned to create an empire by using a strategy of terror and kindness. He would destroy the towns and cities that resisted him, and sell their people into slavery. He would help rebuild the towns and cities that surrendered.

Section 30.4

1. Check that students' shading on their maps corresponds to the shaded areas on the map in Section 30.4 of *History Alive! The Ancient World*.

2. On the map, students should circle at least two of the following labels: Macedonia, Egypt, Persian Empire.

3. Captions will vary. Possible caption: Alexander brought much of the known world at that time under his rule. The vast size of the empire might have created the problem of how to control that many diverse peoples across such a large area.

Section 30.5

Answers will vary. Possible answers: Alexander deeply admired Greek culture and hoped that Greek culture would blend with the varied cultures of the people he had conquered. He built Greek-style cities, including Alexandria. Greeks settled in these cities, bringing with them Greek laws, art, and literature. He also required soldiers and officials to speak only Greek.

Section 30.6

Answers will vary. Possible answers: Alexander used religion to inspire loyalty among his followers and the people he had conquered. He honored Egyptian and Persian gods. He also encouraged the idea that he was a god.

Section 30.7

Answers will vary. Possible answers: Alexander adopted some of the practices of other cultures to show respect for the customs of the people he had conquered. In Persia, he adopted the Persian system of government and borrowed Persian customs. He encouraged marriage between Macedonians and Persians. He himself married the daughter of Darius, the Persian king.

Section 30.8

Answers will vary. Possible answers: After Alexander's death, his empire crumbled. Settlers left the cities he had constructed, and the cities fell into ruin. His generals fought each other for control of the empire. The empire was eventually divided into three separate kingdoms.

The Legacy of Ancient Greece

How did ancient Greece contribute to the modern world?

Overview

In a Social Studies Skill Builder, students learn about the enduring contributions of the ancient Greeks by matching descriptions of modern life to images of Greek achievements in language, literature, government, the arts, the sciences, and sports.

Objectives

In the course of reading this chapter and participating in the classroom activity, students will

Social Studies

- explain how Greek language, literature, and art influence the modern world.
- identify the Greek roots of American democracy.
- describe the achievements of important Greek figures in the arts, sciences, and social sciences.
- evaluate the impact of Greek contributions on modern life.

Language Arts

- recognize the origins and meanings of frequently used foreign words in English.
- use facts and supporting details to write evaluative statements.

Social Studies Vocabulary

Key Content Terms geometry, latitude, longitude, biology

Academic Vocabulary volume, principle, medical, theory, accurately

Materials

*History Alive!
The Ancient World*

Interactive Student Notebooks

Placards 31A–31J

Lesson Masters

- Student Handout 31 (2 copies, cut apart)
- Information Master 31 (1 transparency)
- Vocabulary Development handout (1 per student, on colored paper)

Activity	Suggested Time	Materials
Preview	15 minutes	• Interactive Student Notebooks
Vocabulary Development	30–40 minutes	• *History Alive! The Ancient World* • Interactive Student Notebooks • Vocabulary Development handout
Social Studies Skill Builder	90–120 minutes (2–3 regular periods) (1–1.5 block periods)	• *History Alive! The Ancient World* • Interactive Student Notebooks • Placards 31A–31J • Student Handout 31 (2 copies, cut apart) • Information Master 31 (1 transparency)
Processing	20–30 minutes	• Interactive Student Notebooks
Assessment	40 minutes	• Chapter 31 Assessment

Preview

1 **Have students complete the Preview activity in their Interactive Student Notebooks.** Students use a key of ancient Greek words and meanings to match modern English words to their definitions.

2 **Have students share their responses in pairs or as a class.** Afterward, reveal the definitions for each English word.

- *autocracy*: F, rule by one person
- *autograph*: A, somebody's signature
- *chronic*: G, lasting over a long period of time
- *chronology*: B, study of the order in time
- *geology*: D, study of the structure of Earth
- *geothermal*: E, relating to Earth's heat
- *thermograph*: H, an instrument that records temperature
- *thermometer*: C, an instrument for measuring temperature

3 **Explain the connection between the Preview activity and Chapter 31.** Tell students that these words are just a few examples of the many English words that are derived from ancient Greek language. The ancient Greeks influenced not only modern language but also literature, government, medicine and other sciences, the arts, and sports. In this chapter, students will learn many ways in which ancient Greece contributed to the modern world.

Vocabulary Development

1 **Introduce the Key Content Terms.** Have students locate the Key Content Terms for the chapter in their Interactive Student Notebooks. These are important terms that will help them understand the main ideas of the chapter. Ask volunteers to identify any familiar terms and how they might be used in a sentence.

2 **Have students complete a Vocabulary Development handout.** Give each student a copy of the Vocabulary Development handout of your choice from the Reading Toolkit at the back of the Lesson Masters. These handouts provide extra Key Content Term practice and support, depending on your students' needs. Review the completed handout by asking volunteers to share one answer for each term.

Reading

1 **Introduce the Essential Question and have students read Section 31.1.** Have students identify the Essential Question on the first page of the chapter: *How did ancient Greece contribute to the modern world?* Then have students read Section 31.1. Afterward, have students use information from Section 31.1 and from the chapter opener image to propose some possible answers to the Essential Question.

2 Have students complete the Reading Notes for Chapter 31. Assign Sections 31.2 to 31.11 during the activity, as indicated in the procedures for the Social Studies Skill Builder. Remind students to use the Key Content Terms where appropriate as they complete their Reading Notes.

Social Studies Skill Builder

1 Before class, prepare materials and arrange your classroom. Cut apart the cards from two copies of *Student Handout 31: Legacy Cards* and spread the cards faceup on a table. Post *Placards 31A–31J: Greek Contributions*, spacing them out along the classroom walls.

2 Place students in pairs and introduce the activity. Tell students that they will learn about the legacy of ancient Greece by matching descriptions of modern life to images of ancient Greek achievements. Students will then read to learn more about these contributions and their impact on the modern world. Finally, pairs will become experts on one contribution and share what they learn with the class.

3 Review the steps for identifying Greek contributions. Project *Information Master 31: Identifying Greek Contributions to Modern Life* and review the steps with students. Consider using one of the legacy cards to model the steps.

4 Monitor pairs as they identify and learn about Greek contributions. Have one student from each pair choose a legacy card from the table. Monitor pairs as they match the descriptions on the legacy cards to the placards showing Greek achievements. As pairs complete their Reading Notes for each of Sections 31.2–31.11, use Guide to Reading Notes 31 to check their answers. Continue until most pairs have matched most of the legacy cards.

5 Review the contributions. Remove the placards from the wall and assign one placard to each pair. Each pair will then describe the image on the placard and explain its relationship to modern life. Give pairs a few minutes to prepare. (**Note:** If you have more than twenty students in your class, you may have two pairs of students work together on some of the placards. Or you may create another set of placards.) Have students take notes during the presentations for any of the placards they did not visit, and instruct them to complete the Reading Notes for the corresponding sections for homework.

Processing

Have students complete the Processing activity in their Interactive Student Notebooks. Students illustrate and annotate a spectrum to evaluate the impact of five Greek contributions on modern life.

Student Handout 31

Placards 31A–31J

Information Master 31

Quicker Coverage

Assign One Legacy Card to a Group Rather than conduct the Social Studies Skill Builder by having pairs match legacy cards to placards to identify Greek contributions, put students into ten groups of roughly equal size. Give each group one legacy card and have them find the appropriate placard. Have groups complete the Reading Notes for the corresponding section. Then groups should use their legacy card, placard, and notes to prepare a brief presentation for the class. As each group presents, other groups should complete that section of their Reading Notes.

Skim the Review Sections Before students read Sections 31.3, 31.9, and 31.10, discuss ancient Greek contributions that students are already familiar with, from the reading in Chapters 26 (The Rise of Democracy) and 29 (he Golden Age of Athens). Instruct students to first skim the related sections in Chapters 26 (Section 26.5) and 29 (Sections 29.4 and 29.6) before completing the Reading Notes for the Chapter 31 sections on government, architecture, and theater.

Deeper Coverage

Create a Human Spectrum After students have completed Step 5 of the Social Studies Skill Builder, follow these procedures to have them create a human spectrum:

- Make a spectrum by placing a 10- to 15-foot strip of masking tape across the floor in the front of the room. On the board above either end of the spectrum, write "Least Significant Impact on Modern Life" and "Most Significant Impact on Modern Life."

- Review the purpose of a spectrum. Tell students that they will now rate the Greek contributions according to their impact on the world today.

- Give pairs two to three minutes to discuss where on the spectrum they would place their contribution and why. Then have each pair choose a student representative for their placard. Representatives should stand in the place on the spectrum where they think their contribution belongs, and hold their placards in front of them.

- Encourage audience members to discuss where they think the contributions should be positioned on the spectrum. For example, they might identify ones they believe are misplaced, and explain their reasons. The purpose of this activity is not to find the "correct" locations, but to have students use evidence to support their opinions.

Find Local Examples of Greek Contributions Have students find three examples of Greek contributions in their community. For example, students might notice a public building with Greek-style architecture, a map with longitude and latitude, or a sign containing a word derived from Greek. Tell students to sketch or take a photograph of each example. Then, next to each visual, students should write a caption that describes the example, states where it is located in their community, and explains which Greek contribution it shows.

Assessment

Mastering the Content

1. C	5. B	9. D	13. D
2. D	6. B	10. C	14. A
3. C	7. C	11. B	15. B
4. A	8. A	12. A	

Applying Social Studies Skills

16. The word *acropolis* means "high city"; *acro* = high, *polis* = city.

17. The Greek root *geo* means "earth" and *-metry* means "measuring" so *geometry* means "measuring Earth."

18. a, philosophy; b, democracy; c, autobiography; d, microbiology; e, telescope; f, microscope

19. Answers will vary. Possible answers: autocracy (rule by a single self), autograph (written by oneself), geology (study of Earth, science of Earth), microphone (device to make small sounds bigger), telegraph (writing far away), telephone (sound far away)

Exploring the Essential Question

20. Answers should include all of the elements requested in the prompt.

Scoring Rubric

Score	Description
3	Student completes all three parts of the task (descriptions of places of interest influenced by ancient Greece). Descriptions, explanations, and reasons are clearly stated, supported by details, and demonstrate command of standard English conventions.
2	Student responds to most or all parts of the task, but descriptions and explanations may lack details or not be clearly stated.
1	Student responds to at least one part of the task. Descriptions and explanations may contain factual and/or grammatical errors and may lack details.
0	Response does not match the task or is incorrect.

Painting the Gods

1   **Examine and discuss images of ancient Greek sculpture.** Display an image of an ancient Greek statue and have students look at the photograph on the first page of the Chapter 31 Reading Further in the Student Edition. You may also have students find other examples of Greek sculpture by looking through the Unit 5 chapters in their books. Have students brainstorm adjectives that come to mind when they look at these images of ancient sculpture. Write their suggestions on the board.

2   **Have students read the Chapter 31 Reading Further.** Ask students what adjectives they might use to describe the Brinkmanns' versions of ancient sculpture. On the board, make a second list of these suggestions. Discuss Vinzenz Brinkmann's reasons for colorizing Greek sculpture. Ask, *How does color change the way we view this art?* Encourage students to express their opinions about Brinkmann's work, including reasons why they agree or disagree with his actions.

3   **Have students turn to the first page of the Reading Further in their Interactive Student Notebooks.** Read aloud the first paragraph on the page. Ask students to consider old black-and-white movies they may have seen on TV. Discuss (a) why older movies were filmed in black and white, and (b) whether students or their families have watched such movies at home. Note that in the early days of television, all programming was in black and white because the technology for color television had not yet been developed. Lead students to relate the debate about adding color to old films to the Brinkmanns' research and recreation of ancient sculpture.

4   **Have students complete the Reading Further in their Interactive Student Notebooks.**

5   **Have students share their work.** Invite students to share their points of view as expressed in their paragraphs. Discuss the issue of creating color replicas of ancient Greek and Roman sculpture. Let the class vote on whether they think it is a good idea.

English Language Learners

Offer an Alternative Preview Activity Provide a more visual Preview activity to help students see links between modern life and ancient Greece. Find three or more pictures of ancient Greek temples. It is likely that they will look similar. Find three or more pictures of modern U.S. government buildings with Greek architecture, such as the U.S. Capitol, the U.S. Supreme Court, and the U.S. Department of Treasury. Have students identify the similarities between the ancient and the modern buildings. Then ask them to predict why those similarities might exist.

Review the Areas of Contributions Clarify each of the ten areas of Greek contributions: literature and history, government, medicine, mathematics, astronomy, geography, biology, architecture, theater, and sports. Before conducting the activity, write these terms on the board. Have students work in small groups to define each one and generate a list of examples.

Learners Reading and Writing Below Grade Level

Annotate the Legacy Cards Annotate each legacy card from Student Handout 31. Underline words that students may have difficulty with. On the bottom or back of the legacy cards, provide a brief definition for those words. For example, on the legacy card for biology, you might underline the words *nurseries, bulbs,* and *pollinated.* Consider making a simple sketch of a flowering plant and label it to help define these terms.

Provide Sentence Starters For the Processing activity, provide some or all of these sentence starters to help students explain their placements along the spectrum. Students might use these starters as a resource:

- *[Name of contribution] has the least significant impact on modern life because . . .*
- *[Name of contribution] has some significant impact on modern life because . . .*
- *[Name of contribution] has the most significant impact on modern life because . . .*
- *[Name of contribution] has more/less significant impact on modern life than [Name of other contribution] because . . .*

Learners with Special Education Needs

Support the Reading Notes For the last column on the matrix in the Reading Notes, use Guide to Reading Notes 31 to provide two examples of contributions. Tell students that they have to find one additional example as they read. Students should then choose and draw the one example they think is the most important. You might also consider using Guide to Reading Notes 31 to provide some of the matches for the placards, if necessary.

Reduce the Processing Activity Requirements Rather than have students choose and draw five items to place on the spectrum, have students select two. Students should select the contributions that they think had the least and the most significant impact on modern life. Students should label the spectrum, draw an illustration, and write a sentence for each of the two contributions.

Advanced Learners

Design Commemorative Stamps Tell students that the U.S. Postal Service has decided to issue a series of stamps celebrating the contributions of the ancient Greeks. Students have been asked to use pictures and/or words to design four stamps that represent their choices of ancient Greek contributions. They must also write a speech explaining why they have selected these contributions from all the ones they learned about in Chapter 31. If time permits, have students present their stamps and speeches in small groups. Alternatively, have students post their designs, conduct a gallery walk, and hold a class vote to determine which stamps to use in the postal series.

Create a Gallery of Greek Figures Have students work in pairs or in small groups to research one or more of the ancient Greeks discussed in the chapter. Students should then create a "bust" for a gallery of Greek figures. Each bust should include the following: an image of the figure's head; a nameplate with the figure's name, his or her title, and some biographical information; and a plaque that describes the figure's most important achievements.

Enrichment Resources

Find out more about the legacy of Greece in the modern world by exploring the following Enrichment Resources for *History Alive! The Ancient World* at www.teachtci.com.

Enrichment Readings These in-depth readings encourage students to explore selected topics related to the chapter. You may also find readings that relate the chapter's content directly to your state's curriculum.

Internet Connections The recommended Web sites provide useful and engaging content that reinforces skills development and mastery of subjects within the chapter.

Literature Recommendations

The following books offer opportunities to extend the content in this chapter.

The Ancient Greeks (People of the Ancient World) by Allison Lassieur (Danbury, CT: Children's Press, 2005)

Hippocrates: Father of Medicine by Herbert S. Goldberg (Lincoln, NE: Authors Choice Press, 2006)

Vocabulary from Latin and Greek Roots: Book 1 by Elizabeth Osborne (Clayton, DE: Prestwick House, 2003)

Drawings and lists of contributions will vary, but possible responses are provided below.

Section 31.2

Placard Letter: A

Contributions:

- The English alphabet grew out of the one used by ancient Greeks.
- Many English words have Greek roots.
- English grammar, punctuation, and paragraphing are all based on Greek writing.
- Greeks developed historical writing.

Section 31.3

Placard Letter: D

Contributions:

- Democracy began in ancient Athens.
- The practice of having citizens serve on juries began in Greece.
- Although there are differences between American democracy and Greek democracy, the basic principles are the same.

Section 31.4

Placard Letter: B

Contributions:

- Hippocrates brought a scientific way of thinking to medicine.
- Hippocrates believed diseases had natural causes.
- Hippocrates taught his students to observe and write down what they saw.
- Today's doctors take the Hippocratic Oath, based on Hippocrates' code of ethics.

Section 31.5

Placard Letter: E

Contributions:

- Pythagoras started a school where students developed mathematical theories.
- The Greeks created new and improved methods for measuring shapes and spaces.
- Euclid developed a textbook that has been used as the basis for teaching geometry for more than 2,000 years.
- Hypatia was the first woman to earn fame as a mathematician.

Section 31.6

Placard Letter: C

Contributions:

- Aristarchus was the first to suggest that Earth moves around the sun.
- Hipparchus studied and named more than 850 stars.
- Hipparchus figured out how to estimate the distances from Earth to both the sun and the moon.
- The theories of Hipparchus allowed later scientists to accurately predict eclipses of the moon.

Section 31.7

Placard Letter: J

Contributions:

- Herodotus made the first world map, using information he gathered while traveling and speaking with other travelers.
- Ptolemy invented a system of longitude and latitude.
- Ptolemy wrote a book that listed over 8,000 places in the world.
- Ptolemy's book also contained maps that showed how to represent Earth's curve on a flat surface.

Section 31.8

Placard Letter: I

Contributions:

- The Greeks identified many types of plants and gave names to the different parts of plants.
- The Greeks discovered that plants reproduce by spreading seeds.
- Greek doctors used many plants to treat people.
- The way we classify animals and plants today is based on Aristotle's work.

Section 31.9

Placard Letter: F

Contributions:

- The Greeks used columns to make their temples balanced and stately.
- Greek styles are still used today in many public buildings.
- Greek styles are also used in homes and stores.
- The design of today's covered porches reflects a Greek stoa, which is a covered line of columns.

Section 31.10

Placard Letter: G

Contributions:

- Greek theaters were built as semicircles with rows of seats that rose steeply so everyone could hear.
- Greeks invented special effects.
- Writers have been inspired by Greek myths and stories.
- Greek dramas are still performed all over the world.

Section 31.11

Placard Letter: H

Contributions:

- The first Olympic Games were held in ancient Greece in 776 B.C.E.
- Today's Olympics reflect ancient Greek customs, such as the lighting ceremony.
- Modern Olympic events grew out of Greek contests, such as the pentathlon.

Ancient Greece

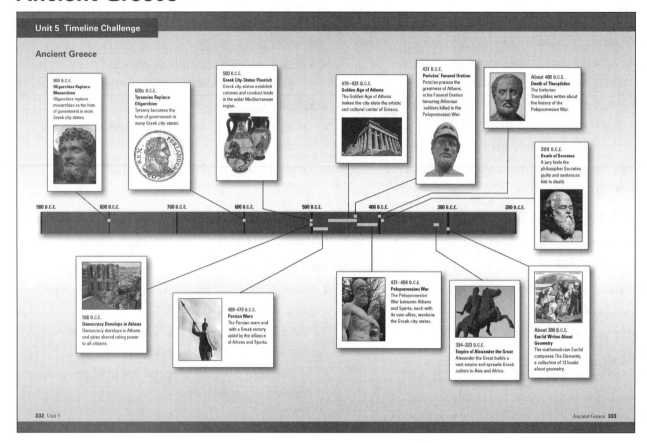

Overview

This Timeline Challenge provides students with a review of the main events and ideas of this unit, as well as practice in reading and interpreting timelines. You can vary and expand the activity according to students' needs and the amount of time available.

Basic Procedure

1 **Introduce the timeline in the Student Edition.** Direct students to the Ancient Greece Timeline at the end of Unit 5 in the Student Edition. You may wish to have students read aloud and discuss the timeline entries.

2 **Introduce the Timeline Challenge in the Interactive Student Notebook.** Direct students to the Unit 5 Timeline Challenge in their notebooks. Point out the two types of questions, "Timeline Skills" and "Critical Thinking," and model how to answer each type.

3 **Have students complete the Timeline Challenge.** Monitor students as they work. Use the Guide to Unit 5 Timeline Challenge to check their answers. You may wish to project a transparency of the Timeline Challenge as you work through the questions with the class and conduct a discussion of the "Critical Thinking" questions.

4 **Complete the KWL chart.** Return to the KWL chart created at the beginning of the unit, and ask students to list the key information they have learned.

Classroom Timeline

1 **Prepare the Timeline Challenge Cards.** Copy and cut the cards from *Student Handout TC5: Unit 5 Timeline Challenge Cards.* You may wish to laminate the cards for future use.

2 **Create a timeline on a classroom wall.** On an empty wall or a large bulletin board, make a timeline with masking tape or colored paper. Mark off the time intervals in advance, or ask students to do so in class.

3 **Have students place the Timeline Challenge Cards.** Distribute cards to pairs or individual students and have them tape the cards in the correct locations on the timeline. Call on students to provide more information on the timeline topics, to review main events and issues.

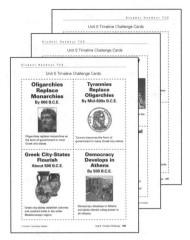

Student Handout TC5

Internet Research

1 **Review students' suggestions for additional timeline entries.** Have students share their answers to the last question of the Timeline Challenge.

2 **Have students conduct Internet research.** Ask students to choose and research one of their suggested events.

3 **Have students create additional Timeline Challenge Cards.** Direct students to research an appropriate image for their cards and then use the computer to create an illustrated card, complete with timeline entry.

Timeline Skills

Score 1 point for each correct answer.

1. Greek city-states were flourishing by 500 B.C.E.

2. Of these forms of government, oligarchy was the first used in ancient Greece, appearing around 800 B.C.E.

3. Democracy appeared about 300 years after the development of oligarchies.

4. Democracy developed in Athens, about 500 B.C.E.

5. The Golden Age of Athens happened after the Persian Wars.

6. The Golden Age ends in 431 B.C.E., at the same time as the Peloponnesian War begins. Because Athens was fighting Sparta in the war, Athens could no longer use resources for cultural achievements.

7. Pericles delivered his Funeral Oration speech during the Peloponnesian War.

8. Alexander the Great was not tutored by Socrates. Socrates was tried and sentenced to death in 399 B.C.E., which is 65 years before the rise of Alexander.

9. Alexander the Great built a vast empire and spread Greek culture to Asia and Africa.

10. Euclid was a mathematician. He was important because he wrote a set of geometry books on which today's geometry books are based.

Critical Thinking

Score 1 to 3 points for each answer, depending on the thoroughness of the response.

11. a. Before democracy was developed, ancient Greek city-states had monarchies, oligarchies, and tyrannies as forms of government. Monarchy was rule by one person, a monarch, who had power over many things. Oligarchy was rule by a few people called aristocrats, who typically used their power only to help themselves. Tyranny was rule by a tyrant, who seized power but had to rely on the support of the people to stay in power.

b. Similarities: In both the people have the power to rule and the citizens serve on juries. Difference: In ancient Greece, every citizen voted on every law.

12. Similarities: Both Athens and Sparta had a government and a system of slavery. Differences: Athens had a democracy, while Sparta had an oligarchy. Athens relied on trade for its economy. Sparta discouraged trade and relied on farming and conquest. Athens educated only boys, in many subject areas. Sparta educated boys and girls, focusing mostly on military training. Finally, women had more rights in Sparta than in Athens.

13. Answer will vary. Students must identify an important Greek figure from the unit, describe his or her contribution to the arts and sciences, and explain why the contribution is significant.

14. Answers will vary. Students must explain why the events they chose merit inclusion.

Using Scores to Inform Instruction

Timeline Skills A score of 7 out of 10 indicates that students understand most of the key events of this unit.

Critical Thinking A score of 8 out of 12 indicates that students are able to think critically about most of the key issues of this unit.

If students score below these levels, consider reviewing timeline and critical thinking skills.

Ancient Rome

Overview

This activity introduces the geographic information essential to Unit 6. Students read and interpret maps to learn key physical features of ancient Rome, as well as to understand the expansion of the Roman Empire. Students annotate an outline map of the Roman Empire, answer questions in their Interactive Student Notebooks, and then discuss critical thinking questions. Students' comprehension of content and proficiency in map-reading and higher-order thinking skills will help you gauge their readiness for the unit. The pages that follow include a completed map, answers to questions, a scoring guide to inform your teaching, and suggestions for modifications to meet specific student needs.

Essential Geographic Understandings

1. Location of ancient Rome

2. Key physical features: Mediterranean Sea, Adriatic Sea, Ionian Sea, Tyrrhenian Sea, Alps, Apennines, Rome, Po and Tiber rivers

3. Gradual expansion of the Roman Empire

4. Impact of location on Roman expansion

Procedures

1 **Introduce the unit.** Tell students they will learn about the history of ancient Rome, from its beginnings as a village, then as a city, and later as an empire that expanded into much of Europe.

2 **Create a KWL chart.** Ask students to identify what they already know about the geography of ancient Rome and what they want to learn. Use their responses to gauge how much additional background information they will need as you progress through the unit. Students will return to the KWL chart at the end of the unit and add the key information they have learned.

3 **Have students read Unit 6 "Setting the Stage" in the Student Edition.**

4 **Have students complete the Geography Challenge.** Monitor students as they work. Use the guide on the next two pages to check answers. You may wish to project the map from the Interactive Student Notebook and have students annotate it as the class works through the map-reading questions. Make sure students have grasped Essential Geographic Understandings 1 and 2.

5 **Discuss the "Critical Thinking" questions.** Help students understand the geographic relationships described in Essential Geographic Understandings 3 and 4.

The Roman Empire, About 117 C.E.

BRITAIN

GAUL

A L P S

CARPATHIAN MTS.

ETRURIA

APENNINES

Po River

Tiber River

Rome

Adriatic Sea

GREECE

ASIA MINOR

ASSYRIA

SPAIN

Tyrrhenian Sea

Ionian Sea

JUDEA

Mediterranean Sea

EGYPT

S A H A R A

N
W E
S

| 0 | 400 | 800 miles |
| 0 | 400 | 800 kilometers |

Azimuthal Equal-Area Projection

Geography Skills

Score 1 point for each correct answer. Use the map on the previous page to check shading and labeling.

1. Students should label the Alps on their maps.

2. Students should label the Apennine Mountains as the range that runs the length of Italy.

3. Students' label should show that Rome is located on the Tiber River.

4. A peninsula is a land mass that is surrounded on three sides by water. Check that students label the seas that make Italy a peninsula—the Ionian, Tyrrhenian, Mediterranean, and Adriatic seas.

5. Check that students label the Po River. The Po River runs in an east-west direction. The Tiber runs in a north-south direction. The Romans could use the Tiber River as a route to the sea. Also, because the city was located at the best place to cross the river, it became a center of trade.

6. The Roman Empire expanded as far north as Britain, and in Europe, as far west as Spain.

7. Students should label the Sahara as the southernmost boundary of the Roman Empire.

Critical Thinking

Questions may have more than one correct answer. Score 1 to 3 points for each reasonable answer, depending on the strength of students' geographic reasoning.

8. The Italian peninsula was centrally located in the Mediterranean region, which made it easier for the Romans to trade with other countries, as well as to transport armies and supplies.

9. The altitude of the Alps would have made it difficult for people to interact with cultures in northern Europe. The Apennines would have made it difficult for people on Italy's east coast to interact with those on the west coast. It is likely that the mountainous geography isolated individual communities in ancient Italy, allowing little contact with other Romans or other cultures. This would change as Roman technological advances made travel easier.

10. The Romans would have been more likely to choose a water route to Spain. A water route would have been much shorter, and stops to restock supplies could have been made at Sardinia and other islands along the way.

11. The evidence lies in the expansion of the Roman Empire itself, eventually extending as far north as Britain, as far east as Spain, south to Africa, and west to Syria. It is unlikely that the Romans could have succeeded without sea travel.

Using Scores to Inform Instruction

Geography Skills A score of 4 out of 7 or better indicates that students have acquired sufficient geographic information to proceed with the unit.

Critical Thinking A score of 7 out of 12 or better indicates that students are beginning to understand the relationships between physical geography and the different ways in which people live.

Modifying Instruction

ELL or Learners with Special Education Needs Consider focusing on map-reading questions or limiting the number of "Critical Thinking" questions.

Students with Weak Map or Critical Thinking Skills Assign appropriate pages from the Social Studies Skills Toolkit in the back of the Lesson Masters.

Geography and the Early Development of Rome

How did the Etruscans and Greeks influence the development of Rome?

Overview

In a Response Group activity, students learn about the founding of Rome, and examine images to identify evidence of Etruscan and Greek influences on Rome.

Objectives

In the course of reading this chapter and participating in the classroom activity, students will

Social Studies

- identify the location and describe the geography of Rome.
- explain the myth of Romulus and Remus.
- analyze the influence of Etruscan engineering and sports on the development of Rome.
- analyze the effect of Greek architecture, writing, art, and religion on Roman culture.

Language Arts

- understand cause and effect.
- identify myths as a form of fiction, and distinguish between the historic and the mythic.

Social Studies Vocabulary

Key Content Terms Rome, Etruscan, cuniculus, gladiator, Greco-Roman

Academic Vocabulary adapt, document, display

Materials

*History Alive!
The Ancient World*

Interactive Student Notebooks

Visuals 32A–32D

Lesson Masters

- Student Handout 32 (1 copy per group of 3)
- Vocabulary Development handout (1 per student, on colored paper)

Activity	Suggested Time	Materials
Preview	10 minutes	• Interactive Student Notebooks • Visual 32A
Vocabulary Development	30–40 minutes	• *History Alive! The Ancient World* • Interactive Student Notebooks • Vocabulary Development handout
Response Group	60 minutes (1–2 regular periods) (1 block period)	• *History Alive! The Ancient World* • Interactive Student Notebooks • Visuals 32A–32D • Student Handout 32 (1 copy per group of 3)
Processing	20 minutes	• Interactive Student Notebooks
Assessment	40 minutes	• Chapter 32 Assessment

Preview

1   **Have students complete the Preview activity for Chapter 32 in their Interactive Student Notebooks.** Project *Visual 32A: Artistic Renditions of Ancient Greece and Rome*, and tell students that these images are paintings of life in ancient Greece and Rome. Have students use the projected images to complete the tasks.

2   **Have students share their answers in pairs or as a class.** Students might identify such common features as columns, statues, arched windows, decorated buildings, or people in togas.

3   **Explain the connection between the Preview activity and Chapter 32.** Tell students that the reason why they were able to point out similarities between the two images is because the ancient Romans were heavily influenced by the ancient Greeks. In this chapter, students will learn about the founding of Rome, and discover the influence of neighboring cultures (such as the Greeks) on its development.

Visual 32A

Vocabulary Development

1   **Introduce the Key Content Terms.** Have students locate the Key Content Terms for the chapter in their Interactive Student Notebooks. These are important terms that will help them understand the main ideas of the chapter. Ask volunteers to identify any familiar terms and suggest how they might be used in a sentence.

2   **Have students complete a Vocabulary Development handout.** Give each student a copy of the Vocabulary Development handout of your choice from the Reading Toolkit at the back of the Lesson Masters. These handouts provide extra practice and support, depending on students' needs. Review the completed handout by asking volunteers to share one answer for each term.

Reading

Introduce the Essential Question and have students read Section 32.1. Have students identify the Essential Question on the first page of the chapter: *How did the Etruscans and Greeks influence the development of Rome?*

1   Then have students read Section 32.1. Afterward, have students respond to these questions:

   • Where is Rome? Describe its location.

   • Who were Romulus and Remus? What was unique about their lives?

   • According to myth, how was Rome founded?

2   **Have students complete the Reading Notes for Chapter 32.** Assign Sections 32.2 to 32.8 during the activity, as indicated in the procedures for the Response Group. Remind students to use the Key Content Terms where appropriate as they complete their Reading Notes.

> **Listening and Speaking: Oral Response to Literature**
>
> Have pairs or small groups of students discuss, develop, and present oral responses to the myth by thinking about why this story was generated and why it has had the staying power that it has had.

> **Vocabulary Development: Multiple-Meaning Words**
>
> Each academic vocabulary word is a multiple-meaning word. Have students generate a list of multiple meanings for each word. Then ask them to consult a print or online dictionary to find more. Challenge students to use a range of meanings for each word in contexts they create.

Response Group

1 **Place students in groups of three.** Make sure that all students can see the screen. You may want to prepare a seating chart that shows students with whom they will work and where they will sit.

2 **Have students read Section 32.2 and complete the corresponding Reading Notes.** Remind students that they now are familiar with the myth of how Rome was founded; next they will learn how historians describe the founding of Rome. After students have completed their Reading Notes, ask, *What might be some of the ways that neighboring cultures influenced Rome?*

3 **Introduce the activity.** Tell students that in this activity they will read about Etruscan and Greek influences on Rome, create a set of cards to represent the influences, and examine images of life in Rome. For each image, groups will identify and discuss the cultural influences that can be seen or inferred. If necessary, clarify that "to infer" means "to use context clues to draw conclusions about something that is not clearly stated nor shown directly."

4 **Have students read Sections 32.3 to 32.8 and complete the corresponding Reading Notes.** Explain that these sections describe the Etruscan and Greek influences on Rome, which students must understand before beginning the activity. Use Guide to Reading Notes 32 to review the answers with the class.

5 **Have groups create "Cultural Influence" cards.** Distribute a copy of *Student Handout 32: Etruscan and Greek Influence Cards* to each group. Tell students to create "Cultural Influence" cards by following these procedures:

Student Handout 32

   • Cut apart the cards from the handout.

   • Use the corresponding images in Chapter 32 to complete an illustration on each card.

   • Use their Reading Notes to add two or three phrases that summarize the influence of that cultural aspect on Rome. For example, on the "Etruscan Engineering" card, students might write "built stone arches" and "used cuniculus to bring water to the city."

   • Review the cards as a group, making sure that every student can explain the six influences.

6 **Model the activity procedures.** Project the top of Visual 32A again, or have students look at the chapter opener image in their book. Follow these steps:

   • Tell groups they will first set aside "Cultural Influence" cards for all the Etruscan and Greek influences they can directly *see* in the image of the Baths of Carcalla. Explain that they might set aside the "Etruscan Engineering" card because they see arches and the "Greek Art" card because they see sculptures.

   • Then challenge groups to use their observation skills to identify cultural influences that are *implied* by the image. Explain that, for example, students could set aside the "Greek Writing" card because Romans might have kept a written record showing when people paid to use the baths.

- At your signal, have groups hold up a card for an Etruscan or Greek influence they identify (by sight or by inference) in the image. Choose a group at random and have them explain the Etruscan or Greek influence for the card they are holding up. Have other groups set down their cards during the explanation.

- Then have each group hold up an influence card for a *different* influence they identified. Choose another group to share. Continue this process until all identified influences have been shared.

- Ask, *What questions do you have about the activity procedures?*

7 **Project *Visual 32B: Roman Street Scene* and have students identify Etruscan and Greek influences.** Tell students this is an artist's version of a street scene in ancient Rome. Have groups neatly line up their "Cultural Influence" cards in the center of their workspace. Allow students adequate time—about 3 to 5 minutes—to identify cultural influences in the image (both seen and inferred) and to set aside the corresponding cards.

Visual 32B

8 **Have groups justify their answers.** Follow the procedures in Step 6 to have groups hold up cards and explain the Etruscan and Greek influences they see in and infer from the image. Some suggested answers follow, but accept any influences that students can justify:

- **Influences that might be seen:** Etruscan engineering (arches), Etruscan sporting events (chariot), Greek architecture (monumental public buildings), Greek art (sculptures on fountain), and Greek writing (on wall)

- **Influences that might be inferred:** Etruscan engineering (water from cuniculi being drawn from a fountain)

9 **Repeat Steps 7–8 for *Visual 32C: The Circus Maximus*.** Tell students this is an artist's rendition of the Circus Maximus. Some possible answers:

- **Influences that might be seen:** Etruscan engineering (arches), Etruscan sporting events (chariot race), Greek architecture (stadium), Greek art (sculptures and monuments), Greek religion (statues of gods and goddesses)

- **Influences that might be inferred:** Etruscan engineering (water for the horses and spectators), Greek writing (accounts of payment and posted scores of the races)

Visual 32C

10 **Repeat Steps 7–8 for *Visual 32D: The Roman Forum*.** Tell students this is an artist's rendition of the Roman Forum. Some possible answers:

- **Influences that might be seen:** Etruscan engineering (arches), Greek architecture (monumental public buildings and columns), Greek art (sculptures and monuments), Greek religion (statues of gods and goddesses)

- **Influences that might be inferred:** Greek writing (laws posted in public, court orders, senators' votes, record of trade)

Visual 32D

11 Wrap up the activity with a class discussion. Ask,

- Which Etruscan and Greek influences did you find the most interesting?

- Which aspects of Etruscan and Greek culture do you think had the most important influence on Rome?

Processing

Have students complete the Processing activity. Explain that the Romans, as Americans do, often celebrated the achievements of their leaders on coins. Tell students that they will honor Etruscan and Greek influences on Roman culture by creating their own coins.

Quicker Coverage

Break Up the Reading Allow groups to divide Sections 32.3 to 32.8 among themselves. Each group member should read about two Etruscan or Greek influences and complete the corresponding Reading Notes. Students should then take turns sharing the information from their assigned sections until all group members have completed their Reading Notes.

Reduce the Number of Images Have students analyze only one or two of the images from Visuals 32B–32D. If using only one image, conduct a longer class discussion by pushing students to speculate further about influences that might be inferred from the image.

Omit the Influence Cards Instead of having students create and hold up influence cards, simply have groups take turns pointing out Etruscan and Greek influences that can be seen or inferred. Challenge groups to find unique examples in the image that have not yet been pointed out.

Deeper Coverage

Debrief, Using a Spectrum To wrap up the activity, draw the following spectrum on the board:

Least Important   Most Important
Influence on Rome   Influence on Rome

◄──►

Tell groups to copy the spectrum on a piece of paper and then line up their six influence cards along the spectrum. The more important they think an influence is, the closer they should place that card to the right. The less important they think an influence is, the closer they should place the card to the left. Consider having groups stand along the board and hold their six cards in the appropriate places. Ask individual students to justify the placement of certain cards, and encourage the class to suggest alternate placements. After the activity, have all students create individual spectrums with all six influences. Tell students to write a sentence justifying the influences they placed farthest right and farthest left.

Hold a Debate Have students debate which influence on Rome was the most important. Assign half the class to represent one influence and the other half, another influence. You can assign influences or let groups choose their own. Give students time to formulate their arguments, using information from the book and from the activity images.

Assessment

Mastering the Content

1. D	5. A	9. C	13. A
2. C	6. C	10. A	14. D
3. A	7. B	11. C	15. B
4. B	8. D	12. B	16. D

Applying Social Studies Skills

17. on the southwest part of the Italian peninsula, near the Tyrrhenian Sea

18. they probably traveled by boat, because the land they settled is near the coast; some of their colonies were on an island.

19. Answers will vary. Possible answer: they controlled the neighboring land on both sides.

Exploring the Essential Question

20. Answers should include all the elements requested in the prompt.

Scoring Rubric

Score	Description
3	Student completes two pictures and two appropriate captions. Captions are clearly stated, supported by details, and demonstrate command of standard English conventions.
2	Student responds to most or all parts of the task, but captions may lack details or not be clearly stated.
1	Student responds to at least one part of the task. Captions may contain factual and/or grammatical errors and may lack details.
0	Response does not match the task or is incorrect.

English Language Learners

Explicitly Teach "Influence" As you debrief the Preview activity, introduce the term *influence* and provide examples of how one country's culture can influence another's. Have students think about ways their native culture might appear in American society (e.g., restaurants, clothing, music), or ways that aspects of American culture appear in their native society.

Scaffold the Concept of Making Inferences Follow these steps:

- Have students discuss how they might know a friend is angry, without being told. Elicit ideas such as the friend refuses to talk, has her arms crossed, or she slammed a door. Explain that when we use nonverbal clues to figure out the emotion another person is feeling, we are making an *inference*.

- Give additional examples of how someone might make an inference about a situation. For example, if students saw a flowerpot broken on the floor and a puppy nearby, they might infer that the puppy knocked over the flowerpot.

- Project Visual 32A and read aloud the sample inference in Step 6 of the Response Group, about Greek writing. Have students identify evidence in the image that may support that inference. Then give them time to brainstorm other influences that they might infer from the image.

Learners Reading and Writing Below Grade Level

Use Presentations to Reduce the Reading Divide up the reading for Sections 32.3 to 32.8 by having groups read and complete the corresponding Reading Notes for only one of the sections (some sections may be assigned to two groups). Have each group create a simple poster that includes the following:

- the section number and title

- a summary of how the Etruscan or Greek influence affected Rome

- an illustration or symbol to represent the influence

As groups present, have all other students fill in their Reading Notes. You may want to create a transparency of the Reading Notes and fill them in as a class.

Learners with Special Education Needs

Distribute Copies of the Images Make a copy of Visual 32A, which you project during the Preview activity. On this copy, circle or draw arrows to three features that are in both images, such as the columns, statues, and arching windows. Tell students to use this for guidance as they complete the Preview activity. During the Response Group activity, provide copies of Visuals 32B–32D, on which you have circled the features you want students to consider. Students will then identify the Etruscan and Greek influences that correspond to the circled features.

Support the Reading Notes Provide students with a copy of Guide to Reading Notes 32 with key words or phrases omitted from each answer. Tell students to fill in the missing words as they read each section of text.

Advanced Learners

Explore More Etruscan and Greek Influences Challenge students to find other Etruscan and Greek influences on Rome. Consider having students research the following cultural elements that were adapted by Romans:

- *Etruscan*: government, metalworking, sculpture, social organization, or mysticism

- *Greek*: coinage, theater, or philosophy

Then have students present these influences in a manner of their choosing. They might create a poster or digital presentation, or perform a skit or pantomime.

Brainstorm Cultural Influences on the U.S. Tell students that geography plays a role in how neighboring countries influence each other's cultures. Just as Greek and Etruscan culture had an impact on Roman culture, the neighbors of the United States—Canada and Mexico—have influenced us. Have students brainstorm specific ways in which our neighbors have influenced aspects of our culture, such as architecture, art, sports, food, and language.

Enrichment Resources

Find out more about the geography and early development of Rome by exploring the following Enrichment Resources for *History Alive! The Ancient World* at www.teachtci.com.

Enrichment Readings These in-depth readings encourage students to explore selected topics related to the chapter. You may also find readings that relate the chapter's content directly to your state's curriculum.

Internet Connections These recommended Web sites provide useful and engaging content that reinforces skills development and mastery of subjects within the chapter.

Literature Recommendations

The following books offer opportunities to extend the content in this chapter:

Brave Cloelia: Retold from the Account in The History of Early Rome by the Roman Historian Titus Livius by Jane Louise Curry (Los Angeles: Getty Publications, 2004)

The Etruscans by Don Nardo (Farmington Hills, MI: Lucent Books, 2004)

Gods and Goddesses of Ancient Rome by Leon Ashworth (Mankato, MN: Smart Apple Media, 2002)

Section 32.2

Cartoons will vary. One cartoon should illustrate the myth of Remus and Romulus; the other should illustrate the Latins' founding of Rome on the Palatine, around 700 B.C.E.

Section 32.3

The Romans used Etruscan arches to build bridges, stadiums, and aqueducts. They adopted the cuniculus from the Etruscans and used it to irrigate land, drain swamps, and carry water to their cities.

Section 32.4

Romans enjoyed watching the dangerous Etruscan sport of chariot racing. Slave fighting was also adapted from the Etruscans. Some Roman slaves that fought against each other or animals were called gladiators.

Section 32.5

The Romans used Greek columns and designs to add to the beauty of their buildings. They constructed buildings that resembled Greek temples and used concrete to create even larger structures, such as the Pantheon.

Section 32.6

The Romans used a modified Etruscan alphabet, which was an adaptation of the Greek alphabet. Like the Greeks, they write in all-capital letters and carved important documents into walls and columns for all to see. Greek poetry also inspired Roman writers.

Section 32.7

Romans copied the Greek technique for making pottery. Wealthy Romans collected Greek art and built monuments in the Greek style. Roman sculptors and painters used Greek art as a model, but their figures were more realistic.

Section 32.8

Roman religion was highly influenced by Greek religion. The Romans made Greek gods as their own, but gave them Roman names. The Romans were more concerned with following the correct rituals than with stories about their gods.

The Rise of the Roman Republic

What were the characteristics of the Roman Republic and how did they change over time?

Overview

In an Experiential Exercise, students assume the roles of patricians and plebeians to learn how the struggle between these two groups led to a more democratic government in the Roman Republic.

Objectives

In the course of reading this chapter and participating in the classroom activity, students will

Social Studies

- describe the founding of the Roman Republic.
- compare and contrast the rights and powers of patricians and plebeians during various phases of the Roman Republic.
- describe how the government of the Roman Republic became more democratic over time.
- summarize the lasting significance of the ideas and organization of the Roman Republic.

Language Arts

- identify the tone, mood, and emotion conveyed in oral communication.
- clearly state a position.

Materials

*History Alive!
The Ancient World*

Interactive Student
Notebooks

Visual 33

Lesson Masters

- Student Handout 33
  (1 copy, cut apart)
- Vocabulary Development
  handout (1 per student, on
  colored paper)

8 or more magazines
with color photographs
or illustrations

books and games

snacks

Social Studies Vocabulary

Key Content Terms patrician, plebeian, republic, Senate, consul, tribune, veto, constitution

Academic Vocabulary dramatic, crisis, publish, civic

Activity	Suggested Time	Materials
Preview	10 minutes	• Interactive Student Notebooks
Vocabulary Development	30–40 minutes	• *History Alive! The Ancient World* • Interactive Student Notebooks • Vocabulary Development handout
Experiential Exercise	50 minutes (1 regular period) (1 block period)	• *History Alive! The Ancient World* • Interactive Student Notebooks • Visual 33 • Student Handout 33 (1 copy, cut apart) • 8 or more magazines with color photographs or illustrations • books and games • snacks
Processing	20 minutes	• Interactive Student Notebooks
Assessment	40 minutes	• Chapter 33 Assessment

Preview

1 **Have students complete the Preview activity for Chapter 33 in their Interactive Student Notebooks.** Students will describe a time when they were treated unfairly and the actions they took to remedy the situation.

2 **Have students share their answers in pairs or with the class.**

3 **Explain the connection between the Preview activity and Chapter 33.** Tell students that when the Roman Republic was founded, some people had more rights than others. Just as students tried to improve the situations they described in the Preview activity, some Romans attempted to gain greater equality and power in their government. In this chapter, students will learn how this struggle for equality led to a more democratic government in the Roman Republic.

Vocabulary Development

1 **Introduce the Key Content Terms.** Have students locate the Key Content Terms for the chapter in their Interactive Student Notebooks. These are important terms that will help them understand the main ideas of the chapter. Ask volunteers to identify any familiar terms and suggest how they might be used in a sentence.

2 **Have students complete a Vocabulary Development handout.** Give each student a copy of the Vocabulary Development handout of your choice from the Reading Toolkit at the back of the Lesson Masters. These handouts provide extra Key Content Term practice and support, depending on your students' needs. Review the completed handout by asking volunteers to share one answer for each term.

Experiential Exercise

1 **Understand the intent of the activity.** In this activity, students will experience the plebeian struggle for equality in Rome. After showing a photo of a Roman mosaic, you will tell students that their task is to produce the "tiles" for a class mosaic by cutting squares from magazines. Six students will be designated as "Pats;" the remaining students will be "Plebs." The working arrangement during the production of the tiles will simulate the relationship between patricians and plebeians in ancient Rome. Students will not actually assemble a mosaic. (**Note:** Consider skimming the teacher notes embedded below to get a feel for the connections between the activity and Chapter 33.)

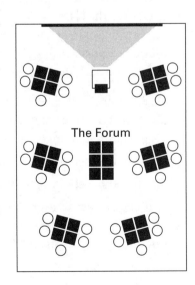

The Forum

2 **Arrange the classroom and prepare materials.** Before class, arrange your classroom according to the diagram. Place one ruler, four pairs of scissors, and at least one magazine at each group of four desks. Create the "Forum" by placing six desks together in the center of the room. Provide various snacks, books to read, and games in the Forum.

Phase 1: Creating Conflict Between Patricians and Plebeians

1 **Introduce the activity.** As students enter the classroom, have them randomly sit at one of the six groups of desks. Project *Visual 33: Roman Mosaic* and describe the elements of a Roman mosaic. Tell students that Romans used fragments of colored tile, glass, and stone to create mosaics that showed scenes of everyday life, nature, and Roman gods. Mosaics were often constructed on the walls and floors of public buildings and in the homes of the wealthy. Explain that students will work in small groups to prepare tiles for a mosaic about ancient Rome. Instead of using tile, glass, or stone, they will use half-inch squares of paper cut from magazines.

Visual 33

2 **Assign students the roles of Pats and Plebs.** Follow these steps:

- Tell students to identify the single student in each group who is wearing the darkest clothing. Announce that these students are now called "Pats" and that they will be the group leaders. The rest of the students are now called "Plebs." (**Note:** The random manner in which students are selected is intended to represent the fact that patricians inherited their power.)

- Have all Pats move to the front of the class. Give each a role card from *Student Handout 33: Role Cards for Pats.* While Pats read the instructions on their cards, have Plebs take inventory at their tables to verify they have the following items: scissors, a ruler, and magazines. Take the Pats aside and answer any questions they may have about their role.

Student Handout 33

- Have Pats quickly choose their two spokespersons and announce these students to the class. (**Note:** The spokespersons represent the two consuls who were selected by the Senate to command the army and run Rome's day-to-day affairs.)

3 **Have Pats stand in front of the class and vote on how Plebs should make tiles.** Tell the Plebs that before they cut out tiles for the mosaic, the Pats will decide for the class the size and colors of the mosaic and how much time the class will have to create it. As the Plebs watch, ask the six Pats to vote on the four questions below. Have the two Pat spokespersons lead the discussion and record each decision on the board.

1. Shall the mosaic have 5, 7, or 10 colors?

2. Which of these colors shall be included: black, brown, gray, blue, green, purple, red, orange, white, yellow, or pink?

3. Shall the Plebs cut out 300, 450, or 600 tiles for the mosaic?

4. Shall the Plebs have 5, 10, or 15 minutes to cut out tiles?

(**Note:** Consider writing the questions on the board before class. Encourage the Pats to select large numbers of colors and tiles. This will create more tension between the Pats and Plebs, which is critical for success in the activity.)

4 **Have Pats return to their groups and supervise as Plebs work.** At your signal, tell the Plebs to begin cutting out tiles. As the Plebs cut, the Pats should make sure each tile is one color only and no larger than a half-inch square—Pats can use rulers to measure them. Have the Pats tell the Plebs to separate the tiles into piles by color. Tell the Plebs that if they do not complete the task in the allotted time, they will be unable to start the mosaic project on schedule and might get a bad grade. (**Note:** The loss of academic points is intended to represent the loss of peace and order in ancient Rome that resulted when patricians and plebeians struggled for power.)

5 **Have Pats relax in the Forum, while you encourage Plebs to voice their complaints.** After two to three minutes, tell the Pats to move to the Forum and relax while the Plebs work. Remind them that a *forum* was an open space in a Roman town where people gathered to engage in various activities. (**Note:** This is designed to represent the aristocratic privileges that patricians enjoyed. Consider having Pats alternate between relaxing in the Forum and supervising their group of Plebs.) Expect the Plebs to be frustrated with the privileges of the Pats. To ensure that a majority of the Plebs are frustrated, encourage them to complain about the task by prompting them with these questions: *Why is your group taking so long to create tiles? Don't you wish you could sit in the Forum with the Pats?* To heighten the tension in the classroom, repeat any complaints Plebs make so everyone can hear.

6 **Have frustrated Plebs move to one corner of the room.** Once a majority of Plebs have become frustrated with preparing the tiles, ask them, *Who is frustrated with this arrangement and wants to take a break?* Have Plebs who respond affirmatively move to one corner of the classroom. (**Note:** This is intended to represent the plebeians' withdrawal from the city of Rome during the Conflict of the Orders.)

7 **Debrief Phase 1.** Hold a class discussion centering on these questions:

- (to frustrated Plebs) Why are you upset? What process do you think should be used to make the tiles?
- (to Pats and remaining Plebs) How do you feel about the complaints of these frustrated Plebs?
- (to everyone) What will happen if the tiles are not completed on time?

Phase 2: Establishing a New Working Relationship for Patricians and Plebeians

1 **Have frustrated Plebs elect four representatives.** Explain that these four students will represent the Plebs and will have the power to approve or disapprove decisions made by the Pats. (**Note:** This represents the historic fact that, after their revolts, plebeians were allowed to elect tribunes with the power of veto.) Encourage Plebs to select representatives who will speak confidently and are capable of negotiating a new working arrangement.

2 Appoint a new spokesperson for the Pats and for the Plebs. Explain that these two new spokespersons will lead the discussion and record on the board any decisions made by the representatives. (**Note:** This is intended to represent the law requiring that one of the two consuls be a plebeian.)

3 Have the Pleb representatives negotiate a new working arrangement with the Pats. Tell the four Pleb representatives and six Pats to move to the front of the classroom. Have the Pleb representatives suggest changes in the previous decisions about colors, tiles, and work time. Allow the Pats to respond to these demands. Encourage the Pleb representatives and the Pats to negotiate a new arrangement for making the mosaic tiles that both sides can accept. If they are unable to compromise, coax them by reminding them that unless the tiles are prepared by the end of the class period, all students will lose points. (**Note:** The new working arrangement may include a minor change, such as decreasing the number of tiles needed. This is intended to represent the Plebeians gaining political equality.) Then have all students return to their desks.

4 Debrief Phase 2. Hold a class discussion centering on these questions:

- How did you feel at the start of the activity?
- How were Pats selected? What do you think of this method?
- Why did some Plebs become frustrated with making tiles?
- Why did the Pats negotiate a new working relationship with the Pleb representatives?
- What groups of people in ancient Rome may have struggled over political power?

Reading

1 Introduce the Essential Question and have students read Section 33.1. Have students identify the Essential Question on the first page of the chapter: *What were the characteristics of the Roman Republic and how did they change over time?* Then have students read Section 33.1. Afterward, have students respond to these questions:

- Who was Lucius Brutus? Why was he important?
- In the activity, which students represented patricians? Which students represented plebeians?

2 Have students read and complete the corresponding Reading Notes for Sections 33.2 to 33.5. Remind students to use the Key Content Terms where appropriate as they complete their Reading Notes. After students complete each section, discuss connections with their experience in the activity. For example, after reading Section 33.2, students might mention that at the beginning of the activity they were divided into two groups—Pats and Plebs—and directed by the teacher, who might represent an Etruscan king.

Processing

Have students complete the Processing activity on a separate sheet of paper in their notebooks. Students will create an illustrated timeline to show how the characteristics of the Roman Republic changed over time.

Quicker Coverage

Modify the Experiential Exercise Consider using some of the following tips to simplify setup and accelerate the activity:

- So that you don't have to gather materials for the Forum, have volunteers bring in their favorite books, games, and snacks (obviously, follow your school's regulations about such items). This will also fuel tensions between the Pats and Plebs as only a few students will be allowed to use the Forum.

- Omit the scissors; instruct Plebs to neatly tear the magazines to create tiles. Tell Pats to reprimand Plebs if they do not tear in straight lines.

- Speed up Phase 1 by acting as the "Etruscan king." Quickly designate the two Pat representatives. Introduce them as your "trusted advisers" who will help you make good decisions about the mosaic. Present your preferences for the four questions about the mosaic, and have the Pats approve your decisions or suggest slight modifications. Thank the Pats for their approval.

Deeper Coverage

Let Students Create a Mosaic Students are sometimes frustrated that they do not actually get to build a mosaic. Consider giving groups 5 to 10 minutes to create mini-mosaics with whatever tiles they have produced. Alternatively, suggest that students create mosaics at home for extra credit. Require that their mosaics relate to the struggle between patricians and plebeians. For example, they might create a simple mosaic of the Twelve Tables and write an inscription about the importance of written laws.

Explore Government Characteristics Further Have students add to their spoke diagrams in their Section 33.5 Reading Notes. For each political characteristic of the Roman republic, instruct students to brainstorm a way they see this characteristic in the structure or values of the United States government. You could also have students research more about Greek and Roman influences on the political culture of the United States. Challenge students to present these influences in some visual manner. They might create a triple Venn diagram to compare the governments of the three cultures or create a flowchart to trace the progression of ideas from Greece to Rome to the United States.

Assessment

Mastering the Content

1. A	5. B	9. C	13. A
2. B	6. B	10. B	14. A
3. C	7. D	11. D	15. C
4. C	8. A	12. D	16. D

Applying Social Studies Skills

17. king; consuls

18. Answers will vary. Sample answers: stir up the plebeians to rebellion; increase conflict between patricians and plebeians

19. Answers will vary. Sample answers: limit the power of the consuls; put the plebeians in charge of the government

Exploring the Essential Question

20. Answers should include all the elements requested in the prompt.

Scoring Rubric

Score	Description
3	Student completes all the tasks, including an appropriate home page and links to two other pages. Home page is clearly stated, supported by details, and demonstrates command of standard English conventions.
2	Student responds to most or all parts of the task, but home page may lack details or not be clearly stated, or links may be absent.
1	Student responds to at least one part of the task. Home page may contain factual and/or grammatical errors and may lack details.
0	Response does not match the task or is incorrect.

English Language Learners

Provide a Checklist for the Experiential Exercise Offer select students the option of being an "observer," instead of a Pat or a Pleb. Provide a checklist of things to watch for during the activity.

Learners Reading and Writing Below Grade Level

Reduce the Amount of Reading In lieu of students reading Sections 33.2 to 33.4, directly teach the historical connections by filling out the T-chart below, as a class. To save time, you might provide students the left side of the T-chart so they only need to record connections to the Experiential Exercise. Afterward, have students read Section 33.5 and complete the corresponding Reading Notes.

Historical Reality	In-Class Experience
• Patricians were a small number of wealthy families who inherited their power and wealth.	• A small group of Pats was selected by the teacher.
• Plebeians made up the bulk of Roman society—working as peasants, artisans, and shopkeepers.	• The majority of the class were Plebs preparing mosaic tiles.
• Patricians elected the senators and held political power.	• Pats voted on the way Plebs would create mosaic tiles.
• Plebeians had fewer privileges than patricians and could not serve in the government.	• Plebs were not allowed to relax in the Forum, nor to make decisions.
• Plebeians left Rome when their political demands were not met.	• Some Plebs stopped preparing mosaic tiles and moved to a corner of the room.
• Plebeians elected Tribunes of the Plebs to protect their political rights.	• Plebs elected two representatives to negotiate with the Pats.

Learners with Special Education Needs

Prepare Students for the Experience Before beginning the activity, summarize the goal and forewarn students about the upcoming tensions between Plebs and Pats. Depending on the level of your students, you may wish to tell them explicitly that the simulation will create classroom conditions so that one group of students will feel frustrated with another group of students. Explain that it is okay for them to feel happy, angry, or frustrated during the activity. Assure students that you will debrief the activity as a class so they can share their feelings and learn how the experience connects to the history of Rome.

Advanced Learners

Graph Plebeian Equality Over Time Modify the Processing activity, an illustrated timeline. Have students create a line graph to demonstrate the increasing equality of the plebeians. Students should title the x-axis "Year" and label the five dates in the Processing activity. Students should title the y-axis "Level of Equality" and label it from 0 to 10. For each date, tell students to evaluate the extent of equality that plebeians experienced at that time. For example, in 616 B.C.E., plebeians were under both patricians and the Etruscan king. Students might suggest that plebeian equality was extremely low, perhaps a 1 on the scale. They would plot the point (616, 2). After students have plotted the "equality level" for all five dates, they can connect the points to create a line graph.

Compare the Plebeian Struggle with Others in History Help students discover that the story of the plebeians has occurred throughout history, as different groups fought to gain economic, political, and civil rights. Encourage students to think of other groups who have fewer rights than a more powerful group. For example, they might consider Native Americans, African Americans, or women in the United States. Ask students to create a Venn diagram, a chart, or another type of graphic organizer that shows the similarities and differences between the plight of Roman plebeians and the plight of the group they have chosen.

Enrichment Resources

Find out more about the rise of the early Roman Republic by exploring the following Enrichment Resources for *History Alive! The Ancient World* at www.teachtci.com.

Enrichment Readings These in-depth readings encourage students to explore selected topics related to the chapter. You may also find readings that relate the chapter's content directly to your state's curriculum.

Internet Connections These recommended Web sites provide useful and engaging content that reinforces skills development and mastery of subjects within the chapter.

Literature Recommendations

The following books offer opportunities to extend the content in this chapter.

The Ancient Romans by Allison Lassier (Danbury, CT: Children's Press, 2005)

Famous Men of Rome by John Haaren (Blacksburg, VA: Wilder Publications, 2009)

The Story of the Romans by H. A. Guerber (Chapel Hill, NC: Yesterday's Classics, 2006)

Section 33.2

1. The Etruscans ruled Rome between 616 and 509 B.C.E.

2. The patricians were a small group of wealthy landowners. They elected the "fathers of the state," who advised the Etruscan king.

3. The plebeians were peasants, laborers, craftspeople, and shopkeepers. They had very little voice in the government.

Section 33.3

1. Illustrations will vary but should show a "happy" patrician on the lower balance pan and a "sad" plebeian on the higher pan.

2. All power was in the hands of the patricians.

3. Power was in the hands of the Senate. Only patricians could be senators and consuls. Patricians elected the senators.

Section 33.4

1. Illustrations will vary but should show a "scared" patrician on the lower balance pan and an "angry" plebeian on the higher pan.

2. Patricians held the power. They made the decisions and interpreted the laws to benefit themselves.

3. Patricians were frightened by the actions of the plebeians because the work on the farms and in the city came to a halt. Also, patricians were afraid that, without plebeians, the army was too weak to defend Rome.

Section 33.5

1. The Tribunes of the Plebs spoke for the plebeians and could veto actions of the Senate. The Council of Plebs made laws for all plebeians.

2. In 451 B.C.E., patricians agreed to write down laws on the Twelve Tables. In 367 B.C.E., one of the two Roman consuls was required to be a plebeian. In 287 B.C.E., plebeian assemblies could pass laws for all Roman citizens and could nominate consuls, tribunes, and members of the Senate.

3. Other countries adopted the following characteristics from the Roman Republic: a written constitution, elected assemblies, citizenship, civic duty, checks and balances, and a spirit of republicanism.

From Republic to Empire

Did the benefits of Roman expansion outweigh the costs?

Overview

In a Problem Solving Groupwork activity, students explore and record events describing the expansion of Roman territory and the creation of the empire.

Objectives

In the course of reading this chapter and participating in the classroom activity, students will

Social Studies

- summarize the major events in Roman expansion between 509 B.C.E. and 14 C.E.

- explain the role of Julius Caesar and Octavian in Rome's transition from republic to empire.

- map the geographic boundaries of Rome at the height of its empire.

- evaluate the positive and negative effects of military expansion on Roman society and economic growth.

Language Arts

- clarify an understanding of text by creating visual and written summaries.

Social Studies Vocabulary

Key Content Terms civil war, dictator, Punic Wars, Julius Caesar, Caesar Augustus, Pax Romana

Academic Vocabulary approximately, collapse, vision, plot

Materials

History Alive! The Ancient World

Interactive Student Notebooks

Visual 34

Lesson Masters

- Student Handouts 34A and 34B (1 per group of 4)
- Vocabulary Development handout (1 per student, on colored paper)

Activity	Suggested Time	Materials
Preview	10 minutes	• Interactive Student Notebooks
Vocabulary Development	30–40 minutes	• *History Alive! The Ancient World* • Interactive Student Notebooks • Vocabulary Development handout
Problem Solving Groupwork	120–140 minutes (3 regular periods) (1.5 block periods)	• *History Alive! The Ancient World* • Interactive Student Notebooks • Visual 34 • Student Handouts 34A and 34B (1 per group of 4)
Processing	20 minutes	• Interactive Student Notebooks
Assessment	40 minutes	• Chapter 34 Assessment

Preview

1   **Have students complete the Preview activity for Chapter 34 in their Interactive Student Notebooks.** Students will assess the costs and benefits of having a much larger family than they currently have.

2   **Have students share their answers in pairs or as a class.**

3   **Explain the connection between the Preview activity and Chapter 34.** Tell students that positive and negative effects occur when any group gets larger. A larger family may give you more people to talk to and play games with, but you may also end up in more arguments. Likewise, an expanding empire may gain more land and resources, but fights may break out among its diverse peoples over civil rights and distribution of resources. In this chapter, students will learn about the events that led to the expansion of Rome from a republic to an empire, and the costs and benefits of this expansion.

Vocabulary Development

1   **Introduce the Key Content Terms.** Have students locate the Key Content Terms for the chapter in their Interactive Student Notebooks. These are important terms that will help them understand the main ideas of the chapter. Ask volunteers to identify any familiar terms and suggest how they might be used in a sentence.

2   **Have students complete a Vocabulary Development handout.** Give each student a copy of the Vocabulary Development handout of your choice from the Reading Toolkit at the back of the Lesson Masters. These handouts provide extra Key Content Term practice and support, depending on your students' needs. Review the completed handout by asking volunteers to share one answer for each term.

Reading

1   **Introduce the Essential Question and have students read Section 34.1.** Have students identify the Essential Question on the first page of the chapter: *Did the benefits of Roman expansion outweigh the costs?* Then have students read Section 34.1. Afterward, have students use information from Section 34.1 and from the chapter opener image to propose some answers to the Essential Question.

2   **Have students complete the Reading Notes for Chapter 34.** Assign Sections 34.2 to 34.6 during the activity, as indicated in the procedures for the Problem Solving Groupwork activity. Remind students to use the Key Content Terms where appropriate as they complete their Reading Notes.

Problem Solving Groupwork

1 Introduce the concept of the expansion of the Roman Empire. Explain that the Roman Empire developed over the course of about five hundred years, and that historians sometimes divide this expansion into four periods. To give students an overview of all four periods of growth, have volunteers read Section 34.2 aloud. Then have students complete the Reading Notes for this section. Use Guide to Reading Notes 34 to review the answers as a class.

2 Project *Visual 34: Detail of Trajan's Column* and introduce the activity. Tell students that this is a detail of a column celebrating a military victory of the Emperor Trajan. (**Note:** An image of the entire column is on the Introduction page of the chapter.) Explain that Romans often had sculptures, reliefs, and inscriptions engraved on columns, to chronicle their accomplishments. Ancient Roman citizens also occasionally expressed their political views by scrawling drawings and sayings—like modern graffiti—on the walls of their cities. Tell students that in this activity they will create columns, out of paper instead of stone, to commemorate one of the four key periods of growth in the Roman Empire. Then students will have an opportunity to write sayings at the bases of the other groups' columns.

Visual 34

3 Arrange students in groups of four.

4 Distribute materials and assign topics. Pass out a copy of *Student Handout 34A: Creating a Column About Roman Expansion* to each group. Assign each of the four topics to two of the groups, and tell them to circle their assigned topic on the handout.

5 Review the steps for creating a column. Review the roles of Historian, Editor, Sculptor, and Engineer in Step 1 of Student Handout 34A. Explain that in his or her role, each student will be responsible for leading the group through one of the steps to prepare their column. Then review Steps 2 through 5 and answer students' questions.

Student Handout 34A

6 Monitor groups as they create their columns.

- Allow students adequate time—about two class periods—to prepare. Monitor their progress by checking their work and initialing their handouts as they complete each step.

- During Step 2, make sure that groups complete the part of the map and the column of Reading Notes that correspond to their assigned period. Use Guide to Reading Notes 34 to check their work.

- When they reach Step 5, give each group a copy of *Student Handout 34B: Top of a Roman Column* and assist students in assembling their columns.

7 Have students post their columns on the wall. When groups are ready, have them display their columns along the wall in chronological order. (**Note:** Consider posting labels for each historical period so that students know exactly where to place their columns. To make the columns more realistic, you may want to attach rolled sheets of poster board to the wall, thus providing a cylinder around which groups can wrap their columns.)

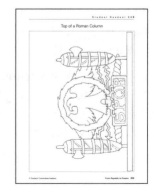

Student Handout 34B

8 **Have groups examine a column and record notes.** Assign each group to a column they have not read about. Tell groups they will now examine a column commemorating one of the periods of Roman expansion that they have not read about in detail. Explain that when inspecting the assigned new column, they should first examine the inscriptions and illustrations, and then read the corresponding section of *History Alive! The Ancient World* and complete the Reading Notes in their Interactive Student Notebooks.

9 **Instruct students to create sayings to add to the columns.** Ask group members to discuss the costs associated with expansion during the historical period they just read about. Then have each group add a saying (motto or slogan), to the base of that column to represent the feelings of those who may have had a *negative* view of expansion during that period. For example, after reading about Julius Caesar in Section 34.5, a student might write, "Stop Caesar! We will not be ruled by kings!" and draw a simple visual of a crown with an *X* on it. Emphasize that they must use language appropriate for the classroom.

10 **Have groups repeat Steps 8 and 9 with the remaining columns and sections of *History Alive! The Ancient World*.** Circulate to verify that students are writing political commentary in an appropriate manner.

11 **When all groups have reviewed all columns and completed their Reading Notes, hold a class discussion.** Ask,

- What areas did Rome control at the height of its empire?
- Why were the Romans able to successfully expand their territory? What were some of the costs of this expansion?
- Did the benefits of Roman expansion outweigh the costs?

Processing

Have students complete the Processing activity in their Interactive Student Notebooks. Students will list the costs and benefits of Roman expansion and write a paragraph answering the Essential Question.

Quicker Coverage

Cut the Groupwork in Half Assign two groups to each time period and have them work together to create a column. For example, assign one group to the first four paragraphs of Section 34.3 and the other group to the last four paragraphs of Section 34.3. In this scenario, the first group would be responsible for two illustrated inscriptions on the base of the column. The second group would be responsible for two illustrated inscriptions on the top section of the same column.

Writing: Punctuation

Use students' paragraphs as the basis for a mini-lesson on punctuation. Before students write, review the rules for linking independent clauses with a semicolon or with a comma and coordinating conjunction. Then require the use of one compound sentence linked with a semicolon and one compound sentence linked with a coordinating conjunction and comma. After students write, call for examples, and use them to review the use of both marks of punctuation in compound sentences.

Modify the Group Activity Instead of creating columns, have groups create posters about their assigned time periods. Each group's poster should have a

- title
- one-sentence summary about Roman expansion during their time period
- T-chart that lists all the costs and benefits related to expansion during their time period
- one illustration to represent the greatest cost to the Roman people and one illustration to represent the greatest benefit

Have groups hang their posters along the wall in chronological order. Give students time to circulate around the room, filling in their Reading Notes for each section as they review the posters. Alternatively, have each group present their poster and tell students to complete their Reading Notes while groups make their presentations.

Deeper Coverage

Create a Mosaic of Roman Expansion Have students create a mosaic with "tiles," illustrating the costs and benefits of Roman expansion. Provide these instructions:

- Give your mosaic an appropriate title.
- Use two main colors of tiles: one for costs and one for benefits.
- Create at least six tiles: three representing the *costs* of Roman expansion and three representing the *benefits* of Roman expansion.
- On each tile, explain the cost or benefit of expansion by writing a short phrase and drawing a simple symbol.
- Make the size of each tile match the importance of its topic. For example, if you think that the greatest benefit of Roman expansion was that it increased trade throughout the Mediterranean, then that should be your largest tile.
- Add additional creative touches.

Debate Roman Expansion Conduct an informal class debate using the Essential Question: *Did the benefits of Roman expansion outweigh the costs?* Write the debate question on the board and divide the class into two teams. Allow students time to formulate their arguments. Encourage them to back up their arguments with specific evidence from the reading and the images in Chapter 34. You might want to have each team come up with a slogan they can chant before the debate. Alternatively, divide students into pairs and have them conduct mini-debates in which they discuss the following issues:

- Should Rome have fought the Punic Wars?
- Was Augustus good or bad for Romans?
- Did the benefits of Roman expansion outweigh the costs?

After pairs have had time to debate, allow them to share their ideas with the class. Then have the class vote on each issue.

Assessment

Mastering the Content

1. D	5. A	9. B	13. B
2. B	6. C	10. A	14. A
3. A	7. D	11. C	15. C
4. C	8. B	12. D	16. D

Applying Social Studies Skills

17. Sicily

18. a. the Danube River (also accept Carpathian Mountains, Rhine River, or Atlantic Ocean)

    b. the Sahara

19. a. the Rubicon R., the Alps, Gaul, water/the Atlantic Ocean (any two)

    b. Spain, Gaul

    c. Answers will vary. Possible answers: land, because the route is shorter and more direct and the Romans built good roads; sea, because a land journey has to cross the Alps but a boat could have a smooth passage the whole distance and could easily carry more goods

Exploring the Essential Question

20. Answers should include all the elements requested in the prompt.

Scoring Rubric

Score	Description
3	Student completes all eight parts of the task. Explanations are clearly stated, supported by details, and demonstrate command of standard English conventions.
2	Student responds to most or all parts of the task, but explanations may lack details or not be clearly stated.
1	Student responds to at least one part of the task. Explanations may contain factual and/or grammatical errors and may lack details.
0	Response does not match the task or is incorrect.

English Language Learners

Support the Preview Activity and Essential Question Before the Preview activity, make sure students understand the phrase "costs and benefits." You might describe it as "advantages and disadvantages" or "good effects and bad effects." After the Preview activity, help students understand the connection between a growing family and an expanding country. Equate having more siblings to gaining more people in an expanding empire. Make sure students understand the Essential Question: *Did the benefits of Roman expansion outweigh the costs?* Explain that when Romans took over more land, both good and bad results occurred. Students will try to determine if the positive outweighed the negative.

Learners Reading and Writing Below Grade Level

Give Specific Topics for the Columns To help groups focus on the important information in their assigned historical period, provide the topics below. Students can divide these among their group members, assigning each student to create an inscription and illustration about one of the topics.

- **Rome's Conquest of the Italian Peninsula, 509 to 264 B.C.E.:** Overthrow and defeat of the Etruscans, Rebuilding of Rome, Defeat of the Samnites and Greek city-states, Treatment of conquered peoples

- **Expansion During the Punic Wars, 264 to 146 B.C.E.:** First Punic War, Second Punic War, Third Punic War, Changes in Roman life

- **Expansion During the Final Years of the Republic, 145 to 44 B.C.E.:** Rebellions of allies and slaves, Civil war between Pompey and Caesar, Caesar's reforms, Caesar's vision for Rome and his assassination

- **Rome Becomes an Empire, 44 B.C.E. to 14 C.E.:** Rise to power of Octavian (Caesar Augustus), Accomplishments of Augustus, Reforms of Augustus, Pax Romana

Learners with Special Education Needs

Provide Costs and Benefits To assist students with the Processing activity, give them the T-chart below. Tell them to highlight the three benefits and the three costs they think were the most important. They can use their highlighted lists to write their paragraphs.

Benefits of Roman Expansion	Costs of Roman Expansion
gained territory	republic ended
wealth	death toll from ongoing warfare
new customs	destruction of farms
Pax Romana	need for large permanent army
education	plebeian and slave uprisings
construction	high taxes
art and literature	civil wars

Advanced Learners

Create a Children's Storybook Have students create a children's storybook that explains the costs and benefits of Roman expansion. Read Remy Charlip's *Fortunately* aloud and have students use the same narrative pattern. Consider writing this example on the board: *"Fortunately, Rome was able to conquer the entire Italian peninsula. Unfortunately, many Romans died while fighting these wars of expansion."* Storybooks should have:

- an illustrated cover page with a catchy title.

- illustrated story pages that describe at least three costs and three benefits of Roman expansion, using the "Fortunately . . . Unfortunately" pattern.

- a "Note from the Author" page that answers the Essential Question in a well-written paragraph.

Compare Roman and U.S. Expansion Challenge students to compare and contrast the expansion of Rome with the expansion of the United States during the 1800s. Students might consider the initial and final sizes of the two nations, the methods they used to expand, and the costs and benefits of their expansion.

Enrichment Resources

Find out more about Rome's expansion and change from a republic to an empire by exploring the following Enrichment Resources for *History Alive! The Ancient World* at www.teachtci.com.

Enrichment Readings These in-depth readings encourage students to explore selected topics related to the chapter. You may also find readings that relate the chapter's content directly to your state's curriculum.

Internet Connections These recommended Web sites provide useful and engaging content that reinforces skills development and mastery of subjects within the chapter.

Literature Recommendations

The following books offer opportunities to extend the content in this chapter.

Everyday Life in the Roman Empire by Kathryn Hinds (Tarrytown, NY: Marshall Cavendish Children's Books, 2009)

The Illustrated Encyclopedia of the Roman Empire by Nigel Rogers (London: Lorenz Books, 2008)

Julius Caesar: Ruler of the Roman World by Zachary Kent (Berkeley Heights, NJ: Enslow Publishers, 2006)

Section 34.2

Flowcharts will vary. Possible answers:

First Period: Rome defeated the Etruscans, Samnites, and several Greek city-states to take control of the Italian peninsula.

Second Period: Rome fought the Punic Wars with Carthage, and Rome became the greatest power in the Mediterranean region.

Third Period: Julius Caesar became dictator of Rome, instituted reforms, and granted citizenship to Gaul and Spain.

Fourth Period: Rome became an empire under Augustus. Rome continued to expand its borders during the Pax Romana.

Section 34.3

509 to 264 B.C.E.

See the map in the student book to check student maps.

1. The Romans defeated the Etruscans, Samnites, and Greek city-states to take control of the Italian peninsula. They also formed alliances with neighbors.

2. Plebeians would have objected to this expansion because they had to serve in the army. Defeated people would have objected because they had to serve in the army, pay Roman taxes, and couldn't always become Roman citizens.

Section 34.4

264 to 146 B.C.E.

See the map in the student book to check student maps.

1. Rome fought with Carthage for control of the Mediterranean region. Rome gained control of North Africa, Spain, Macedonia, and Greece. Riches, slaves, and new ideas came from the conquered lands.

2. Carthaginians would have objected because the Romans sold them into slavery and burned Carthage. Roman farmers would have objected because Hannibal destroyed many farms. Farmers had to neglect their farms to fight, and Rome began importing grain from other lands.

Section 34.5

145 to 44 B.C.E.

See the map in the student book to check student maps.

1. Julius Caesar began construction projects to provide work. He adopted a new calendar. He provided public entertainment for the poor. He also started new colonies and granted citizenship to people in Gaul and Spain.

2. People from conquered lands would have objected to being enslaved. Farmers and laborers did not like losing their jobs to slaves. The Senate might have objected to expansion during this period because Caesar and his military leaders were a threat to the Senators' power.

Section 34.6

44 B.C.E. to 14 C.E.

See the map in the student book to check student maps.

1. The Pax Romana was a peaceful period of Roman rule in the Mediterranean that lasted 200 years. Caesar Augustus encouraged education, art, and literature; started new construction projects and public services; increased the size of the empire; and improved trade.

2. Romans might have objected to the harsh punishments Augustus established for people who did not follow moral standards. They might also have objected to the Praetorian Guard and the need for a huge army to control such a large amount of territory.

Daily Life in the Roman Empire

How did wealth affect daily life in the Roman Empire?

Overview

In a Social Studies Skill Builder activity, students read about eight aspects of ancient Roman life—such as education and family life—and explore how a teenager might have experienced each.

Objectives

In the course of reading this chapter and participating in the classroom activity, students will

Social Studies

- identify cultural features of Rome and the Roman Empire.
- analyze the political, economic, religious, and social structures of the Roman Empire.
- compare and contrast the daily lives of the rich and poor in the Roman Empire.

Language Arts

- recognize the origins and meanings of frequently used foreign words in English and use the words accurately in writing.
- analyze text that uses the compare-and-contrast organizational pattern.

Social Studies Vocabulary

Key Content Terms Forum, rule of law, paterfamilias, Colosseum, Circus Maximus

Academic Vocabulary accompany, ultimate, leisure, estate

Materials

*History Alive!
The Ancient World*

Interactive Student Notebooks

Visual 35

Lesson Masters

- Information Masters 35A–35H (2 copies of each page)
- Student Handout 35 (1 per student)
- Vocabulary Development handout (1 per student, on colored paper)

Activity	Suggested Time	Materials
Preview	10 minutes	• Interactive Student Notebooks
Vocabulary Development	30–40 minutes	• *History Alive! The Ancient World* • Interactive Student Notebooks • Vocabulary Development handout
Social Studies Skill Builder	100–120 minutes (2–3 regular periods) (1.5 block periods)	• *History Alive! The Ancient World* • Interactive Student Notebooks • Visual 35 • Information Masters 35A–35H (2 copies of each page) • Student Handout 35 (1 per student)
Processing	20 minutes	• Interactive Student Notebooks
Assessment	40 minutes	• Chapter 35 Assessment

Preview

1 **Have students complete the Preview activity for Chapter 35 in their Interactive Student Notebooks.** Project *Visual 35: Street Scene in the Roman Empire*. Have students examine the image and answer the questions in their Interactive Student Notebooks.

2 **Have students share their answers in pairs or as a class.** Consider having students come up to the image to point out evidence for their answers.

3 **Explain the connection between the Preview activity and Chapter 35.** Tell students that, as they saw in the image, both rich and poor people lived in ancient Rome. In this chapter, students will learn about daily life in the Roman Empire, and how people's lives were affected by differences in wealth. Students will also explore what it was like to be a teenager living in the Roman Empire.

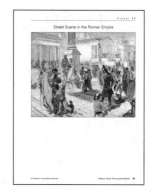

Visual 35

Vocabulary Development

1 **Introduce the Key Content Terms.** Have students locate the Key Content Terms for the chapter in their Interactive Student Notebooks. These are important terms that will help them understand the main ideas of the chapter. Ask volunteers to identify any familiar terms and suggest how they might be used in a sentence.

2 **Have students complete a Vocabulary Development handout.** Give each student a copy of the Vocabulary Development handout of your choice from the Reading Toolkit at the back of the Lesson Masters. These handouts provide extra Key Content Term practice and support, depending on your students' needs. Review the completed handout by asking volunteers to share one answer for each term.

Reading

1 **Introduce the Essential Question and have students read Section 35.1.** Have students identify the Essential Question on the first page of the chapter: *How did wealth affect daily life in the Roman Empire?* Then have students read Section 35.1. Afterward, have students respond to these questions:

- Why was Rome considered the center of the empire?

- What was the most important part of the city?

- What kinds of activities went on in the Forum?

2 **Have students complete the Reading Notes for Chapter 35.** Assign Sections 35.2 to 35.10 during the activity, as indicated in the procedures for the Social Studies Skill Builder. Remind students to use the Key Content Terms where appropriate as they complete their Reading Notes.

Social Studies Skill Builder

1 Arrange the classroom. Create two sets of eight stations by posting the copies of each page of Information Masters 35A–35H at different spots in the classroom. At each station, place desks for students and one copy of *History Alive! The Ancient World*, opened to the corresponding section of Chapter 35.

2 Have students read Section 35.2 and complete the corresponding Reading Notes. Tell students that this section provides background information about daily life in ancient Rome. Use Guide to Reading Notes 35 to review the answers as a class. Then have students propose some answers to the Essential Question: *How did wealth affect daily life in the Roman Empire?*

3 Place students in pairs and introduce the activity. Tell students they will now learn about eight specific aspects of life in ancient Rome. Give each student a copy of *Student Handout 35: Daily Life of a Roman Teenager*. Explain that there are two sets of eight stations. Each station corresponds to one aspect of Roman daily life. At each station, pairs will follow the directions on the Information Master to

- read a section of Chapter 35 and complete the corresponding Reading Notes in their Interactive Student Notebooks.

- review the posted information to learn how a teenager might have experienced the aspect of life they just read about.

- complete the illustration on Student Handout 35 and write a caption.

- have their work checked, and then move to a new station.

4 Have students visit the stations. Instruct pairs to choose a starting station and begin the activity. Monitor students' progress, making sure that they finish their Reading Notes before completing the image and caption on Student Handout 35. As pairs finish, check their work, and then have them choose a new station. Continue this process until most pairs have completed their Reading Notes and Student Handout 35.

5 Wrap up the activity with a brief class discussion. Ask,

- What aspects of Roman life did you find most interesting? Why?

- How did wealth affect daily life in the Roman Empire?

- In what ways is your life similar to that of a teenager in ancient Rome? In what ways is your life different?

Processing

Have students complete the Processing activity on a separate sheet of paper. Students will write a dialogue between a rich Roman and a poor Roman who are comparing and contrasting their daily lives in the Roman Empire.

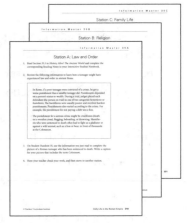

Information Masters 35A–35H

Student Handout 35

Writing: Capitalization

Before students write their dialogue, review the rules for capitalizing words in dialogue. Remind students to begin the first word in a quotation with a capital letter. Also, remind them that when a speaker tag interrupts the words of a speaker, the first word after the break is not capitalized unless it begins a new sentence.

Quicker Coverage

Divide Up the Stations Assign half the pairs to Stations A–D and half the pairs to Stations E–H. When students have completed their Reading Notes and Student Handout 35 for their assigned stations, allow pairs to form groups of four and share their notes. Model the sharing process for students so they understand how to teach each other, rather than simply copy each other's notes.

Deeper Coverage

Pantomime Aspects of Roman Life Allow pairs to perform pantomimes—a popular theatrical form developed by the Romans—about some aspect of daily life, and see if their classmates can guess what it is. Tell students that, as in the game of charades, they will use body movements and facial expressions, but no words, to act out their topic. Assign each pair one of the eight aspects of ancient Roman daily life. Give them two to three minutes to decide what they will pantomime, and to practice. Encourage them to use their books and Reading Notes as resources. Then have each pair perform their pantomime. Encourage classmates to guess what the pair is doing and the aspect of daily life their pantomime reflects.

Play a Trivia Game After the activity, conduct a quick "trivia" game to test how closely students read Chapter 35. Assign students to teams of four, and have them close their books and Reading Notes. Then ask the questions below in random order. (They are listed in the same order as the sections of Chapter 35.) If a team can correctly answer the question from memory, award them two points. If no team can answer, allow students to search their Reading Notes and book. Award one point to the first team to find the answer.

Trivia Questions

- Why would a wealthy Roman man wear an old, dirty toga on purpose? *(to hide his wealth from thieves at night)*
- Why would a Roman put a little clay foot by a statue at a temple? *(to remind the god which part of the body needed to be healed)*
- What did Roman parents place around a newborn infant's neck? *(a bulla for good luck)*
- What do cooked mice, roasted parrots, and salted jellyfish have in common? *(foods that wealthy Romans ate)*
- Why was there such a risk of fire in ancient Rome? *(buildings were made of wood, and people cooked on open grills inside)*
- Why did Roman students make a stop before attending school each morning? *(to buy beans, nuts, and bread to eat as they walked to school)*
- Where was the best place to meet a boyfriend or girlfriend in ancient Rome? *(Circus Maximus)*
- What sweetener was used by the ancient Romans? *(honey)*

Assessment

Mastering the Content

1. B	5. A	9. A	13. A
2. C	6. D	10. C	14. B
3. A	7. C	11. D	15. B
4. D	8. B	12. D	16. C

Applying Social Studies Skills

17. a. taking walks, playing ball

    b. conversation, reading, writing poems (any two)

18. Answers will vary. Possible answers: they are having a good time; they are watching the actors

19. living a peaceful and orderly life

Exploring the Essential Question

20. Answers should include all the elements requested in the prompt.

Scoring Rubric

Score	Description
3	Student completes a response that addresses all four bulleted points. Response is clearly stated, supported by details, and demonstrates command of standard English conventions.
2	Student addresses most or all parts of the task, but response may lack details or not be clearly stated.
1	Student responds to at least one part of the task. Response may contain factual and/or grammatical errors and may lack details.
0	Response does not match the task or is incorrect.

English Language Learners

Highlight the Reading Provide copies of Sections 35.3 through 35.10 from the book. Highlight key words or phrases that will help students follow the text and complete their Reading Notes. In Section 35.3, you might highlight the following: "Romans always believed," "common in Rome," "richer . . . poorer," "rich men . . . rich families," "Any Roman, including the poor," "all citizens," "poor . . . rich." On Information Masters 35A–35H, highlight the portion of the reading students will need to complete their illustrations and captions on Student Handout 35.

Replace the Processing Activity Instead of writing a dialogue, have students create two sensory figures— one for a rich Roman and one for a poor Roman. Each sensory figure should include statements from that person's perspective and describe four aspects of daily life. Consider requiring that students use one of the Key Content Terms in each statement. For example, the "rich Roman" might say, "With my ears, I hear my *paterfamilias* making rules for our family."

Learners Reading and Writing Below Grade Level

Conduct a Prereading Strategy Use the trivia questions (located in the Deeper Coverage section of this chapter) as a prereading strategy. After the Preview, but before the Skill Builder, have students turn to Section 35.3 and read the first question aloud. Reward the student who finds the answer, or have students record their answers instead of shouting them out. Then have students turn to Section 35.4, and continue this process. As students are looking for answers, they will increase their comfort level with the text and be better prepared to take their Reading Notes.

Reduce the Number of Stations Allow students to complete the Reading Notes for just four or five of the eight stations in the time allotted to the rest of the class. For the remaining stations, only require that they complete the pictures and captions. Use Guide to Reading Notes 35 to provide answers for the remaining Reading Notes.

Learners with Special Education Needs

Model the Activity Model the procedures for the Social Studies Skill Builder before sending pairs to the stations. Using a transparency of Information Master 35A and of the Reading Notes for Section 35.3, complete the Venn diagram for this section as a class. Then complete all the steps on Information Master 35A together, asking volunteers to share their answers orally at each step.

Support the Processing Activity Provide the following scripted lines to help students understand how to discuss an aspect of daily life in a dialogue:

> *Rich Roman:* "I enjoy watching the chariot races from my cushioned seat close to the track at the Circus Maximus."
>
> *Poor Roman:* "I also love going to see the chariot races, but I have to sit on a wooden bench far away from the action."

Consider requiring students to include only two or three aspects of daily life in their dialogues.

Advanced Learners

Write a Dialogue Between Teens Have students write a dialogue between a Roman teenager and an American teenager. Encourage students to reference at least four aspects of daily life that were discussed in Chapter 35, from both a Roman perspective and a American perspective. Require that students include Key Content Terms in appropriate parts of their dialogue. You may even wish to challenge students to write a four-character script, involving a rich and poor Roman and a rich and poor American.

Compare Rome to Home Have students create a Venn diagram, digitally or on poster board, comparing daily life in the Roman Empire to life in the United States today. For example, they might compare ancient Roman sporting events to modern sporting events, or family life in the Roman Empire to their own family life. Consider giving students a choice between (1) comparing their personal experience to all eight aspects of daily life on a single Venn diagram, or (2) researching one aspect of Roman and American daily life in depth and creating a more detailed Venn diagram.

Enrichment Resources

Find out more about daily life for the rich and the poor in the Roman Empire by exploring the following Enrichment Resources for *History Alive! The Ancient World* at www.teachtci.com.

Enrichment Readings These in-depth readings encourage students to explore selected topics related to the chapter. You may also find readings that relate the chapter's content directly to your state's curriculum.

Internet Connections These recommended Web sites provide useful and engaging content that reinforces skills development and mastery of subjects within the chapter.

Literature Recommendations

The following books offer opportunities to extend the content in this chapter.

Ancient Rome on 5 Denarii a Day by Philip Matyszak (New York: Thames & Hudson, 2008)

Daily Life in Ancient Rome by Alberto Angela (New York: Europa Editions, 2009)

Tools of the Ancient Romans by Rachel Dickinson (White River Junction, VT: Nomad Press, 2006)

Section 35.2

Answers will vary. Sample answers:

Rich Romans: bought luxury items that came from around the empire, decorated their houses with statues and fountains

Poor Romans: lived in dangerous neighborhoods, worked on small farms or on estates owned by the rich

Section 35.3

Law and Order

Rich Romans: treated more leniently by the law, police patrolled their neighborhoods

Poor Romans: suffered harsher punishments, lived in dangerous neighborhoods

All Romans: could accuse someone of a crime, law applied to all citizens

Section 35.4

Religion

All Romans: adopted many Greek gods, made offerings and sacrifices to please gods or ask for help, celebrated festivals and holidays, honored emperors as gods

Section 35.5

Family Life

Rich Romans: men held political positions and provided for the family, women ran households and trained slaves

Poor Romans: both husband and wife had to work to provide for family

All Romans: paterfamilias ruled the family, only kept healthy babies, held ceremonies to celebrate a boy becoming a man and getting married

Section 35.6

Food and Drink

Rich Romans: had kitchens, ate meat, bread, mice, parrots, jellyfish, snails, and dates for dinner

Poor Romans: cooked on small grills, ate fish, asparagus, figs, and bread for dinner

All Romans: got food from thermopolia (fast-food places), drank water and water with honey, and ate garum

Section 35.7

Housing

Rich Romans: large houses made of stone and marble, indoor pools, kitchens, fancy dining rooms

Poor Romans: small apartments made of wood, no kitchens, cooked on small grills; apartments were noisy, dirty, and filled with disease

All Romans: fire was a danger

Section 35.8

Education

Rich Romans: tutored by fathers or slaves and then sent to school; learned Latin, Greek, math, science, literature, music, public speaking

Poor Romans: usually worked rather than go to school, learned a trade

All Romans: boys may have had some education at home; most girls did not

Section 35.9

Recreation

Rich Romans: attended plays and musical performances, threw fancy dinner parties, sat on cushions in the shade at the Circus Maximus

Poor Romans: sat on wooden benches at the Circus Maximus

All Romans: went to festivals and public baths, watched gladiator contests and chariot races

Section 35.10

Country Life

Rich Romans: owned farms, livestock, and large villas; had time to hunt, read, and relax

Poor Romans: many freedmen and slaves worked on farms; other poor farmers had small farms and lived in huts

All Romans: 90 percent of people lived in the country; farms provided food for Rome and other cities

The Origins and Spread of Christianity

How did Christianity originate and spread?

Overview

In a Social Studies Skill Builder activity, students learn about the development and spread of Christianity in the Roman Empire and analyze New Testament parables as literature.

Objectives

In the course of reading this chapter and participating in the classroom activity, students will

Social Studies

- explain the origins of Christianity in the Jewish Messianic prophecies and the life and teachings of Jesus of Nazareth as described in the New Testament.
- identify the contribution of early Christian leaders to the spread of Christian beliefs.
- describe the role of the Roman Empire in the persecution and spread of Christianity.

Language Arts

- analyze and interpret New Testament parables literature to understand plot, character, and message.
- analyze the effect of character on plot.

Social Studies Vocabulary

Key Content Terms Christianity, Jesus, Messiah, Gospel, disciple, parable, Resurrection, missionary, Constantine

Academic Vocabulary emphasis, convert, stress

Materials

History Alive!
The Ancient World

Interactive Student Notebooks

Visual 36

CD Track 19

Lesson Masters

- Information Master 36 (2 copies of each page, cut apart)
- Student Handout 36 (1 per student)
- Vocabulary Development handout (1 per student, on colored paper)

Activity	Suggested Time	Materials
Preview	15 minutes	• Interactive Student Notebooks • CD Track 19
Vocabulary Development	30–40 minutes	• *History Alive! The Ancient World* • Interactive Student Notebooks • Vocabulary Development handout
Social Studies Skill Builder	60 minutes (1–2 regular periods) (1 block period)	• *History Alive! The Ancient World* • Interactive Student Notebooks • Visual 36 • Information Master 36 (2 copies of each page, cut apart) • Student Handout 36 (1 per student)
Processing	20 minutes	• Interactive Student Notebooks
Assessment	40 minutes	• Chapter 36 Assessment

Preview

1   **Introduce the concepts of *fable* and *parable* to students.** Play CD Track 19, "The Lion and the Mouse," and have students complete the Preview activity for Chapter 36. Tell students to follow along in their Interactive Students Notebooks as the fable is read aloud. Afterward, have students answer the Preview questions to analyze the typical characteristics of fables.

2   **Have students share their Preview activity responses as a class.** After students have identified the characters in the fable and summarized the plot, encourage them to suggest a variety of moral lessons that the fable may be trying to teach. (**Note:** The moral lessons can be stated as aphorisms. You may want to give an example, such as, "Be more ready to forgive, than to return, an injury.") Then tell students that all of the following have been given as the moral of this fable:

   - "No act of kindness is ever too small."

   - "Little friends may prove to be great friends."

   - "Never judge a book by its cover."

3   **Explain the connection between the Preview activity and Chapter 36.** Tell students that fables are loved worldwide because of their ability to teach a lesson through a short creative story, usually involving animals or nature. *Parables* are similar to fables. They are also brief stories that teach a lesson, but the characters are usually people, not animals, and the events could have taken place in real life. As told in the New Testament, the founder of Christianity, Jesus of Nazareth, often used parables to teach his followers. It is said that he told stories about everyday people and situations to illustrate how his followers should live. In this chapter, students will learn about the origins and development of Christianity, the teachings of Jesus, and how Christianity spread throughout the Roman Empire.

Vocabulary Development

1   **Introduce the Key Content Terms.** Have students locate the Key Content Terms for the chapter in their Interactive Student Notebooks. These are important terms that will help them understand the main ideas of the chapter. Ask volunteers to identify any familiar terms and suggest how they might be used in a sentence.

2   **Have students complete a Vocabulary Development handout.** Give each student a copy of the Vocabulary Development handout of your choice from the Reading Toolkit at the back of the Lesson Masters. These handouts provide extra Key Content Term practice and support, depending on your students' needs. Review the completed handout by asking volunteers to share one answer for each term.

Reading

1 **Introduce the Essential Question and have students read Section 36.1.** Have students identify the Essential Question on the first page of the chapter: *How did Christianity originate and spread?* Then have students read Section 36.1. Afterward, have students use information from Section 36.1 and from the chapter opener image to propose some answers to the Essential Question.

2 **Have students complete the Reading Notes for Chapter 36.** Assign Sections 36.2 to 36.6 during the activity, as indicated in the procedures for the Social Studies Skill Builder activity. Remind students to use the Key Content Terms where appropriate as they complete their Reading Notes.

Social Studies Skill Builder

1 **Arrange the classroom.** Cut apart the two copies of *Information Master 36: Literature of the New Testament: Parables.* Create two sets of six stations by posting the parables around the room. (**Note:** The first four parables are quoted from the *New Century Version of the Bible,* a contemporary translation that will be easier for students to understand than an older, more traditional version of the New Testament. Due to length, the remaining two parables have been paraphrased.)

2 **Have pairs complete the Reading Notes for Sections 36.2 to 36.4.** Tell students that these sections will give them information about the origins of Christianity. They will learn about Judea, the Gospels, and the life of Jesus of Nazareth. Use Guide to Reading Notes 36 to review the answers as a class.

3 **Project *Visual 36: Jesus Teaching on a Mountainside* and introduce the activity.** Ask, *What do you see? Why might so many people be gathered on this mountainside? What do you think Jesus is doing?* Tell students that this image shows Jesus seated on the side of a mountain in Galilee, preaching to people of all ages. Remind students that, according to the New Testament, Jesus often used parables to teach his message in a way that was easy for people to understand. In this activity, students will read and analyze some of Jesus's parables that appear in the Gospels.

4 **Review the activity procedures.** Give each student a copy of *Student Handout 36: Analyzing Parables as Literature.* Explain that there are two copies of six parables posted around the room. Students will circulate to read and analyze each parable. As students read each parable, they will do the following on Student Handout 36.

   • List the characters in the parable.

   • Briefly summarize the plot of the parable in one sentence, or in a series of short statements.

   • Explain the lesson they think Jesus was trying to teach his followers.

   Remind students that Christians interpret Jesus's parables in various ways. Pairs should simply do their best to brainstorm the meaning of each parable.

Information Master 36

Visual 36

Student Handout 36

5   **Conduct the activity.** Assign a number of pairs to each parable, according to class size. When they have finished analyzing that parable, pairs should have their work checked and then move to a new parable. Give students adequate time to analyze parables and complete Student Handout 36. (**Note:** Guide to Student Handout 36 provides some possible interpretations of each parable.)

6   **Debrief students' analyses.**

   - After most pairs have analyzed most of the parables, explain that they will present answers for the parable they are currently examining. Have pairs that are working on the same parable form a group.

   - On a blank sheet of paper, instruct groups to create a word web with the the name of their parable, large and clear, in the center circle. Then have them use the Student Handout to add circles for: character(s), main plot points, and a summary of the parable's lesson.

   - Have groups use this word web to present answers for their assigned parable. As groups present, tell students to review their answers on Student Handout 36, and fill in any gaps they may have. (**Note:** Allow students to express different opinions about the lesson of each parable, but make sure they justify their interpretations.)

   - When all the groups have finished presenting their parables, discuss the following questions:

     Based on these parables, what behaviors did Jesus want others to follow?

     Which characters did he approve of? Which did he not approve of? How can you tell?

     Why do you think Jesus used parables in his teachings? How are they an effective teaching tool?

7   **Have pairs complete the Reading Notes for Sections 36.5 to 36.6.** Tell students that these sections will give them information about the spread of Christianity throughout the Roman Empire. They will learn how early Christians defined and spread their beliefs, and the role of Rome in the persecution and spread of Christianity. Use Guide to Reading Notes 36 to review the answers as a class.

Processing

Introduce the Processing activity. Tell students that in this activity they will use what they have learned about parables to write one of their own. Their parable should teach a lesson about some aspect of good citizenship. Examples might include: the importance of voting, the importance of volunteering in the community, the need to follow the law, and so on. If necessary, brainstorm a list of topics with students before they begin the activity.

Quicker Coverage

Modify the Debrief Instead of having students present answers to each parable, simply wrap up the activity with a class discussion. Ask,

- Which parable did you find the most interesting?

- Which parable did you think was the easiest to understand? Which was the hardest to understand?

- Why do you think Jesus used parables to teach his followers?

Deeper Coverage

Map the Spread of Christianity Have students work in pairs to research how Christianity spread throughout the Mediterranean area, and the world. Students might create a series of maps showing the location of Christians at different periods, or they might create a single map with a key. Alternatively, consider having students create an illustrated timeline of major events in the origins and spread of Christianity.

Create a Storyboard Allow students to explore the life of Paul by having them illustrate and annotate a storyboard, a series of several illustrated panels. Students might research some or all of the following topics to use in their storyboards.

- Paul's Persecution of Christians

- Paul's Conversion to Christianity

- Paul's Preaching and Travels

- Paul's Imprisonment and Letters

- Paul's Death and Legacy

Assessment

Mastering the Content

1. C	5. B	9. D	13. A
2. A	6. D	10. C	14. C
3. C	7. A	11. B	15. D
4. A	8. D	12. B	16. B

Applying Social Studies Skills

17. Augustus Caesar; King Herod

18. a republic

19. the death of Paul, the Edict of Milan; Answers will vary. Possible answers:
toleration, accepting Christians, ending persecution

Exploring the Essential Question

20. Answers should include all the elements requested in the prompt.

Scoring Rubric

Score	Description
3	Student completes a dialogue that addresses all three bulleted points. Dialogue is clearly stated, supported by details, and demonstrates command of standard English conventions.
2	Student responds to most or all parts of the task, but dialogue may lack details or not be clearly stated.
1	Student responds to at least one part of the task. Dialogue may contain factual and/or grammatical errors and may lack details.
0	Response does not match the task or is incorrect.

English Language Learners

Support the Preview Activity On the board, write definitions for words and phrases in the fable that students may not know. Some suggestions: shall (will), do you a turn (help you), tickled (amused), plight (a bad or dangerous situation), gnaw (chewed on), or bound (tied up). For Question 3, provide students with the three possible morals found in the Lesson Guide procedures, and have students choose one moral and justify it based on the story.

Provide Moral Lessons for the Parables Give students a list of moral lessons from the Guide to Student Handout 36 and allow them to match each lesson to a parable during the activity. Christians interpret Jesus's parables differently, so students are not necessarily "wrong" if they disagree with some of these suggestions.

Learners Reading and Writing Below Grade Level

Reduce the Reading Have pairs read and complete their Reading Notes for only one or two sections. Then use Guide to Reading Notes 36 to debrief all the answers as a class and to answer questions.

Paraphrase All Parables Before class, paraphrase the four parables that are primary source quotations from the Gospels. This will make them easier for students to read and analyze.

Learners with Special Education Needs

Model the Activity Before students begin to analyze parables, explicitly model the steps of the activity. Create a transparency of Student Handout 36. Read one parable aloud and have students identify the characters. Write their responses in the correct row on the transparency. Repeat for the plot and moral lesson. You also might consider requiring pairs to identify only the characters and plot of each parable. Brainstorm the moral lessons as a class.

Advanced Learners

Compare the Stories of Religious Leaders Students may have now learned about important figures in many religions, including Judaism, Buddhism, Daoism, and Christianity. Have students choose two religious figures and compare their stories and their impacts on the world. Have students write a dialogue in which their religious figures discuss questions such as:

- What was your life like? What challenges did you face?

- What are your main beliefs?

- How should people act according to your religion?

Enrichment Resources

Find out more about the origins and spread of Christianity by exploring the following Enrichment Resources for *History Alive! The Ancient World* at www.teachtci.com.

Enrichment Readings These in-depth readings encourage students to explore selected topics related to the chapter. You may also find readings that relate the chapter's content directly to your state's curriculum.

Internet Connections These recommended Web sites provide useful and engaging content that reinforces skills development and mastery of subjects within the chapter.

Literature Recommendations

The following books offer opportunities to extend the content in this chapter.

Constantine: Ruler of Christian Rome by Julian Morgan (New York: Rosen Publishing Group, 2002)

The Rise of Christianity by Don Nardo (San Diego: Lucent Books, 2000)

The Twelve Apostles by Marianna Mayer (New York: Dial, 2000)

Section 36.2

1. Judea was a small territory on the eastern edge of the Mediterranean. It was important to Jews because it was their homeland, which had been part of the ancient kingdom of Israel.

2. *In 63 B.C.E.*, Romans had Jewish leaders that supported Roman rule, but Jews rebelled against Roman control. *In 37 B.C.E.*, Herod ruled Rome and practiced the Jewish religion, but Jews did not trust him. *In 4 B.C.E.*, Herod's three sons ruled Rome, but Jews rebelled again.

Section 36.3

1. The Gospels are accounts of Jesus's life and teachings written by four of his followers, Matthew, Mark, Luke, and John.

2. According to the Gospels, Jesus was born in a stable in Bethlehem because his parents had to go to Bethlehem to be counted for a Roman census, and there was no room left for them inside the inn.

Section 36.4

1. Jesus said that the two most important Jewish laws were, "You shall love your God with all your heart and all your soul" and "You shall love your neighbor as yourself."

2. In the Parable of the Good Samaritan, an injured man is rescued and cared for by a Samaritan, after two people passed him by at the side of the road. Jesus was teaching us that we should be good neighbors by having mercy on others, even those who are not like us.

3. According to the Gospels, Jesus was condemned to die on a cross because his teachings upset many people and because some feared that he might lead a revolt against Rome.

4. Belief in the Resurrection was important to Jesus's followers because it convinced them that he was the Son of God.

Section 36.5

1. Paul stopped persecuting Christians and became a missionary because he believed he had heard the voice of the Jesus in a vision.

2. Paul helped spread Christianity by preaching throughout much of the empire. While in jail, he wrote letters to other Christians.

Section 36.6

1. Christians were considered a threat to Rome because they refused to worship other Roman gods, would not admit that the emperor was a god, preferred a life of simplicity, and refused to serve in the army.

2. Roman persecution of Christians included making their religion illegal and sentencing them to death. Rome's persecution helped to spread Christianity because people admired the bravery of the Christians. Christianity also offered hope to the poor and to slaves.

3. In 313 C.E., Constantine gave Christians the right to practice their religion. The emperors who succeeded Constantine accepted the new faith, and it eventually became the official religion of the empire.

Below are suggested characters, plot, and moral lessons for each parable. Note that there may be other names used to refer to these parables, and there may be alternative interpretations of their moral lessons. The point of the activity is for students to critically analyze parables as literature, while learning some basic concepts of Christianity.

Parable	Characters	Plot	Moral Lesson
Parable of the Fig Tree	Vineyard Owner, Gardener	Fig tree has no fruit. Man wants to cut it down. Gardener advises to wait one more year.	Give second chances; be patient; be productive.
Parable of the Lost Sheep	Shepherd, Sheep	One sheep out of one hundred gets lost. Shepherd will leave the ninety-nine to searc for it and rejoices when he finds it.	Every individual is important; God loves all people; God forgives those who misbehave and always welcomes them back.
Parable of the Rich Fool	Rich Man, God	Man hoards food and goods for himself. God says he is foolish since he will die tonight.	Avoid greed; focus on important things in life.
Parable of the Tower Builder	Builder, Observers	Builder does poor job planning costs. He doesn't finish tower, and everyone laughs at him.	Plan ahead; make wise decisions; know your abilities.
Parable of the Lost Son	Rich Man, Lost (Prodigal) Son, Older Son	Young son leaves home and wastes money. Returns home. Father is thankful and rejoices.	Forgive others; be thankful.
Parable of the Good Samaritan	Victim, Robbers, Locals, Samaritan	Man is beaten and robbed. Locals pass by without helping. Samaritan helps by giving his time and money.	Show love and compassion for others; treat everyone as your neighbor.

Learning About World Religions: Christianity

How are Christians' lives shaped by the beliefs and practices of Christianity?

Overview

In a Visual Discovery activity, students analyze images of Christian sacraments, worship, and holidays to learn about the key beliefs and practices of Christianity.

Objectives

In the course of reading this chapter and participating in the classroom activity, students will

Social Studies

- summarize fundamental Christian beliefs such as the Trinity, the Resurrection, and salvation.
- describe the history and practices of Christian worship services.
- explain the roots of the Christian calendar and major Christian holidays.
- identify the sacraments, including baptism and Holy Communion, observed by various Christian churches.

Language Arts

- clarify an understanding of text through note-taking and connecting the text to images.

Social Studies Vocabulary

Key Content Terms Trinity, salvation, Roman Catholic Church, Eastern Orthodox Church, Protestant, sacrament, baptism, Holy Communion

Academic Vocabulary widespread, interpretation, symbolize, interval

Materials

History Alive! The Ancient World

Interactive Student Notebooks

Visuals 37A–37C

Lesson Masters

- Vocabulary Development handout (1 per student, on colored paper)

Activity	Suggested Time	Materials
Preview	10 minutes	• Interactive Student Notebooks
Vocabulary Development	30–40 minutes	• *History Alive! The Ancient World* • Interactive Student Notebooks • Vocabulary Development handout
Visual Discovery	60 minutes (1–2 regular periods) (1 block period)	• *History Alive! The Ancient World* • Interactive Student Notebooks • Visuals 37A–37C
Processing	10 minutes	• Interactive Student Notebooks
Assessment	40 minutes	• Chapter 37 Assessment

Preview

1 **Have students complete the Preview activity for Chapter 37 in their Interactive Student Notebooks.** Students will list three things they already know about Christianity and then generate three questions they have about Christianity.

2 **Have students share their answers in pairs or with the class.**

3 **Explain the connection between the Preview activity and Chapter 37.** Tell students that they may already know some things about Christianity because it is the most common religion in the United States. In this chapter, they will learn more about the major beliefs and practices of Christianity. During the activity and the reading, they should look for answers to the questions they posed on the T-chart in the Preview activity.

Vocabulary Development

1 **Introduce the Key Content Terms.** Have students locate the Key Content Terms for the chapter in their Interactive Student Notebooks. These are important terms that will help them understand the main ideas of the chapter. Ask volunteers to identify any familiar terms and suggest how they might be used in a sentence.

2 **Have students complete a Vocabulary Development handout.** Give each student a copy of the Vocabulary Development handout of your choice from the Reading Toolkit at the back of the Lesson Masters. These handouts provide extra practice and support, depending on your students' needs.

Reading

1 **Introduce the Essential Question and have students read Section 37.1.** Have students identify the Essential Question on the first page of the chapter: *How are Christians' lives shaped by the beliefs and practices of Christianity?* Then have students read Section 37.1. Afterward, have students use information from Section 37.1 and from the chapter opener image to propose some answers to the Essential Question.

2 **Have students complete the Reading Notes for Chapter 37.** Assign Sections 37.2 to 37.6 during the activity, as indicated in the procedures for the Visual Discovery. Remind students to use the Key Content Terms where appropriate as they complete their Reading Notes.

Visual Discovery

1 **Have students read Sections 37.2 and 37.3 and complete the corresponding Reading Notes.** Tell students that these sections will introduce them to the main beliefs of Christianity. Use Guide to Reading Notes 37 to review students' answers.

2 Place students in pairs and introduce the activity. Explain that students will learn about the practices of Christianity by analyzing images of Christian sacraments, worship, and holidays. After examining each image, they will read to learn more about that particular aspect of Christianity.

3 Project *Visual 37A: Christian Baptism*. Tell students that these images represent the Christian sacrament of baptism. Ask,

- What interesting details do you see?
- What do you think is happening in these images?
- What can these images tell you about the sacrament of baptism?

4 Have pairs complete the Reading Notes for Section 37.4. Tell students that this section will give them more information about Christian sacraments. Have pairs read Section 37.4 and complete the corresponding Reading Notes in their Interactive Student Notebooks.

Visual 37A

5 Have students re-examine Visual 37A. Encourage students to use their Reading Notes to answer these questions:

- What is the purpose of baptism?
- What do all baptisms have in common?

6 Project *Visual 37B: Christian Worship*. Tell students that these images represent activities that might occur during a Christian worship service. Explain that the rituals (or rites) of Christian services can differ, but they all share some common characteristics. Ask,

- What interesting details do you see?
- What types of activities are these people doing?
- What do these images tell you about Christian worship services?

7 Have pairs complete the Reading Notes for Section 37.5. Tell students that this section will give them more information about Christian worship. Have pairs read Section 37.5 and complete the corresponding Reading Notes in their Interactive Student Notebooks.

Visual 37B

8 Have students re-examine Visual 37B. Encourage students to use their Reading Notes to answer these questions:

- What types of worship described in the book do you see in these images?
- What other activities might occur during a Christian church service?

9 Project *Visual 37C: Palm Sunday Procession*. Tell students that this image was taken during the celebration of Palm Sunday. Ask,

- What interesting details do you see?
- What do you think is happening in this scene?
- Why do Christians celebrate this event as a holiday?

10 Have pairs complete the Reading Notes for Section 37.6. Tell students that this section will give them more information about Christian holidays, such as Christmas and Easter. Have pairs read Section 37.6 and complete the corresponding Reading Notes in their Interactive Student Notebooks.

Visual 37C

11 **Have students re-examine Visual 37C.** Encourage students to use their Reading Notes to answer these questions:

- Why and how do Christians celebrate this holiday?
- What other holidays do Christians celebrate? Why?

12 **Wrap up the activity with a quick class discussion.** Ask,

- What did you learn about Christianity that you did not know before this activity?
- What information about Christianity do you think you will most remember from this activity?
- How are Christians' lives shaped by the beliefs and practices of Christianity?

Processing

Have students complete the Processing activity in their Interactive Student Notebooks. Students write the answer to one of their Preview activity questions, and then identify three ways in which Christians' beliefs and practices affect Christians' lives.

Quicker Coverage

Skip the Follow-Up Questions Instead of projecting each visual twice, ask only the first set of spiral questions for each visual (Steps 3, 6, and 9 in the procedures). Then have students complete the Reading Notes that correspond to the image. Use Guide to Reading Notes 37 to review their answers as a class.

Deeper Coverage

Explore the History of Christian Holidays Have students research holidays on the Christian calendar, such as Ash Wednesday, Easter, All Saints' Day, or Christmas. Challenge students to find the roots and significance of these holidays. Because students are likely to find many varying descriptions, use this as an opportunity to talk about bias and the difficulty of historical interpretation. Alternatively, focus on the present-day celebration of holidays. Have students compare and contrast how these holidays are celebrated around the world.

Compare Christian Denominations Students are often amazed at the number of different Christian denominations. Consider having them create a list of all the groups of Christians they may already know (such as Catholic or Baptist). Then have students find a list of denominations worldwide. Allow interested students to research basic facts about the different denominations, such as their origins, primary locations, number of adherents, major beliefs, and major practices. Make sure to limit the number of denominations and type of information that students are assigned to research.

> Writing: Research Report
>
> This assignment may be developed into a research report. If so, ask students to narrow the scope to a specific holiday. Remind students that their report must have a thesis and be supported by facts, details, and explanations from multiple sources. Require a bibliography.

Assessment

Mastering the Content

1. B	5. D	9. B	13. C
2. D	6. C	10. A	14. A
3. C	7. A	11. D	15. B
4. A	8. C	12. B	16. D

Applying Social Studies Skills

17. Baptist

18. 7

19. less than 39%

Exploring the Essential Question

20. Answers should include all the elements requested in the prompt.

Scoring Rubric

Score	Description
3	Student completes all three parts of the task. Paragraphs are clearly stated, use the meaning of the word *church* as designated in each box, include information from the chapter about beliefs and practices, and demonstrate command of standard English conventions.
2	Student responds to most or all parts of the task, but paragraphs may lack details or not be clearly stated.
1	Student responds to at least one part of the task. Paragraph(s) may contain factual and/or grammatical errors and may lack details.
0	Response does not match the task or is incorrect.

English Language Learners

Create Symbols for the Sacraments The sacraments can be very difficult to understand. Before starting the activity, consider summarizing each sacrament in simple terms and creating descriptions as a class. Then have students brainstorm an appropriate symbol for each sacrament to add to each description.

Learners Reading and Writing Below Grade Level

Support the Reading Notes For relevant sections of the Reading Notes, explicitly model how to complete the graphic organizer. Create a transparency of the Reading Notes, read a portion of the section text aloud, and then brainstorm as a class what information should be added to the graphic organizer. Record that information on the transparency and then allow students to read and complete the rest of the notes independently. Debrief the notes by calling on students to explain their answers, and then record them on the transparency.

Learners with Special Education Needs

Support the Preview Activity Students may have a tough time brainstorming general questions they have about Christianity. Consider suggesting some different types of questions they might ask, such as

- questions about Christian beliefs

- questions about Christian practices

- questions about Christian history

- questions about Christians in other countries

- questions about types of Christianity

Advanced Learners

Create Thematic Maps and Graphs Have students research and create thematic maps that illustrate Christianity in the United States or around the world. Students might create a

- world map showing the percent of Christian population by country.

- U.S. map of Christian population by state.

- U.S. map of predominant Christian denominations by state.

Alternatively, have students graph information about Christianity, such as creating a bar graph of denominations in your own state.

Compare and Contrast the Sacraments Remind students that Christian denominations observe the sacraments differently. Assign students to compare either baptism or Holy Communion. Have students compare different beliefs and practices related to their assigned sacrament. (**Note:** Even within denominations, individual churches may have different beliefs and traditions.) Students might create a matrix comparing the sacrament in different denominations or a visual presentation illustrating similarities and differences in the observance of the sacrament.

Enrichment Resources

Find out more about Christianity by exploring the following Enrichment Resources for *History Alive! The Ancient World* at www.teachtci.com.

Enrichment Readings These in-depth readings encourage students to explore selected topics related to the chapter. You may also find readings that relate the chapter's content directly to your state's curriculum.

Internet Connections These recommended Web sites provide useful and engaging content that reinforces skills development and mastery of subjects within the chapter.

Literature Recommendations

The following books offer opportunities to extend the content in this chapter.

Catholicism and Orthodox Christianity by Khaled Anatolios and Stephen F. Brown (New York: Chelsea House, 2009)

Christianity by Trevor Barnes (New York: Kingfisher Publications, 2005)

Martin Luther by Samuel Willard Crompton (New York: Chelsea House, 2004)

Section 37.2

Answers may vary but should include:

the Trinity: the union of three beings in one God

the Resurrection: the miracle when Jesus arose from the dead after he was executed by the Romans

salvation: the belief that God can save people from sin and can grant them everlasting life

Section 37.3

1. The patriarchs in Constantinople believed that they had authority over all Christians, while the pope in Rome believed that he had authority over all Christians. In 1054, the eastern part of the Church split with the western part. The eastern Church under the patriarchs became the Eastern Orthodox Church, and the western Church under the pope became the Roman Catholic Church.

2. Martin Luther was a German priest who called for reforms in the Catholic Church. In 1517, Luther and his followers left the Catholic Church and formed their own. They, and others like them who protested against corruption in the Catholic Church, became known as Protestants.

3. The main result of the Reformation is that today the Protestant branch of Christianity is separate from Roman Catholicism and includes thousands of denominations.

Section 37.4

1. A sacrament is a sacred rite of Christian churches, such as baptism.

2. Baptism is a sacrament that uses water to symbolize a new phase in someone's life. Some Christians apply only a little water to an individual's head, while others lower the individual completely underwater. Some denominations baptize babies, while others let people decide when they grow up if they want to be baptized. Baptism marks a person's entry into the Christian church.

3. Holy Communion is a Christian sacrament that commemorates Jesus and his Last Supper. Christians have different views of its meaning. Some see the bread and wine as the body and blood of Christ. Others see both as symbolic.

Section 37.5

1. Almost all Christian churches display a cross, the universal symbol of Christianity. But churches range in size from very small chapels to huge cathedrals. Some churches are richly decorated with paintings and stained glass windows. Others are very plain so that nothing will distract worshippers from focusing on the word of God in the Bible.

2. Sunday is the day of the week when Christians believe that Jesus rose from the dead.

Section 37.6

[first, at the end of December] Christmas: the holiday that celebrates Jesus's birth

[between Christmas and Palm Sunday] Lent: marks the 40 days that Jesus spent in the wilderness before he started to preach

[before Easter] Palm Sunday: the first day of Holy Week; it marks when Jesus went to Jerusalem to celebrate Passover

[after Palm Sunday, but before Easter] Good Friday: the day that Jesus died on the cross

[last] Easter: this is the most important Christian holiday; it celebrates the Resurrection

The Legacy of Rome in the Modern World

To what extent does ancient Rome influence us today?

Overview

In a Response Group activity, students play the "Rome to Home" game to discover how aspects of Roman culture, such as art, architecture, and language, influence modern life.

Objectives

In the course of reading this chapter and participating in the classroom activity, students will

Social Studies

- describe internal weaknesses of the Roman Empire and trace the fall of the empire in the west.
- explain the founding of Constantinople and the rise of the Byzantine Empire.
- evaluate the extent to which Roman art, architecture, engineering, language, philosophy, and law influence modern society.

Language Arts

- recognize the origins and meanings of frequently used foreign words in English.
- write a thesis statement and support it with relevant evidence.

Social Studies Vocabulary

Key Content Terms Byzantine Empire, patron, Renaissance, triumphal arch, aqueduct, Latin, Stoicism, natural law

Academic Vocabulary enormous, transfer, dissolve, generation

Materials

History Alive! The Ancient World

Interactive Student Notebooks

Lesson Masters

- Information Master 38 (1 transparency)
- Vocabulary Development handout (1 per student, on colored paper)

various magazines, such as news, home, and general-interest magazines

sticky notes

Activity	Suggested Time	Materials
Preview	10 minutes	• Interactive Student Notebooks
Vocabulary Development	30–40 minutes	• *History Alive! The Ancient World* • Interactive Student Notebooks • Vocabulary Development handout
Response Group	70–90 minutes (2 regular periods) (1 block period)	• *History Alive! The Ancient World* • Interactive Student Notebooks • Information Master 38 • various magazines, such as news, home, and general-interest magazines • sticky notes
Processing	15 minutes	• Interactive Student Notebooks
Assessment	40 minutes	• Chapter 38 Assessment

Preview

1 **Have students complete the Preview activity for Chapter 38 in their Interactive Student Notebooks.** Students will predict the extent to which they think Roman art, architecture and engineering, language, philosophy, and law influence us today.

2 **Have students share their answers in pairs or as a class.** Expect that many students will say that ancient Rome has little impact on us, or will be unable to support their opinions with examples.

3 **Explain the connection between the Preview activity and Chapter 38.** Tell students that it may surprise them to learn that Roman culture has influenced our own. Ancient Roman art, architecture, language, thinking, and laws all contribute something to our modern society. In this chapter, students will evaluate the extent to which ancient Rome influences us today.

Vocabulary Development

1 **Introduce the Key Content Terms.** Have students locate the Key Content Terms for the chapter in their Interactive Student Notebooks. These are important terms that will help them understand the main ideas of the chapter. Ask volunteers to identify any familiar terms and suggest how they might be used in a sentence.

2 **Have students complete a Vocabulary Development handout.** Give each student a copy of the Vocabulary Development handout of your choice from the Reading Toolkit at the back of the Lesson Masters. These handouts provide extra Key Content Term practice and support, depending on your students' needs. Review the completed handout by asking volunteers to share one answer for each term.

Reading

1 **Introduce the Essential Question and have students read Section 38.1.** Have students identify the Essential Question on the first page of the chapter: *To what extent does ancient Rome influence us today?* Then have students read Section 38.1 Afterward, have students respond to these questions:

- Who was Edward Gibbon?
- Why was Gibbon interested in the Roman Empire?
- What does it mean that "Rome perished, yet it lived on"?

2 **Have students complete the Reading Notes for Chapter 38.** Assign Sections 38.2 to 38.6 during the activity, as indicated in the procedures for the Response Group activity. Remind students to use the Key Content Terms where appropriate as they complete their Reading Notes.

Response Group

1 **Have students read about the fall of Rome.** Tell students that Section 38.2 describes the factors and events that led to the fall of the Roman Empire in the west. Have students read this section and complete the Reading Notes. Use Guide to Reading Notes 38 to review the answers as a class.

2 **Project the top of *Information Master 38: The "Rome to Home" Game*.** Cover the visual so that only the title and illustration are visible. Ask, *What interesting details do you see? What do you think this illustration represents?* Explain that the illustration is an example of visual metaphor. It is intended to show how aspects of Roman culture have "traveled" to modern times.

Information Master 38

3 **Introduce the activity.** Explain that students will form groups to play a fast-paced game called "Rome to Home." In each round, students will read about an aspect of Roman culture, such as art or language. Then they will earn points by finding examples in magazines that show how that aspect of Roman culture is found in modern life.

4 **Place students in groups of three.** Make sure that everyone can see the screen.

5 **Provide groups with magazines and sticky notes.** Make sure that each group has at least three different types of magazines. This will allow them to broaden their search for specific examples of Roman culture in modern life.

6 **Have students read Sections 38.3 through 38.6 and play the game "Rome to Home."** One at a time, reveal the steps on Information Master 38 to help students play the game. Here are some suggestions to ensure that each round unfolds smoothly:

- *Step 1*: Make sure that groups have all completed their Reading Notes before proceeding to Steps 2 and 3.
- *Step 2*: If necessary, decrease the time limit to create a sense of urgency, or increase the time limit if groups need longer to find examples.
- *Step 3*: You may want to extend the time limit if you feel groups do not have enough time to compile their final lists of unique examples.
- *Step 4*: Appoint a different Presenter for each round of the game. After each Presenter shares, ask if another group has identified the same examples. If so, have all Presenters cross the duplicate examples off their lists. Continue the process until all Presenters have shared their examples.
- *Step 5*: Record the points for each group on the board.

7 **Wrap up the activity by having students re-examine their Preview activity answers.** Tell students to turn back to the Preview activity for Chapter 38. Using a different color pen or pencil, have students reassess each statement and add specific evidence from their Reading Notes or Chapter 38.

Processing

Have students complete the Processing activity in their Interactive Student Notebooks. On a separate sheet of paper, students will write a thesis statement assessing the extent to which Roman culture influences us today. Then they will list evidence from the activity to support the thesis statement.

Quicker Coverage

Shorten the Game Instead of playing Round 1, use it to quickly model how the game will be played. Then have students follow the appropriate steps to play Rounds 2 and 3 of "Rome to Home." In Step 3, you might require that students list only two or three unique examples, rather than five. This will decrease the required time for sharing answers and scorekeeping. In place of Round 4, conduct a class discussion by having students compare and contrast Roman law with law today.

Eliminate the Magazines If you are unable to gather magazines, find some images online or make transparencies of some magazine pages that illustrate the influence of Roman culture today. Instead of playing the game in rounds, have students complete all their Reading Notes first. Then project an image and have groups use their Reading Notes to determine the Roman influence or influences in the image. Tell groups to record answers on a sheet of paper (instead of randomly calling out answers). Then project each image again, one at a time, reviewing the answers, giving points for all correct answers, and allowing students to "challenge" if they see a connection you had not intended.

Deeper Coverage

Find Local Roman Influences Have students find three examples of Roman cultural influences in their community. For example, they might notice a building with a dome, a mosaic, or a sign containing a word derived from Latin. Tell students to sketch or take a photograph of each example. Then, next to each visual, students should write a caption that describes the example, states where it is located in the community, and explains the Roman cultural influences it contains.

Judge the Influence of Greece and Rome Students have now learned about both Greek and Roman contributions to modern society. Have students review their Reading Notes for Chapters 31 and 38, and then write a persuasive paper answering the following question: *Does ancient Greece or ancient Rome have a greater influence on our culture?* In their essays, students should write a strong thesis statement and incorporate specific evidence from their books, Reading Notes, and observations about modern culture. Have students bring their papers to class and conduct an informal class debate to determine which ancient culture has the greater influence.

Writing: Spelling

Before students write, review the difference between the frequently confused words *affect* and *effect*. Provide an example of correct spelling and usage by using the words in the context of *effects* of the Roman Empire, as well as in the context of how Roman ideas have *affected* us. At the proofreading stage, have peer reviewers find and correct, if needed, every use of *affect(s)* and *effect(s)*.

Assessment

Mastering the Content

1. A	5. C	9. D	13. C
2. B	6. A	10. D	14. D
3. B	7. B	11. B	15. C
4. A	8. C	12. D	

Applying Social Studies Skills

16. Ostrogoths

17. Byzantine Empire

18. Mediterranean, Africa

19. Franks

Exploring the Essential Question

20. Answers should include all the elements requested in the prompt.

Scoring Rubric

Score	Description
3	Student completes all seven parts of the task (ranking plus examples and explanations). Examples and explanations are clearly stated, supported by details, and demonstrate command of standard English conventions.
2	Student responds to most or all parts of the task, but examples and explanations may lack details or not be clearly stated.
1	Student responds to at least one part of the task. Examples and explanations may contain factual and/or grammatical errors and may lack details.
0	Response does not match the task or is incorrect.

Lessons from Pompeii

1 **Discuss the concept of urban planning.** Ask whether students think a city should be developed according to a plan or whether it is better for people to be allowed to build whatever, wherever, and however they choose.

2 **Have students read the first two pages of the Chapter 38 Reading Further in the Student Edition.** Elicit students' opinions on whether the urban planners who studied Pompeii had the right ideas about what principles help to create a well-planned city. Ask whether there is any area in their city or town that is like a "forum." Do any other features of Pompeii remind students of their own community, or of a city they have visited?

3 **Have students read the rest of the Reading Further.** Have students consider the issues that urban planners would have faced in planning the students' community: where the streets would lie; how wide those streets would be; which areas should be reserved for business, industry, and housing; where facilities such as schools, parks, and hospitals should go. Encourage opinions about which aspects of their town or city are well planned and which are not.

4 **Have students complete the Reading Further activity in their Interactive Student Notebooks.**

5 **Invite students to share their ideas about how their city or town could be improved.** Suggest that interested students create models or draw pictures of what their city or town would look like according to their plan.

English Language Learners

Adapt Round 3: Language Students may have a difficult time scanning for words in Round 3. Tell students that they may also brainstorm and record any words they know that begin with a Latin prefix or contain a Latin root word, regardless of whether the word is in the magazine. For example, the prefix *re-* is in the table in Section 38.5, so they could write down *recall*, *review*, and *redo*. You might also encourage students whose first language is a Romance language to identify words in that language with Latin roots or prefixes.

Learners Reading and Writing Below Grade Level

Do the Reading Notes Together In Step 1 of each round of "Rome to Home," have volunteers read each of Sections 38.3 through 38.6 aloud while the rest of the class follows along. This will ensure that all groups move to Step 2 at the same time. Complete the Reading Notes as a class and make sure that students understand the aspect of Roman culture discussed in the section. Then play the rest of the game in the same manner, moving quickly from step to step as a class.

Support the Processing Activity As you introduce the Processing activity, remind students that a thesis statement is a single sentence that clearly states the writer's position on the topic. Have students review their answers in the Preview activity. Give groups time to brainstorm ways to phrase a thesis statement answering the question in the Processing activity, and then have each individual write a thesis statement. When finished, have students use this checklist to evaluate their statements:

- Does my thesis statement clearly express my opinion?

- Is my thesis statement a claim that deserves further discussion?

- Would I be able to prove, defend, or explain my thesis statement in an essay?

Learners with Special Education Needs

Frontload the Game To give students a head start in preparing for the "Rome to Home" game, assign the reading for Chapter 38 in advance. For each of the four sections in the Reading Notes, tell students to write down two examples of Roman influences in modern society. They can use these examples as guides when they are hunting for pictures to use in the "Rome to Home" game.

Simplify the Scorekeeping Eliminate the requirement that groups must come up with unique answers for points. On Information Master 38, delete the second instruction line of Step 3. After students have compiled their lists of items, allow them to read their items aloud and give a point for each correct answer, whether or not other groups found the same answer.

Advanced Learners

Explore Roman Influence Worldwide Have pairs research and create a presentation showing how a particular aspect of Roman culture has affected the world. For example, students might compare the many variations of triumphal arches or the many languages that borrow from Latin. Presentations should

- show visual representations of the examples—either pictures downloaded from the Internet or from a digital camera, or sketches scanned and inserted.

- explain how the aspect of Roman culture is shown in the images.

- compare and contrast how different nations have been influenced by this aspect of Roman culture.

Compare Ancient Rome to the United States Have students synthesize information from Unit 6 by creating a Venn diagram to compare and contrast the United States and the Roman Empire. They might consider politics, values, daily life, or other categories of their own choosing. Then challenge students to evaluate whether the factors that caused the fall of Rome might also weaken the United States. Consider having students present their conclusions in a one-page statement to the American public.

Enrichment Resources

Find out more about the legacy of Rome in the modern world by exploring the following Enrichment Resources for *History Alive! The Ancient World* at www.teachtci.com.

Enrichment Readings These in-depth readings encourage students to explore selected topics related to the chapter. You may also find readings that relate the chapter's content directly to your state's curriculum.

Internet Connections These recommended Web sites provide useful and engaging content that reinforces skills development and mastery of subjects within the chapter.

Literature Recommendations

The following books offer opportunities to extend the content in this chapter.

City: A Story of Roman Planning and Construction by David Macaulay (Boston: Houghton Mifflin Company, 1983)

The Greek and Latin Roots of English by Tamara M. Green (Lanham, MD: Rowman & Littlefield Publishers, Inc., 2007)

Legacies from Ancient Rome by Anita Ganeri (Amarillo, TX: Chrysalis Education, 2000)

Section 38.2

1. On the three illustrated "cracks," students write the chief problems of the Roman Empire: political instability, economic issues, and weakening frontiers. Illustrations will vary.

2. 330 C.E., Constantine moves capital from Rome to Constantinople.

   410 C.E., Germanic tribe attacks and loots Rome.

   476 C.E., Roman Empire in the West ends when the last emperor is dethroned.

3. On the map, students should label Rome, Constantinople, and the Byzantine Empire; draw an arrow from Rome to Constantinople; and shade in the area of the Byzantine Empire.

Section 38.3

1. Answers will vary but should describe four art-forms of ancient Rome, such as statues, mosaics, frescoes, blown glass, gem cutting, metalworking, or cameos.

2. Some examples of Roman artforms that influence modern life are murals in restaurants, banks, and other buildings; lifelike statues; cut gems and cameos.

Section 38.4

1. Answers will vary but should describe four architectural or engineering achievements of ancient Rome, such as the use of arches, vaults, and domes; the use of cement to create massive buildings and stadiums; triumphal arches; and the building of roads, bridges, and aqueducts.

2. Many modern churches, banks, and government buildings include Roman designs. Many communities have stadiums that include features like those found in the Roman Colosseum. Some modern freeways are built over Roman roads, and parts of Roman aqueducts are still used today.

Section 38.5

1. The Latin alphabet had 23 letters while the modern English alphabet has 26 letters.

2. The Roman numerals I, V, and X are used to write the numbers 1 through 10. The number 50 is written as *L*, 100 is *C*, 500 is *D*, and 1,000 is *M*.

3. Some examples of Roman language that influence modern life are the use of Latin proverbs, Latin root words such as *civis*, and Latin prefixes such as *pre-*.

Section 38.6

1. Answers will vary but should describe three important ideas in Roman philosophy and law, such as: live in a way that agrees with nature; have a good character; apply laws to all people; and believe that natural law says everyone has certain basic rights.

2. Roman philosophy and law affect modern life in several ways. Today, we describe someone who bears pain and suffering bravely as stoic. Some modern law codes in Europe are based on Roman laws. The U.S. Declaration of Independence and the U.S. Constitution are based on some Roman ideas. Many today believe that all humans have basic rights that are guaranteed by natural law.

Ancient Rome

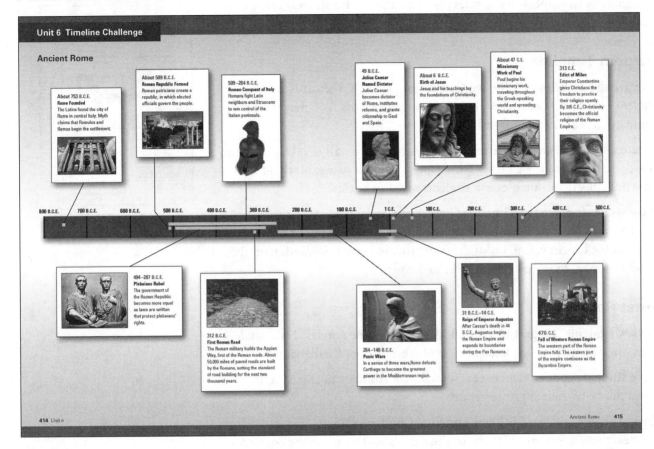

Overview

This Timeline Challenge provides students with a review of the main events and ideas of this unit, as well as practice in reading and interpreting timelines. You can vary and expand the activity according to students' needs and the amount of time available.

Basic Procedure

1 **Introduce the timeline in the Student Edition.** Direct students to the Ancient Rome Timeline at the end of Unit 6 in the Student Edition. You may wish to have students read aloud and discuss the timeline entries.

2 **Introduce the Timeline Challenge in the Interactive Student Notebook.** Direct students to the Unit 6 Timeline Challenge in their notebooks. Point out the two types of questions, "Timeline Skills" and "Critical Thinking," and model how to answer each type.

3 **Have students complete the Timeline Challenge.** Monitor students as they work. Use the Guide to Unit 6 Timeline Challenge to check their answers. You may wish to project a transparency of the Timeline Challenge as you work through the questions with the class and conduct a discussion of the "Critical Thinking" questions.

4 **Complete the KWL chart.** Return to the KWL chart created at the beginning of the unit, and ask students to list the key information they have learned.

Classroom Timeline

1 **Prepare the Timeline Challenge Cards.** Copy and cut the cards from *Student Handout TC6: Unit 6 Timeline Challenge Cards.* You may wish to laminate the cards for future use.

2 **Create a timeline on a classroom wall.** On an empty wall or a large bulletin board, make a timeline with masking tape or colored paper. Mark off the time intervals in advance, or ask students to do so in class.

3 **Have students place the Timeline Challenge Cards.** Distribute cards to pairs or individual students and have them tape the cards in the correct locations on the timeline. Call on students to provide more information on the timeline topics, to review main events and issues.

Student Handout TC6

Internet Research

1 **Review students' suggestions for additional timeline entries.** Have students share their answers to the last question of the Timeline Challenge.

2 **Have students conduct Internet research.** Ask students to choose and research one of their suggested events.

3 **Have students create additional Timeline Challenge Cards.** Direct students to research an appropriate image for their cards and then use the computer to create an illustrated card, complete with timeline entry.

Timeline Skills

Score 1 point for each correct answer.

1. The Roman Republic was formed about 250 years after Rome was founded.

2. The Roman Republic was created when patricians overthrew the last Etruscan king and formed a government in which elected officials govern the people.

3. The plebeians rebelled against patrician rule for about 200 years. In the end, the government became more democratic because laws were written that protected plebeians' rights.

4. Rome conquered Italy before it conquered Carthage.

5. The Punic Wars were fought from 264 to 146 B.C.E.

6. Of Julius Caesar, Augustus, and Constantine, Constantine was the last to rule Rome.

7. The Pax Romana happened during the rule of Augustus.

8. Paul helped spread Christianity in the Greek-speaking world. He traveled, preached, and wrote letters.

9. Rome allowed Christians the freedom to openly worship in 313 C.E.

10. Roman workers constructed about 50,000 miles of roads.

Critical Thinking

Score 1 to 3 points for each answer, depending on the thoroughness of the response.

11. The Roman Republic was a government run by elected officials. The Senate was a group of 300 men who held most of the power. Two consuls shared control of the army. At first, only patricians could participate in the government. The plebeians revolted. Over time, the plebeians won the right to elect officials to tribunes, which had the power to veto the Senate. Eventually, plebeians gained the right to pass laws. Roman leaders wrote down a set of laws called the Twelve Tables.

12. One event that helped spread Christianity during Roman times was the missionary work of Paul. He traveled throughout the Greek-speaking world, preaching about Christian beliefs. Even after he was jailed, he continued writing letters to other Christians. Another event that helped spread Christianity was the recognition of the religion by Emperor Constantine in 313 C.E. He gave Christians the freedom to practice their religion openly.

13. Answers will vary. Students should identify and describe a Roman contribution, and explain their rationale for choosing this contribution.

14. Answers will vary. Students must explain why the events they chose merit inclusion.

Using Scores to Inform Instruction

Timeline Skills A score of 7 out of 10 indicates that students understand most of the key events of this unit.

Critical Thinking A score of 8 out of 12 indicates that students are able to think critically about most of the key issues of this unit.

If students score below these levels, consider reviewing timeline and critical thinking skills.

This pacing guide suggests how many instructional days to allot to each chapter, including activities and assessment, for teaching the course in 50-minute classes, five times per week.

Unit 1: Early Humans and the Rise of Civilization		Unit 4: Ancient China	
Geography Challenge	1 day	Geography Challenge	1 day
Ch. 1: Investigating the Past	3 days	Ch. 19: Geography and the Early Settlement of China	5 days
Ch. 2: Early Hominids	5 days	Ch. 20: The Shang Dynasty	4 days
Ch. 3 From Hunters and Gatherers to Farmers	5–6 days	Ch. 21: Three Chinese Philosophies	5 days
Ch. 4: The Rise of Sumerian City-States	5 days	Ch. 22: The First Emperor of China	5 days
Ch. 5: Ancient Sumer	4 days	Ch. 23: The Han Dynasty	5 days
Ch. 6: Exploring Four Empires of Mesopotamia	3–4 days	Ch. 24: The Silk Road	3 days
Timeline Challenge	1 day	Timeline Challenge	1 day

Unit 2: Ancient Egypt and the Middle East		Unit 5: Ancient Greece	
Geography Challenge	1 day	Geography Challenge	1 day
Ch. 7: Geography and the Early Settlement of Egypt, Kush, and Canaan	4–5 days	Ch. 25: Geography and the Settlement of Greece	3 days
Ch. 8: The Ancient Egyptian Pharaohs	4 days	Ch. 26: The Rise of Democracy	4 days
Ch. 9: Daily Life in Ancient Egypt	5–6 days	Ch. 27: Life in Two City-States: Athens and Sparta	4 days
Ch. 10: The Kingdom of Kush	4 days	Ch. 28: Fighting the Persian Wars	4 days
Ch. 11: The Origins of Judaism	4 days	Ch. 29: The Golden Age of Athens	6 days
Ch. 12: Learning About World Religions: Judaism	3–4 days	Ch. 30: Alexander the Great and His Empire	4 days
Timeline Challenge	1 day	Ch. 31: The Legacy of Ancient Greece	5 days
		Timeline Challenge	1 day

Unit 3: Ancient India		Unit 6: Ancient Rome	
Geography Challenge	1 day	Geography Challenge	1 day
Ch. 13: Geography and the Early Settlement of India	4 days	Ch. 32: Geography and the Early Development of Rome	3 days
Ch. 14: Unlocking the Secrets of Mohenjodaro	3–4 days	Ch. 33: The Rise of the Roman Republic	3 days
Ch. 15: Learning About World Religions: Hinduism	4 days	Ch. 34: From Republic to Empire	5 days
Ch. 16: Learning About World Religions: Buddhism	4–5 days	Ch. 35: Daily Life in the Roman Empire	5 days
Ch. 17: The First Unification of India	4 days	Ch. 36: The Origins and Spread of Christianity	3 days
Ch. 18: The Achievements of the Gupta Empire	5–6 days	Ch. 37: Learning About World Religions: Christianity	3 days
Timeline Challenge	1 day	Ch. 38: The Legacy of Rome in the Modern World	4 days
		Timeline Challenge	1 day

History Alive! The Ancient World Skills Correlation	Map Skills	Comparing and Contrasting	Sequencing Events	Creating a Timeline	Analyzing Cause and Effect	Making Predictions	Recognizing the Role of Chance, Error, and Oversight in History	Framing Questions to Research	Distinguishing Fact from Opinion	Selecting Useful Information	Selecting Credible Sources: Primary Sources	Selecting Credible Sources: Secondary Sources	Drawing Sound Conclusions	Identifying Frame of Reference and Point of View	Identifying Bias, Stereotyping, and Propaganda	Conducting a Cost-Benefit Analysis	Interpreting Political Cartoons
Unit 1: Early Humans and the Rise of Civilization																	
Geography Challenge	•					•							•				
Ch. 1: Investigating the Past		•				•		•		•	•	•	•				
Ch. 2: Early Hominids	•		•	•	•	•		•		•			•				
Ch. 3: From Hunters and Gatherers to Farmers	•	•						•									
Ch. 4: The Rise of Sumerian City-States	•		•		•	•							•			•	
Ch. 5: Ancient Sumer								•		•			•			•	
Ch. 6: Exploring Four Empires of Mesopotamia		•	•			•		•		•	•				•	•	
Timeline Challenge		•	•	•									•				
Unit 2: Ancient Egypt and the Middle East																	
Geography Challenge	•					•							•				
Ch. 7: Geography and the Early Settlement of Egypt, Kush, and Canaan	•	•			•	•		•					•			•	
Ch. 8: The Ancient Egyptian Pharaohs			•	•		•				•	•		•		•	•	
Ch. 9: Daily Life in Ancient Egypt		•	•		•	•		•					•	•	•		
Ch. 10: The Kingdom of Kush	•	•	•	•	•			•	•	•	•	•	•				
Ch. 11: The Origins of Judaism	•	•	•		•	•		•		•			•		•		
Ch. 12: Learning About World Religions: Judaism		•	•	•				•		•							
Timeline Challenge			•	•	•								•				

History Alive! The Ancient World **Skills Correlation**	Map Skills	Comparing and Contrasting	Sequencing Events	Creating a Timeline	Analyzing Cause and Effect	Making Predictions	Recognizing the Role of Chance, Error, and Oversight in History	Framing Questions to Research	Distinguishing Fact from Opinion	Selecting Useful Information	Selecting Credible Sources: Primary Sources	Selecting Credible Sources: Secondary Sources	Drawing Sound Conclusions	Identifying Frame of Reference and Point of View	Identifying Bias, Stereotyping, and Propaganda	Conducting a Cost-Benefit Analysis	Interpreting Political Cartoons
Unit 3: Ancient India																	
Geography Challenge	•					•							•				
Ch. 13: Geography and the Early Settlement of India	•				•	•				•			•			•	
Ch. 14: Unlocking the Secrets of Mohenjodaro	•	•				•			•		•		•				
Ch. 15: Learning About World Religions: Hinduism					•	•			•	•			•				
Ch. 16: Learning About World Religions: Buddhism		•	•			•	•		•	•	•						
Ch. 17: The First Unification of India	•	•	•			•				•	•			•			
Ch. 18: The Achievements of the Gupta Empire	•	•	•	•		•				•	•						
Timeline Challenge			•	•	•					•			•				
Unit 4: Ancient China																	
Geography Challenge	•					•							•				
Ch. 19: Geography and the Early Settlement of China	•	•				•			•	•			•		•	•	
Ch. 20: The Shang Dynasty	•				•	•			•	•	•		•				
Ch. 21: Three Chinese Philosophies		•	•		•				•				•				
Ch. 22: The First Emperor of China	•	•								•				•	•	•	
Ch. 23: The Han Dynasty	•	•	•		•					•							
Ch. 24: The Silk Road	•				•	•	•			•			•			•	
Timeline Challenge			•	•	•					•			•				

History Alive! The Ancient World Skills Correlation

	Map Skills	Comparing and Contrasting	Sequencing Events	Creating a Timeline	Analyzing Cause and Effect	Making Predictions	Recognizing the Role of Chance, Error, and Oversight in History	Framing Questions to Research	Distinguishing Fact from Opinion	Selecting Useful Information	Selecting Credible Sources: Primary Sources	Selecting Credible Sources: Secondary Sources	Drawing Sound Conclusions	Identifying Frame of Reference and Point of View	Identifying Bias, Stereotyping, and Propaganda	Conducting a Cost-Benefit Analysis	Interpreting Political Cartoons
Unit 5: Ancient Greece																	
Geography Challenge	•					•							•				
Ch. 25: Geography and the Settlement of Greece	•	•	•		•					•			•			•	
Ch. 26: The Rise of Democracy		•	•	•	•				•	•				•		•	•
Ch. 27: Life in Two City-States: Athens and Sparta	•	•			•				•	•			•		•		
Ch. 28: Fighting the Persian Wars	•	•	•			•	•		•	•			•				
Ch. 29: The Golden Age of Athens	•	•							•	•	•		•				
Ch. 30: Alexander the Great and His Empire	•				•	•	•	•	•	•					•	•	
Ch. 31: The Legacy of Ancient Greece								•	•	•	•						
Timeline Challenge		•	•	•	•								•				
Unit 6: Ancient Rome																	
Geography Challenge	•				•								•				
Ch. 32: Geography and the Early Development of Rome	•	•	•		•					•		•					
Ch. 33: The Rise of the Roman Republic		•	•	•	•						•				•		
Ch. 34: From Republic to Empire	•				•	•				•	•				•	•	
Ch. 35: Daily Life in the Roman Empire		•									•	•					
Ch. 36: The Origins and Spread of Christianity			•		•					•	•	•		•			
Ch. 37: Learning About World Religions: Christianity		•	•		•			•									
Ch. 38: The Legacy of Rome in the Modern World	•	•						•		•							
Timeline Challenge			•	•	•								•				

Placards

Chapter 5
9: Greenstone seal of Hashhamer, at www.britishmuseum.org.

Lesson Guide

Photographs

Cover: Ian Mckinnell/Getty Images

Title page: Ian Mckinnell/Getty Images

Art

Chapter 16
200–202: Len Ebert.

Placards

Photographs

1: Sylvain Julienne/Woodfin Camp and Associates **2:** RF/N. Frey Photography/Shutterstock **3:** David L. Brill **4:** Sisse Brimberg/National Geographic Image Collection **5:** Sisse Brimberg/National Geographic Image Collection **6:** © Gianni Dagli Orti/CORBIS **7:** © Scala/Art Resource, NY **8:** The Oriental Institute of the University of Chicago **9:** © Copyright Trustees of The British Museum, London **10:** © Scala/Art Resource/NY **11:** Boltin Picture Library **12:** © Scala/Art Resource/NY **13:** Boltin Picture Library **14:** © Jehangier Gazdar/Woodfin Camp & Associates **15:** © Borromeo/Art Resource, NY **16L:** Robert Harding **16R:** Robert Harding **17:** © Borromeo/Art Resource, NY **18:** © James Blair/National Geographic Image Collection **19:** Robert Harding **20:** © Jehangir Gazdar/Woodfin Camp & Associates **21:** © CORBIS **22:** © Asian Art Museum of San Francisco. The Avery Brundage Collection. Reproduced by permission **24:** © Asian Art Museum of San Francisco **27:** © Asian Art & Archaeology, Inc./CORBIS **29:** © Chris Hellier/CORBIS **31:** Giraudon/Art Resource, NY **32:** Xinhua/Sovoto **33:** The Art Archive **34:** © Bettmann/CORBIS **35:** © Royalty-Free/CORBIS **36:** Science & Society Picture Library **37:** © The Gallery Collection Corbis **39L:** © RF/Jiss | Dreamstime.com **39R:** Bildarchiv Preussischer Kulturbesitz/Art Resource, NY **40:** North Wind Picture Archives **41:** North Wind Picture Archives **42:** © Robert Harding World Imagery/Corbis **43:** © Erich Lessing/Art Resource, NY **44:** © Erich Lessing/Art Resource, NY **45:** © Bettmann/CORBIS **46:** © Copyright The Trustees of the British Museum **47:** © Bettmann/CORBIS **48:** Art Resource, NY **49:** RF/Purestock/Alamy **50:** RF/Shutterstock **51:** National Library of Medicine **52:** © Giraudon/Art Resource, NY

Art

Chapter 14
14B–14H: Doug Roy.

Chapter 29
29B–29F: Doug Roy.